HANDBOOK OF JOURNALISM AND MASS COMMUNICATION

By the same Authors

– *Media Policy and Nation Building – Select Issues and Themes*

– Translation of two AMIC publications (in Hindi)

- *Press Systems in SAARC* and
- *Role of Media in National Crisis*

About the Authors

Vir Bala Aggarwal, a senior researcher and academic, had a brilliant scholastic career in MJ and B.Tech (Printing Technology). She worked on role of mass media in development, for her dissertation for Ph.D.

She has published and presented a large number of papers on media issues in journals, and regional and national seminars. Presently working as the Chairperson, Department of Journalism and Mass Communication, Himachal Pradesh University, Shimla, she specialises in communication theory, printing technology and development issues; and is associated with a number of journalism departments as a resource person.

V. S. Gupta, a senior media and communication academic, is a former Professor, Haryana Agricultural University. A recipient of several awards and fellowships, Professor Gupta conceptualised and implemented a number of training programmes in journalism and communication at the university. As the Country Representative for the Asian Media Information and Communication Centre (AMIC), Singapore, for a number of years, organised numerous seminars and colloquia throughout the country. He has written and edited, jointly and singly, nine books and a number of manuals, besides having been widely published in India and abroad.

HANDBOOK OF JOURNALISM AND MASS COMMUNICATION

VIR BALA AGGARWAL
Chairperson,
Department of Journalism
and Mass Communication,
Himachal Pradesh University
Shimla

V. S. GUPTA
Former Professor
Haryana Agricultural
University,
Hisar

CONCEPT PUBLISHING COMPANY, NEW DELHI-110 059

ISBN 81-7022-881-6 (PB)

First Published 2001
Reprinted 2002

Reprint : 2023

Published and Printed by
Ashok Kumar Mittal
Concept Publishing Company
A/15-16, Commercial Block, Mohan Garden,
NEW DELHI-110059

Phones : 5351460, 5351794
Fax : 091-11-5357103
Email : publishing@conceptpub.com

PREFACE

This book is designed for the students of journalism and mass communication studying for their post-graduate degree in the subject; and also for all those interested in keeping themselves acquainted with the latest trends and developments in this area of study.

The book discusses comprehensively major aspects of mass communication theories and models, communication landscape in the country, latest trends in broadcasting, history and growth of journalism in India, besides public relations and advertising as well as media management.

A significant feature of the book is the compilation of Annexures painstakingly undertaken for supplementing the information included in the text. The Glossary which appears at the end of the book has been compiled to include terms from a multi-disciplinary point of view. It encompasses subjects like computer and printing technology, broadcasting, advertising, mass communication and public relations.

Whereas most of similar books cover limited aspects of mass communication, here an effort has been made to include wide range of topics such as models, types and functions of communication. Likewise the authors have discussed principles and tools of public relations, public relations practice in different sectors, public opinion, propaganda and publicity so as to afford the students a broad perspective of all the topics in the section. The section on media management discusses organisation and working of different departments of a newspaper establishment. It also includes various legal enactments applicable to the profession.

When writing this book, we have tried to use all the good knowledge on the subject we could find. Our debt of gratitude is therefore so large that it is impossible to acknowledge all cases of direct and indirect influence. The ideas of leading scholars and researchers who have been active in a number of academic fields have been incorporated so as to enrich the contents of the book. Some of the authors whose works we have consulted are : Denis McQuail, John R. Bittner, John Fiske, Joseph R. Dominick, Gulab Kothari, Cutlip and Center and several others. Relevant facts and data have been collected from the Reports of the Ministry of Information and Broadcasting, *India 2001*, and *Mass Media–2001*, and other publications brought out by the Publications Division of the

Government of India; references to some other authors have been included in the text and in the bibliography at the end of the book.

The authors wish to acknowledge their debt of gratitude to the writers mentioned above and also to any other writer whose name has been inadvertently omitted.

The book does not discuss practical aspects of the subject such as reporting, sub-editing and newspaper production because it forms an altogether distinct area of study. The authors propose to bring out shortly a companion volume covering these aspects. The authors also plan to bring out revised edition of the book every alternate year so as to equip the students with the latest information in this area of study. We propose to incorporate suggestions from all sections of readership for the improvement of the book and remove deficiencies, if any, in the forthcoming editions.

It is our hope that the book would be a step in the direction of the better understanding of the subject.

VIR BALA AGGARWAL and V. S. GUPTA

ACKNOWLEDGEMENTS

We wish to gratefully acknowledge our deep gratitude to :

Prof. Dr. S. K. Gupta, a renowned historian, and presently Vice – Chancellor, Himachal Pradesh University, and also formerly Head of the Department of Journalism and Mass Communication, for his consistent support and encouragement;

The Publisher, Mr. Ashok Mittal for cheerfully bearing with us the delay on our part in completing the manuscript.

CONTENTS

SECTION VI

LIST OF TABLES

SECTION–I

MASS COMMUNICATION—
ORIGIN AND DEVELOPMENT

MEDIA OF COMMUNICATION—
THE INDIAN CONTEXT

Mass Communication– Origin and Development

Communication is the process of sending and receiving information. It is the vehicle through which we develop, maintain and improve human relationships. At times it becomes the tool through which human relationships are undermined or even destroyed. Communication word is drawn from *communis* (Latin derivation) which means common, the idea of commonality is frequently stressed in talking about communication. Denis McQuail defines, communication is a process which increases commonality, but also requires elements of commonality for it to occur at all.

The definitions of communication, as the saying goes, are dime a dozen. Depending upon one's perception and point of view, communication is : transmission of information to elicit a response; coordinating favourable response between a person and an audience, sharing information, an idea or an attitude, or "a meeting of minds, a bringing about of a common set of symbols in the minds of the participants – in short, an understanding".[1]

It would be in order to refer to the following important observations about how communication is all pervasive :

Communication is part of the very fabric of society. It takes place at all levels between peoples and between institutions, from government to people, from people back to government, and through many channels both inter-personal and mediated.

– *National Communication Systems, UNESCO*

---

[1] John C. Merrill and Ralph L. Lowenstein, *Media, Messages and Men*, New York, David McKay, 1971.

Communication maintains and animates life. It is also the motor and expression of social activity and civilization; it leads people and peoples from instinct to inspiration, through variegated processes and systems of enquiry, command and control; it creates a common pool of ideas, strengthens the feeling of togetherness through exchange of messages and translates thought into action, reflecting every emotion and need from the humblest tasks of human survival to supreme manifestations of creativity–or destruction. Communication integrates knowledge, organization and power and runs as a thread linking the earliest memory of man to his noblest aspirations through constant striving for a better life.

– *Many Voices, One World, UNESCO*

Communication presupposes a shared environment, a social relationship between those who participate. When man communicates, he shares his own knowledge, attitudes and skills with others in the form of gestures, spoken or written messages. Man has to decide how to send his message. Human beings can only receive messages through one or more of their five senses of hearing, seeing, smelling, tasting and touching.

In nutshell, communication can be described as an act of transmission of ideas, thoughts, beliefs, knowledge and opinion, etc. The purpose of communication is to establish commonness.To communicate effectively, the sender's words and symbols must mean the same thing to the receiver that may do, to the sender.

Birds chirp, frogs croak, honeybee dances and convey messages to their fellows. But here we are concerned with human communication. Human communication is the sending from one person to another of meaningful messages (Denis McQuail). These messages could be oral or written.

Berlo says, "Communication does not consist of the transmission of meaning. Meanings are not transmitted or transferable. Only messages are transmitted and meanings are not in the message, they are in the message users."

NEED FOR COMMUNICATION

Man's need for communication is as strong and as basic as his need to eat, sleep and love. The severest punishment for a child is to leave him alone and tell, "I refuse to talk to you". Grown-ups too, and especially the aged need company, need to communicate. Society punishes criminals by locking them in solitary cells, thus starving them of that basic need to communicate. Only for a short time can man do without communication but for modern man it would be impossible to function without the mass media of communication.

Communication involves interaction with our environments–physical, biological and social. Deprived of this interaction we would not be aware of whether we are safe or in danger, whether hated or loved. This basic need for communication can perhaps be traced to the process of man's evolution. In Ramapithecus age our prehistoric ancestors emerging from caves possessed the basic senses of sight, hearing, touch, smell and taste. Different from creatures of the twentieth century, their brains and central nervous systems began slowly to evolve and later generations gradually acquired the basic tools for communication. They began to distinguish between pleasurable and unpleasurable experiences. More refined perception and a more sophisticated brain and central nervous system developed simultaneously and aided in satisfying basic needs–light to see, air to breathe, food to eat, water do drink, sleep to strengthen and shelter to protect them from the environment. By about 300,000 B. C. their nervous systems and brain, as well as their genetic features began to resemble those of present humans.

In the Mnemonic stage, wise persons were those who could remember something. Actually, this was memory aiding stage which was in existence about 50,000 years earlier. Communication was social and language was not developed.

By about 7000 B. C., the ability to communicate gained another medium–Pictographics. Communication took place by drawing pictures. These wall etchings inside caves and temples remain vivid picture messages that depict the life and religious beliefs of these first humans. Thus, creativeness and imagination developed in this stage but outlet of this creativeness was not there. Man was merely cave-dweller.

In the period from 3000 to 2000 B. C. these etchings became highly stylized, and the first symbols came into existence. This stage came to be known as Ideographic stage. Man started living in social groups and started building houses. Humans were now able to record socio-cultural events, attitudes, values and habits and to trace the development of moral codes. In this stage pictures were reduced to symbols for example :

Man λ, House 9
Bull ∀, Gates Δ, Camel 7

Symbols were used for act of writing in the Phonetic stage, suppose, if they were to write क, they used the symbol † and if न the symbol used was ⊥ and so on.

Functional Requirements of Society

1. *A System of Communication* : A system through which people could exchange symbols and thus propagate learning at a much accelerated rate.
2. *A System of Production* : To create goods and services both for their needs and for barter and exchange.
3. *System of Defence* : To protect their domain against intruders.
4. *System of Member Replacement* : Sufficient to counteract disease and other elements of member destruction.
5. *System of Social Control* : To maintain order in the society.

In the following centuries each of these functional requirements was and is still, fulfilled by even more sophisticated and efficient systems, especially in communication. As civilization progressed, inter-personal communication was used cross-culturally. Relay runners would carry messages to distant places and different people. Learning about people living in different ways was still very slow, however, mostly determined by how fast a messenger could run or ride. In some cases the messages took months and even years to reach their destination.

The story of modern mass communication begins in the fifteenth century with Johannes Gutenberg's invention of printing from movable types. People could now produce and send messages much faster. From this point on, breakthroughs in communication technology mushroomed because accelerating the recording of knowledge made possible a much more rapid exchange of information. Two important developments followed the invention of movable type. First, the use of a paper making machine in the eighteenth century made it possible to mass produce and cut paper in specific sizes, reducing the cost of production. Second, the application of steam power to the printing press, an alternative to human labour, made possible true mass production of printed material. Sources of power and improved printing presses developed continuously during the nineteenth century.

Three other inventions in the nineteenth century further aided the ability to communicate. First, the development of major Transportation Systems permitted large quantities of newspapers to be carried to people residing far away. Second, the development of Telegraph permitted people to communicate over long distances with considerable speed. The third major development of this century was the invention of telephone–which helped to communicate vocally with each other over long distances.

Electronic Communication

Just as the twentieth century dawned, radio was invented by which electromagnetic impulses could be sent through the air without wires, carrying voice transmission over long distances. For the first time in civilization, people had a medium of mass communication. In the same century the ability to capture moving visual images with the camera was perfected. People also discovered ways of capturing movement as well as sound on film to produce the motion picture and the electronic system called Videotape. Scientists and technologists, in deciding how these motion pictures could be transmitted over wires, and subsequently without wires, created a new medium called Television.

Satellite Communication

Satellite is a space vehicle that relays electromagnetic signals from one or more transmitters to one or more receiving stations, usually at long distances. These are being used for telecommunication, both direct and indirect. But here, we are concerned only with the indirect telecommunication facility of the satellites. These transmit the biggest possible treasure of information to the mass media which further relay it to the masses. Satellites are mainly of two types :

Intelesat Satellites : Such types of satellites extend global trunk line communications to different countries and are used mainly for telephone, telegraphic and other cable transmissions.

Domestic or Regional Satellites : They provide communication facilities only to the television transmission.

The other forms of communication satellites are–Direct Broadcast Satellites (DBS), Defence Satellite Communication System (DSCS) and Tracing and Data Relay Satellites (TDRS).

So far we have answered mass communication partially. It includes newspapers, radio and television which will be discussed under sub-section "Media of communication". Let us define other types of communication : intra-personal and inter-personal communication, group communication and public communication.

Intra-personal Communication

Intra-personal communication is communication within ourselves. Even early man used his senses to help understand his world and thus to perceive, to judge and to act accordingly. He learnt that on a hot, raining day, he should go outside the cave to cool off. When it was cold, they should build a fire—all were the result of communication taking place within the individual. This is the electrochemical action of the body taking part in the process of intra-personal communication. Intra-personal communication is the basis of all other forms of human communication. Without an effective system of intra-personal communication, an organism is unable to function in its environment. Ideally this communication system allows one to make decisions based on information received through the senses. For instance, when we watch television, our eyes and ears receive information and communicate it to our brain. If what we see and hear is pleasant or interesting, our intra-personal communication system indicates that we are attending to it. If we do not like it, our brain sends a message to our muscles that results in a decision to change stations or to push the button off.

Just as the electronic component in the television set prohibits more than one station from being received at a time, this central nervous system also concentrates on one immediate thought. In intra-personal communication our eyes and ears become the Senders, electrochemical impulses Messages, central nervous system Medium and the brain becomes the Receiver of these impulses, which transmits additional electrochemical impulses in the form of feedback to muscles, producing such physical activity as changing the station, etc.

Inter-personal Communication

It is a face to face communication. It is a communication between two persons. Wilmot suggests, the uniqueness of two-person communication hinges on the high degree of potential intimacy and involvement between the participants. This type of communication includes most of the informal, everyday exchanges that we engage in from the time we get up until we go to bed. Such activities can also be thought of as transactions. Inter-personal communication is the kind of communication we experience most frequently. It tends to have three following basic characteristics :

One, both parties are in close proximity.

or

Two, both parties send and receive messages.

or

Three, these messages include both verbal and non-verbal stimuli.

Obviously, physical distance between us must be limited when we say that these messages include both verbal and non-verbal stimuli. We tend to think of such communication solely as speech communication. Yet we respond to a person's facial expressions, eye movements, hand gestures, dress and posture as well as to other non-verbal stimuli he or she transmits. Sometimes non-verbal stimuli supplement verbal stimuli; sometimes they contradict them, sometimes they replace them.

For the inter-personal communication to be effective, field of experience of one person should be the same as that of the other. Our background, knowledge, beliefs and virtually anything about us make up our field of experience. When we communicate inter-personally, our fields of experience begin to overlap. A reporter who does not share common knowledge about political issues with a politician cannot ask intelligent questions. Thus the politician and reporter cannot carry on an intelligent dialogue. The further a relationship between two people advances; the more fields of experience will overlap. This overlapping of fields of experience is called homophily. The greater homophily that is present, the more chance for effective meaningful inter-personal communication. Everyday we use inter-personal communication. However, the number of people we can reach with our ideas is limited.

Group Communication

Group communication is distinct in that it occurs between three or more persons who perceive themselves as belonging to, or being identified with, a group. Interaction and intimacy depends upon the size of group. The larger the group the less personal and intimate is the possibility of exchange. In fact, as the group grows in size communication tends to become more and more of a monologue, and participation becomes problematic.

Shaw (1976) has identified six ways in which a group may be defined.

1. *Perceptions:* Do members make an impression on other members?
2. *Motivation:* Is membership in the group rewarding?
3. *Goals:* Do group members work together for a purpose?
4. *Organization:* Does each member have a specialized role like moderator, note-taker and so on?
5. *Interdependency:* Is each member somewhat dependent on the other?
6. *Interaction:* Is the group small enough to allow face to face communication between members?

These criteria represent guidelines for defining a group. A small group may meet some but not necessarily all these criteria. One that does meet all six would be described as a collection of people who influence one another, derive some satisfaction from maintaining membership in the group, interact for some purpose, assume specialized roles, are dependent on one another, and communicate face to face. Using this definition of a group, small group communication may be defined as "the process by which three or more members of a group exchange verbal and non-verbal messages in an attempt to influence one another."

Types of groups

1. *Primary groups :* This is the basic social unit to which we belong e.g. family.
2. *Casual or social groups :* It is in the company of adult friends, neighbours and others with whom we socialize. While these relationships may be relatively short lived, their influence on our thinking and behaviour is often considerable.

3. *Learning or educational groups :* When we come together to teach or learn something about a given subject e.g. seminars and conferences, etc.
4. *Work groups :* Such types of groups have specific goals to achieve, often within the context of a job. Membership may be required by virtue of employment in an organization rather than owing to individual interest in the group. Group members may have little in common except that their jobs require them to interact. The consequences of not participating in a work group may be severe.
5. *Therapeutic groups :* These are groups whose members come together to learn about themselves and to improve their interpersonal relationships.

Public Communication

Public communication tends to occur within a more formal and structured setting. It is different from small group communication. In public communication, however, one person is designated the speaker, and the rest are cast in the complementary role of listeners, or audience members. Participants are face to face and are still sending and receiving communicative stimuli. Anyone who has tried to speak before an audience whose members are reading a paper, sleeping or doing other things that denote lack of attention knows all too well that audiences send messages as well as receive them. But the balance of message sending is quite uneven–the speaker initiates most of the verbal messages, and, though, audience members often send non-verbal messages (applause, laughter and so on), audiences in general are not usually expected to contribute verbal messages except in a question-and-answer period following the speech. Despite this imbalance, public communication is still face to face communication, and we frequently find ourselves participating in it as either speakers or listeners. Hart *et al.* (1975) identified several distinctive aspects of the public communication context.

Public communication occurs in "public" rather than "private" places–that is in classrooms, auditoriums, conferences, seminars, rather than in homes, offices, etc.

Public communication is a "pronounced social occasion" as opposed to a relatively informal, unstructured occasion. Usually the event is planned in advance. There is an agenda. Some people are designated to perform certain functions.

There are behavioural norms that are relatively clear cut. For example, questions are usually addressed to the speaker after his or her address is completed.

For all these reasons public communication often demands that the speaker be much more deliberate and organized.

Mass Communication

It is the process of delivering information, ideas and attitudes to a sizable and diversified audience through use of media developed for that purpose. The art of mass communication is much more difficult than that of face to face communication. The communicator who is addressing thousands of different personalities at the same time cannot adjust an appeal to meet their individual reactions. An approach that convinces one part of the audience may alienate another part. The successful communicator is one who finds the right method of expression to establish empathy with the largest possible number of individuals in the audience.

The mass communicator's task breaks down into two parts, knowing what to communicate and how to deliver the message to make the greatest possible impact on an audience. A message of poor content told to millions of people, may have less total effective impact than a well presented message placed before a small audience. Effectiveness of the message leaves the last impression.

The audience in mass communication, according to Wright (1975) is relatively large, heterogeneous and anonymous to the source. The experience is public and rapid. The source works through a complex organization rather than in isolation and the message may represent the efforts of many different people. Consider again the first element in this definition : the audience. Although in some person-to-group and organizational settings the audience is quite large, face to face interaction is often possible. In mass communication, the size of the audience makes it impossible for the mass communicator and audience members to interact face to face. In addition to being a diversified group, the receivers in mass communication are, for the most part, unknown to the source.

The second element, the experience is public rather than private because the messages are not addressed to particular individuals. It is intended for rapid consumption by large number of people.

The third element in this definition of mass communication–the source of the communication, is not working in isolation but rather from within a complex organisation. There are two points to be made here. First, the message itself represents the efforts of many different individuals. Second, these individuals represent a complex organization which is usually concerned with making a profit.

Characteristics of Mass Communication

Mass Medium : A mass medium makes it possible for the message to reach far beyond the immediate proximity of the sender. A few hundred feet may be all the distance the human voice can project to a crowd without the aid of public address system. A mass medium can take that same message around the world.

Limited Sensory Channels : The presence of a mass medium also limits the number of sensory channels upon which we can draw. When we sat in the auditorium and listened to the politician, all of our senses could take part in the communication process. For example, after the speech we might have shaken hands with the politician. With mass communication we might only be able to hear and see the politician.

Impersonal Communication : In inter-personal communication the first meeting may be impersonal but as the relationship grows, the communication becomes more and more personal. But in mass communication, it is impersonal.

Gatekeeper : A gatekeeper is a person who, by selecting, changing and rejecting messages, can influence the flow of information to a receiver or group of receivers. A gatekeeper can be a news editor who edits the reporter's copy, a film producer, who cuts a scene from the original script and so on. There are three functions of the gatekeeper (i) to limit the information we receive by editing this information before it is disseminated to us; (ii) to expand the information we receive by giving us additional facts or view; and (iii) to reorganize or reinterpret the information.

Delayed Feedback : The feedback in mass communication is not as immediate or complete as it is in face to face communication. And since mass communication usually involves a chain or network of individuals, the feedback intended for one person in the chain is likely to reach a different member of the chain. Moreover, it is sometimes impossible for the source in mass communication to respond to make public all the feedback that is received.

Elements of Communication

According to Wilbur Schramm, communication requires at least three elements : (a) the source, (b) the message and (c) the destination. The *source* may be an individual speaking, or gesturing, etc., or a communication organization like the newspaper, movie, etc. The *message* may be in the form of sound waves in the air, or a wave of the hand, or some ink on the paper, or impulses in an electric current; the important thing is that it is something which can be interpreted meaningfully by somebody else. The *destination* may be an individual who is listening, or reading, on watching, or it may be a group of people who are listening to a lecture, or watching a movie.

In 1948, political scientist Harold Lasswell suggested a convenient way to describe an act of communication is to answer the following questions?

Who
To Whom
In which channel
Says what
With what effect?

Who — The Communicator : The communicator is the source of the message. He may be a primary or a secondary source of message. When he is the secondary source of the message he may get the information from other sources; but it is the responsibility of the communicator to communicate the message to the people in the form they can understand.

With What Purpose — The Objective : The communicator must be clear about the response from the audience. The objectives must be defined clearly which could be–informing, educating, reasoning or may be lobbying.

To Whom — The Audience : Communication requires receivers and consumers of messages, *the people* with whom he communicates. Communication involves the joint conduct or transaction of source and receiver. The receivers are active participants in communication with the source. It is, therefore, necessary, in order to communicate effectively, not only to know the general audience characteristics, but also to know the specific audience. If the audience or the particular target group is clearly defined, it will be easier for the communicator to put across the message effectively.

In Which–Channel (s) : This portion of Lasswell's model pertains to the media. It is more aptly phrased in the plural, "*in which channels*", for there is a complex variety of media people use when communicating about public purposes. The channel can also be regarded a vehicle that takes the message to the audience.

For thousands of years messages were communicated through spoken voice when the source and the receiver were in a face-to-face situation. Even today a large majority of population in India, due to lack of literacy, depend upon oral communication. Chances of successful communication in a face-to-face situation are far greater. The communicator gets an immediate feedback, about the need, if any, to modify his message for the appropriate impact.

In spite of the vastly expanding media of mass communication, inter-personal communication through spoken word continues to enjoy a predominant position in villages : the extension workers, political and opinion leaders rely on spoken word communication for the dissemination of the desired message and putting across their point of view.

Chances of successful communication in a face-to-face situation are far better because the pace of communication is regulated by the participants. Since the communicator gets an immediate feedback about the need, if any, to modify his message for appropriate impact, the chances of establishing effective understanding with the audience are greater. Even with all the wonders of modern technology the face-to-face communication is still the most effective and persuasive means of communication. A face-to-face dialogue, conference or speech can cut through all the bottlenecks, barriers or blocks.

It is usually the use of various combinations of basic forms of communication–spoken, written and visual–that carries the maximum impact. In a classroom situation a teacher uses a black board or shows a chart, while speaking or delivering a lecture; he also combines a written word with a spoken word. The use of photographs, models, slides, charts, etc., while speaking to the audience is an ideal combination for effective communication.

Different forms of communication appeal to different people.

Messages are received through all the five senses–sight, hearing, smell, taste and touch. The message is likely to be understood better if it appeals to more than one senses at a time. It is, therefore, evident that no single channel can reach all the people we want to reach. Since there is a great variation in the experiences, abilities, attitudes and skills of the people, the choice of channel will have to be carefully done. Research has also proved that a single exposure is not sufficient to get the desired impact for all kinds of audiences and all kinds of messages. It is important for a communicator to know as to which channel will work better for the particular type of message and the particular type of audience. A communicator may use one or several channels depending upon the nature of the message and the target audience.

The invention of printing made it possible for a single written message to reach many receivers and thus increase the potential effectiveness of individual writer communicators. The written message is used in many forms–posters, charts, leaflets, circular letters, wall newspapers, and of course–books, magazines and newspapers constitute a major segment of print medium.

The electronic media–Radio, Television and Cable Television–constitute major channels of mass communication ushering in, Communication Revolution.

Says What? The Message : Three factors are pertinent to the message produced by the source : the code, content and the treatment.

Message is a set of codes that has its own meaning to the communicator and receiver. The code could be verbal, non-verbal or written. A code can be defined as group of symbols that can be structured in a meaningful way. Languages are codes, which contain elements–sounds, letters, words, etc. Music is a code, which has notes, syntax, etc. Any form that communicates requires a code.

The content can be defined as the material in the message selected by the source. The communicator must define the contents of the message which could be information, ideas, attitude, appeal, etc. The contents of message must be specific, accurate and precise. The information must be timely and updated. Other important questions that need to be answered are : Does the audience need the message? Is the message specific? Has the message been recommended by appropriate authorities ?

Again style or treatment (presentation) determines the effectiveness of the message. The treatment of the message refers to the decision the communicator makes as to how he should deliver his message. In preparing copy for the newspaper, journalists select the contents which would be interesting to the reader, give the stories proper heading, decide about the type size and page placement according to the appeal and importance of the story.

With What Effect? : The impact of a message depends upon whether it can be used within the frame of reference that is already available. The frame of reference consists of a number of beliefs and the information already available with the receiver. A good information background is necessary for the message to have any impact. Again the kind of people with whom the receiver is associated will also affect the success of the communicator. The short-term effect of communication is judged by the change it has produced in people's knowledge, attitude and behaviour; whereas the long-term effect is assessed by people's actions.

Barriers of Communication

There are a number of barriers, which prevent the achievement of the desired results. Some of these are : lack of communication environment or a common frame of reference, noise, badly coded messages, disturbance in the transmission channels, mistrust between the sender and the receiver, different perception of reality and vagueness about the objectives achieved.

The common frame of reference implies the social context in which communication takes place. Communication is related to social systems. Communication increases the likelihood of similarities among people, increases the chances that people can work together to accomplish a goal. The allocation of position, the specifications of role behaviour are all accomplished through communication. The common frame of reference in the individual and reference group to which he belongs influences the effect of the message given by the communicator. Both the sender and the receiver would be able to focus their mind meaningfully on the message, if the social context is well defined.

Differing norms in different social systems also affect communication. In his book,

The Process of Communication, David K. Berlo gives one of the situations of communication breakdowns.

> An American's concept of punctuality is quite different from a Tunisian's or an Indonesian's. In the American system, if you arrive at a man's office fifteen minutes after you said you would

> be there, you have violated a norm. In a Tunisian system, you might arrive at a man's office an hour late, sometimes half a day late and not violate a norm at all. An American who works in a Tunisian system has to alter his concepts of group norms. If he does not, he will be insulted, hurt, and critical of the Tunisian's behaviour–because he is bound by the norms of his own system, and does not realize that they are neither "right" nor "true" for another system.

Likewise the concept of cultural context is equally important for meaningful communication to take place. Culture broadly denotes shared beliefs, values, ways of making things, behaving, etc. It includes songs and dances, language, shared concepts, establishment of norms within a social system. Cultural gap between two parties or lack of sensitivity towards cultural and social norms constitutes a serious obstacle to effective communication. Unless the experiences–in the social and cultural context–of the two persons have a good deal in common, meaningful communication becomes difficult.

Noise constitutes barrier between the sending and receiving of communication signals. Shannon and Weaver in, *The Mathematical Theory of Communication*, postulates two levels of noise problem. At level A is the engineering noise and at level B is the semantic noise. Level A is physical and technical and is defined as any distortion of meaning occurring in the communication process which is not intended by the source, but which affects the reception of the message carrying signals and their clarity. The semantic level is noise or bottleneck in terms of codes–linguistic, personal, psychological and cultural.

Several communication scholars use the term Noise in a wider ambit. Noise can occur not only in the primary channel but also in the source, and in the receiver. The noise in the source refers to the confused thinking prior to the communication. This prevents the communicator from imparting clearly his idea to the receiver because he himself does not understand clearly what he wants to communicate.

The use of ambiguous expression or highly specialized jargon, inappropriate to the situation, also makes communication difficult. At times the attitude of the sender is at variance with that of the receiver and in case attitudinal clash occurs, communication is bound to suffer. Being out of tune with oneself, mental or physical fatigues are also obstacles to effective communication.

An other important factor to be noted is the limited information processing capability of an individual. Most people can retain only six to eight separate bits of information in their short-term memory, hence we tend to be selective. We tend to select only those bits of communication, which are relevant to us and ignore others.

Some other barriers to effective communication are : no perceived benefit to audience, variation in language and listening skills, personal biases, etc. It is, therefore, essential that a communicator must continue to adjust and adapt his approach to communication with others– those of different cultures, different attitudes and having different expectations of communication. It is equally imperative that, in order to remove all barriers or blocks to effective communication, a communicator will have to be sensitive to the signals reflected by the audience. There will always be need to re-tune our approach to communication–in order to get across our message effectively.

Lippman's Barriers to Communications	Roper's Hypothesis	Gallup's Regulators of Absorption Rate of New Ideas
1. Artificial censorships.	GREAT THINKERS Adam Smith, Jefferson	1. Complexity of the idea
2. Limitations of social contact.	GREAT DISCIPLES Robert Taft, FDR	2. Factors of differences from accustomed patterns.
3. Meagre time available for paying attention to public affairs	GREAT DISSEMINATORS Lippman, Reston, Meany, Murrow	3. Competition with prevailing ideas.
4. Distortions because events must be compressed into short messages.	LESSER DISSEMINATORS Clergy, Editors, etc.	4. Is idea susceptible to demonstration and proof?
5. Difficulty of making small vocabulary to express a big, complicated world.	POLITICALLY ACTIVES 10 to 15 million citizens who take active interest in public affairs and provide local leadership.	5. How strong are vested interests which will block proposed change?
6. Fear of facing those facts which seem to threaten established routine of men's lives.	POLITICALLY INERT 80 to 90 million citizens who seldom voice opinions but who vote, buy, decide.	6. Does proposal meet a felt need?
7.		7. Frequency with which public is reminded of new idea.

Source : Cutlip and Center, *Effective Public Relations*, New Jersey : Prentice-Hall, 1971.

Diffusion and Adoption Process

Ideas are first disseminated and then adopted. Elmo Roper formulated a hypothesis which he named 'Concentric Circle Theory'. He assumes that ideas penetrate the whole public very slowly. They do so by a process similar to osmosis. They move out in concentric circles from great thinkers to great disciples to great disseminators to lesser disseminators to the politically active to the politically inert. The flow of ideas as hypothesized by Roper is described in the following diagram :

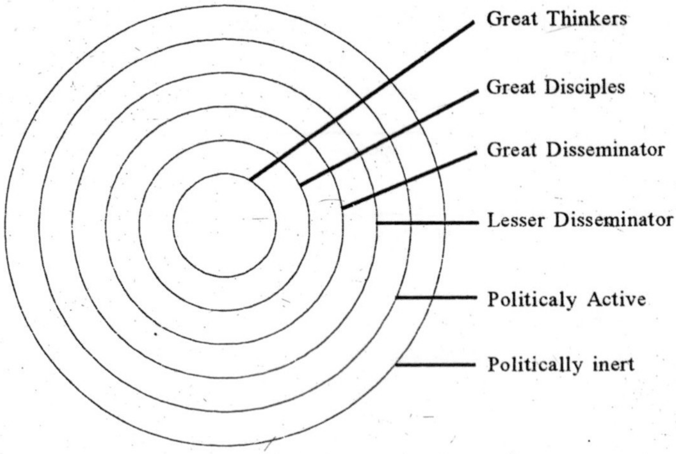

Concentric Circle Theory

This theory does not explain the rate of flow in the transmission and acceptance of ideas which is governed by many factors. These include Lippman's barriers to communication described above and George Gallup's 'Regulators of Absorption Rate' listed below :

Gallup's Regulators of Absorption Rate of New Ideas

1. *Complexity of the idea :* If the idea is more complex it will take more time in diffusion and adoption.
2. *Factors of difference from accustomed patterns :* If the ideas are different from the accustomed pattern these will not easily be diffused and accepted.

3. *Competition with prevailing ideas :* More competition with the prevailing ideas, more time in diffusion and acceptance.
4. *Is idea susceptible to demonstration and proof :* If the ideas can be demonstrated these will be soon diffused and accepted.
5. *How strong are vested interests which will block proposed change :* Vested interests slow down the progress in diffusion and acceptance process.
6. *Does proposal meet a felt need :* Particular ideas in demand will help in diffusion and acceptance process.
7. *Frequency with which public is reminded of new ideas :* Repetition of ideas will foster the process of diffusion and acceptance.

Agricultural sociologists have concluded that acceptance goes through five stages.

(i) *Awareness :* This is the first stage when he has little knowledge of the idea and learns of its existence.

(ii) *Interest :* In the second stage, the individual develops interest in the idea. He seeks more information and considers its general merits.

(iii) *Evaluation :* The individual makes mental application of the idea and weighs its merits for his own situation. He obtains more information and decides to try it.

(iv) *Trial :* The individual actually applies the idea or practice–usually on a small scale.

(v) *Adoption :* If the idea proves acceptable, it is adopted.

The 7 C's of Communication

1. *Credibility :* Communication starts with a climate of belief. This climate is built by performance on the part of the communicator. The performance reflects an earnest desire to serve the receiver. The receiver must have confidence in the sender. He must have a high regard for the source's competence on the subject.
2. *Context :* The context must confirm, not contradict the message. It must provide for participation and playback.
3. *Content :* The content determines the audience. Hence, the

message must have meaning for the receiver, and it must be compatible with his value system. It must have relevance for him.

4. *Clarity :* The message must be put in simple terms. Words must mean the same thing to the receiver as they do to the sender. Complex issues must be compressed into theme slogans that have simplicity and clarity. The farther a message has to travel, the simpler it should be.
5. *Continuity and Consistency :* Communication is an unending process. It requires repetition to achieve penetration. The story must be consistent.
6. *Channels :* Only the established channels of communication should be used–channels that the receiver uses and respects, creating new ones is difficult. Different channels have different effects and serve effectively in different stages of the diffusion process.
7. *Capability of Audience :* Communication must take into account the capability of the audience. Communications are most effective when they require the least effort on the part of the recipient. This includes factors of availability, habit reading ability and receiver's knowledge.

Functions and Uses of Mass Communication

For a society to exist, certain communication needs must be met. These needs existed since earlier times. Primitive tribes had sentinels who scanned the environment and reported dangers. Councils of elders interpreted facts and made decisions. Tribal meetings were used to transmit these decisions to the rest of the group. Other members of the tribe may have been story-tellers and jesters who functioned to entertain the group. As society became larger and more complex, these jobs grew too big to be handled by single individuals. With the advent of a technology that allowed the development of mass communication, these jobs were taken over by the mass media and this change was an important one. Sometimes, dysfunctions were also performed by the mass media. Dysfunctions are the consequences that are undesirable from the point of view of welfare of the society.

Lasswell (1948) presented a summary statement of the basic communication functions in the following manner :

(a) Surveillance of the environment.
(b) Correlation of the parts of the society in responding to its environment.
(c) The transmission of the cultural heritage.

These functions refer to the provision of information, the giving of comment and interpretation to help make sense of the fragments of information and also the formation of consensus; the expression of cultural values and symbols which are essential to the identity and continuity of society, respectively. Wright (1960) developed this basic scheme to describe many of the effects of the media and added 'entertainment' as a fourth key media function. This may be part of the transmitted culture but it has another aspect–that of providing reward, relaxation and reduction of tension, which makes it easier for people to cope with real life problems and for societies, to avoid breakdown (Mendelsohn, 1966).

Denis McQuail (1987) added one more function : that is mobilizing function of media. Nearly everywhere, the media are expected to advance national interests and promote certain key values and behaviour patterns, but especially so in times of crisis. And in certain developing societies, as well as in many socialist states, a mobilizing role is formally allotted to the media.

The following set of basic ideas about media purpose in society has been taken from Denis McQuail's book '*Mass Communication Theory.*'

I. *Information*

- providing information about events and conditions in society and the world.
- indicating relations of power.
- facilitating innovation, adaptation and progress.

II. *Correlation*

- explaining, interpreting and commenting on the meaning of events and information.
- providing support for established authority and norms.
- socializing.
- co-ordinating separate activities.
- consensus building.
- setting orders of priority and signalling relative status.

III. *Continuity*

- expressing the dominant culture and recognizing sub-cultures and new cultural developments.
- forging and maintaining commonality of values.

IV. *Entertainment*

- providing amusement, diversion, the means of relaxation.
- reducing social tension.

V. *Mobilization*

- campaigning for societal objectives in the sphere of politics, war, economic development, work and sometimes religion.

Dominick (1990) in his book *'The Dynamics of Mass Communication'* has described the main functions of media-surveillance, interpretation, linkage, transmission of values and entertainment. These functions are not mutually exclusive. The actual content or activity representing the functions will also vary a good deal according to whose purpose is being served. Let us discuss these functions one by one.

Surveillance

Of all the media functions, surveillance is apparently an important function and the degree of audience dependence on the media for news supports this observation. Surveillance refers to what we popularly call the news and information role of the media. The media have taken the place of sentinels and lookouts. Correspondents for wire services, TV networks, and newspapers, are located across the globe. These individuals collect the information for us which we could not get for ourselves. Their reports are funnelled back to mass media organizations that, in turn, produce in newspapers or magazines, radio or TV.

Surveillance function can be divided into two categories one is warning or beware surveillance and the other is called instrumental surveillance.

1. *Warning surveillance :* It occurs when the media informs us about threats from depressed economic conditions, floods, droughts, increasing inflation, terrorist attack or erupting volcanoes, etc. These warnings can be about immediate threats (a television station interrupts programming to broadcast a flood warning) or they can be about long

term on chronic threats (a newspaper series about air pollution or unemployment).

2. *Instrumental surveillance :* It has to do with the transmission of information that is useful and helpful in every-day life. News about new products, share prices, fashion shows, heroes, new films or matches, etc. are some examples of instrumental surveillance. Not all examples of surveillance occur in traditional news media, but appear in different magazines also. In fact, the surveillance function can be found in content that is primarily meant to entertain. A soap opera might perform an instrumental function by portraying new fashions and hair styles, etc.

Interpretation

The mass media do not supply just facts and date. They also provide information on the ultimate meaning and significance of those events. Not all the happenings are included in the newspapers or in a TV or radio newscast. Only those items or events are selected by the media organizations which are of prime importance. Those stories which are given page-one space and eight-column headings are obviously judged to be more important than those which are given one or two paragraphs in inside pages. In a TV or radio newscast, those stories that are given two minutes at the beginning of the show are deemed more newsworthy than the item that gets two minutes toward the end. Stories that ultimately make it into the paper or the newscast have been judged by various gatekeepers sitting in the media organizations. The most obvious example of this function can be found on the editorial pages of a newspaper. Interpretation, comment and opinion are provided for the reader so that he or she gains an added perspective on the news stories carried on the other pages.

Interpretation is not confined to editorials only. Articles devoted to an analysis of the causes behind a particular event or a discussion of implications of a new government policy are also examples of the interpretation function. Why is the price of onions going up? What impact will a prolonged drought have on food prices? Treatment of these topics may deal with more than the factual information that might be contained in a straight news story. At special events such as world cup matches, satellite launches, elections, etc. commentators are on hand to interpret the meaning behind what is going on.

Interpretation can take various forms. Critics are employed by the various media organizations to review books, films and to rate different kinds of programmes. The consequences of the interpretation function of the mass media can be that the individual is exposed to large number of different points of view, probably far more than he or she could come in contact with through personal channels. Because of this, a person can evaluate all sides of an issue before arriving at an opinion. Additionally, the media make available to the individual a wide range of expertise that he or she might not have access to through interpersonal communication.

There are, however, certain dysfunctions that might occur. Since media content is public, any criticism or praise of a certain individual or group is also public and might have positive or negative consequences for the medium involved. Therefore, media might discourage critical evaluation of controversial topics. On the other side, there is also danger that an individual may in the long run come to rely too heavily on the views carried in the media and lose his or her critical ability and becomes passive and allows others to think for him or her.

Linkage

Closely allied with surveillance function is the linkage function. It is the ability of the mass media to join different elements of society that are not directly connected by interpersonal channels. For example, mass advertising attempts to link the needs of the buyers with the products of sellers. Legislators in Delhi may try to keep in touch with their constituents by reading regional papers. Voters, in turn, learn about the doings of their elected officials through newspapers, TV and radio. Poor people that attempt to raise money for the treatment of certain diseases are another example of this linkage function. The needs of those, suffering from the disease, are matched with the desires of others who wish to see the problem eliminated.

Another type of linkage occurs when geographically separated groups that share a common interest are linked by the media. In 1988, when government did not accept the UGC recommendations about revised pay scale norms, protests took place at many places across the country. These demonstrations were covered by the media and people saw what was happening in Delhi and *vice-versa*. This coverage provided an informational as well as an emotional linkage among these various groups and helped to foster a general feeling that they are part of a nationwide movement. Media raised an alarm to help those families who had been killed in the Kargil fighting. The people watched the sacrifices made by these heroes for the sake of country and the suffering of the young widows. Such coverage provided an information as well as emotional linkage among the countrymen. Resultantly, huge donations were pouring in to help the deserted families.

Linkage function also helps a person who dials a number and is linked up with similarly minded folks. It is also possible that the media can create totally new social groups by linking members of society who have not previously recognised that others have similar interests. Some writers call this function the "public making" ability of the mass media.

Transmission of Values

The transmission of values is a subtle but nonetheless important function of the mass media. It has also been called the socialization function. Socialization refers to the ways in which an individual comes to adopt the behaviour and values of a group. The mass media present portrayals of our society and by watching, listening and reading we learn how people are supposed to act and what values are important. Media portrayals picture motherhood and childrearing as activities that have a positive value for society. Individuals who are exposed to these portrayals are likely to grow up and accept this value. Thus, a social value is transmitted from one generation to another.

The mass media also teach us about people; they show us how they act and what is expected of them. In other words, the media present us with role models that we may observe and perhaps initiate. A study once indicated that many adolescents learnt about killing and robbery by watching films and television programmes that featured this activity.

Sometimes, the media consciously try to instil values and behaviour patterns in the audience. There are countless examples of values and behaviours that are in part at least, socialized through the media. However, at this point let us examine some of the consequences of having the mass media serve as agents of socialization. At one level, value transmission *via* the mass media will aid the stability of society. Common values and experiences are passed down to all members, thereby creating common bonds between them. On the other hand, the kinds of values and cultural information that are included in mass media content are selected by large organizations that may select values and behaviours that encourage the *status quo*.

Of all the mass media, it is probably television that has the greatest potential for the socialization of young children. By the time, an individual has reached eighteen, he or she will have spent more time in watching television than any other single activity. Television is flooded with many musical and entertainment channels. Because of this wide exposure, several writers have warned of possible dysfunctions that might occur if television became the most important channel of socialization. For instance, since so many TV programmes contain violence, it has been feared that youngsters who watch many violent programmes might be socialized into accepting violence as a legitimate method of problem solving.

Entertainment

The most obvious of all media functions is that of entertainment. The newspapers devote much space to cover the events of the day, gossip, humour, comics, sports, share prices, horoscopes, puzzles and general entertainment features. Whereas television is primarily devoted to entertainment. The entertainment content of radio varies widely according to station format.

The scope of mass media entertainment is awesome. The importance of the entertainment function has grown as people have accumulated more leisure time which they will probably fill with entertainment provided by the media.

In the past, the entertainment function was fulfilled by interpersonal communication : storytelling, folk songs, folk dances, nautankies, puppet shows, folk theatres and magicians.

The consequences of having this task taken over by mass communication are clear : the media can make entertainment available to a large number of people at relatively low cost. This helps make leisure and recreational time more enjoyable. Entertainment that is carried by the mass media appeals to mass audience. The ultimate result of this state of affairs is that media content is designed to appeal to the lowest common denominator of taste. Many critics have argued that the media have lowered the level of Indian culture and have cheapened taste.

One other consequence of the widespread use of media for entertainment is that it has encouraged passivity. Instead of reading newspapers and magazines, they flick on the TV sets and watch entertainment programmes. Instead of playing games, people might simply watch it on TV critics charge that the mass media will turn Indians into a nation of watchers and listeners one day.

THEORIES OF COMMUNICATION

There has been enormous interest among social scientists to find out the effects of the mass communication within society. This has resulted in a number of theories which essentially trace the relationship between mass communication and society. A theory is someone's conceptualisation of an observed set of events. Any attempt to explain or represent a phenomenon is a theory. The term communication theory usually refers to the body of theories for understanding of the communication process. They are based on the studies of signs, symbols and meaning and their relation to the objects or concepts to which they belong. So far no single integrated theory of communication has yet emerged which is universally accepted. However, some of the important theories that have been described here help us to understand how mass communication operates in society.

Earlier theories were based on the assumptions that mass media have enormous and direct influence upon society. But later researches provide evidence against any direct cause and effect relationship between mass communication and society, rather they underline the importance of individual differences and personal influences on transmission, acceptance and retention of message, sociological theories stated mass media, as an outcome of changes in society. There are other theories that express ideas on how the mass media ought to or can be expected to operate under prevailing political and economic circumstances. Some of the theories which have been discussed here will provide insights into the role of mass communication in society and the way in which an audience utilizes different mass media.

1. Hypodermic or Bullet Theory

As the name implies, bullet theory suggests the messages were thought to be like magic bullets that were shot directly into the receiver. It assumes that receivers are passive and defenceless and take whatever is shot at them. The magic bullet theory also portrays that the media have direct, immediate and powerful effects on those who pay attention to their content. The theory assumed that they reached every eye and ear in the same way and brought about the same changes of thought and behaviour in the entire audience. Two assumptions that can easily be drawn from such an approach are : (1) people receive information directly from the mass media and not through an intermediary, and (2) that reaction is individual, not based on how other people might influence them.

This theory still holds good by many critics of the mass media who assume the media are extremely powerful institutions and the media consumers are woefully naïve and malleable. They see media gatekeepers as highly manipulative and somehow much more clever than their audiences. Contemporary media, especially television are accused of creating insidious influences, alongwith shortening the public's attention span, rushing children into adulthood and even reducing all public discourse to fluffy, trivialized amusement.

If one believes in bullet theory, one has to maintain that the audience is made up of an enormous undifferentiated mass of humanity and each mumber of the audience would react identically to the mass mediated messages but this is incorrect. The media do not have simple and uniform influences that cause individual's thoughts and actions. The influence of media on individuals depends on many factors, including individual psychological differences, membership in social categories, and patterns of social relationships that serve as alternative channels of communication. All of these shape and limit a person's exposure to the media and how he or she will eventually interpret media content. Therefore, we must anticipate that the media's role in shaping public's views of current issues in the news and of the importance of social problems will be similarly complicated.

2. Individual Differences Theory

The individual differences theory proposes that each of us has unique qualities that result in our reacting differently to media messages. In other words, the reaction to media content differs according to motivation of audience members, their position to accept or reject a given message, intelligence, beliefs, opinions, values, needs, moods, prejudices, perceptibility, etc. Professors Melvin De Fleur and Sandra Ball-Rokeach in their book *Theories of Mass Communication* state : Individual differences perspective implies that media messages contain particular stimulus attributes that have differential interaction with personality characteristics of audience members. Since there are individual differences in personality characteristics among such members, it is natural to assume that there will be variations in effect which correspond to these individual differences.

Thus, an individual's needs, attitudes, values, prior beliefs and other cognitive and emotional states play an important part in screening and selecting media exposure and interpretation. This means that members of an audience are very selective in what they read, listen to, or view from the media. It also means that the pattern of understanding and interpretation of one person may be very different from that of another who is attending to identical media content. Hence, variables in these differing effects are partially caused by the audience's selective exposure, selective perception and selective retention of media content. These factors act as barriers between message and effect, thereby limiting the scope of direct impact of mass communication on people. These concepts are discussed as below :

Selective Exposure

Selective exposure occurs when people tend to expose themselves to various messages or stimuli that are in accordance with their existing opinions and interests and avoid communications which cause dissonance to their beliefs. Bittner (1986) states that the theory of selective exposure suggests we will select those media which support our beliefs and which have programming and information appealing to our own interests. Furthermore, the more we use those media, the more the people responsible for programming will send information that appeals to us. Will a medium's continual reinforcement of our beliefs and opinions and will our continual reinforcement by choice selective exposure of programming that supports our interests make us a society of psychological isolates with narrow and dogmatic views continually fed by programmers sending more and more specialized messages?

Selective Perception

Once the individuals have selectively exposed themselves to the messages in accordance with their preferences, they read only those messages which are in accordance with their existing attitudes. Thus, they may either ignore or misinterpret those messages, or parts of a message, which conflict with or are dissimilar to held attitudes and expectations. For example, if the individual is extremely loyal the politician, he might agree with everything the politician says regardless of what he says, so much so that if his opponent said the same thing, he might completely disagree with him. We can say the individual would be guilty of selective perception. It is not a serious crime, but one that can considerably distort how the individual react to messages.

Selective Retention

Selective retention means that we tend to remember things that are familiar to us or that we perceive as corresponding to our preconceived ideas. For example, if a politician is making a speech we might retain only those portions of the speech with which we agree. If we perceive the entire speech as favourable, we may remember all of it. If we perceive it as unfavourable, we may wipe it entirely from our mind. If parts of the speech affect us positively, we remember those parts while forgetting the negative ones. Or the negative ones may be the very ones we remember. Either way, how we originally perceived the address determines what we retain, a process called selective retention. Thus, factors influencing selective retention include the importance of the message for later utility, the extent to which the message coincided with predispositions, the intensity of the message, the means by which it was transmitted.

3. Cognitive Dissonance Theory

This theory was coined by L. A. Festinger in 1957. The theory predicts that people will seek out information which confirms existing attitudes and views of the world or reinforces other aspects of behaviour. Similarly, it predicts that people will avoid information which is likely to increase dissonance. If someone dislikes a person, he will dislike his or her views, what he or she says is unlikely to cause cognitive dissonance for there is a congruence here. Dissonance is acute when a liked person says something seemingly 'out of character' or fails to accord with expectations or the image held of him or her. Festinger states his theory thus : Any time a person has information or an opinion which considered by itself would lead him not to engage in some action, then this information or opinion is dissonant with having engaged in action. When such dissonance exists, the person will try to reduce it either by changing his actions or by changing his beliefs and opinions. If he cannot change the action, opinion change will ensure. This psychological process, which can be called dissonance reduction, does explain the frequently observed behaviour of people justifying their actions. When dissonance exists, dissonance reduction attempts do occur.

Essentially the dissonance concept suggests that persons avoid information adverse to their views or situation and seek out information consonant with their world.

Festinger portrays the following typical sources of dissonance between two beliefs :

(i) Logical inconsistency, (ii) Cultural mores, (iii) Past experience, and (iv) When one specific opinion is launched by definition in a more general opinion, this theory states that behaviour can cause persuasion. Many researchers support this point and provide suggestions for involvement and self-persuasion.

Melvin De Fleur and Sandra Ball Rokeach (1981) have concluded that "from the vast available content, individual members of the audience selectively attend to interpret and retain messages, particularly if they are related to their interest, consistent with their attitude, congruent with their beliefs and supportive of their values".

These studies which tried to discover psychological characteristics as intervening (between media and audience) were admirable which could serve as barriers between message and effects emerged from the political studies and gave rise to personal influence theory.

4. Personal Influence Theory

This theory is the outcome of a classic study of the 1940 presidential elections in the United States. This study was conducted by Lazarsfeld, Berelson and Gaudel in 1948. They were interested in the general impact of mass media on voting behaviour and especially in the people who changed their voting intention during the course of the campaign. Their findings were that broad coverage of the campaign by the mass media simply reinforced the initial preferences of the voters, it was only the personal influence or interpersonal relationships that changed the voting behaviour of the voters. Researchers suggest that within the group to which we belong, certain people have a particularly strong influence. These people have been called opinion leaders –"individuals who, through day-to-day personal contacts, influence others in matters of decisions and opinion formation" (Wright,1975). These opinion leaders can come from any social, economic or occupational level. Within different levels of society, there are different opinion leaders. Opinion leaders themselves tend to be better informed and to be heavy users of the various mass media. They read more newspapers and magazines; they watch the coverage of political and social issues by the broadcast media, they tend to be influenced by them. This influence, in turn, is passed on others in face-to-face communication. It was this discovery that generated a two-step flow of communication theory.

Two-step Flow of Communication

This concept was poised by Paul Lazarsfeld and his associates. According to this theory communication flows in two directions–horizontal as well as vertical. Horizontally opinion leaders are cultivated and the information is passed from the various mass media to certain opinion leaders and vertically message is passed on from these opinion leaders to the other people within the population. The authors found little evidence of the direct influence of the media; indeed people seemed more influenced by face-to-face contact with others. Lazarsfeld and his fellow researchers suggested that the flow of communication to the individual was often directed through an opinion leader who played a vital role in both spreading and interpreting the information. They thus proposed a two-step mode of communication flow which later research has found to be generally useful. In highlighting the importance of the social context of the receiver in the process of the interpretation of mass communication messages this model differs significantly from earlier ones. It presents the mass audience as being composed of interacting and responsive individuals rather than of the socially isolated, passive atoms of earlier mass society theories.

Like other theories, two-step flow has its shortcomings too; it diminishes the original, direct influence of mass media, its effects are evident only in political studies that were conducted decades ago when there was no television influence and, therefore, may not be as applicable to the contemporary political scene.

Multi-step Flow of Communication

It is a development of two step flow of communication in the sense that opinion leaders may also be consulting with others whom they consider opinion leaders. It is not specific about the number of steps, there will be in the relaying process nor does it specify that messages must originate from a source and then pass straight through the agencies of mass media. This theory suggests a variable number of relays in the communication process and the receivers may receive the message at various stages along the relay network. The exact number of steps in the process depends upon the :

(i) intentions of the source,

(ii) availability of mass media,

(iiii) the extent of audience exposure to agencies of communication,

(iv) the nature of the message, and
(v) the importance of the message to the audience.

Multi-step flow of communication process is important in the sense it allows the researcher to account for different variables in different communication situations.

It is important to note that both two-step flow and multi-step flow theories clearly discredit the direct influence of the mass media because of extraneous influences, interpersonal channels and social relations of audiences which are often complex, multi-directional and multi-dimensional.

Sociological Theories of Mass Communication

The sociological approach to communication theory is based on the assumption that there exists a definite relationship between mass communication and social change. Some of the relevant theories which we are going to discuss are : The Cultivation Theory, Social Learning Theory, Agenda Setting Theory, Play Theory and the Uses and Gratification Theory.

1. *The Cultivation Theory*

This theory was developed by George Gerbner in 1967. It is based on the assumption that mass media have subtle effects on audiences who, unknowingly, absorb the dominant symbols, images and messages of media. He calls it "Cultivation of dominant image pattern". According to this theory, a long, persistent exposure to TV is capable of cultivating common beliefs about the world. Gerbner and his colleagues are of the view that the messages of television do not portray reality in society, but repeated exposure to such distortions leads to development of particular beliefs about the world; and these beliefs get reinforced once they are developed. He also strongly suggests that the powerful effect of mass media act as moulders of society. Additionally, cultivation analysis concentrates on the long-term effects of exposure rather than the short-term impact on attitudes and opinions.

Gerbner and his associates have detected a phenomenon called 'mainstreaming' whereby differences apparently due to cultural and social factors tend to diminish among heavy TV viewers. They have also found evidence for what they call 'resonance', situation in which the respondent's real life experiences are congruent with those of the television world, thereby leading to a greater cultivation effect.

The recent emphasis in cultivation studies has been on specifying the conditions that are most likely to encourage or hinder cultivation. Although results are not as clear cut as we might like, cultivation appears to depend on the motivation for viewing. Individuals who watch TV simply to pass time or because it becomes a habit appear to be more affected than people whose viewing is planned and motivated. Moreover, cultivation appears to be enhanced when the viewer perceives the content of entertainment shows to be realistic. Audience members who look with skepticism on the accuracy of TV shows seem less likely to display the cultivation effect. Finally, some studies have noted that cultivation seems to work best when audience members have only indirect or distant contact with the topic. Interestingly enough, this finding seems to run counter to the resonance notion.

2. *Social Learning Theory*

It is one of the most widely used theories in mass communication. According to this theory, the media are active but subtle educators in teaching readers, viewers and listeners about the world. Due to audiences, frequent exposure to television, the medium is deemed capable of teaching viewers a number of both positive and negative social behaviours and attitudes that they might not personally come into contact with. An important component of this theory is that it explains how people can learn from observations alone.

3. *Agenda Setting Theory*

The term was coined by Maxwell McCombs and Donald L. Shaw (1972) in the context of election campaign where politicians seek to convince the voters about the party's most important issues. An agenda is a selection of items arranged to give some items more importance than others. Agenda theory says that the news media present the public net with a picture of the world as it is but with an agenda of their own–a selection of reports about what is happening in the world. Agenda theorists try to describe and explain (a) how stories are selected, packaged and presented–a process–known as gatekeeping, (b) the resulting agenda, and (c) how this agenda affects what people think about the relative importance of the issues presented. The theory also 'predicts' that if a particular news item is presented prominently and frequently by the press, the public will come to believe that it is important. Thus, the press does not necessarily tell us what to think, but it does tell us what to think about. A host of research studies of newspapers, television and other news sources has confirmed that our personal agendas are indeed set in this manner.

Newspapers receive an abundance news in their offices and only a few of them are selected. This process is called gatekeeping. It results in some stories being in the news and some not, in some being given strong emphasis and others being buried. Thus, gatekeeping results in a news agenda presented by the media to the public.

The study of gatekeeping has a long tradition in the study of the media. A whole series of factors cultural, social, psychological and so on operate at various stages to influence what is presented and how. Some journalists maintain that economic considerations often outweigh conceptions of the public interest in determining what is reported. In accordance with the law of large numbers, the media present what people will find interesting in order to attract the largest audience possible.

There are numerous factors which affect gatekeeping at various stages, including the ethics of individual journalists, the policies of editors or publishers, a desire to get ahead, to protect one's job, or to avoid conflict; time and space limitations, dependence on handouts from government or from public relations offices as the source of news.

Shaw, McCombs and their associates found substantial correlation between the agendas set by the media and the public's beliefs about the importance of the issues. It was found that audience had different sets of beliefs depending on their social categories. That is, young people's perceptions of the important issues differed from other people's and men's patterns were different from women's. Differences in attention to issues and evaluations of their importance also varied among people with different income levels and different political preferences. But the authors did find strong support for the Agenda Setting Theory. Among their additional conclusions were these :

- There is a progressive increase in the use of mass communication during a presidential campaign.
- The influence of the media's agenda on an individual's concern with issues is directly related to how much he or she is exposed to mass communication. Those individuals most frequently exposed to mass communication show higher levels of agreement between personal agendas and mass media agendas.

Thus, the study established agenda-setting as an important influence on our political process. At the same time, the researchers concluded that the influence of the media's agenda must be interpreted in long-range terms and depends on social categories, changing patterns of media use and frequency of media exposure. Generally, then, agenda-setting appears to be one indirect way in which the media can change society over a long period of time. A host of subsequent studies has confirmed this conclusion.

4. *Play Theory*

In theory of mass communication, William Stephenson counters those who speak of the harmful effects of the mass media by arguing that first and foremost the media serve audiences as play experiences. Even newspapers, says Stephenson, are read for pleasure rather than information and enlightenment. He sees the media as a buffer against conditions which would otherwise be anxiety producing. The media provide communication-pleasure. Stephenson argues that what is most required by people within a national culture is something for everyone to talk about. For him mass communication should serve two purposes. It should suggest how best to maximize the communication-pleasure in the world. It should also show how far autonomy for the individual can be achieved in spite of the weight of social controls against him.

5. *Uses and Gratification Theory*

This theory has emerged out of the studies which shifted their focus from what the media do to the people to what people do with the media (Katz, 1959). The uses approach assumes that audiences are active and willingly expose themselves to media and that the most potent of mass media content cannot influence an individual who has "no use" for it in the environment in which he lives. The uses of the mass media are dependent on the perception, selectivity and previously held values, beliefs and interests of the people.

The term "gratification" refers to the rewards and satisfaction experienced by audiences after the use of media, it helps to explain motivations behind media use and habits of media use or the actual needs satisfaction by the media are called media gratifications. In nutshell, this theory which deals in *individual* functions and dysfunctions view that mass media audiences make active use of what the media have to offer arising from a complex set of needs which the media in one form or another gratify. Several researchers have classified the various uses and gratifications which are as follows :

Cognition : Cognition means the act of coming to know something. When a person uses a mass medium to obtain information about something then he or she is using the medium in a cognitive way. At the individual level, however, researchers have noted that there are two different types of cognitive functions that are performed. One is to use the media to keep up with information on current events e. g. I want to know what is going on in the world. The other is using the media to learn about things in general or things that relate to a person's general curiosity e.g. 'the media give me ideas'.

Psychologists and sociologists point out that using the media in this fashion seems to address a person's cognitive needs. These needs are related to strengthening our knowledge and understanding of the world we live in and are based to a certain extent on a desire to explore and master the surrounding environment. Thus, the use of the media in this way is linked to the fulfilment of a basic human need.

Diversion : Another basic need of human beings is for diversion. Diversion can take many forms. Some of these forms identified by researchers include :

(a) Stimulation, or seeking relief from boredom or the routine activities of everyday life–Viewers watch the programme when they are bored and have nothing else to do or simply to pass the time.

(b) Relaxation, or escape from the pressures and problems of day-to-day existence–Too much stimulation, however, is undesirable. Psychological experiments have indicated that human beings are negatively affected by a condition called "sensory overload". When faced with sensory overload, people tend to seek relief. The media are one source of this relief.

(c) Emotional release of pent-up emotions and energy–The use of media for emotional release is fairly obvious. Emotional release can take many subtle forms. One of the big attractions of soap operas, for example, seems to be that many people in the audiences are comforted by seeing that other people have troubles greater than their own. Other people identify with media heroes and heroines and participate vicariously in their triumphs. Such a process evidently enables these people to vent some of the frustrations connected with their normal lives.

(d) Reality exploration or advice–The programme is used to help solve problems in the viewer's own life. Some of the programmes help the viewer understand his or her own life as well as others' and to provide an accurate reflection of reality.

Social utility : Psychologists have also identified a set of social integrative needs, including our need to strengthen our contact with family, friends and others in our society. The social integrative need seems to spring from an individual's need to affiliate with others. The media function that addresses this need is called social utility. When the programme is used as a tool for social interaction with others and the people view the programme with friends and enjoy talking about the programme with friends then we are using the media as conversational currency.

Social utility is apparent in other instances as well. Going to the movie with friends is the most common factor among adolescents. In fact, many times, the actual film is of secondary importance, and the social event of going out has the most appeal.

Other people report that they use the media, particularly TV and radio, as a means to overcome loneliness. The TV set represents a voice in the house for people who might otherwise be alone. Radio keeps people company in their work places. People who might otherwise be deprived of social relationships find companionship in media content and media personalities. In fact, some viewers might go so far as to develop feelings of kinship and friendship with media characters. Audience members might react to media performers and the characters they portray as if the performers were actual friends. This phenomenon is called parasocial relationship.

Withdrawal : In our earlier discussion, we have noted that humans occasionally needed to escape from certain activities, in this connection, they use the media not only for relaxation but also for withdrawal uses. At times, people use the mass media to create a barrier between themselves and other people or other activities. For example, the media help people avoid certain chores that should be done. Perhaps many of us put off our work until we finish watching a TV programme or reading the newspaper. Children are quick to learn how to use the media in this fashion.

In closing we should emphasize that it is not only media content that determines audience usage, but also the social context within which the media exposure occurs. For example, soap operas, filmfares, comedies, etc. all contain material that audiences can use for escape purposes. People going to a movie, however, might value the opportunity to socialize more than they value any aspect of the film itself. Here the social context is the deciding factor.

This theory is so functional in orientation that it ignores the dysfunctions of media in society and culture. It is conservative at heart and sees media primarily as positive ways in which individuals meet their needs without any attention to the overall negative cultural effects of media in society. This theory fails, to take into account that the mass media compete with other sources of satisfaction. Relaxation, for example, can also be achieved by taking a couple of drinks and social utility needs can be satisfied by joining a club or playing football.

The uses-and-gratifications approach assumes that people are aware of their own needs and are able to verbalize them. This approach relies heavily on surveys based on the actual responses of audience members. Thus, the research techniques assume that people's responses are valid indicators of their motives.

A great deal of additional research needs to be done in connection with the uses-and-gratifications approach. In particular, more work is needed in defining and categorizing media-related needs or drives in relating these needs to media usage. Nonetheless the current approach provides a valuable way to examine the complex interaction between the various media and their audiences.

6. *Dependency Theory*

This theory relates to the degree to which audiences are dependent upon the mass media. S. J. Ball Rokeach and Melvin De Fleur believe 'The potential for mass media messages to achieve a broad range of cognitive and behavioural effects will be increased when media systems serve many unique and central information systems'.The fewer the sources of information in a media world, the more likely the media will affect our minds and thoughts, our attitudes and how we behave. Further, that influence will have increased potential 'when there is a high degree of structural instability in the society due to conflict and change'.

However, just as the audience may be changed by information/ messages it receives, in turn the media systems themselves are changed according to audience response. It is not one-way traffic. In the words of De Fleur and Rokeach, both the media and their audiences are integral parts of the society. This surrounding socio-cultural context provides controls and constraints not only on the nature of media messages but also on the nature of their effects on audiences. In the cognitive or intellectual sphere, the authors cite the following possible media roles : (i) The resolution of ambiguity, and relatedly limiting the range of interpretations of situations which audiences are able to make, (ii) Attitude formation, (iii) Agenda-setting, (iv) Expansion of people's systems of beliefs and (v) Clarification of values through the expression of value conflicts.

The media play a significant role in the establishment and maintenance of communal solidarity and oneness, equally they may work towards the alienation of sections of the population who are traditionally discriminated against– women, police atrocities, child exploitation and reserved classes, etc.

At critical decision making times, such as elections, people have become increasingly dependent on the media, especially TV, for election information and guidance. Ball Rokeach and De Fleur argue that the greater the uncertainty in society, the less clear are people's frame of reference, consequently there is greater audience dependence on media communication.

Normative Theories of Mass Media

These theories explain how the media 'ought to' or can be 'expected to' operate under the prevailing set of political-economic circumstances. Since each society controls its mass media in accordance with its policies and needs, it formulates its own separate press theory. Therefore, the media system that exists in a country is directly related to the political system in that country. The political system determines the exact relationship between the media and the government. Siebert and his colleagues (1956) mentioned four theories, based on classification of the world's national media systems. Denis McQuail (1980) added two more theories to the original set of four. He concedes that these theories "may not correspond to complete media systems" but "they have now become part of the discussion of press theory and provide some of the principles for current media policy and practice". A brief description of these theories has been given as below :

1. *Authoritarian Theory*

This theory evolved in the sixteenth and seventeenth centuries, spreading throughout Europe with the invention of the printing press. The authoritarian theory views humans as subservient to the state. They held the belief that the ruling elite should guide the masses, whose intellectual ability was held in low esteem. Public dissent and criticism were considered harmful to both government and the people and were not tolerated. The press in such a society is viewed as an instrument for disseminating the state's position to the public, informing the public what is right and wrong based on the state's interpretations of issues, and providing official policy statements of the ruling elite. The state, after determining its objectives, uses the press as a means of obtaining those objectives. The press becomes a means to an end rather than an instrument of criticism of either means or ends.

Authoritarians used various devices to enforce cooperation of the press including licensing censorship of material before publication, the granting of exclusive printing rights to favoured units of the press, and the swift-harsh punishment of government critics. In fact, in certain societies, not only is the press prohibited from criticizing the government, but it is also required to perform functions for the good of the state. These might include omitting certain news reports that would be embarrassing or harmful to the government and explaining other events in a light favourable to the ruling powers. The main principles of the theory can be briefly summarized:

- Media should do nothing which could undermine established authority or disturb order.
- Media should always be subordinate to established authority.
- Censorship can be justified to enforce these principles.
- Media should avoid offence to majority, or dominant, moral and political values.
- Unacceptable attacks on authority, deviations from official policy or offences against moral codes should be criminal offences.
- Journalists or other media professionals have no independence within their media organizations.

Today the authoritarian system of the press is still in operation in many parts of the world. In communist countries, in nations under dictatorial control, and in some third world countries, a free press is little more than a theory without practice.

2. *Libertarian Theory*

The libertarian theory developed slowly in the sixteenth century being refined in the eighteenth century as libertarian principles found their way into nation's constitutional framework. In theory, a libertarian press is the exact opposite of an authoritarian press. Libertarians assume that human beings are rational and are capable of making their own decisions and that governments exist to serve the individual. Unlike the authoritarians, libertarians hold that the common citizen has a right to hear all sides of an issue in order to distinguish truth from falsehood. Since any government restriction on the expression of ideas infringes on the rights of the citizen, the government can best serve the people by not interfering with the media. In short, the press must be free of control.

Fred Siebert in discussing the development of libertarianism, credits its transition from authoritarianism to the efforts of four men : John Milton in the seventeenth century, John Erskine and Thomas Jafferson in the eighteenth century and John Stuart Mill in the nineteenth century. Milton argued that people had the capacity to distinguish between right and wrong and good and bad. As a result, to make decisions, people should have "unlimited access to the ideas and thoughts of other men". Erskine argued that people seeking to enlighten others, and not intending to mislead, should be able to address the universal reason of a whole nation on what is believed to be true. John Stuart Mill believed that people had the right to think and act as they pleased if they did not infringe on the rights of others. Jefferson, borrowing from Milton's ideas, believed that the collective aggregate of a people, if intelligent and informed, could arrive at sound decisions. The press was the instrument to inform the people and, therefore, had to be free of control. Gradually, the rights of the press and libertarianism began to gain ground and became part of the constitutional doctrine both in the United States and later in England.

This theory is criticized on the following grounds. First, it is very unclear to what extent the theory can be held to apply to public broadcasting, which now accounts for a large part of media activity in many societies. Secondly, the theory has been most frequently formulated to protect the owners of media and cannot give equal expression to the arguable rights of editors and journalists within the press. Thirdly, the theory seems designed to protect opinion and belief and has much less to say on 'information'. Fourthly, the theory prescribes compulsory control but provides no obvious way of handling the many pressures to which media are subject. In nutshell, the theory can be expressed in the following principles :

- Publication should be free from any prior censorship.
- Attacks on any government, official or political party, should not be punishable, even after the event.

- There should be no compulsion to publish anything.
- No restriction should be placed for gathering the information for publication.
- The act of publication and distribution should be open to a person, a group without licence or permit.
- There should be no restriction on getting or sending information overseas.
- Journalists should have professional autonomy within their organization.

3. *Social Responsibility Theory*

The theory was constructed in 1947 by the Commission on Freedom of the Press, a private organization financed by magazine publisher Henry Luce. According to this theory, although the press had a right to criticize government and other institutions, it also had a responsibility to preserve democracy by properly informing the public and by responding to society's interests and needs. Probably the most significant contribution of the social responsibility theorists is their view that it is more important for citizens to have the right of access to information than it is for the press to achieve complete freedom of speech. It is not enough that increasing by large media and economic structures have the freedom to do as they please. They are also obliged to respond to society's needs.

Social responsibility theory has a wide range of application since it covers several kinds of private print media and public institutions of broadcasting, which are answerable through various kinds of democratic procedure to the society. The theory has thus to reconcile independence with obligation to society. It is assumed that the media do serve essential functions in society, especially in relation to democratic politics. Media should accept an obligation to fulfil those functions–not only in the sphere of information and the provision of a platform for diverse views, but also in matters of culture. It should give maximum emphasis on media independency, consistent with their obligations to society. The theory states that media should also follow certain standards in work.

It can be seen that social responsibility theory has to try to reconcile three somewhat divergent principles : of individual freedom, of media freedom and of media obligation to society. There can be no single way of resolving the potential inconsistencies but the theory has favoured two main kinds of solution. One is the development of public and the other is the development of professionalism as a means of achieving higher standards of performance, while maintaining self-regulation by the media themselves.

The main principles of this theory can be stated as follows :

- Media should accept and fulfil certain obligations to society by setting high or professional standards of truth, accuracy, objectivity and balance, etc.
- In accepting and applying these obligations, media should be self regulating within the framework of law and established institutions.
- Journalists and media professionals should be accountable to society as well as to employers.

4. *Soviet Communist Theory*

Wilbur Schramm while writing this theory begins his discussion by noting that when a reporter from the United States and one from the Soviet Union get together, "The talk is apt to be both amusing and frustrating". Their different frames of reference are simply incompatible. The American loathes the Soviet reporter's life with a government controlled press. The Soviet reporter loathes the American's association with a "corrupt", "venal", "irresponsible press" controlled by special interests.

The Russian press and other media were completely reorganized after the Revolution of 1917. This theory is derived from the basic postulates of Marx and Engels. It envisages media to be under the control of the working class. The working class by definition holds power in a socialist society.

To understand the Soviet media theory of the press, one must examine the Soviet interpretation of the word "freedom". The Soviet constitution guarantees both free speech and a free press. In addition, the principle tenet of Soviet political life is one of unity. The rise of the working class, the revolution, was a movement of unity within Soviet Society. This joining together of the people into a classless society has become the philosophy of the Soviet state. Thus, freedom from the Soviet point of view is freedom from the oppression of a upper, middle and lower class.

Schramm explains that mass communication in the Soviet media theory is an instrument of the state. It (media) do not have integrity of their own. Their integrity, such as it is, that of the state. They are "kept" instruments, and they follow humbly and nimbly the gyrations of the party line and the state directives. Mass communication is integrated with other instruments of the state, such as schools, the police, and even assemblies as instruments protecting the communist philosophy. Yet while the press is considered an instrument of unity, it is also considered an instrument of revelation to provide enlightenment and to prepare the masses for unity and eventually revolution. The press is an "agitator, propagandist, and organizer".

Broadcasting under the Soviet-Communist theory likewise is designed not so much to serve the public but to inform it. Programming is again the instrument of the state, and the medium is important to it because of the large number of people that broadcasting can reach.
The theory can be summed as follows :

- Media should not be privately owned.
- It should serve the interests of, and be in control of the working class.
- Media should respond to wishes and needs of their audience.
- Media should serve positive functions for society by education, information, motivation and mobilization.
- Society has a right to punish for the anti-societal publication.
- Media should provide a complete and objective view of society.
- Journalists' aims and ideals should coincide with the best interests of the society.

5. *Development Media Theory*

The limited application of the four established theories of the press to Third World countries has led to the birth of a new media theory whose main task is that communication be used to carry out the development functions in a society. The absence of some of the conditions in these countries which are necessary for a developed mass communication system are as follows :

- Communication infrastructure; the professional skills; the production and cultural resources and the available audience, etc.
- Technology, skills and cultural products.
- Devotion of these societies to economic, political and social development as a primary national task.
- Developing countries' awareness of their similar identity and interest in international politics.

The normative elements of emerging development theory are shaped by the conditions described above and have both negative and positive aspects. They are as below :

- Opposed to dependency and foreign domination and to arbitrary authoritarianism.
- For positive uses of the media in national development.
- For the autonomy and cultural identity of the particular national society.

Development media theory favours democratic grass-roots involvement to a certain extent. It emphasized on a 'right to communicate based on Article 19 of the Universal Declaration of Human Rights : Everyone has the right to freedom of opinion and expression; this right includes of freedom to hold opinions without interference and to seek, receive and impart information and ideas through any media regardless of frontiers'. The main principles of this theory can be summed as follows :

- Media should accept and carry out positive development tasks in line with nationally established policy.
- Media should give priority to the national culture and language.
- Freedom of media should be restricted to an extent keeping in view the economic priorities and development needs of the society.
- Journalists and other media workers have responsibilities as well as freedom in their information gathering and dissemination tasks.
- The state has a right to intervene in or restrict, media operations and devices of censorship and direct control in the interest of the development of a country.

6. *Democratic-Participant Media Theory*

Denis McQuail states that it is most difficult to formulate this theory, partly because it lacks full legitimisation and incorporation into media institutions and partly because some of its tenets are already to be found in some of the other theories.

The main feature of the democratic-participant theory relates to the needs, interests and aspirations of the active "receiver" in a political society. It is concerned with the right to relevant information, the right to answer back, the right to use the means of communication for interaction in small-scale settings of community, interest group and sub-culture.

This theory has a mixture of theoretical elements, including libertarianism, utopianism, socialism, egalitarianism, environmentalism and localism. Media institutions constructed according to the theory would be involved more closely with social life than they are at present and more directly in control of their audiences, offering opportunities for access and participation on terms set by their predecessors rather than by controllers.

The main principles of this theory can be stated as below :

- Individual citizens and minority groups have rights to communicate.
- Groups, organizations and local communities should have their own media.
- The organization and content of media should not be subject to centralized political or state bureaucratic control.
- Small scale, interactive and participative media forms are better than large-scale, one-way and professionalized media.

Our discussion of the theories of the press should be viewed not so much as categories in which various mass media can be placed but rather as different variations of media systems. These systems can apply to different media across different countries or even different media within one country. They represent the roots of not the press in society but also of mass communication in general.

Some Important Models of Communication

A model is a pictorial presentation to show the structure of communication process in which various elements are linked. It is an abstracted representation of a reality. A good model comes as close to reality as possible and it discusses and explains the reality as clearly as possible. But being an abstraction, a model is not a reality, it only represents the reality of communication for better understanding of the communication process. Models are based on assumptions that theorists make as to how communication functions and what effect it has upon individual and society.

The earlier models of communication were simple but inadequate. Most of them were linear i.e. one directional. Aristotle constructed a model which had only three elements essential for communication to happen i.e. speaker-speech audience. Such type of communication takes place in face-to-face situations. Another model, constructed during World War-II, saw communication as a magic bullet that transferred ideas, feeling or knowledge almost automatically from one mind to another. For example, sender A sends a message to receiver B who is considered passive and is assumed to be accepting whatever is shot at him. This one-way model of communication became redundant as more researches on the subject showed communication as a dynamic two-way process. By 1950s, models became more elaborate and adequate.

Shannon and Weaver and Gerbner's models are considered to be universally applicable for they can explain any example of communication. The widely quoted model of Lasswell verbalizes communication in terms that can be applied to mass media. Osgood, however, emphasizes the dynamic relationship between source and receiver. Schramm on the other hand explains communication as a process of sharing of experiences on the basis of commonness and stresses the importance of feedback and noise in the process. Newcomb's triangular linear form of model is designed specifically in the interpersonal and social communication context. Finally, Westley and MacLean's model of communication is considered useful to the mass media and is often associated with news.

Westley and MacLean's Model (1957)

Bruce Westley and Malcolm MacLean's model is an extension of Newcomb's model and specifically adapted for the mass media. They have introduced a new element, C, which is the process of deciding what and how to communicate. This model explains that messages in mass communication pass through different check points called'gatekeeper' before they are actually received by the receiver. This model emphasizes the role of gatekeepers within the media organization. They decide on which messages are to be transmitted and which are not to be transmitted. How much information need to be given to the audience and how their contents are to be modified. The model can be explained as follows :

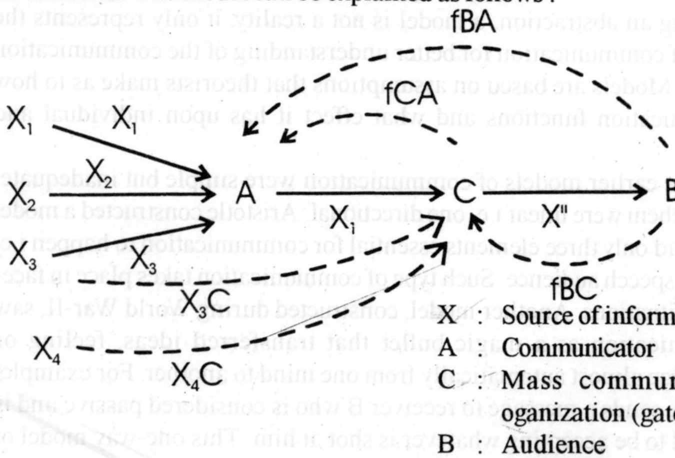

X : Source of information
A : Communicator
C : Mass communication oganization (gatekeeper)
B : Audience
f : feedback

Fig. 1. Westley and MacLean's model of communication, 1957.

The messages C transmits to B (X") represent his selections from both messages to him from A's (X') and C's selections and abstractions from Xs in his own sensory field (X3c, X4), which may or may not be Xs in A's field. Feedback not only moves from B to A (fBA) and from B to C (fBC) but also from C to A (fCA) Joseph.

A, here, is communicator or reporter who receives messages from many sources $X_1, X_2, X_3, X_4 \ldots\ldots\ldots X_\infty$ and according to his perception writes a report and sends it to C (the gatekeeper or the mass communication organization) who performs the editing function; that is the process of deciding what and how to communicate. Edited message, C sends it to the audience B. The audience, therefore, receives the reporter's and editor's version of the events and not necessarily what may be the reality.

In this model C is both channel and mediator of A's transmission of X to B, and B's contact with X is more remote than in the Newcomb's model, if it exists at all save through the combined 'processing' of AC. A and C now play dominant roles. B is very much at their mercy.

It can also be seen from the model that X need not go through to B via A and C but via C alone. The role of C as intermediary has a dual character, purposive when the process involves conveying a message through C from an 'advocate' a politician, for example, and non-purposive when it is a matter of conveying the unplanned events of the world to an audience.

The main thrust of the model appears to be emphasizing the dependency of B upon A and C. What is missing from the model, and what later thinking about mass media processes insists upon, are the numerous message sources and influences which work upon B other than AC, and counter- balance the influence of AC such as the family, friends, members of peer groups, colleagues, workmates or wider influences such as school, church, trade unions, etc.

Osgood's Model (1954)

Charles E. Osgood's model is different from the earlier models, in the sense that it does not follow the conventional pattern of communication from source to channel to receiver. He describes communication as a dynamic process and says that a given communication event may begin with receiving stimuli as shown below :

Osgood stressed that each participant in the communication process sends as well as receives messages and as such encodes, decodes, and interprets messages. Thus, according to Osgood, communication is a dynamic process in which there is an interactive relationship between the source and the receiver where a person may be a source one moment, a receiver the next and again a source the following moment. This is particularly true in interpersonal communication.

Harold D. Lasswell's Model (1948)

Lasswell argues that to understand the process of mass communication we need to study each of the stages in his model :

Who (Sender)
Says what (message)
In which channel (channel)
To whom (audience)
With what effect? (effect)

It is still 'linear' it sees communication as the transmission of messages : it raises the issue of 'effect' rather than meaning. 'Effect' implies an observable and measurable change in the receiver that is caused by identifiable elements in the process. Changing one of these elements will change the effect.

Assuming that the effect would include the notion of feedback, Lasswell's model could still do with an additional question–In what context (social, economic, cultural, political) is the communication process taking place? Also Lasswell makes no provision of intervening variables, those mediating factors which have impact on the ways in which messages are received and responded to.

Theodore M. Newcomb's Model (1953)

It is a triangular model and represented chiefly interpersonal communication. It tries to introduce the role of communication in a society or a social relationship. According to it, communication maintains equilibrium within the social system. The model works like this :

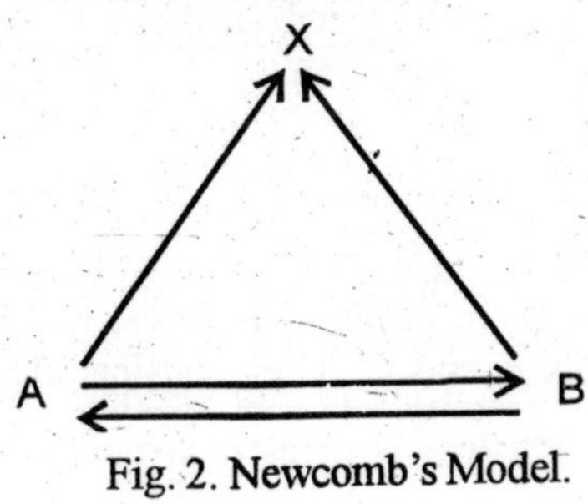

Fig. 2. Newcomb's Model.

A and B are communicator and receiver, they may be individuals, or management and union or government and people. X is part of their social environment. ABX is a system, which means that its internal relations are interdependent : of A changes, B and X will change as well; or if A changes his relationship to X, B will have to change either his relationship with X or with A. ABX will be in equilibrium only if A and B have similar attitude to X. But if A likes X and B does not, then A and B will be under pressure to communicate until both adopt similar attitude to X. The more important a place X has in their social environment, the more urgent will be their drive to share an orientation towards it.

This model assumes significance in the light of people's increasing need for information. In fact, in a democracy, people need adequate information about their social environment so that they can identify their problems and share with the fellow members and know-how to react.

Claude Shannon and Warren Weaver's Model (1949)

Shannon and Weaver's Mathematical Theory of Communication is widely accepted as one of the main seeds out of which communication studies have grown. It is essentially a linear process-centred model. For them, the main channels were the telephone cable and the radio wave. They produced a theory that enabled them to approach the problem of how to send a maximum amount of information along a given channel, and how to measure the capacity of any one channel to carry information. They claim for their theory a much wider application to human communication than solely the technical one. Within the framework of their model of transmission, the authors identify three levels of problems in the analysis of communication. These are :

Level A (technical problems)	How accurately can the symbols of communication be transmitted?
Level B (semantic problems)	How precisely do the transmitted symbols convey the desired meaning?
Level C (effectiveness problems)	How effectively does the received meaning affect conduct in the desired way?

Shannon and Weaver's model was constructed mainly to tackle level A problems and the assumption seems to be that to sort out the technical problems by improving encoding will almost automatically lead to improvements at levels B and C. They consider that the meaning is contained in the message : thus improving the encoding will increase the semantic accuracy. But there are also cultural factors at work here which the model does not specify : the meaning is at least as much in the culture as in the message.

Both claim that the three levels are not watertight, but are interrelated, and interdependent : and that their model, despite its origin in level A, works equally well on all three levels. The point of studying communication at each and all of these levels is to understand how we may improve the accuracy and efficiency of the process.

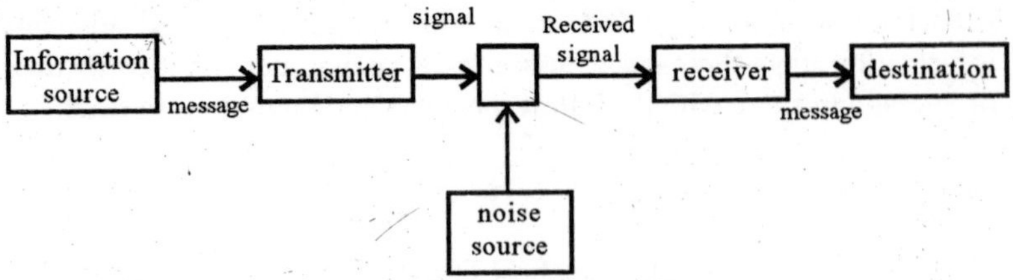

Fig. 3. Shannon and Weaver's model of communication.

In this model, the source decides which message to send out of many messages. This selected message is then changed by the transmitter into a signal which is sent through the channel to the receiver. For a telephone the channel is a wire, the signal an electrical current in it, and the transmitter and receiver are the telephone handsets. In conversation, our mouth is the transmitter, the signal is the sound waves which pass through the channel of the air and our ear is the receiver. Shannon and Weaver's model is important as it introduces the concept of 'Noise'. Noise whether it originates in the channel, the audience, the sender or the message itself, always confuses the intention of the sender and thus limits the amount of desired information that can be sent in a given situation in a given time.

In this model, no provision has been made for medium and feedback. The medium is basically the technical or physical means of converting the message into a signal capable of being transmitted along the channel. Media can be divided into three main categories.

1. *The presentational media* : the voice, the face, the body, etc.
2. *The representational media* : books, paintings, photographs, etc.
3. *The mechanical media* : telephones, radio, television, etc.

Feedback is also very important concept which Shannon and Weaver do not use, but is one that later workers have found useful. Briefly, feedback is the transmission of the receiver's reaction back to the sender.

In this model, there is also no acknowledgement of the importance of context–social, political, cultural–in influencing all stages of the communication process. Nevertheless, the Shannon and Weaver model arguably gave birth to what has come to be termed communication studies.

George Gerbner's Model (1956)

George Gerbner attempts to produce a general purpose model of communication in which the communication act is seen as a transmission of messages. The model assumes significance as it is seen as an advancement over earlier models in two ways. It relates the messages to 'reality' and thus enables us to approach the question of perception and meaning; further it sees the communication process as consisting of two alternative dimensions–the perceptual or receptive dimension and the communicating or means and control dimension. The complex model of Gerbner looks like this :

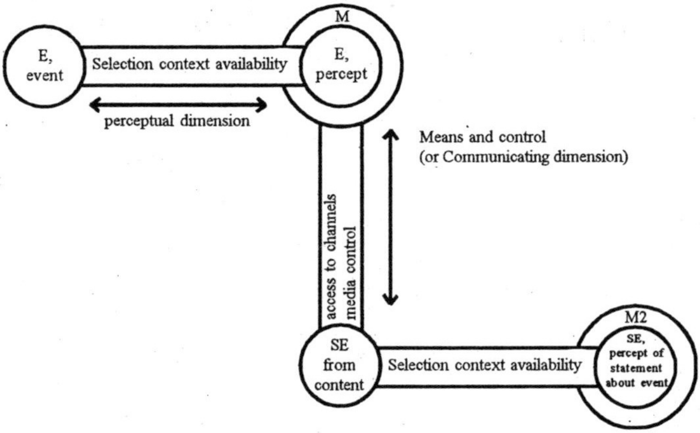

Fig. 4. Gerbner's Model (modified).

In this model, the communication process can be explained in three stages. The first step is referred to as the horizontal dimension. It starts with an event E (external reality) as perceived by M (Human being directly or through a machine such as a camera or a microphone). M selects E according to his perception of the event. Since human perception is a complex phenomenon, the process involves interaction and negotiation. In this way, we try to match external stimuli with internal pattern of thought or concept and arrive at some perception of the event.

In the second stage, the vertical dimension, we give meaning to whatever we have perceived. It is then converted into a signal about SE. This is called message, that is, a singular statement about the event SE. Here, it is important to select the appropriate 'means'–the medium channel of communication. In this context, access to media assumes significance. So, who makes the selection and whose picture of the world is transmitted as SE is obviously of prime importance. The media, especially television, often dubbed 'elitist', naturally would produce the elite biased version of an event.

The third stage of the process is again horizontal, M2 is not an event E, but a signal or statement about an event, or SE. The process here is something like we have explained in stage one i. e. the meaning of the message is not 'contained' in the message itself, but is the result of an interaction or negotiation between the receiver and the message. M2 brings to SE a set of needs and concepts derived from his culture and sub-culture and if he can relate SE to them, we can say that he finds meaning in the message. And this can be realised only by interaction or negotiation between M2 and SE, the resulting meaning is SE. For example, the government's policy of not showing programme containing sex and violence is a way of restricting their availability to people.

NEW WORLD INFORMATION AND COMMUNICATION ORDER (NWICO)

The concept of the New World Information Order (NWIO), which is also referred to as New World Information and Communication Order (NWICO), was born out of the strong conviction regarding imbalance, bias and disequilibrium inherent in the ownership and working of information and communication resources between the developed and the developing countries.

The determined efforts made by the non-aligned countries to take remedial measures to correct the above imbalance and disequilibrium, so as to usher in a more equitable and balanced information and communication order constitutes the backdrop of the demand in which the NWICO issue was raised. While discussing the working of news agencies, A *Manual for News Agency Reporters (1980)*, brought out by the Indian Institute of Mass Communication says : Among the results of the prevailing pattern of information flow with which developing countries are most concerned are :

1. Despite the size of their population and territory, developing countries get hardly any notice in the world media. Whatever is reported is lopsided and projects a distorted picture.
2. The values that foreign media force down on developing countries have tended to undermine the self-confidence of these peoples.
3. Even for information about each other, developing countries have had to depend on western media. This leads to inadequate understanding and sometimes needless apprehensions.

Decolonisation of Information

The concept was used for the first time in the report from a symposium on the mass media in the non-aligned countries in Tunis in March 1976. This symposium was manifestation of the cooperation which had developed among the non-aligned countries regarding news transmission and information development. At the fourth summit of non-aligned countries in Algiers, in September 1973, a programme of action had been adopted which encouraged the member countries to work for "reorganisation of existing communication channels, which are the legacy of the colonial past and which have hampered free, direct and fast communication between them". On a more practical level the programme proposed revision of cable tariffs, agreements on joint use of and guidelines for communication satellites, and increased contact and exchange of experience between the media institutions in the non-aligned countries. The Tunis symposium endorsed this programme. "Since information in the world symposium shows disequilibrium in favouring some and ignoring others", said a resolution adopted by the symposium, "It is the duty of the non-aligned to change this situation and obtain the decolonisation of information and initiate a new international order in information".

The call for the "New Order" gathered momentum during the 1970s even though its beginning can be traced to the history of "decolonisation" or freedom movement in the Third World countries. The dissolution of the old colonial empires after World War II, was also the beginning of a new awareness in the Third World countries. The Bandung Conference in 1956 was the first forum at which information and cultural imperialism practised by a few western big powers was questioned by several member countries. At this Conference, it was pointed out that the western media– all powerful, dominant and pervasive–were highly biased against the interests and needs of the people living in the developing countries whether independent or still struggling against the colonial rule. It was strongly felt that the reporting in the western media was negative and unsympathetic to the aspirations of all the people coming from the countries which were newly liberated or struggling for liberation. There was resentment against the western media, which were and continue to be privately owned. These media were used both to support the commercial interests of the media organisations and the global political and economic interests to the big powers.

New Delhi Declaration, 1976

In 1976, the first ever conference of the information ministers and representatives of news agencies from the non-aligned countries, was held in New Delhi. The conference expressed its determination to rectify the imbalance and concretise arrangements for effective cooperation in all fields of information, mass media, social and cultural information. A linkage was also sought to be established, perhaps for the first time, between economic and political dependence on the one hand and the information monopoly, on the other was sought to be established.

The conference adopted a declaration which stated, among other things, that the present global flow of information was characterised by serious deficiencies and inequalities. The great majority of countries are reduced to passive recipients of information which is transmitted from a few centres. In a situation in which the means of information are dominated and monopolized by a few agencies to spread information as they wish, at the same time that the rest are denied the right to inform and to be informed objectively and accurately. The declaration stated that the major international news agencies had ignored or distorted the foreign policy efforts of the non-aligned nations and that these nations had few possibilities of getting to know about each other through other channels.

The conference, which was attended by 59 countries as participants and seven countries or international organisations as observers, reaffirmed the determination of the non-aligned countries not to continue to suffer individually or collectively because of the present inequitable global situation. It was clear that it could be rectified by encouraging constructive and wide-ranging cooperation among themselves for achieving greater collective self-reliance. They expressed commitment to the improving of the flow of direct information and fast communication between each other, thereby promoting both greater mutual beneficial cooperation in the social and cultural fields. They stressed that the decolonisation of information was essential for these purposes and that the establishment of a New International Order for Information was as necessary as the New International Economic Order.

Since the early 1960s, the United Nations Educational, Scientific and Cultural Organisation (UNESCO) became a forum where developing countries raised the above issues concerning the inequitable and imbalance in information and communication resources between the western countries and the Third World countries.

The General Conference of UNESCO, at its nineteenth session held in Nairobi in 1976, instructed the Director-General "to undertake review of all the problems of communication in the contemporary society, seen against the background of technological progress and recent developments in international relations, with due regard to their complexity and magnitude". In 1977, the Director-General, Mr.Amad-Mahtar M'Bow set up a "brain trust", the International Commission for the Study of Communication Problems under the presidentship of Mr. Sean MacBride. The MacBride Report, as it came to be called, was sent to the UNESCO Director-General in 1980, although its Interim Report had been submitted in 1978.

The above report, also popularly known as *Many Voices, One World,* Communication and Society : Today and Tomorrow, is one of the best, most well known, widely referred and useful documents in the discipline of communication and media. It has been produced by an international group of prominent persons drawn from different countries of the world which included journalists and authors, broadcasters, academics, public men and scholars. Mr. B. G. Verghese, former editor of the *Hindustan Times* and an eminent author and thinker, who later headed the Working Group on Autonomy of Akashvani and Doordarshan (1977) and produced the well known Verghese Committee Report represented India.

The MacBride Report discussed the issue of imbalances and inequalities in the communication sector in information flow from the developed to the developing countries. It observed : Such imbalances are today not only limited to news flows in the usual sense. They also affect, to an increasingly serious extent, the collection and diffusion of data necessary for scientific purposes, technological innovations, commercial needs, trade development, exploitation of natural resources, meteorological forecastings, military purposes, etc. In short there is an imbalance regarding strategic information for political and economic decision-making.

The gap between the fully-informed and the under-informed continues to widen as the imbalance between those imparting and those receiving information becomes accentuated. Although it is only fair to recognise that the international flows have enormously increased and that communication sources have enormously increased their output, it is necessary also to stress that communications have strengthened their power to control the impact of the messages transmitted, as well as the selection of information available. Also, the attendant distortions and imbalances reflect in some way the dominant interests of the societies from which they emanate.

This situation cannot continue without being detrimental both to international understanding and to cooperation between nations, without affecting the socio-political and socio-cultural conditions prevailing in different countries and without prejudicing the efforts to satisfy the basic needs, to solve the essential problems of the world's populations and to safeguard world peace.

The observations, by and large, sum up the issues raised in the NWICO debated. The commission also took note of the imbalances in the flow of news through technology. The western nations, because of supremacy of technology, were primarily responsible for promoting alien values across cultural frontiers. Thus, they were practising *cultural imperialism* through their control of communication infrastructure, news circulation, cultural and entertainment products, educational software, etc.

The commission concluded that the primary factor in imbalance and inequalities was an economic one. The report said that one-way flow in communication is basically a reflection of world's dominant political and economic structures.

The Final Report of the Commission was approved at the General Conference of UNESCO held at Belgrade in 1980. The Resolution accepted on NWICO covered a wide range of issues such as :

- elimination of the imbalances in information flow,
- elimination of negative effects of monopolies,
- removal of internal and external obstacles to free and wider flow of information,

- freedom and responsibilities of journalists, and
- improving the capacity of developing countries to improve their own infrastructures.

The second resolution concerned the International Programme for the Development of Communication (IPDC). One of the main objectives of the programme is : to promote in developing countries, according to their communication policies and development plans, the creation or extension of infrastructures for the different communication sectors, in order to increase particularly the contribution of the means of communication to endogenous economic, social and cultural development, as well as to promote improved international exchange of information.

India and the NWICO

India has been the leading light and inspiration in strengthening the concept and cause of NWICO. India has steadfastly pursued the policy of advancing the cause of NWICO in the UNESCO and in the non-aligned movement. The contribution of India in the following areas is more specific :

1. The Non-Aligned News Agency Pool (NANAP) was started in January 1975, as a voluntary effort on the part of the non-aligned countries to promote flow of news within the community. India's premier news agency, Press Trust of India (PTI) has been one of the seven redistribution centres of the pool news ever since 1976. The pool has now about 100 members.
2. *Inter-Press Service* : A Third World cooperative, the news agency was founded in 1964 by a group of journalists from Latin America. With headquarters in Rome, the agency has attracted international notice. The agency places emphasis on analysis, interpretation and background.
3. *Diploma Course in News Agency Journalism for Non-aligned Countries :* India took commendable initiative in starting a training programme for news agency journalism for journalists from non-aligned countries. The training programme, started in 1978, is conducted by the Indian Institute of Mass Communication (IIMC), New Delhi. A large number of journalists from various non-aligned countries have been trained under this programme.

It may, however, be pointed out that there had been a degree of hostility to the demand of the non-aligned countries for a fair and balanced flow of international news, information and data. The hostility led to the withdrawal of the United States from UNESCO, subsequently followed by Britain and Singapore. Since then NWICO has been off the agenda for the western media.

MEDIA AND DEVELOPMENT

Before we discuss how mass media can play an effective role in the development of a nation, it would be appropriate to understand what development means.

Development is a concept which has varied connotations. To some it means modernisation, to others social change and yet some others would take development as enhancing quality of life. Economic development involves mobilisation of national resources, augmentation of skilled manpower, capital and technical know-how, and their utilisation for the attainment of constantly rising national goals, higher income standards and the change from a traditional to a modern society. Streeth (1981) defined, *"Development is an attack on the chief evils of the world today : malnutrition, disease, illiteracy, slums, unemployment and inequality".*

Development is much more than mere economic growth. It means the development of society as a whole, and of all its institutions–economic, social and political. It calls for the improvement of the lot of the poor through an equitable sharing of the resources–social and economic.

Some development economists sought to identify "development" with increase in real per capita income on the plea that it takes into account the changes in population yet their ultimate emphasis remained on the growth of the total product. If the rate of development is greater than the rate of population growth, then the per capita real income source increases. Thus, most of the definitions are given on economic development whether based on the concept of realised levels potential stages of economic growth, per capita income or availability of goods and services aim at maximisation of material well-being.

In nutshell, development is both a physical reality and a state of mind in which society has, through some combination of social, economic and institutional processes, secured the means for obtaining a better life.

Whatever be the specific components of better life, development in all societies must have at least three objectives :

1. To increase the availability and widen the distribution of basic life sustaining goods such as food, shelter, health and protection.
2. To raise levels of living including addition to higher incomes, the provision of more know-how, better education and greater attention to cultural and humanistic values, all of which will serve not only to enhance material well-being but also to generate greater individual and national esteem.
3. To expand the range of economic and social choices available to individuals and nations by freeing them from servitude and dependence not only in relation to other people and nation states but also to the forces of ignorance and human misery.

Social Development

The term social development is used to indicate development planning for the so-called social sectors, such as, health and education or for the target groups deserving of special treatment, e.g. scheduled castes, backward classes, woman, etc. Accordingly, there came about a sort of paradigmatic shift in the concept of development. There emerged the conception of development as provision for the basic needs of people, such as food, clean water, health, shelter and education.

Taken literally, social development of society can be viewed as an arrangement devised by men to secure fulfilment. Accordingly, development of the society would mean development of such arrangements as may bring greater and greater fulfilment to its members. There are many facets of these arrangements; but four of them are of key importance for developmental purposes. These are material, structural, normative and integrative. The ultimate mark of social development is the development of a sense of social solidarity. Society is just not an assembly of people, it is a manifestation of human craving for reaching out to others. Only if this fact is reorganised, will society be understood as it should. Viewed in this way, the development of a sense of community. In the so-called developed societies, man today has become more solitary. The forces of modernisation have tremendously undermined the sense of community leaving man alienated. Indeed, the more modern a society, the more alienated the people.

In nutshell, development in socio-economic terms may be described as improvement in material welfare especially for persons with the lowest incomes; the eradication of poverty and illiteracy alongwith combating of disease and early death; and changes in the composition of inputs and outputs that generally include shifts in the underlying structure of production from agriculture towards industrial activities. Hence, it is a process of accelerating the growth with greater social justice aiming at utilising of resources and opportunities in order to improve the quality of life of the people with special reference to the weaker section of the society.

National Development

National development generally means mobilising human potential through : Access to material resources like good health, education, housing and food and personal self respect.

In case of India the national development process has been identified around the creation of a realm of cultural values as embodied in the preamble of the Constitution in the creation of a secular, socialist and democratic society and would entail removal of caste, regional, ethnic inequalities. This is possible by decentralised planning by involving local groups and leaders; detribalisation of a large section of population, removal of income inequalities, wealth disparity, gender bias and ensuring employment.

Apart from building human capital, other major elements of national development have been spelt out in communication policy of national development.

The progress of a nation depends first and foremost on the progress of its people. Unless it develops the spirit and potential ties, it cannot develop much else.....materially, economically, politically and culturally. Hence, the first task must be to build up their human capital. To put it in more humanistic terms, it refers to improving the education, skills and hopefulness, alongwith the mental and physical health of the men, women and children.

It further adds that to raise educational standards in developing countries there is an urgent need of dissemination of knowledge on farming, industrial skills, health, nutrition and community development, as well as provisions for 'mass education' to overcome limitations of illiteracy. This therefore underlines the need for the MASS MEDIA to achieve progress in a national development in a holistic manner.

Mass media should not be used blindly–there should be some social control. It has to be guided by some communication policies.

Communication Policies and Functions of Media

Communication policies are sets of legislative measures, principles, norms and directions established to guide the functioning of communication system in a country. The policies are shaped over time in the context of country's general approach to communication systems, emanating as they do from political ideologies, and are related to the socio-economic development of the society.

While defining 'National Media Policy', Pran Chopra is of the view that decisions of the national government might help the media fulfil certain functions that are appropriate for them in a democratic and pluralistic country, like India. In this context, following functions of the media can be considered as most appropriate :

1. The media should be accessible to largest possible number easily.
2. Information provided therein should be reliable, relevant and abundant.
3. Media so selected should provide reasonably free channels of expression of opinion that are well informed, responsible and adequately reflect the relevant point of view.
4. It should be a two-way-channel not only addressing messages to the audience but also giving the audience a forum for the expression of their concerns.
5. The fifth one overrides all aforementioned functions, that is the media must preserve credibility.

Role of Media

Media should promote socio-economic development of the country. It must feel the responsibility to exercise their function in environmental surveillance, consensus building and socialisation in order to strive for the protection of a sustainable environment. The programmes on ecology, deforestation and conservation in rural areas can be dubbed in Hindi and major regional languages, so that they could be telecast in regional slots from local centres.

Media should uphold the unity and integrity of the country and the democratic and social values enshrined in the Constitution. Thus, use of mass media against the security of the state, the public order, morality and good habits should be prohibited. It should promote equality and fraternity among people and act as catalyst in strengthening the cohesive forces and in weakening the decisive forces.

Emphasis should be given on commercial ethics and not encouraging unnecessary consumption.

It must promote research and development activities in order to get proper feedback of peoples' participation.

Media must play due attention to the field of education, adult literacy, child education, higher education and distance education. Besides its emphasis on education, stress should also be given on information culture and healthy recreation. The overall tone of the programme should be of humanism and nationalism with a general orientation towards the limitation of potentially negative influence of programme content (*especially those of violence and sex*).

Special attention should be paid to the development news, quiz programmes, in an attempt to increase their positive contribution to educational processes.

Media must play its role as an instrument of social change and national cohesion by upholding progressive values and involving the community in a free dialogue. It will have to shun an elitist approach and consumer value system and evolve a true national model.

It must play a major role in development, especially in conveying informative and persuasive messages from a government to the public. Modern theorists like Lerner and Moore have also showed how mass media could serve as a kind of magic multiplier for development in under developed countries. Media must take up gender issues and help how the women can be more empowered. It must create awareness among women about abolishing of dowry system, choice of life partner, equal share in the property, freedom to do jobs outside homes, equal pay for equal work, etc.

Apart from providing entertainment or recreation to the viewers, media also owes its responsibility of highlighting the issues of health and hygiene. Emphasis should be given on the required calories in the food, vaccination of infants, cleanliness and use of contraceptives for the desired family norms and prevent deadly diseases like acquired immune deficiency syndrome (AIDS). General awareness must be created about infant mortality rate and cleanliness to ensure better quality of life.

The Indian social situation is in a bad shape as a result of exploitation and corruption. People unaware of their rights are often misused by the affluent for their selfish motives. Bribery, favouritism and nepotism are some of the contagious social diseases which have established its roots in the society. Thus, media can play a very effective role in keeping alive the sentiments of the people.

India is a country of different religions, sects and communities. In such a situation inter-community or inter-religious conflicts are bound to arise. Hence, media can play an important role in promoting the communal harmony by giving equal treatment to each and everyone.

It is observed that a section of people still believes in superstitions and black magic, etc. In the past, many instances have been reported in which people remained victims of this disbelief. In a society with conservative values and orthodox outlook, a total revolution in mental disposition is needed. Therefore, media can play a very successful role in breaking the barriers of orthodoxy and infusing scientific temper among masses.

Media must also promote research and development activities in order to get proper feedback of peoples' participation.

The Indian Constitution is based on the principle of equality. The problem of the backwardness of the masses who are at the lower side of dubious caste hierarchy, is still prevalent in many parts of the country. The government from time to time has made some efforts by granting reservation, free education, scholarships and many other benefits to ameliorate their social status. These policies and programmes of the government should be properly reflected in the mass media for the development of the country.

The youth, particularly in urban areas, often indulge in drugs and other related intoxicants. Media can educate the masses about the harmful effects of the drugs through various programmes and other advertisements.

Since mass media are regarded as an instrument of social change, they are supposed to play a dominant role in the process of development by conveying information and persuasive message of the government.

Media should inculcate scientific techniques in enhancing agricultural production, encourage small scale industries, especially agro-based co-operative methods for better farming and marketing.

International issues like cold war, energy crisis, globalisation and GATT, etc. should be given due importance in coverage.

Media must pay proper attention to rural poverty, unemployment, urban slums, weaker sections, destitute children, handicapped people, blind, aged and other vulnerable sections of the population. It must emphasise a mass campaigning in order to step up the attention of the people to the development problems and to help them to realise how they can contribute to national development through their individual efforts.

Innovations and ideas help the masses in changing their lifestyle. Various programmes and advertisements provide an opportunity to the individuals to tune their living in accordance with the demand of time, indirectly helping them in raising their economic position in the society. Thus, mass media can be powerful means to initiate mass campaigns for development.

There exists inequalities of income among various sections of the society. Economic development is possible only when there is reduction in income disparities that is possible by providing economic support in the form of loan or employment to the poor. Such issues should also be dealt with properly by mass media.

Another problem of our country is indebtedness. It is generally felt that landlords and money lenders exploit the people by keeping them under indebtedness and by using them as bonded labour. Media in such instances are expected to educate the people of their rights and help them to free themselves from social stigma.

Hence mass media can be used in a variety of ways for various purposes and can aim at increasing the tempo of national development.

Let us discuss the mass communication situation in the Indian context.

MEDIA OF COMMUNICATION : THE INDIAN CONTEXT

Since times immemorial, India has a rich legacy of various modes of communication; oral communication, traditional forms of communication, and mass communication comprising print and electronic media. Before the advent of printing the Indian ethos, culture and traditions were primarily oral in form. The ideas and messages contained in folk tales, myths, epic stories, and hyms were disseminated by the wandering monks through oral communicaiion methods. Similarly, traditional forms of communication primarily–folk theatre, folk songs, puppet shows, ballads, folk religious discourses constitute a rich resource which can be usefully harnessed for bringing about desirable societal changes for accelerating the development process. The print and electronic media are the two modern means of mass communication which have expanded rapidly and are imperceptibly competing with and, in some cases, overtaking the oral and traditional media of communication. A discussion on the role and development of all the four media of communication in India constitutes a fascinating aspect of the history and growth of media in the country.

Oral Communication

Speech is beyond doubt the most important vehicle of human communication. The culture of the Indian nation has been predominantly oral. The spoken word had a sanctity of its own. It was revered as the source of knowledge and inspiration for good conduct. Before the advent of printing technology, traditional beliefs were disseminated orally. In ancient days oral communication was the only technique available to the religious preachers and philosophers for propagating their point of view.

Large masses of people were illiterate. The general masses were not aware of the advantages of literacy or education. Their outlook towards life was determined by fate and accident of birth. In such a situation the oral tradition of communication was harnessed to perpetuate ideas in support of the *status quo* and the social system prevailing at the time. The Brahmin priests used highly sanskritised language which carried an aura of scholarship and erudition. The religious teachings were confined to the *elite*, far beyond the access of the general masses.

Although the means of transport were primitive, communication by religious preachers was still possible. These religious preachers who were known as *parivrajakas* (wandering monks) travelled from, and between, various centres of pilgrimages and delivered discourses on religious matters, epics and scriptures. It will be interesting to point out the difference in the methods and use of language by the preachers of Brahminism and Buddhism. As stated earlier, the Brahmin priests used sanskritised, literary and scholarly language, whereas the Buddhist method of communication was through local language. People were, therefore, more receptive to the Buddhist mode of communication.

During the modern times Mahatma Gandhi was one of the most successful practitioners of oral communication. In order to communicate his plans of action during freedom struggle, his views and philosophy, Gandhi was not contented with his writings alone. He spoke with conviction and sincerity of purpose; his expressions were chosen with utmost care. His words and sentences were most appropriately chosen to convey his meaning. He used *Padayatra* (literally journey on foot; but also included journey by train) and Prayer Meetings for establishing direct and personal rapport with his listeners. In his book–*Religious Communication in India, Vol. I,* J. V. Vilanilam pointed out : The other interpersonal channel which carried Gandhiji's message to people was his regular prayer meeting. Silent prayer was followed by singing of hymns and chanting of *Ramanam* by the audience. These prayer meetings ended with a brief statement by Gandhiji on some vital issue.

The regular national and international media looked forward to these statements from the greatest leader of the Indian freedom movement. Thus, the prayer meetings became a very potent means for the dissemination of the Gandhian ideas on politics, economics, village uplift, untouchability, *ahimsa, satyagraha* and *swadeshi.*

Even today, in spite of the vastly expanding media of mass communication, interpersonal communication through spoken word continues to enjoy a predominant position particularly in villages; the extension workers, political and opinion leaders rely on spoken word communication for the dissemination of the desired message and putting across their point of view.

Traditional Forms of Communication

> Even where modern media have penetrated isolated areas, the older forms maintain their validity, particularly when used to influence attitudes, instigate action and promote change. Extensive experience shows that traditional forms of communication can be effective in dispelling the superstitions, archaic perceptions and unscientific attitudes that people have inherited as part of tradition, and which are difficult to modify if the benefits of change are hard to demonstrate. Practitioners of the traditional media use a subtle form of persuasion by presenting the required message in locally popular artistic forms. This cannot be rivalled by any other means of communication.
>
> –*Many Voices, One World*

The traditional forms of communication constitute a potential source for conveying messages for economic and social development. Communities and individuals have utilized a wide range of media–local fairs, puppet shows, street theatre, folk songs and ballads for social purposes and as a support to local development schemes for health and family welfare campaigns, for creating political awareness.

In India, the most effective means of communication, specially in villages continue to be the traditional forms–folk theatre, folk tales, and of course, religious discourses. Folk forms which have been traditionally used as a means of disseminating information are diverse in nature and include different combinations of drama, dance, song, mime, story telling and puppetry.

India has a rich tradition of using folk media for nation building activities; even during the freedom struggle folk songs were used to popularise *satyagrah* and conveying political messages. Gurudev Rabindranath Tagore, in his famous *swadeshi samaj* speech in July 1904 advocated the use of *Jatra*, festivals and songs in order to reach the rural masses. Likewise, the eminent Tamil poet Subramanya Bharathi started using folk music to invoke patriotic feelings. Folk tunes were used to popularise songs on glories of spinning-wheel, need to boycott British goods and other diverse themes associated with the freedom struggle. Even during the recent parliamentary elections, *Jatra* was one of the popular modes used for campaigning.

The relevance of traditional form of communication–*Nukkad Natak* (street plays) was brought in bold relief when this form was utilised in states like Orissa, Uttar Pradesh and Bihar to apprise the rural population of the Kargil conflict. In this day and time, when there has been exponential growth in broadcast media and means of transport and travel are within the reach of common man; one is confronted with a sense of dismay that there would be some people in the rural areas of the country who would be still ignorant of the national happenings in the country. These street plays were perhaps one of the few successful channels to inform the people of various aspects of the conflict as also the valour and sacrifices made by the Indian soldiers. The plays were equally successful in instilling a feeling of patriotism in the audience.

The authors, never sure about the efficacy of folk media in transmitting development messages was pleasantly surprised when the participants of the Rural Press Seminar organized at Jaipur in 1994 were treated to a first rate performance by the folk artists in Lal Sot village near Jaipur. The artists, divided in two groups of singers, would take up one after the other through songs, the issues of corruption, maladministration and lack of development in the villages; and hold the elected representatives in the Panchayats and legislative assembly squarely responsible for the state of affairs. The performance not only entertained the audience through their presentation but also informed and educated them about the goings-on in the state politics. Nothing was considered sacrosanct, nobody was above reproach; it was an open house performance with village people as participants. That was an example of traditional media being utilised for creating awareness amongst people about the problems and lack of progress in the rural areas with telling effect.

The outcome of various researches has established the importance of folk media in development communication. Traditional uses of folk media were primarily for entertainment, social communication and religious activity. These media have an element of motivational and persuasive communication. There have been sporadic efforts to involve folk media for conveying development messages through mass media agencies.

These efforts have not gone very far as a number of traditional media experts have expressed the view that presenting messages through folk media which is spectator-oriented would alienate these media from their basic philosophy and cultural setting.

Radio and television have added new dimensions to folk music, making different styles known outside their language area. The mass media have made people aware of the unexpected wealth of folk and tribal music and exposed musicians to the cultural diversity of India and folk musical styles live again for millions to be heard and viewed over a vast media network for all times. They have created a new interest in folk music, not only among the musicians and sophisticated audiences, but also among the people themselves. The effect of the renewed interest in folk forms among urban circles, brought about partly by the mass media agencies has given stimulus to folk music of different regions.

The Government of India set up a Song and Drama Division in 1954 for tapping the traditional and folk forms of the media for plan publicity. The Division has ten regional centres and nine sub-centres in different parts of the country. The Division also has tribal centre at Ranchi. The centre utilises the folk forms by the tribal artists from Madhya Pradesh, Bihar and Orissa. The basic idea in establishing this centre is to provide and encourage development of suitable programmes in tribal idiom and dialect. The Division puts up field programmes in coordination with other units of the Ministry of Information and Broadcasting, government departments and voluntary organizations. During 1999-2000, the Division organised, mostly in rural and semi-urban areas, 38,576* programmes on broad national themes and government policies.

Much of social usage of folk medium has been related to preindustrial societies in which cultural expression has been primarily oral and essentially localized. Traditional performing arts are functional and interpersonal, have a contextual base and would be able to carry

* *Mass Media– 2001.*

the message of change, development and growth. However, there have been differing opinions in India on the wisdom of using mass media to broadcast folk media for social and development purposes. Successful publicity through folk arts depends on a happy synthesis of writing skill (at the script level) and theatre skills (at the performance level).

However, creative or innovative talent in the governmental organisations is lacking. There is a severe dearth of talent and imagination also. That's why the productions remain essentially ineffective.

There is also the aspect of inadequate funds at the performance level. As a result average or below average troupes perform who fail to build up the required effect. The most important lacuna is the absence of commitment of the management. This aspect becomes conspicuous when we consider the fact that certain Yatras and "street dramas" performed by the Communist workers in Bengal are much better produced and presented than the ones by the governmental organisations (Pillai, 1998).

Interpersonal Communication

Since the modern means of mass communication had not been in place till such time as printing was invented in the 15th century in Europe, vast majority of people lived within the context of their small village or tribal community with interpersonal communication being the main form of social contact. The International Commission for the Study of Communication Problems in its report says : Such interpersonal communication has been ever present, unceasing and specially within a small community, unrivalled in its importance. In the past it must have served to strengthen the values of comradeship and cooperation to counterbalance the fragmentation imposed by subjection to external authority. In any case, it has always had a socializing dimension, encouraging work, harmonious group living, banding together in the struggle against natural forces and in collective decision making. It remains an irreplaceable facet of human communication.

Interpersonal communication usually occurs in social situations, whereas the mass media inform decisions, interpersonal contacts support and legitimate them. Interpersonal influence is a two-way communication, the audience can talk back and convince itself. It is flexible, it is more trustworthy. If a goal of interpersonal communication is to achieve a changed attitude, to this end as a rule interpersonal communication is more effective than mass communication. The great advantage that the mass communication has over interpersonal communication is that of multiplier factor in circulating messages and information. With the rapid proliferation of mass media in India, the mass communication process is reaching out to large number of people. However, the number of people to whom the mass communication process reaches out cannot be ascertained, and from whom the feedback is not immediately available. In the mass communication process, the active participation of the recipients is comparatively small. In this context, Melkote refers to Schramm as under : Only when communication can build itself into the social structure, is it going to show any real hope of extensive results. Only when media channels can mix with interpersonal channels and with organisation in the village, are you going to have the kind of development you will like.

The communication system in the People's Republic of China is a good example of this model. The mass media in this country work with and through a complex web of interpersonal channels and groups, feeding people with information they need and at the same time can feedback to the party cadres.

Several communication scholars have emphasized the more effective use of interpersonal communication in combination with media channels, in situations which call for reaching people with new ideas and persuading them to utilize these innovations. Rogers in his study, *Mass Media and Interpersonal Communication*, enumerates media forum (small groups of individuals who meet regularly to receive a mass media programme and discuss the contents) to Canada, Japan, India, Nigeria, Ghana and Brazil, linked to radio or television as one such example. Such a media forum programme in India was Rural Radio Forum or *Charcha Mandals* which made farmers aware of agricultural and health innovations and encouraged them to try new ideas. These forums were later on discontinued as the government felt that these had fulfilled the objectives for which these were initially planned.

It, however, needs to be stated clearly that efficient use of media to bring about social change must take into account adequate knowledge of local culture. The new practices sought to be introduced should generally conform to the societal norms of the group or the unit. In India interpersonal channels, in combination with mass media, have been used effectively for conveying social and political messages to the people. This in fact is the most favoured communication method of reaching to millions of people in the shortest possible time. In the recent parliamentary elections this combination–political and public rallies were organised in large numbers including street corner meetings in towns and villages; and the news–at times even live coverage through television, was successfully utilised to get across to the people from all sections of society.

Communication through Mass Media

Mass communication, or communication through mass media, has been an ever-evolving process since the invention of printing by Gutenberg in the 15th century in Germany. Several historians believe that the modern age of communication dates from the invention of printing. Printing was initially used for dissemination of knowledge and ideas through books.

The beginnings of press in India as a part of mass communication and to propagate news and views about the current happenings in the contemporary society are credited to James Hicky who published the first newspaper in India called *Bengal Gazette* in 1780. Since then the Indian press struggled for survival and growth during the British rule in the country, made significant contribution tc the freedom movement and articulated the aspirations of the people. During this period several of India's top freedom fighters were excellent journalists and public leaders with mass following who were excellent communicators as well, chief among them were Mahatma Gandhi and Tilak.

Since independence the print media in the country has proven its resilience. The Indian press is characterized by pluralism and range of diversity in terms of socio-economic, linguistic and cultural interests. The press in India is one of the freest in the world and has emerged as a strong pillar of democracy and rights of citizens.

The print media at present continues to be in a state of buoyancy in terms of growth in circulation, number of newspapers as also the languages in which the newspapers are published.

Print Media

A country's press reflects the society it lives in, and the excessive space devoted in newspapers and magazines to politicians and political parties doings is a mirror of what excites the readers. The newspapers are full of politicians' election speeches and minute details of elections and electoral politics. The politicians recycle their speeches times without number every day, the newspapers dutifully publish the same speeches day after day. This excessive preoccupation with politics of the country is a legacy from the freedom movement when the press played an important role in mobilising public opinion against the foreign rule. It has, however, been observed that during the recent years economic policy issues and financial reporting are getting due importance, primarily because of the policy of economic liberalisation introduced since 1991, bringing in its wake far reaching changes in the business and economic sectors.

The circulation of newspapers in India increased 20% in 1998 over the previous years despite the marginal fall in the number of publications registered during the year. According to the Registrar of Newspapers in India's Report, *Press in India 1999,* the growth in the print media in 1998 was 5.09 per cent over the previous years, it has registered an increase of 6.47 per cent in 1998. The circulation in 1999 was 13,00,87,493 copies.

The newspapers were being published in 101 languages and dialects including 18 national languages and English, Hindi continues to top both the numbers as well as circulation with 17,836 newspapers commanding a circulation of 5,72,89,398. *The Times of India* was the top multi-edition daily, followed by *Malayala Manorama. The Anand Bazar Patrika*, published from Calcutta, claimed the highest circulation during 1998 among the single edition dailies.

Significantly ABC has also pointed out that the circulation of newspapers continued to rise phenomenally. The total average net paid circulation certified by the Bureau over the past ten years had increased from an average of 25.9 million to 40.9 million copies*.

As literacy levels in India are relatively low at 52 per cent and the physical distances to cover are huge, it is indeed a challenging task for newspapers to tackle the problems of time and distance in a country of India's dimensions and diversities. In terms of total newspaper circulation, India is at third place after Japan and USA. An other interesting feature of the Indian press is that newspapers in the country are amongst the lowest priced anywhere in the world.

Newspapers cover a broad area which includes every conceivable subject from offering hard news to entertainment, analysis and interpretation. Politics is, however, a major obsession of the Indian press. Barring a few exceptions, serious journalism devoted to an understanding of human condition and of deeper developmental concerns is at a major

---

**Times of India*, 29 September, 1999.

disadvantage. Newspapers are becoming more and more commercial and fiercely competitive in their approach. So different from the idealistic service inspired pre-independence period. The press has been captured by the big business; and dependence on revenue from advertisements is quite noticeable. The power and potential of the press, and the media as a whole in reaching out to the masses is quite perceptible.

Over the past few decades, the Indian press has witnessed a three tier growth. The mainline English language newspapers, published mostly from the metropolitan centres and state capitals, constitute the upper crust of the press, The English language press, catering to less than 5 per cent of the readers has a major share of advertising revenue because it is seen by the advertisers as aimed at the upper class clientele credited with purchasing power.

Leading Hindi and regional language newspapers, which during the past more than a decade have registered phenomenal increase in circulation, constitute the second tier of the Indian press. The statistics show that the domination of English language newspapers is receding, as more and more regional language papers from non-metropolitan areas are being published. The regional language press is increasingly making use of advanced means of telecommunication and printing technology.

The third tier of the Indian press is constituted of the small newspapers, mostly in Hindi and Indian languages, are brought out from district centres, having grassroot contacts. This segment of print media has progressed rapidly because of the three factors–gradual spread of literacy, rise in people's purchasing power and increasing level of political and general awareness and interests in the affairs of the country.

Interestingly there has been general scepticism regarding the useful purpose that host of small district newspapers serve. It would, however, be worthwhile even after more than 34 years of the publication of the book, *Communication and Change in Developing Countries,* to refer to the assessment about the district newspapers, and their contribution in encouraging local participation and mobilizing local effort : I have regarded these district papers as of immense value, for they focus the attention of the local population on local development effort and assist in creating interest in the local affairs. I personally know of a number of cases in which these small newspapers have exercised considerable influence on local administration and have helped to build local opinion on political and economic issues. If development requires local participation, these district papers have to play an important role in mobilizing local effort. It may be conceded that all of them are not motivated by the highest ideals, and some of them may be instruments of local politicians, but as a whole they are of great assistance to local development. Political decentralization and establishment of Panchayati Raj have created a new political structure in local administration. The Zila Parishads and Panchayat Samitis have been entrusted with wide powers in the spheres of local administration and local development. The small district newspapers have the same significance in local affairs as provincial papers in state matters and metropolitan papers in national problems.

Responding to the demands and requirements of its readers, the language press has evolved its own pattern. It accords proper importance to local and regional news as compared to national and international news which is generally received through news agencies. The events, problems and region specific news, which are generally not treated adequately by the metropolitan press are of special interest to the language press.

An emerging feature of the language press is the single daily domination in several states with circulation ranging from one-third or more of total circulation, and readership from half or more of the total readership in the language of the State. These States include Andhra Pradesh, Gujarat, Punjab, West Bengal and Kerala. Infact, in Andhra Pradesh, *Eenadu* dominates with half of total circulation and over 90 per cent of total readership in the State. In Kerala and Gujarat, two dailies have been dominating, both with significant share in circulation and readership as indicated in Table 1.

Table 1. State with Dominant Newspapers

State	Newspaper	In per cent	
		Share in total circulation	Share in total readership
A.P.	Eenadu	55	92
Gujarat	Gujarat Samachar	38	58
	Sandesh	30	47
Karnataka	Prajavani	26	57
Kerala	Malayala Manorama	42	63
	Mathrubhumi	31	54
Punjab	Punjab Kesari	37	50
Rajasthan	Rajasthan Patrika	34	50
Maharashtra	Navakal	8	27
	Lokmat	6	26
Tamil Nadu	Dinathanthi	18	66
	Dinamani	7	20
West Bengal	A. B. Patrika	24	45

Source : ABC : *Vidura*, Jan.-March 1999, p. 36.

The language newspapers, closer as they are to the local communities, reflect the cultural and social traditions of the people they serve.

Because of the highest rate of literacy in the country, the people of Kerala enjoy a high degree of awareness and can therefore claim a large slice of language press. The country's highest circulated daily paper, the *Malayala Manorama*, enjoys a high level of prestige in terms of editorial quality, introduction of latest printing technology and taking initiative in promoting agricultural and rural development in the state. A multi-edition newspaper it has been the highest circulated daily in the country for several years.

Broadcast Media

Over the years and particularly so during the preceding two decades, India has developed a fairly extensive electronic media infrastructure. Radio and television, and cable television since the advent of Gulf war in 1991, have seen exponential growth in terms of reach and impact. Presently, All India Radio network comprises 199 radio stations. The flagship of Doordarshan–the Primary channel–operates through a network of 1042 terrestrial transmitters of varying powers to make available TV signals to over 87 per cent of population.*

Radio, which continues to be a very important medium, has not matched the growth of television. It is indeed a sad commentary on the priorities of government media planners in our country that radio, which has been the most widely used medium for development purposes, is cost effective and has the capacity to reach large audiences, has been marginalised.

The well-known radio personality, Mark Tully making a comparison between Radio and TV says : Radio, as a means of mass communication, is friendly and has a far bigger reach. When you are listening to radio, you are personally involved, your mind is working. This is because mind is picturising the piece of information being communicated. In television, it is like spoon feeding your audience. The pictures are there before you and voice over is nothing more than captions to a series of visuals.

There could not have been more unequivocal and categorical assertion about utilitarian qualities of radio than what has been stated in the UNESCO report on communication–*Many Voices, One World.* In developing countries, radio is the only medium that can really be labelled mass where a large proportion of the population can be reached by radio broadcasts and possesses the means to receive them. No other medium now has the

* *India 2001.*

potential to reach so many people so efficiently for information, educational, cultural and entertainment purposes. Radio can be used easily and economically to reach outlying regions and for communication in the many vernacular, often unwritten languages, existing in developing countries. Almost all countries have a certain capacity to produce radio programmes in line with their political needs, cultural patterns and basic values.

In the above context, one cannot help recalling the observations made by the Working Group on Autonomy for Akashvani and Doordarshan that India should have given first priority to the development and densification of radio for atleast next 10-15 years. Radio is far cheaper and the availability of cheap transistors has made it ubiquitous.

In the beginning of the nineties, the sudden arrival of satellite channels had affected the popularity of radio and it remained virtually dead, at least in urban areas. With the opening of FM channels, introduction of new programmes and application of latest technologies, the radio is fast coming back in the reckoning.

Radio continues to be most frequently used mass medium in development programmes. Development broadcasting originated primarily to carry information on agriculture and rural development, health and family welfare. Some of the important programmes where AIR has been making significant contribution are : radio support for distance education programmes launched by universities, schools and other organisations, pulse polio immunisation campaign, and in the broadcast of Radioscope, National Science Magazine started since April 1995. These programmes, as well as others concerning rural development and other sectors, would come up for detailed discussion in the respective chapters.

Radio is essentially a people oriented medium, a medium of the poor man, who is central to all the development strategies of the national and state governments. It is non-elitist and is ideally suited for dissemination of information at the local/community level. It would, therefore, be appropriate to briefly refer to India's experience in setting up the first local radio station at Nagercoil in 1989; as well as the lead taken by a Bangalore based media NGO, *Voices* and initiating the first ever community radio programme from Shimoga district in Karnataka.

The broad outlines of the initiative were finalized at the International Consultation on Media Policy and Community Radio organised in September 1996 at Bangalore. The outcome of the Consultation was embodied in a valuable document – Bangalore Declaration on

Community Radio. The Declaration states : Community radio is public service broadcasting in its most decentralised form. A community radio station serves a defined geographical area of a village or groups of villages, and is owned and managed by organization serving a given community. Such a radio station would, besides educating and entertaining people, connect people with people through participatory or circular communication, connect with organizations and communities, and finally connect people with government and public service agencies. In a number of ways, community or public interest broadcasting can be termed Equal Opportunity Broadcasting, which is essential not only for effective democratisation of a public resource but also in the context of our plural society with a multiplicity of languages, cultures and ethnic groups. In terms of programming the community radio stations will build linkages between private broadcasters, local self-government institutions, educational and professional bodies and special interest groups. It is important that these groups are provided access to the medium in order to serve the public interest in all its dimensions. Community radio stations should also work in concert with government agencies in reaching out to and promoting economic and social welfare of the marginalised and disadvantaged groups within the community.

Television made its beginning in the country as a modest pilot project in September 1959; when the President Dr. Rajinder Prasad inaugurated the Experimental Television Service, operated from improvised studio. The programmes were telecast twice a week for a duration of one hour each and the signals were limited to 25 km from Delhi. The regular service with a news bulletin was started in 1965.

It would be interesting to recall, in retrospect the delay in starting television in India was due to the general feeling in the government that television was a luxury, a status symbol with limited utility and, therefore, could not be treated on priority for allocation of funds in a poor country like India where the need was pressing for more important necessities for the people. However, the role of television from the very beginning as an aid to education and social change was clearly recognised. There was also a realization of the immense potential of television as an instrument of rapid socio-economic transformation.

Doordarshan, the National Television Service in India, is also one of the largest terrestrial networks in the world. The flagship of Doordarshan– the Primary Channel–operates through transmitters of varying powers to make available TV signals for over 87 per cent of population. Doordarshan uses a large number of transponders of the Indian National Satellite. Doordarshan programmes are watched by 350 million viewers in their homes (Table 2). During 1997-98, Doordarshan earned around Rs.5 billion as revenue through commercial advertisements. It has its production facilities in 42 cities across the country.

To meet the regional aspirations, 10 regional language satellite channels on Doordarshan were introduced in 1994. Since the footprints of INSAT satellites cover the whole country, regional language programmes are available throughout the country regardless of one's place of residence.

Table 2. Pattern of Increase in Television Transmitters and TV Households

Year	No. of transmitters	No. of TV households (in millions)
1980	18	–
1985	172	6.8
1990	519	27.8
1995	672	52.3
1996	743	–
1997	868	57.7
1998	1027	63.2

Source : Doordarshan 1997 and Doordarshan 1998 (Prasar Bharti Broadcasting Corporation of India).

The Satellite Instructional Television Experiment (SITE) in 1975, primarily undertaken to experiment with television through satellite communication to broadcast special programmes in 2400 villages in six states aroused wide international interest. Subsequently the Ninth Asian Games in 1982 proved to be a significant milestone in the growth of Indian television because it heralded the introduction of colour television in the country. In 1983, a Special Plan for television expansion was approved. The plan was historic because beginning July 1, 1984, one transmitter was commissioned every day for a period of almost four months. During 1984, India's first soap opera *Hum Log* was introduced with the object of promoting women's welfare, family planning and reinforcing positive social values. The programme became very popular and made headway for other serials.

The Gulf War coverage by CNN in 1991 was a defining moment in the beginning of a new era in television broadcasting in India which ushered in far-reaching changes at a dizzy place. This was also the beginning of multi-channel TV in the country. The Special Edition of *India Today*, caught the spirit of the moment when it heralded the arrival of CNN in January and of STAR TV in April 1991, as "easily the most dramatic revolution took place on the TV screen. 1991 was the year when India ended decades of isolation from the rest of the world". Subsequently also the fortnightly news magazine wrote : The mundane television set has suddenly turned into an incredible technicolour dream boat.... and like a lost tribe discovering an oasis in the desert, lakhs of Indians are hot wired into this superbazaar of soaps, sports, news, music, sex and much more .... Hungry for any kind of news or entertainment, lakhs of people in cities and towns across the nation are now only too familiar with the names of the new electronic media companies, an alphabet soup of initials promising round the clock entertainment–MTV, CNN, BBC, ATN, Zee TV.

If any thing, the number of satellite channels has increased rapidly. The Sengupta Committee, while referring to Satellite channel universe, lists 52 channels operating in the country.

Today TV is no longer an urban phenomenon. Its penetration, in the sub-urban and mofussil areas, and even in villages, is not considered a big deal any longer. There has, in fact, been a virtual paradigm shift from state monopoly of electronic media to virtual *laissez-faire;* from the position of monopoly national broadcaster to one of the players is indeed a metamorphosis in the media landscape in the country. What does this metamorphosis augur for channelising communication media for development purposes?

Television was started in India for the purpose of development communication as vehicle of social change and national cohesion by unhesitatingly upholding progressive values and involving the community in a free dialogue, but it has gradually steered away from the enshrined development goals and chartered a course contrary to its development pursuits. Today entertainment has become the primary function of this medium.

The Working Group on Software for Doordarshan, under the chairmanship of P. C. Joshi (1982) indicated : Today development and communication are entirely unrelated. On the one hand, we have a powerful medium like Doordarshan not being used for development task, on the other hand we have developed programme and action without any media or communication support. The two should work hand in hand, reinforce each other if planning has to be effective. The Group also expressed its unhappiness on the VIP orientation of the programmes and said : It is a pity that a television system which is not only publicly funded but is also directly run by the government, on the ground that is necessary to make television serve the purpose of development in the direction of socialism, should show so little orientation towards the common people in its news and current affairs programmes. Doordarshan news should be gathered and presented from perspective not only of the government, the ruling party and the urban well-to-do, but also of the many other social, economic and political groups, who constitute the nation.

The Indian television industry has become completely entertainment oriented; telecast of feature films, *chitrahar*, soaps and other serials has made Indian TV a tool of entertainment with development being relegated to a subordinate slot. Television commenced with the aim of promoting socio-economic development of rural people by disseminating of knowledge, through education and information. During the course of expansion, however, Doordarshan now fulfils the three widely accepted principles : entertainment first, information second, and education last. The entertainment element has gone increasing at the cost of education and information dissemination.

Doordarshan, despite its great potential to communicate for millions of the illiterates, has its own constraints. Being mainly a unichannel operation, in most of the cities, it has to satisfy its viewers by compromising on its declared objectives. It is far behind in rural development communication, as the urban viewers, being in majority, can lobby and exert pressure to get the balance tilted in favour of entertainment programmes. Almost all the production centres of Doordarshan are located in cities and most of the programme producers have an urban background. Majority of the participants in its programmes are drawn from urban areas. Naturally rural issues are least projected.

Many programmes related to development subjects are broadcast regularly which bring about consciousness among the people. Educational programmes prepared by UGC, NCERT, etc. and agriculture broadcasting are good examples of development communication. Programmes based on health, environment, science and technology, etc. are also telecast from time to time. But these programmes contain many drawbacks including elitist nature. Similarly, the programmes on social awareness also need many improvements.

Development programmes are shabbily produced. They lack aesthetics and necessary visuals. Dull production leaves the viewer cold. Development programmes are never telecast on prime time and they fail to attract advertisement revenue. The viewers often consider such programmes as government propaganda and surf channels. TV can be most effective medium of mass communication only if it provides good programmes.

There has been pervasive concern over the impact of advertising on the quality and contents of the television programming at various levels; it has unleashed the forces of consumerism; which is spreading like wildfire, whereas access to the basics of life remains a serious problem for a large number of population. Several studies, seminars and reports of working groups have expressed concern that in order to meet the requirement of sponsors and advertisers, TV channels telecast programmes which threaten family values and usher in a life style out of sync with the Indian traditions. Suggestions have been in place to find solution to this situation which is becoming more and more intractable issue.

Multi-media Communication

In the Indian context which has a rich tradition of oral and traditional communication and a vibrant print and electronic media, Internet has emerged as an important factor in the fast developing communication landscape. With internet expanding rapidly the Information Age is well and truly upon us. The worldwide web is a challenge because of the interactive opportunity it offers for instant communication and is racing ahead at a breath taking speed. A large number of newspapers are available on internet. The *Hindu* was the first Indian newspaper to go on the net in 1995. Soon, other newspapers, both in English and Indian languages followed suit as also magazines. As is the predominant practice, the world over, access to Indian newspapers is also free. A major newspaper group chain operating from the capital has sites for all its publications, as well as for classifieds, jobs and careers, property, education, computing, etc. All these sites are easily available. It also offers Web Directory which has 9000 websites on Art and Culture, Business and Economy, Health and Fitness, News and Media, People and Society, etc.

Internet access in India has not reached a critical mass yet in view of the limitations of the infrastructure and bandwidth. Ever since the internet space was deregulated by the government, the number of internet subscribers is growing. Till date there are more than 2.5 lakh internet subscribers in India and according to a report there will be a quantum leap in the next twenty-four months. More than 2 million internet subscribers are expected by the end of 2001.

This technology is impacting print media as well. More and more online editions of newspapers will be available. Colour and graphics will play an increasingly important role in newspaper publishing. The newspapers will become increasingly digital in its production processes.

Another India? The other face of India, far different from the wandering monks depending upon oral communication in hoary days of distance past.

Non-dominant Communication

Non-dominant communication processes are media forms, which run contrary to dominant values, ideological propositions and organisational norms. Non-dominant communication consists of those media processes which have been marginalised by the homogenizing zeal of an industrial economy, and which are largely sustained through an intrinsic local ethos in addressing social issues of the moment.

These forms, amorphous and scattered as they are, may include street theatre based on folk songs and puppetry to convey messages of social importance, write-ups and feature stories on important contemporary issues which the mainstream media may not take up (or would take up only when the issue has been articulated through non-dominant processes) and has already become important enough to receive attention at a regional or national level. The way the issues concerning Narmada Dam were articulated through the vernacular press at the local level before these found space in the national press, cyclostyled bulletins, leaflets and letter on video films, were all instances and forms of non-dominant communication used for serving an important purpose. These processes have provided several feminist groups and voluntary organisations means to express their point of view and represent the ideology these stand for. The noted free lance journalist, Bharat Dogra, who publishes *News from Fields and Slums*, has found a novel method to articulate his views on poverty, environmental problems and concerns of the common person. He finds that small booklets, 16-32 pages, economically priced helps him focus on an issue and create the necessary impact. The production costs are low; he has managed to carry on the *News* with financial support from his wife, who later on joined him after giving up her government job. He has been, on principle, opposed to foreign funds, and hopes the feature service will motivate the next generation to create necessary climate wherein issues concerning the poor and slum dwellers could be properly focussed.

Communication Policies and Five-Year Plans

In the First Five-Year Plan (1950-56), it was recognised that all available methods of communication will have to be developed.

The Second Five-Year Plan (1961-66), stressed that the plan has to be carried into every home in the language and the symbol of the people and expressed in terms of their needs and problems.

In the Third Five-Year Plan (1965-71), it was as proposed to intensifying the existing arrangement for bringing home the implication of rapid development and carrying the message of the Plan to the masses throughout the country. The subsequent Plan documents also emphasised different aspects of communication strategy for development.

The Fourth Five-Year Plan (1969-74), felt the need to inform the people in the rural areas particularly those in the backward regions, about the specific schemes in agriculture, forestry, road construction, marketing, the supply of credit and other inputs so that the benefits of these programmes are more widely stressed.

In Fifth Five-Year Plan (1974-79), expansion of the television network to provide much needed support to education and to promote social and economic development was stressed.

From the Sixth Five-Year Plan (1980-85) onwards, fund allocation for electronic media and particularly television progressively increased which led to massive expansion of the television.

In the Seventh Five-Year Plan (1985-90), the objectives of the media policy were :

1. National and emotional integration of various regions of the country.
2. Utilisation of the medium as a means of development and social upliftment.
3. Dissemination of information and entertainment.

The Eighth Five-Year Plan and subsequent plan visualised an unprecedented growth in terms of extension of coverage, satellite services, software schemes and production facilities. Even in the earlier Five-Year Plans the role of media has been greatly emphasised to provide the general masses with the information about the objectives, targets and benefits of the Plan.

SECTION–II

PRINT MEDIA

Print Media

Journalism in India — Past and Present

The growth and development of journalism in India has had a chequered history. In India, journalism has been a product of struggle against the continuing repressive measures of the British rulers over a long period of time, right from the beginnings in 1780, when James Hicky, who published *Bengal Gazette*, the first newspaper in the country, was deported from India, till the final phases of the freedom movement–the Quit India Movement, when some of the leading papers had got their printing machines confiscated and hefty security deposits forfeited, repeatedly for defying the repressive laws against the press.

Journalism in India was nurtured by some of the greatest men that this country has produced–freedom fighters, social reformers, intellectuals and men of letters who gave their best to its development and growth. The tallest stalwarts of the freedom movement–Mahatma Gandhi, Lokmanya Bal Gangadhar Tilak, the social reformers and liberal thinkers Raja Rammohun Roy, Surendranath Bannerji and Gopal Krishan Gokhle were themselves either editors or pioneers in establishing well known newspapers. The history of journalism has, therefore, been inextricably linked with the growth of national consciousness and the progress of freedom movement. In fact the press journalism nurtured the national consciousness and freedom movement in the country and was in turn nurtured by it.

Pioneers of Indian Journalism

Modern journalism in India, which began towards the end of the eighteenth century, attracted government attention since its very inception. The first attempt to start a newspaper in Calcutta was made by William Bolts in 1776. Bolts had resigned from the service of East India Company after a court stricture for private trade under the Company's authority. He thought of exploiting the untouched field of newspapers publishing for ventilating his grievances against the Company. His efforts to publish a newspaper were not approved by the Company and he was asked to go back to Europe. This way the first cherished efforts to publish a newspaper came to a naught.

Beginning of Press in India

James Augustus Hicky made history by starting the *Bengal Gazette* on *Calcutta General Advertiser*, the first newspaper published from India on January 29, 1780. In the first issue, he introduced himself as the first and late printer to the Honourable Company though he did not seem to have enjoyed a high reputation. About his venture he said, "I have no particular passion for printing of newspapers; I have no propensity! I was not bred to a slavish life of hard work, yet I take a pleasure in enslaving my body in order to purchase freedom for my mind and soul." The journal described itself as, "A weekly political and commercial paper open to all parties but influenced by none".

It was the sheet paper with a size of 12" × 8" having three columns on each side. It published extracts from English newspapers at home, letters from local and mofussil readers and items of gossip and scandal of interest to the European community. The items were divided by rules or stars. The issue had more advertisement than reading matter. The news were mostly related to private lives of individuals. Hicky had a column to himself through which he used to talk to his readers directly. It was described as a 'witty and scurrilous' paper and very soon earned the enmity of Warren Hastings, the Governor General and Chief Justice Elijah Impey and generally the administration. Hicky's Gazette gained popularity within weeks. The individuals he attacked were not happy but others were. In fact they looked forward to reading the issue. Its readership was among the traders and merchants and non-officials European class community. In Hicky's Gazette there were regular columns–'poet's corner', 'Bon-ton', 'a women column' where new fashions and modes were discussed. News varied from political, individual, and local stories to weather or the arrival of some pretty women from England. Besides carrying a belated account of the debates in the British Parliament, Hicky's Gazette had editorials on the army and on the reported plans of individual rulers, letters to the editor also found a space.

Hicky knew his reading public. Spicy news about individual lives interested his European readers most. He had his "informal sources" and his own kind of investigative reporting.

Hicky's fortunes began to decline when a rival paper '*Indian Gazette*' appeared in the same year. It was a much better newspaper with four pages, each 16 inches long with three columns and well printed. It was published by Messink and Reed who followed Hicky and benefited from his experiences. When Hicky found that his customers were deserting him, he launched attacks against its proprietors, Peter Read, a salt agent, and B. Messink, a theatrical producer, John Z. Kiernander, whom he suspected of supplying types to his rival and Droze who did publicity for this journal. What aggravated his feelings was the grant of postal facilities to the *India Gazette* and their denial to him. He bitterly complained his readers that undue pressure had been brought to bear of Hastings through his wife to withhold postal facilities to him. It was suggested that he should seek Mrs. Hastings intervention in the matter but he rejected it, saying, "There is something so sneaking and treacherous in going clandestinely to fawn and take advantage of a good-natured woman to draw her into a promise to getting that done which I knew would be highly improper to ask her husband, though his unbounded love for his life would induce him to comply with.

There was no love lost between Hicky and Warren Hastings, nor was he popular with officials and many merchants and businessmen. The publicity which he gave to the social life of the European community in Calcutta was touched by malice and ridicule. While announcing marriages and engagements he also published news of engagements anticipated and he utilised this to hit people he disliked.

In June 1781 Hastings patience was at an end. The Chief Justice of India sent an army of 400 people to arrest Hicky at his house and to seize his printing types. He put up resistance and did not allow them to take away his types. He was arrested and was granted bail in the sum of Rs. 80,000. Since he could not pay that amount, he was tried and was sentenced to a year's imprisonment and a fine of Rs. 2000. Even from prison he continued to edit his papers which was allowed because there were no prelaws at that time to bar him. So the attacks continued. Although some of the writings were scandalous yet the journal exposed many malpractices.

In March 1782, Warren Hastings instituted four fresh actions and an order was procured to seize Hicky's printing press. A number of pleas made by Hicky were of no use. He was due to get some money from the Government for printing jobs done earlier. Even this payment was delayed and when it came, it was much smaller than what he expected. In the grip of poverty he set his plight in one of his letters to the Governor General.

> "It would be painful to you to read a long and particular account of the distress of myself and my children, let it suffice that everything which I had has been sold and mortgaged for my unhappy family, and none but God and ourselves knew the keenness of our distress."

Hicky was treacherous, colourful, irresponsible, irrepressible, impetuous, inventive, plucky, and unlucky. He was a fighter who went down. He was not interested in money. He had the courage to face the consequences of his writings and actions. His defence of the freedom of press in the following words was the manifesto of a fighter.

> "Mr. Hicky considered the liberty of the press to be essential to the very existence of an Englishman and a free government. The subjects should have full liberty to declare their principles and opinions, and every act which tends to coerce that liberty is tyrannical and injurious to community."

James Silk Buckingham was another pioneer born in England in 1786 and was recognised as a man of principles by all in Calcutta, including the Governor-General and the Bishop. Jawahar Lal Nehru has described him as among the earliest champions of the freedom of the press in India as one 'who is still remembered' in this country. He came to India in 1818 as the editor of the '*Calcutta Chronicle*' which was started by some Calcutta merchants to propagate their views and protect their interests. He indicated that it would be a chronicle of political, commercial and literary news and views. And it bore the impress of a versatile editor. He brought a breath of fresh air to an atmosphere polluted by the intrigue, scandal mongering, flippancy and easy going life of the European community. He had travelled widely in Arab countries. Buckingham was a scholar whose studies included anthropology and literature and he was interested in steam navigation, horseless carriages and air filled balloons for quick transport. He was a keen observer of the customs and habits of the people among whom he lived. He introduced to his readers Byron and Walter Scott and Washington Irving.

'*Calcutta Journal*' was started by him in October 1818. It was a bi-weekly paper consisting of eight pages. The editor's functions were described as admonishing, "Governors of their duties to warn them furiously of their faults and to tell disagreeable truths." The correspondence columns were open to all who had a grievance. This set a new standard in Calcutta journalism. There were local reports as well as letters from correspondents. These letters revealed the changes that had taken place in the Calcutta society since the days of Hicky. His criticism was instructive. In this respect Buckingham was a contrast to Hicky. Buckingham's paper was interested in discussing the acts and policies of Bengal government, the postal service, the police, the military establishment and government's attitude to various matters of public interest. Buckingham criticised the policy of *sati* and denounced the government's failure to put an and to this system. Buckingham laid emphasis on news of local conditions rather than fashions. The life of the people rather than the social round and criticism rather than invective. He gave prominence to news and views in Bengali and Persian journals and published a summary in his paper. He was a friend of the native (Indian) press and defended its right to exist and voice the opinion of the Indian people.

It will not be an exaggeration to claim that Buckingham was the inspiration behind the growth of Indian journalism. He was truly the father of Indian journalism just as Allen Octavian Hume, the founder of the Indian National Congress, was the father of Indian nationalism. It was with the advent of Buckingham that the press really began to discuss public questions and for the short period he was active in Indian journalism. He concentrated on the public conduct of bureaucrats and state functionaries and educated public opinion.

Buckingham considered a well conducted press essential to promote knowledge and dispel ignorance. He wrote "if knowledge is a blessing and ignorance a curse, a well conducted press that dispels the latter and promotes the former must be as deserving of our support as the schools and other public institutions established for the same purpose since they are only different branches of the same tree; and as the influence of the press may be made to extend much wider than that of the seminaries if each be well regulated and directed to equally worthy ends, the former will be the more effectual engine of the two. The union of both is perhaps the greatest advantage that any nation can possess to excite a taste for reading and a spiril of enquiry among the community generally and to gratify that taste must, therefore, be a task of merit."

He was a stout champion of the freedom of the press and he held views which could be called revolutionary in the background of the prevailing nations about the press. He wrote, "If all remedies proposed for checking evils inseparable from authority exercising almost absolute power, there is none that can be compared with a free press."

The *Calcutta Journal* under Buckingham was acknowledged to be the best produced newspaper and the best in content and presentation. The financial success of the enterprise enabled a new building to be erected and a new improved press to be imported from England. In 1822, the estimated value of the enterprise was placed at £ 40,000 three-fourth of it belonging to the editor and one-fourth being owned by the shareholders. Buckingham's yearly income was about £ 8,000. Buckingham managed to run his paper successfully without getting into any serious problem. Upto this time he had the protection of the trading community and had the support of the Hindu intellectuals. He also had the political tolerance of Lord Hastings.

Buckingham's first encounter with the authorities came when he criticised the suppression of Col. Rubison of the 20th regiment of the East India Company. Objections were raised to the publication and prosecution was started against him. In this case, however, no action was taken against him but Col. Rubison was asked to leave India within 24 hours because it was presumed that the cause of the whole trouble was Col. Rubison.

Hastings followed a liberal policy. He stood in the way of the deportation of Buckingham who had many encounters with the government. John Adam inspired a criminal libel suit against Buckingham for writing that if grievances brought to the notice of the government through the press were not to be given a hearing only those who enjoyed the favour of secretaries and public officers would secure redress. Buckingham was acquitted but it cost him Rs. 600. In spite of Adam's campaign against Buckingham, Hastings did not give up his liberal attitude. When Buckingham criticised the appointment of Dr. Jameson as Superintendent of the Medical School for Indians as he already held three other appointments, Dr. Jameson was angry and Adam wanted Buckingham to be deported.

Buckingham's crime was that he came too close to topics that touched the very roots of the administration. His repeated disclosures of official malpractices and his success in securing redressal of grievances proved a danger to the East India Company and its reputation.

Buckingham's example of courage set a tradition and was met with the government's alternate policy of repression and liberalism. This duality was to continue throughout British rule.

In England, Buckingham started the '*Oriental Herald*' in which he continued to expose the administration in India. He even filed a suit in the House of Commons for the compensation of damages.

Buckingham also advocated an elected Indian legislature composed of an equal number of Indians and Englishmen, and recruitment to the Indian Civil Service by open competition instead of by nomination. He was vigorous dominating and persistent and though he had the airs of an adventurer, he had vision and was ahead of his times.

The significant contribution by Buckingham to Indian journalism has been expressed as under : He made the newspaper the mirror of the people. He manifested at its keenest and most persistent, the spirit of enquiry and criticism. And he imparted to the press the quality of leadership. The bureaucracy wanted, by deporting him, to make him a warning to others but it could not put out the spark he had kindled. Buckingham was one of those journalists who are born rather than made.

Raja Rammohun Roy, whom Nehru considered as founder of the Indian Press, was a linguist, scholar-statesman, social reformer and liberal thinker. He was a champion of freedom of the press. In pursuit of his mession of politico-religious and social reforms he recognised the power of print media as a vehicle for propagating his liberal ideas. As a social reformer, he launched a campaign against *sati* and encouraged the efforts of Lord William Bentinck to abolish it by law. He used his powerful pen to eradicate social evils like caste system, idol worship, animal sacrifice from the Hindu society. He published *Brahmanical Magazine* in English (1821), *Sambad Kaumudi* in Bengali (1821) and *Mirat-ul-Akhbar* in Persian (1822). *Brahmanical Magazine* ceased to exist after the publication of a few issues only. *Sambad Kaumudi*, a news weekly dealt with political, literary, religious, and social subjects. This magazine espoused liberal outlook and became a great champion of civil liberty and rule of law. It stood against the racial discrimination and arrogance on the part of Englishmen. The paper was of the view that education was for social betterment and awakening and favoured spread of western medical science, technical and women education. *Sambad Kaumudi* became biweekly in January 1830 and continued for 33 years.

Rammohun Roy started publishing a weekly *Mirat-ul-Akhbar* in Persian with the objective of laying before public such articles of intelligence as may increase their experience and tend towards their social improvement. However, Roy relinquished the publication of the newspaper in order to register his protest against the introduction of

Press Ordinance of 1823 and injustice done to Buckingham, the editor of *Calcutta Journal.*

It would be pertinent to recall what had been said about freedom of press. Every good ruler must be conscious of great liability to err in managing the affairs of a vast empire and therefore he will be anxious to afford to every individual the readiest means of bringing to his notice whatever may require his interference. To secure this important objective, the unrestrained liberty of publication is the only effective means that can be employed.

He also protested against the introduction of Press Ordinance by Governor General John Adam. The Ordinance required that a licence from the Governor General-in-Council would be mandatory to publish any newspaper. The Ordinance evoked strong protest all-over Bengal. Roy submitted petition against the Ordinance which was signed by a number of politically conscious leaders including Dwarkanath Tagore. This remarkable document, drafted by Roy, has been called as the *Areopagitica of Indian History.*

Bengal was the birth place of journalism in India as well as of the language press. The first periodical in an Indian language was *Dig Darshan* in Bengali, a monthly magazine issued in April 1818. It published a range of subjects concerning politics, history, science, trade, economics, etc. The weekly *Samachar Darpan* also in Bengali (later on began to appear both in English and Bengali) started publication in 1818 and survived uptill 1890. Both these newspapers, although were part of the effort of the Baptist Mission at Calcutta for religious propaganda, also advocated women's education and became quite popular.

Subsequently several newspapers came into existence in Bombay, Calcutta and Madras. During this period, Bombay was emerging as a busy commercial centre of India with foreign and coastal ships engaged in commercial transactions and transport of goods. The Indian merchants in Bombay were mainly from Gujarat who were eager for news about the rates of commodities and shipping intelligence. In response to this need, the English newspapers started publishing advertisements in Gujarati from 1797. In 1822, Marzban started a Gujarati weekly, *Bombay Samachar*, with news of commercial interest. It is considered to be the oldest living Indian language newspaper of India.

Thus, the birth of Indian journalism could be traced to the second and third decades of the 19th century. These journals were started in Bengali and Gujarati. While the aim of Rammohun Roy was to educate the people about Hinduism and propagate social reform, that of Marzban was to serve commercial interests. Thus, social reform and commercial interests were the prime motives to start journalism in India languages. Another characteristics of Indian journalism in the first decade of 19th century was the co-existence of the British owned press and the Indian owned press operating in two water-tight compartments. However, both fought for the freedom of press (*Communication and Social Development in India,* pp. 135-36).

Struggle against Repressive Measures

The early years of nineteenth century saw Indian press struggling against the regulations meant to restrict its freedom. The first such threat emanated on 13 May 1799 when Wellesley issued guidelines for the papers published in Calcutta which required every printer to print his name at the bottom of the paper and pre-censorship of the papers. The penalty for infringement of the law was to be immediate deportation. The censor was instructed to prevent publication of matter relating to subjects like "Public Credit." Comprehensive regulations were issued in 1823 by John Adam, the acting Governor General which made the restrictions on the press more stringent. These regulations provided for obtaining a licence before printing or publishing anything. Adam looked upon the freedom of the press as threat to country's rule. The regulations also provided that a licence could be recalled and unlicensed printing presses could be attached by government and disposed of in the case of offending newspapers. The regulations, especially the clause regarding pre-publication licensing were greatly resented but they continued to hold the field till Sir Charles Metcalfe revised the press laws of the country.

Notwithstanding this restriction, the press in India continued to proliferate but the fact remains that there was no journalistic freedom. The government servants were prohibited to have any connection with the press.

Sir Charles Metcalfe's name is also deserved to be remembered in the history of journalism in India as it was he who even in those authoritarian days, had the foresight to realize the need and importance of a reasonably unrestricted press fulfilling the functions of providing information as also subjecting the government to healthy criticism. Metcalfe was not a politician. He was a whole time servant of the East India Company. He came to India at the age of 19 with General Lake during his Maratha campaign. After a brilliant career in diverse posts, he became a member of the Governor-General's Council in 1827 and acted as Governor-General for some time. It can be said that he freed the press in India and made English the official language. He stood for the freedom of the press and was instrumental in shaping the views of Lord Bentinck, Governor-General on this question. Hence, Bentinck not only followed a policy of tolerance towards the press but also actively assisted it. When leaders of the Indian and European press in Calcutta submitted to him a petition in 1835 seeking the repeal of the restrictions on the press, he assured them a system would be evolved which, while it gave security to every person engaged in the fair discussion of public measures, would effectively secure the government against sedition and individuals against calumny. He told them that the government had no intention of restricting the liberty which they already enjoyed.

Metcalfe when succeeded Bentinck for a short period, got an opportunity of revising the press laws in response to a memorandum received from the profession. The most significant aspect of Metcalfe's revision was a repeal of the most criticised provision of the Adam's regulations regarding pre-publication licensing and its substitution by registration under which an individual was free to print without permission but was liable for punishment if he printed seditious and calumny. So, Metcalfe was the first Britisher who as Governor-General repealed all the press restrictions existence i.e. of 1823, 1825 and 1827. For this act, he has been bestowed with the title of Liberator of Indian Press. He referred the question of revising the press laws to the law counseller, John Macaulay for changing licensing into registration. Macaulay favoured a uniform law for all the company's territories which leave the journalist free to print without permission but still render him liable for punishment for printing seditious and defamatory material. A law on these lines was passed by Metcalfe and he earned the gratitude of the press. Metcalfe said :

1. There is no use of having strict laws on the statute book which was never consulted.
2. He favoured the diffusion of knowledge than the perpetuation of ignorance. He said, "Do what we can, we cannot stop spread of knowledge. It is our duty to promote it whatever be the consequences."
3. He spurned the advice of his counsellors for special vigilance over the Indian language press and said there would not be any discrimination, as between Indian and English newspapers.

4. He held that an administration which depended on attempt to suppress public opinion could not be lasting both because "such a tenure must be rotten and because such attempts must fail." In this way, he admitted a considerable latitude of discussion.
5. He said that press sought to be free provided it be not dangerous to the stability of an Indian Empire.
6. He always advocated the liberty of the press, believing its benefits to outweigh its mischiefs.
7. Admitting that the liberty of the press like the other liberties of the subject, may be suspended when the safety of the press requires such a sacrifice. "I cannot, as a consequence, acknowledge that the present instance ought to be made an exception to the usual practice of the Government, for if there were dangers to the state, either way, there would be more. I should think, in suppressing the publication of opinions than in keeping the valve open by which bad rumours might evaporate".
8. To prevent men from thinking and feeling is impossible, and I believe it to be wiser to let them give vent to their temporary anger, in anonymous letters in the newspapers, the writers of which letters remain unknown, then to make that anger permanent by forcing them to smother it within their own breasts, ever ready to burst out. The government which interferes at its pleasure becomes responsible for all that it permits to be published.
9. He said, "It is better to have steady operation of the censorship, or any fixed rule, to the occasional interference of the government by its arbitrary will".

By promulgating the law relaxing the restrictions of the press which continued to be in force till 1856, Metcalfe earned the disapproval of the Board of Directors at home who charged him with going back on past directives. But Metcalfe would not relent and thereby he lost the chance of being the Governor-General permanently. He was demoted as Governor of north-west provinces and then of Madras. He sacrificed his career but launched the Indian journalism on its long and eventful journey.

He gave five regulations of the press which are as follows :

1. He said that the printer and publisher should make a declaration about the name and the place of their residence and

of the printing press.

2. Fresh declaration needed to be filed in case of change of address and names.
3. The punishment of Rs. 5000 plus two years' imprisonment was constituted against the non-filing of the declaration.
4. Anyone could close his or her press by making simple declaration.
5. As far as the prohibition on the company servants was concerned, Charles Metcalfe limited the restrictions only on the commissioned servants and not otherwise. The Government of India made it clear that the prohibition referred only to the covenanted and commissional servants of the company and not uncovenanted servants employed by the government and liable to be removed without reference to the Court of Directors.

The Court of Directors was angry with Metcalfe for having substituted the new law for the old without a reference to them. They said, "We are compelled to observe that this proceeding must be considered the most unjustifiable in as much as it has been adopted by a government only provisionally and also when a commission for framing a code of laws for three Presidencies was about to commence its important hearings."

The Court of Directors did not stop reminding Metcalfe that his conduct had not been forgotten or forgiven. As a result, due to liberating of the press from previous restrictions, there was considerable increase in the circulation and the number of newspapers in Indian and English languages grew rapidly from 11 in 1824 to 68 by the end of 1830 and it went up about 104 newspapers by the year 1856. Hence, Charles Metcalfe was the champion of the freedom of the press and surpassed all the previous advocates of freedom of press including Raja Rammohun Roy and James Silk Buckingham. He never bothered about his welfare while seeking redemption of the Indian press from the shackles of so many tough and rigid restrictions imposed by previous rulers. Charles Metcalfe was thus as a British Governor-General, a pioneer in the direction of improvement of the structure of the Indian press in India.

In the wake of first war of independence of 1857, the Governor-General Lord Canning, promulgated 1857 Act, which is also called 'Gagging Act.' This Act reintroduced the Adam's regulations of 1823 and required the printing presses to obtain a license to function or to print a newspaper or book. The government was empowered to ban the publication or circulation of any newspaper, book or printed matter.

These rules were applied to English as well as language press. The Act operated for one year. Many newspapers were prosecuted. However, before the Gagging Act could do much harm to the structure of press, the law became defunct on June 13, 1858 and the Indian administration passed into the hands of Queen Victoria on November 1, 1858.

Thus, the period from 1776 when the first attempt was made to start a newspaper in Calcutta by William Bolts till 1857, when the great leader Azimullah Khan started *Payam-e-Azadi*, which forcefully and boldly wrote against the British regime and gave impetus to the national movement, leaving the British government with no alternative except to muzzle the voice of this newspaper. Journalism in India proved not only eventful but also significant period.

The failure of the War of Independence, brought the administration of East India Company to a close, with the Crown taking over the country promising religious toleration and the freedom of the press.

Political journalism in India is traced to 1861, when the Indian Council Act empowered the government to nominate distinguished Indians to the legislature. Many of the great Indian newspapers which flourish even today were established during this period. *The Times of India* was established in 1861, the *Pioneer* in 1861, the *Statesman* in 1875 and the *Hindu* in 1878. This period also witnessed a boom in the Indian language press in the country. Several newspapers in almost all major Indian languages made their appearance.

At about the same time, the government promulgated the Vernacular Press Act in 1878 to stringently control the press. The Act required the printers and the Indian publishers of language newspapers to execute a bond that they would not publish anything that would excite the feelings of disaffection against the government. Under these regulations, any district magistrate or police commissioner was empowered to force the printer and publisher of a newspaper to agree not to publish certain kind of material, to demand security and to confiscate any printed matter it deemed to be objectionable. The Vernacular Press Act of 1878 was the greatest blow to the freedom of the Press in India and the Indian language newspapers suffered most heavily because of this law.

FREEDOM MOVEMENT AND THE INDIAN PRESS

The role of the Indian Press in strengthening and espousing the cause of freedom movement is one of the glorious chapters in the growth and development of the Indian Press. The establishment of the Indian National Congress in 1885 further strengthened the nationalist aspirations of the Indian people. Most prominent members of the Congress were eminent journalists and editors of newspapers. These included such towering personalities as Dadabhai Naoroji, Ranade, Narendranath Sen, etc. The Indian language Press was particularly strong in expressing its views against the government. The Press also took up the cause of social reform.

A number of India's greatmen, social reformers, leaders and crusaders in the struggle of freedom movement used Press for furthering their philosophy and the causes they espoused. Some of these–Aurobindo Ghosh, Annie Besant, Lajpat Rai, Surendra Nath Banerjee, Lokmanya Tilak and Mahatma Gandhi were eminent journalists in their own right.

Tilak carried on struggle for national liberation through journalism. He used the Marathi weekly *Kesari* and the English weekly *Maratha* for writing on social, political and economic subjects for the education and enlightenment of the people. Tilak used journalism for "popular education and public agitation."

Gandhi—The Great Communicator and Journalist

The emergence of Gandhiji at the helm of freedom movement changed the course of Indian history. He shaped national movement and influenced public opinion on various issues.

According to Chalapathi Rau : Gandhi was probably the greatest journalist of all time, and the weeklies he ran and edited were probably the greatest weeklies the world has known. He published no advertisement; at the same time he did not want his newspapers to run at a loss. He had gained considerable experience in South Africa, where he had taken over in 1904 the editorship of the *Indian Opinion* and published it in English, Tamil and Gujarati, sometimes running the press himself. *Young India* and *Harijan* became powerful vehicles of his views on all subjects. He wrote simply and clearly but forcefully, with passion and burning indignation. One of the objects of a newspaper, he said, is to understand the popular feeling and give expression to it; another is to arouse among the people certain desirable sentiments, and the third is fearlessly to expose popular defects.

Gandhiji's papers published no advertisements. They enjoyed wide circulation. His approach to journalism was totally devoid of ambitions. To him it was not a vocation to earn his livelihood; it was a means to serve the public. Writing in the *Young India* of 2 July 1925 he wrote : I have taken up journalism not for its sake but merely as an aid to what I have conceived to be my mission in life. My mission is to teach by example and present under severe restraint the use of the matchless weapon of *satyagraha* which is a direct corollary of non-violence. To be true to faith, therefore, I may not write in anger or malice. I may not write merely to excite passion.

Gandhiji looked upon journalism as a means to serve the people. He said in his autobiography:

> "The sole aim of journalism should be service. The newspaper is a great power, but just as an unchained torrent of water submerges whole countrysides and devastates crops, even so an uncontrolled pen serves but to destroy. If the control is from without, it proves more poisonous than want of control. It can be profitable only when exercised from within. If this line of reasoning is correct, how many journals of the world would stand the test? But who would stop those that are useless? And who should be the judge? The useful and the useless must, like good and evil, go on together, and man must make his choice."

Apart from being a national leader and social reformer, Gandhiji was also a great communicator. More than any one else, he recognized that communication is the most effective tool to shape opinion and mobilise popular support. He was successful because he had a latent skill in communication that surfaced in South Africa where he had gone initially to set up practice as a lawyer. The practice of communication started by him in South Africa gave him the clue to rally millions of his countrymen when he returned to India.

Gandhiji was associated with six journals, for two of which he was the editor. His first paper, *Indian Opinion* was started in South Africa. In order to ventilate the grievances of Indians and mobilise public opinion in their favour, Gandhiji started writing and giving interviews to newspapers. He focussed on Open Letters and letters to the Editor, but soon realized that occasional writings and the hospitality of newspapers were inadequate for the political campaign he had launched. He needed a mouthpiece to reach out to the people; so in June 1903 he launched *Indian Opinion*. It served the purpose of a weekly newsletter which disseminated the news of the week among the Indian community. It became an important instrument of education. Through the columns of the newspaper Gandhiji tried to educate the readers about sanitation, self-discipline and good citizenship.

Gandhiji launched *satyagraha* against the Rowlatt Act and the massacre in Jallianwala Bagh. He had learnt in South Africa how important the press and public opinion could be in politics and had taught himself how to use the written word most effectively.

The two journals *Young India* and *Navajivan* were used by him to ventilate his views and to educate the public on *satyagraha*. In 1933, Gandhiji started *Harijan*, *Harijanbandhu* and *Harijansevak* in English, Gujarati and Hindi, respectively. These newspapers were the vehicles of his crusade against untouchability and poverty in rural areas. These papers published no advertisements even then they enjoyed wide circulation. His note of defiance and sacrifice gave a new stimulus to the evolution of Press as a weapon of *satyagraha*.

Today, when there is widespread concern over the growing influence of market forces on media, and regret over journalism being no longer a social service, Gandhiji said : It is often observed that newspapers publish any matter that they have, just to fill in space. The reason is that most newspapers have their eyes on profits.... There are newspapers in the west which are so full of trash that it will be a sin even to touch them. At times, they produce bitterness and strife even between different families and communities. Thus, newspapers cannot escape criticism merely because they serve the people.

The Second World War brought about a change in the attitude of the government towards newspapers. For the first time the government agreed to self regulation by the organisations of the newspapers themselves, thereby avoiding much of the bitterness caused by the government control. The two important newspaper organisations formed were : The Indian and Eastern Newspapers Society (IENS) and the All India Newspaper Editor's Conference (AINEC). A Press Advisory Committee was formed with the assistance of AINEC. The result was that whatever restrictions that were to continue during the subsequent years were administered by the press bodies themselves or by independent authorities other than the government.

With the approval of Independence Act in August 1947 the role of Press changed. It had to shoulder the new responsibilities of national reconstruction. India's first Prime Minister, Jawaharlal Nehru was the champion of the liberty of press. About the contribution of Nehru in strengthening the Indian Press Chalapathi Rau says : In the period after independence, Nehru played a large part in shaping all thinking about the Press, as Gandhiji had done before independence. He was opposed by powerful sections of the Press, but he could carry on easily because he was a product of adult suffrage, had mass appeal and vast majorities, while newspapers still represented a small segment of opinion. But he stood for tolerance and accepted that a vigorous critical Press was a vital part of democracy. He was a passionate defender of press freedom as of all other freedoms. The traditions which grew in his time are becoming deep-rooted.

The print media in India in recent years has made rapid strides and can now be compared with the best in the world. The freedom of the press being a fundamental right, as guaranteed by the Constitution under article 19(1)(a), the people have made abundant use of this right. The print media has played a very significant role in the democratic process. The mainstream press in India has been the front runner in the issue-based investigative, interpretative and development reporting.

A detailed account of language, number and circulation of dailies and other newspapers taken together in 1998 is as under :

Table 3. Number of Newspapers in 1999 (Language and Periodicity wise)

Languages	Dailies	Tri/Bi weeklies	Weeklies	Fort-nightlies	Month-lies	Quarter-lies	Bi-mon-thlies Halfyearlies	Annuals	Total
English	371	30	881	671	2,734	1,210	731	162	6,830
Hindi	2,305	125	9,609	2,878	3,180	589	185	33	18,903
Assamese	15	3	75	38	59	12	10	1	213
Bengali	99	14	594	494	681	458	169	17	2,526
Gujarati	118	11	776	182	492	58	47	14	1,698
Kannada	314	6	354	231	589	44	19	4	1,561
Kashmiri	0	0	1	0	0	0	0	0	1
Konkani	1	0	3	1	1	0	0	0	6
Malayalam	213	6	174	156	732	57	27	8	1,373
Manipuri	14	0	6	5	10	6	3	0	44
Marathi	346	20	1,108	189	504	110	41	113	2,431
Nepali	3	2	20	6	8	16	5	0	60
Oriya	71	2	142	83	267	88	23	4	680
Punjabi	107	15	350	89	237	32	18	1	849
Sanskrit	3	0	8	4	16	15	6	0	52
Sindhi	11	0	38	11	35	8	2	0	105
Tamil	352	43	93	227	786	32	22	8	1,863
Teluga	151	3	245	187	480	26	12	2	1,106
Urdu	519	20	1,317	361	506	60	17	3	2,803
Bilingual	73	19	593	334	1,148	336	142	34	2,679
Multilingual	17	4	103	63	208	67	34	12	508
Others	54	14	83	30	123	49	11	0	364
Total	5,157	337	16,872	6,240	12,796	3,273	1,564	416	46,655

Source : India 2001.

LANGUAGE PRESS AND NATIONAL DEVELOPMENT

The growth of the language press in India during the closing decades of the twentieth century truly reflects the diversity and plurality of rich linguistic and cultural heritage of the century. Apart from the 19 official recognised languages in the Indian Constitution, the 1971 census is an expression of India's cultural richness and diversity. In the modern mass media, as well as in traditional communication, the use of variety of languages is an advantage, bringing a large segment of user population on to equal terms of comprehension with other linguistic groups.

Interestingly, the Report of the International Commission for the Study of Communication Problems, *Many Voices One World*, lists 16 languages which are spoken by more than 50 million people; out of which there are five languages in which newspapers are published in India. These languages are Hindi, Bengali, Urdu, Telugu and Tamil.

Small newspapers coming out from district centres and having grass-root contacts, mostly in Hindi and Indian languages, constitute another important segments of the Indian Press. These papers articulate the aspiration-demands, difficulties and problems of their readers and have been able to establish strong emotional affinity with them.

The Indian language press has played a historic and memorable role not only in the growth and development of journalism in the country, but also in the struggle for freedom movement. In the early nineteenth century, it also concerned itself with the social reforms and religious issues of the period. With the emergence of Mahatma Gandhi on the Indian political scene and his non-cooperation movement, language papers extended the moral strength to the movement.

In his book, *Journalism in India*, Rangaswami Parthasarathy recapitulates the glorious contribution of the language press as under:

> "Ill-equipped and with poor resources they managed to survive the onslaught and persecution of the alien rulers for over three decades and many of them fell on the wayside after writing a glorious chapter in the history of the freedom struggle during their brief existence. Many were the acts of courage and patriotism and sacrifice by the men who conducted these papers and their staff. They were dedicated to a cause and nothing could stop them from completing their mission. They endured privation and penury and even suffered imprisonment and when not there to enjoy the fruits of a hard-won battle but their spirits must have hovered over the

battlements where they fought and sacrificed their lives to shed tears of joy. The contribution of Hindi and Urdu journalism to the struggle for freedom and the political awakening of the masses is immense.

"The establishment of the Indian National Congress in 1885 further strengthened the nationalist aspirations of the Indian people. Most prominent members of the Congress were eminent towering personalities as Dadabhai Naoroji, Ranade, Narendranath Sen, etc. The Indian language press was particularly strong in expressing its views against the government.

"A number of India's greatmen, social reformers, leaders and crusaders in the struggle of freedom movement used press for furthering their philosophy and the causes they espoused. Some of these–Aurbindo Ghosh, Annie Besant, Lajpat Rai, Surendra Nath Banerji, Lokmanya Tilak and Mahatma Gandhi were eminent journalists in their own right. Tilak carried on struggle for national liberation through journalism. He used the Marathi weekly *Kesari* and the English weekly *Maratha* for writing on social, political and economic subjects for the education and enlightenment of the people. Tilak used journalism for "popular education and public agitation."

A unique feature of the language press in the East and North-East Bengali, Assamese and Oriya is the vibrant practice of bringing special numbers and literary supplements on festive occasions of Rangoli Bihu and Durga Puja. These special issues are brought out in large numbers and contain short stories, poems, creative writings and novels in full or serialised. Buying a Puja number is a part of the traditional festival shopping. Thus, these newspapers meet the higher literary and cultural aesthetics of the people and help mould their tastes. Elaborating the contribution of the language press in Orissa, Bhatt says :

> In Orissa's march ahead and particularly its cultural revival journalism has played no mean part. The press took literature to the people instead of allowing it to remain the preserve of the elite, the result is there for all to see the recognition that Oriya literature has earned by way of the Jananapeeth awards for its poetry and other forms of literature. The Prajatantra group brings out an English weekly, *the Eastern Times*, its *Jhankar* monthly has a high standing in Orissa for the quality of its literary material and for the awards it gives to writers which are prized.

The language press in the South has been particularly vibrant. Several newspapers, *Eenadu* in Andhra Pradesh and *Malayala Manorama* in Kerala have established a new genre of journalism in different ways.

The Telugu daily *Eenadu* launched in 1974, first from Visakhapatnam and a year later from Hyderabad has district editions from almost Andhra districts, with circulation crossing 4 lakhs. The success of *Eenadu* is attributed primarily to the rising public demand for information. Ramoji Rao played crucial role in the victory of N. T. Rama Rao and the *Telugu Desam Party* in 1983. The newspaper has diversified its activities by launching its own regional TV channel and supports an English daily *Newstimes* from Hyderabad.

Several other Indian language papers have also rendered valuable service in shaping different aspects of economic development, social awareness and cultural rejuvenation. This paper has attempted a short overview of the progress of the Indian Language Press in the country about which Mark Tully in his book from *Raj to Rajiv* in 1989 had said : The Indian press, on the one hand, must be most free and lively in the Third World. It does act as a watching on the government which is essential if democracy is to survive in India. There has been an explosion of papers and magazines in both English and Indian languages over the last fifteen years and journalism has become much more vigorous.

Language press constitutes one of the most important media for reaching out to the hundreds of millions of people in all parts of the country. As an important link between planners, bureaucracy and the people at the grassroot level, language press is a viable mean for the promotion of literacy, social awareness and development.

However, it may be noted with concern that in their struggle for existence, the language newspapers sometimes do not adhere to the ethics of journalism i. e. truthfulness and responsibility, objectivity and fair play. Development or literacy related news is far from their mind. Their main objective is to increase sales. The contents and presentation of such papers have a focus on the entertainment, negative news, mainly pertaining to violence, theft, political instability, scams, etc. No doubt these are required for wider dissemination. But the coverage of news of positive side of human life and society should also be there.

Problems Encountered by Language Press

The language press is not only ignored but also scorned by the elite as well as the government. It is felt that the language press is to face more years of persistent struggle ahead before it is recognised as a significant segment of the Indian press alongwith English/National dailies.

The various other recognised problems which come in the way of reporting in case of language press because of main concern being local and to some extent state and nation and hence because of limited target population are financial problems, availability of information and authenticity thereof, infrastructural facilities, risks and threats involved keeping in view the castes, communities and groupism factors. The main challenge before the language reporting is to sensitize the elite readership towards developmental issues affecting the Indian masses, the vast majority of which is inhabiting the rural areas. The nexus of illiteracy, poverty and poor health can be broken by the language press by focusing on the developing schemes, in vogue, and promoting the role of voluntary organisations to break the bureaucratic bottlenecks in the welfare and development schemes. It has been observed that the personnel working in the language press lack adequate training required to handle their multifaceted responsibilities. It may be suggested that an appreciation course in language problems preferably by a language institute or an agricultural university would go a long way in redressing this deficiency.

Language press is promising medium for disseminating information and knowledge about nutrition, health and hygiene, improved farm practices, family planning measures and development plans to those sections of society where the information is needed most. Hence, it becomes all the more important to help in the promotion and sustenance of language press through various measures.

What is needed is to make language press relevant to the Indian situation. It has to encompass in itself the cultural ethos of the Indian life in all its aspects mainly the rural poor and unrepresented people in the press. Its subjects would include profile of an artisan, success story of a farmer, neoliterate women, literacy workers or even the failure stories for reflection, problems faced in marketing of agricultural produce, social superstitions and taboos inhibiting the economic growth and productivity. Such kind of language press shall not only mirror the true life in the Indian people, but shall also provide a different perspective and frame of reference for the planners and policy makers to improve the quality of life of people through literacy and development. The language press is required to assume the role of the information centre about various schemes, plans, projects, weather forecast reports and facilities available like credit, seed, fertilizer besides new development projects e.g. construction of a new road or a bridge in the far flung areas.

Promoting the Language Press for Literacy and Development

Some of the important policy and remedial measures which may help in the promotion and sustenance of language press are :

- Local papers should be allowed to be printed at the Government Press on official rates.
- Provision of free bus and railway passes for the editors of language papers should be made at par with big newspapers.
- Journalists of language newspapers should be provided free insurance and legal protection. There should also be proper police protection for them.
- Paper quota for these papers should be provided on subsidised rates by the government.
- Facilities for loans under various schemes of the government should also be made available as for other cottage industries.
- The advertisements of various government departments, banks and public sector undertakings should be routed through the D.P.R.O. who should then distribute it proportionately to the local press.
- Language/Local papers should not be discouraged by the local administration but due importance must be given to their coverage. They should rather be encouraged and given positive direction by organising workshops/camps from time to time.
- It should be the endeavour of the language press to associate itself with various organisations and departments working in the Indian society.
- The language press is required to have closer association and links with the local bodies such as village panchayats and also with the opinion makers in the villages to promote the development in indigenous situation.
- Indian Languages Press Commission should be appointed to go into whole gamut of the working of language press and should come out with concrete recommendations.

- Language press should aim at the community service and development. It should be the mirror of the true life of contemporary society. It should be true source of feed-back to the government and policy makers. But at the same time, while having such expectations from the language press, the latter should also expect co-operation from the government and the public at large.

PRESS ORGANISATIONS

Press Council

The Third International Conference on Press Council was held in New Delhi a few years back. The conference decided to establish a World Association of Press Council. India and Sweden abstained from voting although they did not approve the motion. Sweden abstained from voting on the grounds that the members of the team had not been given the mandate to vote. India abstained for different reasons. The Press Council of India felt that an informal body would be preferable to a formal body. Proposals to form an International Code of Ethics were dropped, instead countries had been asked to form their own codes.

The institution of Press Council emerged for the first time in Sweden in 1916 known as the Court of Honour. Now it has been established in more than 40 countries. In all the countries, except Italy and Holland, Press Councils have been set up voluntarily. The functions of the Press Councils differ from country to country. The British Press Council came into existence in 1953. It has served as a model for many countries.

In India it is an autonomous, non-official but statutory body. The First Press Commission (1954) recommended the setting up of a statutory Press Council to look after the editorial independence, objectivity of news presentation and fairness of comments, etc. on the part of the newspapers. The council, according to the commission, was also to foster the development of press, protecting it from external pressures and regulate its conduct matters of such objectionable writing as was not legally punishable. In persuance of this recommendation, the Press Council of India was constituted by the Govt. of India in 1966 under the Press Council Act of 1965, with Justice J. R. Mudholkar, the judge of the Supreme Court, as its Chairman, which was later amended in 1970. After the first chairman, Justice Mudholkar, the PCI was headed by Justice N. Rajagopala Ayyangar and (after its revival) by

Justice A. N. Grover, Justice A. N. Sen and Justice R. S. Sarkaria. The present Chairman of the Press Council is Justice P. B. Sawant.

During the internal emergency, the Press Council was abolished on the expiry of the term on 31 December 1975. The Press Council Act was repealed. It was stated that the council was being abolished because it was not able to carry on its functions effectively to achieve the objects for which the Council was established. The Annual Report of the Ministrv of Information and Broadcasting for 1975-76 said : The Press Council during the nine years of its existence had failed to curb the tendentions, provocative and unrestrained writings in the press. It was unable to frame a code of conduct for editors and complaints of minor character mostly engaged its attention. Accordingly the Press Council of India was abolished w.e.f. 1st January 1976.

A fresh legislation providing for the establishment of a Press Council was enacted in 1978. The Act came into force on Ist March 1979. The objectives of the revised Press Council are :

1. To preserve the freedom of press.
2. To improve standards of newspapers and news agencies in the country.

One of the main functions of the Council is to enquire into complaints received by it and building up a code of conduct for newspapers, news agencies and journalists in accordance with high professional standards.

Term

The term of the members of the Press Council is of three years. After every three years new members are appointed to the Council. The term of the present seventh Press Council will expire in 2000 under the chairmanship of Justice P. B. Sawant.

Constitution of the Press Council

Total members	:	28
Chairman	:	01

(Chairman is nominated by a committee consisting of a Chairman of Rajya Sabha, Speaker of Lok Sabha and one elected representative of Council members). Chairman is always a retired judge of Supreme Court.

Among twenty-eight members :

–	Working Journalists (6 editors of newspapers, 7 working journalists other than editors)	:	13
–	From management, big, medium and small newspapers (who own or carry on the business of management of newspapers)	:	06
–	News agencies	:	1
–	Members of Parliament nominated by Speaker of Lok Sabha (Three from Lok Sabha and two from Rajya Sabha)	:	5
–	Persons having special knowledge or practical experience in the following fields :		
	(a) Education and science (nominated by UGC)	:	1
	(b) Law and Literature (nominated by Bar Council)	:	1
	(c) Culture (nominated by Sahitya Academy)	:	1

For the purpose of performing its functions or holding an enquiry under the Act, the Council has been clothed with powers exercisable throughout India as are vested in a civil court while trying a suit under the Code of Civil Procedure, 1908. Thus, the Council can summon and enforce the attendance of persons and examine them under oath. It can require discovery and production of documents. receive evidence on affidavits, requisition public records or copies thereof from any court or office, issue commissions for the examination of persons or documents and finally for any other matter which may be prescribed. The Act, however, recognises immunity of a journalist from disclosing his source of information.

In his book, *The Journalists Handbook*, M. V. Kamath says : The Council, it is important to remember, is NOT a court of law. It is a court of honour. Its verdicts are not judicial pronouncements. Therefore, there is no question of punishment imposed on an offending journalist or newspaper. By that same token the Council cannot award damages to the aggrieved party. As Mudholkar puts it : The only weapon in its armoury is moral authority. The sole strength of the Council lies in its appeal to conscience.

Who can lodge a complaint against a newspaper or journalist to the Council? Anybody. The Council does not even have to wait for someone to make a complaint if it thinks that a case against a newspaper can be made on its own. The complainants, incidentally, need not necessarily have a personal interest in the matter complained against.

A complaint can merely be filed where the complainant has "reasons to believe that a newspaper has offended against the standards of journalistic ethics or public taste or that an editor or a working journalist has committed any professional misconduct or a breach of journalistic ethics."

Objectives and Functions of the Council

The objectives, some of which are given below, of the Council shall be to preserve the freedom of the Press and to maintain and improve the standards of newspapers and news agencies in India :

(a) to help newspapers and news agencies to maintain their independence;
(b) to build up a code of conduct for newspapers, news agencies and journalists in accordance with high professional standards;
(c) to ensure on the part of newspapers, news agencies and journalists, the maintenance of high standards of public taste and foster a due sense of both the rights and responsibilities of citizenship;
(d) To encourage the growth of the sense of responsibility and public service among all those engaged in the profession of journalism;
(e) to keep under review any development likely to restrict the supply and dissemination of news of public interest and importance;
(f) to keep under review cases of assistance received by any newspaper or news agency in India from any foreign source including such cases as by any individual, association of persons or any other organization;
(g) to undertake studies of foreign newspapers, including those brought out by any embassy or other representative in India of a foreign State, their circulation and impact;
(h) to promote a proper functional relationship among all classes of persons engaged in the production or publication of newspapers or in news agencies;
(i) to concern itself with developments such as a concentration of, or other aspects of, ownership of, newspapers and news agencies which may affect the independence of the press; and

(j) to undertake such studies as may be entrusted to the Council and to express its opinion in regard to any matter referred to it by the Central Government.

The Chairman, Press Council of India, Justice P. B. Sawant, in his paper-Press Council : the Conscience Keeper, has said : During the last thirty years, the Council received 8939 complaints. Out of them, 2693 were by the Press against the police, the publicity department and revenue authorities, individual politicians or bureaucrats. The rest 6246 were against the press. The complaints against the government and governmental authorities were mainly of false and malicious charges, false arrests and detentions in police custody, threats to life and property, non-cognizance of and inaction by the police on complaints filed by the journalists, the collusion of the police with the anti-social elements criticised by the press, and connivance at their violence, and threats to life, liberty and property of the journalists and owners of the newspapers, vindictive suspension and cancellation of advertisements, and non-payment or delayed payment of the advertisement bills, cancellation or suspension of accredition passes, withholding of or reduction in news-print quota, stoppage of electricity and water supply, attempt to demolish the premises where the newspapers were published or raids on newspaper offices, seizure of the copies of the newspapers and their destruction, etc. The complaints against the press have been mainly for publication of unverified and abusive language, printing of obscene pictures, communal and casteist writings and attempts to inflame communal passions, refusal to publish replies, encroachment on privacy, distorted and prejudiced reporting, suppression of facts, sensational and misleading headings completely at variance with the contents of the report, malicious reporting and writings, non-publication of the other side of the views expressed, mixing comments with facts, fratricial conflicts, plagiarism, *et al.*

Since the Council has no punitive powers to punish violations of the professional ethics by the press or the encroachment on the freedom of the press by the authorities, the Council has come to be looked upon as a toothless tiger. The critics, however, forget that the Council has been designed essentially as an internal regulatory mechanism of and by the press. Consequently, disapproval, warning, admonition and censure of the newspapers, news agencies and the journalists and strong observations against the authorities are the only weapons kept in its armoury. The exercise of punitive powers by the Council will not only destroy the character of the Council as an internal mechanism of the press, but will also embroil it in a large number of court cases defeating the very objectives for which the Council was established.

The Registrar of Newspapers for India

The Office of the Registrar of Newspapers for India (RNI) also commonly known as the Press Registrar was created on 1st July 1956, pursuant to a recommendation of the First Press Commission by an amendment of the Press and Registration of Books Act 1867.

Functions

It functions as a central government body responsible for the completion of a Register giving particulars like ownership and circulation of all newspapers published in India.

It oversees the allocation of titles, newsprint and certificates for the import of printing and allied machinery required by newspaper establishments and also sees to the enforcement of the provisions of the Press and Registration of Books Act, and has the authority to inspect newspaper records and documents.

The RNI carries out frequent checks to find out whether the newspapers registered with it are published regularly and also whether the circulation figures claimed by newspapers are credible.

It is the duty of the Press Registrar to register all newspapers published in the country to issue certificate of registration to them, to maintain the particular rating to them in a register and to submit to the Central Govt. an annual report containing a summary by the information obtained by him during the previous year in respect of newspapers in the country. These annual reports entitled, 'Press in India' contain valuable information and statistics relating to the press.

The Press Registrar requires information about circulation figures to ensure that :

1. the newsprint used is in proportion with the circulation figures,
2. the printing capacity is in proportion with the circulation figures,
3. the newsprint waste is normal,
4. the payment of newsprint has been made in accordance with rules, and
5. the details (paging, printing and circulation dates, etc.) pertaining to number of supplements printed in advance are correct.

Audit Bureau of Circulations (ABC)

ABC is an independent, self-financing, private body, charged with the responsibility of conducting regular audit of the 'net circulation of newspapers' and issues certificates of Net Paid circulation every six months. It has a very high reputation for reliability and impartiality and is, therefore, quoted with authority.

Need

During the early 1900's, with the growth of mass advertising, some newspapers and magazine publishers began inflating the number of readers for their publications in order to atleast get more revenue from advertisers. In an effort to check this deceptive practice, advertisers and publishers joined together to form the ABC in 1914. The organization's purpose was to establish ground rules for counting circulation, to make sure that the rules were enforced, and to provide verified reports of circulation date. In India, it came into existence in 1948.

Objectives

1. To issue standardised statements of the circulation of members.
2. To verify the figures shown in these statements by auditor's examination of necessary records.
3. To disseminate circulation date for the benefit of advertisers, advertising agencies and newspaper publication.

What does ABC consider?

It considers the following :

1. Whether the changes in the supply desired by agents have been done timely or not,
2. Whether the supply is in accordance with the demand of agents or not,
3. Whether payment is received from the agents in time or not,
4. Action taken by the circulation department on the complaints of agents,
5. The timeliness of payment made to the different modes of transport used for supplying newspapers,
6. The agreements made with the dealers/agents,

7. The preparation of the newsprint used and the circulation.

Functions

The ABC functions in the following manner :

Publishers keep detailed records of circulation data. In the case of a newspaper, these records would include such information as the number of copies delivered by carriers, the number of papers sold over the counter and the number delivered by mail. Twice a year, publishers file a circulation statement with the ABC which the ABC in turn disseminates to its clients. Once every year, the ABC audits publications to verify that the figures that have been reported are accurate. An ABC representative visits the publication and is free to examine records and files that contain data on press runs, invoices for newsprint and transcripts of circulation records.

ABC report helps the advertisers as well as the newspaper. From the verified facts, the advertisers can draw their conclusion and prepare advertising plans. Newspapers are also benefited by the ABC report. Firstly, they gain respect and confidence of advertisers. Secondly, on the basis of the report, they can peep into their own activities and programmes and make a modest review of the progress made by the newspaper. Thirdly, the report is an evidence of the newspaper's worth.

There are a number of special institutions dealing with the press.

Table 4 : Special institutions dealing with Press

Name of institution	Year of establishment
Indian and Eastern Newspapers Society	1939
All India Newspaper Editor's Conference	1940
Indian Languages Newspapers Association	1941
Advertising Agencies Association of India	1945
Press Trust of India	1948
Audit Bureau of Circulation	1948
All India Federation of Working Journalists	1951
Indian Society of Advertisers	1952
United News of India	1961
Press Council of India	1966

Leading Newspapers

The Hindu

Published from Chennai, Coimbatore, Bangalore, Hyderabad, Madurai, Delhi, Vishakhapatnam and Thiruvananthapuram, *The Hindu* is regarded as one of the world's best newspapers. The American Newspaper Publishers' Association selected it for the World Press Achievement Award in 1968.

The Hindu Group was conceived by six patriotic young men to fight the British rule, it has come along way since then. The paper was started as a weekly in 1878 by G. Subramania Aiyer and five other young men to fight its battle to rid Hinduism of its social evils. Among the reforms–for which the campaigned were widow remarriage, raising the age of marriage, abolition of caste and uplift of the touchable. Besides taking interest in social reforms, Subramania Aiyer was equally enthusiastic in participating in India's battle of freedom. He was one of editors who attended the first session of Indian National Congress held in 1885. *The Hindu* has a series of pioneering initiatives to its credit :

1. It was the first newspaper to acquire a fleet of four aircraft and operating them on its own, which was just like operating a small airline with all its problems and headaches.
2. It was again the first newspaper to have launched its facsimile editions in Coimbatore and later extended to Bangalore, Hyderabad and Madurai. It also introduced phototype setting for printing the paper. It was the second newspaper in Asia to introduce the fax system.
3. It has been a pioneer in introducing technological advances and innovations. It has been the first Indian newspaper to go on the net in 1995. Soon other newspapers, both in English and other languages followed suit as also the magazines.

Ever since its inception, *The Hindu* has espoused the cause of first rate journalism, non-partisan, independent and fair. In an editorial in 1967, it wrote what may be considered as its testament. The editorial said : We must make it clear *that we are an independent, non-party newspaper, wedded to the national interest as we see it. We are not the mouthpiece of any party.* We have been more often critical of the ruling party perhaps than singing its praises. We have always made a distinction between programmes and measures on the one side and personalities and parties on the other. Our criticisms have been primarily concerned with the non-wisdom or inappropriateness of certain policies or decisions and whatever governments may come to power we shall continue to judge them not by their professions but by their performance.

The Hindu has postulated three basic principles to make freedom of the press real. The first is that the press must keep its own house clean and exercise reasonable restraint on its functioning. *Freedom should not be allowed to degenerate into licence which would open the door to government interference.* The second is the response of authority to the smooth functioning of the press by removing physical restraints and to enable it to reach as wide a readership as it would wish. The third and the most important is the attitude of society as a whole, which besides the public, includes politicians, trade unions, advertisers, etc. The press has been subjected to pressure from one or another of these sources and the less viable among the press have found it difficult to withstand it. Press freedom can come to prevail only when all sections of the body politic resolve to make it prevail by removing all impediments in the way (*Journalism in India*, Rangaswami Parthasarathy). Parthasarathy, a senior journalist with *The Hindu* for 35 years has also written–*100 Years of the Hindu.*

The Hindu is known for high quality journalism and substantial output of literary, academic and scholarly discussion in terms of book reviews, features on sciences, arts and education and other subjects which several other newspapers are overlooking in favour of high society, fashion and life style features. The paper is also known for good editorials some of which have been praised as "excellently readable pieces," by an eminent editor The newspaper also had some of the most distinguished Indians on its staff as correspondents—notable being Subhas Bose in Vienna and V. K. Krishna Menon elsewhere in Europe.

The Hindu has branched out journalism : spectacularly into several other aspects of sports journalism-*Sportstar*, the leading sports weekly with wide coverage of Indian and international sports; magazine journalism, *Frontline*, the general interest fortnightly news magazines with first rate photographs and pictures particularly on subjects like environment, nature and wild life; and business journalism with *Business Line*, a financial daily. Its Annuals on Industry, Agriculture,

Environment and Cricket are authentic contribution in the respective areas.

There is a lot in the banner headline of its advertisement : If trust, credibility and truthfulness are old fashioned, we really haven't developed at all. *The Hindu* has not only maintained all the above attributes of a good newspaper, it has developed in all branches of journalism.

The Hindustan Times

The Hindustan Times was the first Indian daily coming out from the capital. The paper, which was established in 1923, was inaugurated by Mahatma Gandhi and the first issue contained articles by Motilal Nehru, Jawaharlal Nehru and Mahomed Ali. The great historian K. M. Panikkar was its first editor. Since it was the only English newspaper in the capital, it attracted wide notice right since its inception. Panikkar, with support from K. C. Roy of the Associated Press of India, was able to establish high standards of journalism in *The Hindustan Times*.

The paper made its mark for being the leading paper from the capital despite severe competition from *The Times of India*, which, of late, has posed a major challenge to its supremacy. For several years after independence, *raddiwalas* (those who collect waste paper) used to say Hindustan when they meant any paper. The paper has also been known for its matrimonial columns, which have been taking more pages than before. The paper is read as much for its news content as for its matrimonials.

In the initial years, some of the leading figures of the freedom movement were associated with its management—Pandit Madan Mohan Malaviya, M. R. Jayakar and Lala Lajpat Rai. G. D. Birla took over the paper in 1927 and since then it has been run by the Birla group.

The Hindustan Times, like many other nationalist papers, suffered during the independence movement for supporting the freedom struggle. The paper put up a brave fight against the restrictions imposed by the government and covered prominently, in bold type the news of *Satyagraha*. During the Quit India Movement its editor Devadas Gandhi was arrested for defying the instructions of the Chief Commissioner of Delhi and sent to a prison term.

The paper had a galaxy of distinguished journalists as its editors—Devadas Gandhi, Durga Das, J. N. Sahni, B. G. Verghese and Khushwant Singh. The paper was embroiled into controversy when the owner of the paper G. D. Birla sacked the editor-B. G. Verghese within months of declaration of Emergency in 1975. A group of journalists working with the paper and certain others filed a complaint with the Press Council of India saying that removal of Verghese was an assault on the freedom of press. Journalists led by the Indian Federation of Working Journalists protested against this action and went on strike. The management of *The Hindustan Times* filed a writ petition before the Delhi High Court saying that the issue was purely a matter of employee-employer relationship and the question of freedom of press was not involved.

Many years later the noted writer and columnist Khushwant Singh also had to quit as the editor of *The Hindustan Times* in similar circumstances.

The Hindustan Times pioneered development journalism and the Sunday supplement of the paper carried articles on water policy and famine. The feature on Our Village Chethra, carried on for several years, is remembered as an example of first rate rural reporting.

Hindustan, the sister paper of *The Hindustan Times*, in Hindi started in 1936, is held in high esteem by the Hindi newspaper reading public. The paper launched its Patna and Lucknow editions a few years back.

The Indian Express

Established by the doyen of Indian journalism, Ramnath Goenka in Madras in 1937, the *Indian Express* is the only newspaper which has a national presence in almost all parts of the country. Its nineteen editions are published from Ahmedabad, Bangalore, Belgaum, Bhubaneswar, Chandigarh, Chennai, Coimbatore, Hyderabad, Kochi, Kozhikode, Madurai, Mumbai, Nagpur, New Delhi, Pune Thiruvananthapuram, Vadodara, Vijayawada and Visakhapatnam.

The *Indian Express* is a fully and truly a national paper in the real sense of the term. Regarding the *national* dimensions of a newspaper, S. C. Bhatt makes an interesting comment in his book, *Indian Press since 1955* : It has been a fashion in India for the newspapers coming out from Delhi to be called national dailies following the British pattern for London newspapers to be called national and those from Manchester, Birmingham and Glasgow to be called provincial. But if any newspaper could be called national in India it would only be the *Indian Express*; that too partially.

Partially because it does not have any presence in the vast Hindi heartland–Uttar Pradesh, Madhya Pradesh, Bihar and Rajasthan.

Besides its national presence, the *Indian Express* is known for its crusading journalism; the newspaper was always found equal to the task of fighting battles–battles for the freedom of the press and against repression during the Emergency; battle against the Defamation Bill 1988 which was considered a threat to the freedom of expression and many more. The newspaper was in the forefront of the protest launched by journalists all over the country. The *Indian Express* wrote: Rather than investigate vigorously the instances of wrong doing brought out in the Fairfax, HDW, Bofors and other controversies, the government has, first by branding the disclosures as the result of a 'destabilisation' plot and then by launching a whitewash enquiry by a Parliamentary Committee strengthened the suspicion that there is a great deal to hide. If the Defamation Bill passed in a raging hurry by the Lok Sabha is meant to be a political counter-attack to stem the tide of disclosures, it is an affront to the nation, democratic conscience.

Goenka, who died in 1991, was amongst the tallest figures of the Indian newspaper publishing. He took a leading part in the negotiations with *Reuters*, the British News agency to make it give up its domination on India's news coverage through Associated Press of India resulting in the formation of PTI. After Madras and Bombay, Goenka covered Delhi; the *Financial Express* was also started which has been lagging behind its rival, *The Economic Times*.

The tenacity and dogedness with which the *Indian Express* fought for the freedom of press during emergency elicited a warm tribute from Rangaswamy Parthasarathy : However, there has been at least one newspaper which fought grimly and with determination the assault on the press and became the special target of persecution, and vindictiveness. The *Indian Express* with its proprietor Ramnath Goenka and editor V. K. Narasimham wrote a glorious chapter in the battle for the freedom of the press and when the nightmare ended and press became free again they were hailed as heroes.

The *Indian Express* was on the firing line once again when its offices in 12 centres across the country were raided simultaneously with the involvement of armed police present inside the office and involvement of some 600 intelligence men in September 1987. The paper had emerged as the most powerful cutting edge of the opposition to the Rajiv Gandhi government. The government had accused it of evading customs duties and violating FERA regulations, although the

Editors' Guild of India said : Whatever the reasons given to launch the raids, the government's motives are too clear to hoodwink anyone. In a cover page story, the *India Today* highlighted the background of the controversy with the profile of the newspaper and an interview with Goenka and the editor Arun Shourie.

Frank Moraes and Arun Shourie were the two most well known editors of the *Indian Express*, known for their sturdy independence. Moraes was a fearless critic of the government regardless of the personalities involved. Arun Shourie, who considered "Job of a good newspaper is to ensure accountability and to force a regime to unmask itself" became the first Indian journalist to become a nationally respected figure. He exposed emergency excesses and abuse of authority of Indira Gandhi; uncovered the misuse of official authority by a Chief Minister to collect funds and tackled several other issues: prison reforms, bonded labour, the plight of undertrials, human rights, etc.

The *Indian Express* group continues with the zeal of a crusader what it calls to be the "journalism of courage."

The Tribune

In its 121st year of publication, *The Tribune* has emerged as North India's premier newspaper. It is the largest circulated English daily in Northern India—Punjab, Haryana, Himachal Pradesh and the Union Territory of Chandigarh.

The Tribune was started as a weekly in Lahore in 1881 by Sardar Dyal Singh Majithia, who was a highly educated nationalist and patriot. He had inherited a vast estate from his father which he wanted to utilise for awakening the people of Punjab and India. Since the *Civil and Military Gazette* expressed only the official point of view, the need for a nationalist English daily was acutely felt.

The first issue of *The Tribune* appeared on 2 February 1881. Its editorial captioned, 'About Ourselves,' read : The projectors and conductors of *The Tribune* have no pet theories to maintain, nor any personal interest to serve through the medium of this journal. They profess simply to act for the public weal and they are conscious that the public weal is more advanced by charity and moderation than by rancour and high words. Our appearance in the field of journalism is to meet a crying want of this part of India, namely, an English journal for the representation of the native opinion. The aim of *The Tribune* will be, as its name imports, fairly and temperately to advocate the cause of the masses. In its columns we shall seek to represent the public opinion of India, specially of upper India.

With the advent of the Indian National Congress in 1885, *The Tribune* aligned with popular cause. *The Tribune* condemned the partition of Bengal in 1905. Since *The Tribune* condemned the atrocities committed during the martial law regime in 1919, it was asked to furnish a security of Rs. 2000. The Editor, Kalinath Ray was tried for seditious writings.

Gandhiji said in 1932 : *The Tribune* is the newspaper ... Its editor's reading and analysis of events are unsurpassed. About Kalinath Ray, Gandhiji said : Long live Kalinath Ray. His articles now-a-days on the communal problem and on joint electorates for *Harijan*s bear witness to his deep knowledge and wide experience.

Kalinath Ray was a fearless writer who bravely faced the risks involved in fighting an alien government. When he was sent to rigorous imprisonment for two years in 1919, the whole of Punjab and the press; the people and the leaders rose as one man; because he had emerged as 'undisputed leader for the press in Punjab'. In the face of determined opposition, he was released after three months.

During India's long struggle for independence, *The Tribune* played a distinctive role as an exponent of public view. On the eve of independence when the partition of the country rocked Lahore, the offices of *The Tribune* were ransacked. It had to migrate to India and the Home Minister Vallabhbhai Patel assured all facilities to *The Tribune* to resume publication from the Indian soil. It moved to Simla and later on to Ambala in May 1948. It found a permanent home and habitation in Chandigarh in 1957.

The Tribune is a truly trust-managed newspaper. The policy of paper is to continue to be liberal in politics, secular in outlook, balanced and objective in reporting and temperate in language, official acts and measures may be boldly criticised, but in a fair and candid spirit and in temperate language. Subjects possessing provincial and local interest should receive prominent treatment, alongwith questions of national importance. Religious controversies shall be avoided in the columns of the paper and an attitude of strict neutrality shall be maintained in regard to all creeds and sects.

According to *The Tribune's* code for journalists : Members of the editorial staff shall refrain from publishing matter which is obscene or is likely to encourage vice, crime and unlawful activities. Also no tendentious report of speculative nature shall be published. Good faith with the reader is the foundation of good journalism. Every effort must be made to ensure that the news content is accurate, free from bias and in context, and that all sides are represented fairly.

Members of the editorial staff should perform their duties without fear or favour, adopting an attitude of professionalism and complete objectivity and impartiality. They will not accept patronage or largesse of any type from politicians, civil servants, business houses, governmental bodies, private individuals or institutions or accept any pecuniary benefits from any quarters*.

The Tribune group launched two sister publications in Hindi and Punjabi–*Dainik Tribune* and the *Punjabi Tribune* in 1978. Both the newspapers have been a modest success, primarily because they share the glory and the prestige, as well as the heritage of the better known English counterpart, which has become a byword for good journalism.

The Tribune has recently revamped several of its printing and editorial features with theme pages on week days and supplements on Saturdays besides Sunday Reading. Its Book Review section is quite satisfying, considering the fact that some of the better known metropolitan dailies have discontinued such important activities under the pressure of space and market forces. After all books and scholarships do not attract too much ad revenue.

The Times of India

The Times of India is the oldest English daily in India. The BBC in 1991 featured *The Times of India* among world's six great newspapers. The paper is the flagship of the Bennett, Coleman & Company Ltd. (BCCL); the other important newspapers and journals being *Nav Bharat Times* (Hindi daily), *The Economic Times* and *Femina*. BCCL is the world's tenth largest, old style publishing house with revenues of Rs. 1200 crore. The newspaper has been a trend setter in ways more than one : marketing, economic journalism and management. No other newspaper has changed the rules of the games as *The Times of India* has.

Let us have a look at the BCCL group of papers. According to the Audit Bureau of Circulation, in 1999 the paper consolidated its lead as the country's largest selling English language broad sheet with an average daily circulation of 17.34 lakh copies. It crossed the 20 lakh

* The excerpts from *The Tribune's* Code for Journalists have been taken from the issue dated 21 November 1977. Focus : Media Power.

mark in March 2000 compared to *The Hindu* (7.26 lakh) and the *Indian Express* (6.86 lakh). *The Economic Times*, the country's largest business daily claims to have crossed 4 lakh in April 2000.

The Times of India traces its heritage from *The Bombay Times* in 1838, the paper was published on Wednesday and Saturday only. In 1852, *The Bombay Times* absorbs *The Bombay Standard* and *Bombay Telegraph and Courier*. In 1861, the name of the paper was changed to *The Times of India* under editor Robert Knight who gave it a national character. The Bennett, Coleman & Co.–a joint stock company was formed in 1892. The Delhi edition was launched in 1950.

The Times of India, alongwith *The Pioneer* and *The Statesman*, was one of three newspapers which represented the Anglo-Indian opinion, opposing most violently the advancement of the Indian people.

The newspaper could claim high class printing and news service (it was the earliest newspaper in India to subscribe to the Reuter's news service) and made rapid progress. In his book, *Journalism in India*, Rangaswami Parthasarathy recapitulates several instances when the paper attacked the Indian citizens in a most objectionable tone.

The eminent journalist and editor, Frank Moraes, who joined the paper as junior assistant editor in 1934 stated that since the paper was British owned, it was the first supporter of the government. He later became the first Indian editor.

Apart from Frank Moraes, the paper had several distinguished journalists as its editors–Sham Lal and Giri Lal Jain. Sham Lal, who had joined *The Hindustan Times* more than sixty years ago and was named as the winner of B. D. Goenka Award for Excellence in Journalism in 1993, talking about the transformation in the field of journalism said : Commodification of news may be a fact of life but there is always a question of degree. While the process of commodification cannot be prevented, the excesses of commodification can. Take the British newspaper scene. There are many that remain committed to being serious even at the cost of low circulation. *The Sunday Times* editor once told me that his paper devotes two or three pages to book reviews even though a readership survey showed that only 11 per cent readers read the news. You see, those 11 per cent readers mattered a lot to them.

The above remarks of a former editor of the newspaper are an expression of regret over the extent to which commodification of news and impact of market forces has started influencing the policies of the newspaper. The editorial department is losing its pre-eminence to the management, administration and the advertising departments of the paper. Today BCCL is entering into music software, entertainment, Radio FM broadcasting, music retailing business with Planet M and of course on line journalism–indiatimes. com.

The emphasis is on attracting the advertisement; the price war with *The Hindustan Times* in 1999 was a part of the same strategy. Says one of the BCCL directors : We believe we are not in the newspaper business but in the business of attracting advertising. By offering the advertiser a comprehensive package right through our portfolio of *The Times of India, The Economic Times*, Times FM and the Websites, we have the platform to bring ad revenues earlier than any other websites in the country. We are the specialists in target audience. We will give the advertisers the target audience.

The Times of India has indeed shown that rules of the game have drastically changed and journalism has no longer any social commitment; its bottom lines is *ad revenue.*

Magazine Journalism

The magazine journalism, also termed as periodical press, bristles with excitement. There are more magazines in English, and more than that, in regional languages on the newsstands, bookstalls and stores today than ever before. And there is place for all kinds of magazines; general-interest magazines, speciality magazines, newsmagazines, house magazines, etc. In fact, magazine journalism, in India has been, in a way, trendsetter; young editors got a chance to break new grounds, innovate and improvise-posing challenge to their creative ability and talent in the face of stiff competition.

Magazine journalism is vitally different from newspaper journalism in several important aspects. Magazines lend perspective to contemporary events, they serve as interpreters and analysts of trends and events. Comparatively free from the deadline rush of the daily press, magazines are in a position to add a bit of background, researched effort and back reference to the contemporary events. With a more durable cover and stitched pages, magazines are not ephemeral things, to be flipped over and cast aside.

Magazines perform a middle distance role between newspapers and books while newspapers report events as they occur and the books interpret them in historical perspective, magazines add a new dimension–that of investigation, data and analysis. Another basic difference between the magazine and newspaper is; while a newspaper does not aim at a single special group, and must have something of everything for almost everybody, magazines are generally designed for specific target groups. Magazines provide immense diversity, almost in every aspect–cover design and layout, contents and perspective, variety of subjects, etc

The modern magazine is essentially a product of advances in printing technology fostered in America in the later quarter of the nineteenth century. In the early twentieth century America witnessed phenomenal industrial growth which perked up magazine industry. In order to create market outlets for consumer goods, publicity and advertisement campaigns launched through magazines helped reduce their production costs and expand circulation. Thus dawned the era of mass circulation magazines. Heavily dependent upon advertising as the main source of revenue, the magazine industry had to face stiff competition from television and films and some magazines were eliminated.

Television offered the advertisers cheaper and more efficient means of reaching the mass audience. When the once–great and eminently successful magazines, *Life* and *Look* disappeared in the seventies for lack of advertising, it heralded the beginning of the specialized-audience magazines, which catered to limited groups. These mass magazines were victims of mounting production costs, high mailing rates and diversion of advertisement to television. *Reader's Digest*, with the largest circulation of any American magazine (it has come out with an Asian edition, is, however an exception).

In the Indian magazine world, general-interest magazine is flourishing and special interest periodicals are growing in number. The *Illustrated Weekly of India*, after having completed a century of publication was a popular general-interest English magazine, was closed down. It is indeed a sorry state of affairs because the magazine was fairly successful in what may be termed as "pictorial story telling", and in informing and apprising the Indians about India itself, its various communities, castes and sub-castes.

Indian newsmagazines flourished in aftermath of emergency–political gossips, scandals and shady deals all filled the bill. Subsequently some of the newsmagazines, *India Today*, *Sunday*, *Week*, *Frontline* and *Outlook* have been quite successful in catching the attention and imagination of the reading public.

The growth of *India Today*, which started as a fortnightly

newsmagazine in 1975, in a way, mirrors the progress of journalism in the country during the quarter century. The birth of the newsmagazine heralded the emergence of a magazine boom. This magazine boom could not have occurred without the improvements and innovations in printing technology, and support from the advertising industry. Analyzing the factors for the growth and progress of *India Today*, its editor, Aroon Purie wrote in the Tenth Anniversary Issue (31 December 1985–The Decisive Decade) as under:

> Fortunately for the country, and *India Today*. the last decade has been a period of enormous innovation and advancement, once the Emergency was ended. There has been a new freshness, a new breed of journalists breaking new ground, new technologies such as the world processor and computer terminal, a broad-basing of mass media ownership following from a new entrepreneurship in journalism, increased advertising support, and much more. If journalists and publishers have benefited from all these, the readers have benefited even more.

The newsmagazine covers a wide range of subjects from politics, which dominates its pages, to sports and films, social themes, human interest stories from Aids and women's rights to human rights. In 1986, the new magazine branched out into Hindi with the same name from its base in Delhi. This was later extended to other languages like Gujarati, Malayalam and Tamil.

Film magazines, which are referred to as mags by the film writers, have a large readership both in English and regional languages. These magazines inculcate in the readers a sense of film appreciation about Indian and foreign films, undertake detailed coverage of film events, but more than that they trade gossips, rumours and stories about the heroes and heroines. The foremost film magazine is *Stardust of Bombay* with the height circulation followed by *Filmfare*, *Femina*, *Women's Era* and *New Women* are the magazines brought out by the Times of India group.

In America special interest magazines form a very large segment of the magazine industry–magazines about family living, science-interest publication, youth magazines, travel guides, etc. In India too such magazines–like *Femina*, *Eve's Weekly*, *Science Today* have achieved a very good standard in matters of content, popularity and impact.

Business newsmagazines–specialized business publications serving specific business industrial or professional audience include *Business India*, *Business World* and *Business Today*. Magazines, for instance those dealing exclusively with photography, gardening, cookery and architecture have also come up. A magazine like *Design* in the field of architecture urban planning, fine arts, graphic arts, can be compared with the best anywhere.

Table 5 : Top Twenty Dailies

S. No.	Paper/Centre of Publication	Language
1.	*Malayala Manorama*, Kottayam, Kozhikode, Kochi, Thiruvananthapuram, Palakkad	Malayalam
2.	*Times of India*, Bombay, Delhi, Ahmedabad, Bangalore, Patna, Lucknow	English
3.	*Punjab Kesari*, Jalandhar, Ambala, Delhi	Hindi
4.	*Aj*, Varanasi, Kanpur, Gorakhpur, Patna, Allahabad, Ranchi, Agra, Jamshedpur, Lucknow	Hindi
5.	*Gujarat Samachar*, Ahmedabad, Baroda, Rajkot, Surat, Bombay	Gujarati
6.	*Indian Express*, Bombay, Delhi, Ahmedabad, Baroda, Chandigarh, Coimbatore, Hyderabad, Kozhikode, Kochi, Nagpur, Madras, Madurai, Pune, Vijayawada, Bangalore, Visakhapatnam	English
7.	*Jagran*, Kanpur, Agra, Bareilly, Delhi (Noida), Gorakhpur, Jhansi, Lucknow, Meerut, Varanasi	Hindi
8.	*Mathribhumi*, Kozhikode, Kochi, Thiruvananthapuram, Trichur	Malayalam
9.	*Hindu*, Madras, Bangalore, Coimbatore, Delhi, Hyderabad, Madurai, Visakhapatnam	English
10.	*Eenadu*, Hyderabad, Visakhapatnam, Vijayawada, Tirupati, Anantapur, Karimnagar, Rajamundri	Telugu
11.	*Ananda-Bazar Patrika*, Calcutta	Bengali
12.	*Sandesh*, Ahmedabad, Baroda, Surat, Rajkot	Gujarati
13.	*Navbharat Times*, Bombay, Delhi, Patna, Jaipur	Hindi
14.	*Hindustan Times*, Delhi, Patna	English
15.	*Dinathanthi*, Madras, Madurai, Coimbatore, Tirunelveli, Tiruchirapalli, Vellore, Cuddalore, Salem, Bangalore, Pondicherry	Tamil
16.	*Rajasthan Patrika*, Jaipur, Jodhpur, Bikaner, Udaipur, Kota	Hindi
17.	*Hindustan*, Delhi, Patna	Hindi
18.	*Navbharat*, Nagpur, Bhopal, Raipur, Indore, Jabalpur, Bilaspur	Hindi
19.	*Navakal*, Bombay	Marathi
20.	*Amar Ujala*, Agra, Bareilly, Meerut, Moradabad	Hindi

Acknowledgement : Advertisers Handbook–95.

Magazine journalism has boosted creative talent in many areas including free lance writing and photojournalism. Magazines have a comparatively smaller number of staff, for they invite and accept articles and commission writings on specific subjects from writers and journalists who free lance for several newspapers and magazines. Young aspiring writers, with luck, find outlet in magazine journalism. Apart from free lance journalists and cartoonists, magazine editors employ photographers, illustrators and designers for giving aesthetic and bold look to their publications.

The future of magazine journalism is assured. With the growth in literacy, reading habits of the people, urbanization and improvement in purchasing power magazines definitely have a promising future.

NEWS AGENCIES

A news agency, according to UNESCO, is "an undertaking of which the principal objective, whatever its legal form, *is to gather news and news material of which the sole purpose is to express or present facts, and to distribute this to a group of news enterprises, and in exceptional circumstances to private individuals with a view to providing them with as complete and impartial a news service as possible against payment, and under conditions compatible with business laws and usage.*"

News agencies attained great importance with the invention and progress of telegraph, teleprinters and other technical departments in the field of quick transmission and long distance transmission. They reduce the cost of gathering news.

A news agency generally deals with news coverage. It combines spot coverage with interpretation of the important political and economic events. Although its emphasis is limited, the news agency plays a very important role in shaping public opinion on crucial national and international affairs.

The news agency does not deal directly with the public. It works through the intermediary of the other means of mass communication, namely, the press, radio and television. Essentially, *it plays the role of a wholesale supplier of news*. The media depend on material supplied by the news agencies mainly put of economic necessity. In order to have a wide coverage the newspaper has to maintain a costly network of staff reporters, correspondents, offices, bureaus and telecommunication equipments on a world-wide scale. We are however aware that many newspapers of our country, and more so most of the newspapers of the Third World countries *cannot even maintain a proper network of correspondents within their own country of operation.* Only a few newspapers can afford this investment and recurring expenditure. For a majority of the news media, the news agencies are a major source of news supply. The subscribers to the news agencies include the daily newspapers, the radio and TV stations, the local newspapers, magazines, offices and institutions, particularly government agencies, large corporations in the private and public sector, banks and commercial establishments. The news agencies account for 40-50 per cent of the total content of a daily paper. For many of the medium and small newspapers which cannot afford to have a number of reporters at outstations, news agencies supply bulk of news, sometimes even 100 per cent. The news agencies contribute almost 40 per cent of news to the AIR; the rest being from its own correspondents. No news organisation can do without the services of a news agency.

The first news agency in the world Reuters was started in Germany by Reuter in 1850, which shifted before long from Germany to London. At present Reuters news service has become a worldwide organisation providing news for thousands of papers in different countries. It is truly regarded as global news agency. The other three large *transnational* news agencies are : Agence France Presse (AFP), Associated Press (AP) and United Press International (UPI). In addition there are major agencies like Kyodo of Japan and Deutsche Press Agenteur (DPA) of Germany.

Press Trust of India (PTI)

India's largest news agency, PTI is a non-profit sharing cooperative owned by the country's newspapers, to provide efficient and unbiased news to its subscribers.

In 1948 several important editors of the Indian dailies established the PTI which took over the entire business of the Reuters in India. The PTI emerged as a cooperative news agency with its zone from Cairo to Singapore for covering news for the Reuters World Pool. Registered on August 27, 1947, PTI began functioning from February 1, 1949 taking over the Associated Press of India and the Indian operation of Reuters.

Major services of the agency are headed by Editors. The agency has a staff of over 1,600 including 400 journalists. There are over 100 bureaus across the country and 10 bureaus abroad. The agency also has about 300 stingers spread all over the country. The news services are provided at speeds upto 1,200 bits per second (about 1400 words) by satellite, data channels and ticker lines. For operational purposes, the country is divided into four regions with the offices in Delhi, Mumbai, Calcutta and Chennai functioning as regional headquarters. In Delhi there are also separate bureaus for political, economic and sports coverage. Major services offered by PTI are :

English News Service : PTI news service in English is available in two forms. The 'Core' service covers major developments segmented service allows papers to pick up additional inputs from segments of their choice—National/Regional News, Economics/Commercial News, International News, and Sports News. Core Service puts out about 40,000 words and the full segmented service over 100,000 words per day.

Bhasha : Launched in 1986, the Hindi language news service has its own network in the Hindi-speaking states. Drawing on PTI files as well, *Bhasha* puts out about 40,000 words per day.

Photo Service : Launched in 1987, PTI Photo Service accounts for the bulk of the agency photos in the Indian media. Broadcast by satellite the service is available all over the country. The full colour service of Associated Press of America (AP) is made available with the authorisation of PTI.

Economic Service : The fortnightly economic journal provides analytical reports besides a data update on the Indian economy.

Science Service : Reports on the developments in science and technology both in India and abroad in a fortnightly mailer.

PTI Feature : A package of four weekly features provides an analytical insight on topical national, international and general events.

PTI Mag : Provides ten special stories on topics ranging from Arts to Business to Science in mailer weekly package. Also available on the wire service.

Graphics : A weekly mailer package of 14, PTI Graphics covers all major developments–be it economic, sports or elections. On special occasions like the budget the graphics are broadcast via satellite with the photo service.

News-Scan : Displays news in capsule form on video monitors. Major developments in the country and abroad are covered.

Stockscan : Provides stock market information on video terminals for group display. Stockscan Select of individual users is an interactive version of the service.

Asia Pulse : An on-line data bank on economic developments and business opportunities in Asian countries. Formed by PTI and four other Asian media organisations, Asia Pulse International is registered as a company in Singapore.

PTI-TV : Provides spot and documentary cover for the small screen on contract. Among the more famous programmes done by PTI-TV are 'Money Matters' and 'Tana Bana'.

Non-Aligned News Agencies Pool (NANAP) : PTI is a redistribution centre for this part of the world for news exchange among news agencies of the non-aligned countries. NANAP came into being in 1976.

Organisation of Asia-Pacific News Agencies (OANA) : A grouping of about 30 news agencies of the Asian-Pacific region, includes PTI and UNI of India. Founded in 1961, OANA has been acting as a forum for exchange of news, besides facilitating professional interaction. PTI has covered 50 years of its operation. Its services are available on net too.

United News of India

UNI, founded by newspapers themselves to promote competition between the country's two news agencies, started operations in March 1961.

Since 1968, the agency's communication network has expanded and it now has one of the largest news agency teleprinter networks in the developing world.

The number of subscribers has increased seven-fold. The agency was reaching about 1100 subscribers by teleprinter. These included a dozen in six Gulf countries, linked to UNI through an exclusive satellite channel. The agency now has reporters in 400 big and small towns manned by 300 staffers and 400 stringers.

The agency's pioneering Gulf news operations launched in 1980, now cover the UAE, Bahrain, Quatar, Kuwait, Oman and Saudi Arabia. The UNI news service now also goes to Singapore and Mauritius.

In May 1982, UNI went bilingual when it launched its Hindi Service–UNIVARTA. Today, *UNIVARTA dominates the news columns of Hindi newspapers in all the Hindi states and even in places as far away as Hyderabad, Ahmedabad and Calcutta.* The service grew fast and in fifteen years, nearly 250 newspapers published from more than 60 centres in Hindi heartland have begun subscribing to UNIVARTA. More than 100 of these newspapers depend exclusively on UNIVARTA.

UNI's foreign news comes mainly from the Associated Press of America (AP) which has been collaborating with UNI from the very first day of its operation. Another foreign collaborator from the agency's early days is DPA. UNI also has collaboration arrangements with 15 other wire services, including most of the Gulf agencies. UNI's own correspondents ably supplement agency news coverage from abroad. Nepal was the first country where UNI posted a correspondent way back in 1968. Now foreign reports come in from 22 UNI correspondents based in 20 countries in five continents.

From Cycle to Satellite

Initially, UNI news messages were sent out on cycle to subscribers in New Delhi. This was on March 21, 1961. Today, UNI news reaches out to subscribers over a dedicated teleprinter network stretching over 85,000 kilometres, linking more than 100 towns and cities of India.

UNI was the first news agency in India to go on to satellite communication. The Bombay-New York satellite channel was commissioned on June 6, 1979, for receipt of AP service. An exclusive UNI Bombay-Dubai channel was commissioned on April 1, 1981. UNI computerised its news operations in metropolitan centres, and at present is poised to upgrade the system all over the country with state of art technology. The present UNI activities include: *Wire Services* : UNI General Service, UNI Overseas Serivce, UNI Financial Service, UNI Banking Service, UNI Stock Exchange Service, UNI Language Service (UNIVARTA), UNI World TV News Service (UNISCAN) and UNI Urdu Service.

Mailer Services : UNI Backgrounder Service (Weekly), UNI Agricultural Service (Weekly), UNI Energy Service (Twice a week), and UNI Economic Service (Weekly).

In his book, *The Dynamics of Mass Communication*, Joseph R. Dominick says :

> *The next time you read your local newspaper, you will probably notice that many stories have the initial AP or UPI in the datelines. The AP stands for Associated Press and the UPI for United Press International. These two organisations are called wire services, and together they provide you with most of the news about what's going on outside your local community.*

*

All in all, the wire services are the eyes and ears for local papers and broadcasting stations that can't afford to have people stationed all over the country.

*

The wire services are putting new technology to work virtually all of their material is now delivered by satellite. Noisy typewriters and clattering teletypes have been replaced by computer data based and is linked to several systems that provide teletext services.

Press Laws in India

Press laws in India have a long history dating back to colonial period. In order to restrict the expression of disaffection and protest against foreign rule, the British government enacted several laws and regulations with the objective of imposing censorship, licensing of the Press and gagging the freedom of the Press.

The earliest regulatory measure was introduced in 1799 when the first Press Regulations were promulgated by Lord Wellesley. Under these regulations the newspapers were called upon to print the names and addresses of printers, editors and publishers. However, these regulations were abolished during the administration of Warren Hastings in 1813.

In 1857 the government passed a legislation which came to be known as the *Gagging Act*. This piece of legislation, among other things, introduced mandatory licensing for the owning or running of printing presses, empowered the government to prohibit the publication or circulation of any newspaper, book or other printed matter, and banned the publication or dissemination of statements or news stories which had a tendency to cause hatred or contempt for the government, incite disaffection or unlawful resistance to its orders, or weaken its lawful authority. The Act was however allowed to expire in June 1858.

Another important piece of legislation was the "Vernacular Press Act", passed in 1878. There was a far reaching measure which allowed government to clamp down on the publication of writings deemed seditions and to impose punitive sanctious on printers and publishers who failed to fall in line. Under the Act, any district magistrate or police commissioner could demand security from the printer and publisher of a newspaper, forfeit such security, or confiscate any printed matter considered objectionable without the aggrieved party having recourse to a court of law.

The rigours of the Vernacular Press Act continued until the appointment of Lord Ripon as Viceroy in 1880. One of Ripon's first acts on assuming office was to repeal that unpopular measure. Ripon also introduced several liberal reforms and earned considerable goodwill amongst Indians.

The founding of the Indian National Congress in 1885 proved to be a turning point in the history of the Indian Press. The birth of the Indian National Congress gave the newspapers an opportunity to give expression to the nationalist feelings with greater force and unprecedented boldness. With the intensification of the nationalist agitation against the British rule and the Press playing supportive role a panic stricken administration responded with the Indian Press Act, 1910—a comprehensive law aimed at increasing government control over the mass media. Under the Act, owners of presses were required to tender security deposits; these would be forfeited if they printed any 'objectionable' matter and further action, including seizure of presses, could be taken if they persisted in such conduct. The Act also authorized customs and postal authorities to detain and search mail suspected of containing 'objectionable' matter. In addition, the police were given extensive powers of search and seizure. The harshness of the legislation was matched by vigorous enforcement of its provisions—no fewer than 355 cases were initiated by the government between 1910 and 1914 alone.

The Indian press continued to be under constant pressure throughout the pre-independence period in varying degree. The newspapers and presses were quite often asked to furnish security or additional security, quite often the newspapers got their security forfeited and several of them ceased publication. Even as the nationalist movement continued to grow, and the uneasy relationship between the government and the Press persisted, the Second World War broke out. This resulted in the creation of an entirely new framework of regulations : pre–censorship was introduced. The nationalists had, in the meantime, revived their civil disobedience movement under Gandhi and this increased the pressure on the government. It became increasingly clear around the time Lord Wavell took office as Viceroy in 1943 that independence would soon have to be granted to India, and in the circumstances, any intensification of the repressive measures would prove futile. Consequently, as the War ended, talks on the transfer of power began and most of the controls on the Press were dismantled. There are, however, a number of laws with which a journalist should be familiar.

Defamation : The law of defamation has been described by the Second Press Commission as "a tale of two interests". These interests are : the interest of the individual in his reputation, and the interest of the society that information should pass freely.

In news gathering activities, the press often collides with the government. In addition, the right of free speech and the right of free press sometimes come into conflict with the right of an individual to protect his or her reputation. Protection for a person's reputation is found under the law that deal with defamation.

In order to understand this somewhat complicated area, let us start with some general definitions.

Libel : Libel is a written defamation or statement that tends to damage a person's reputation or good name that brings the person into hatred, contempts or ridicule or injures his or her business or occupational pursuits. Properties must be extremely careful about what they write.

In many cases, a police officer may arrest a person with the intent of asking the prosecutor to file a certain charge. Then, when the prosecutor examines the evidence, the evidence may warrant only a lesser charge. For that reason, most newspaper editors prefer to print the name of an arrested person only after the charge has been filed. Unfortunately, deadline, constraints, sometimes make that impossible, and many newspapers publish the names of those arrested before the charge is filed. A decision to publish a name in such circumstances requires extreme caution. If an individual were arrested in connection with a rape and the newspaper printed that information only to learn later that the prosecutor had filed a charge of assault, a libel sint could result.

Slander : It is a spoken defamation (It may state, if a defamatory statement is broadcast, it is considered to be libel even though technically the words are not written). Libel is considered more harmful and usually carries more serious penalties.

Libel per se : Some words are always libelous. Falsely written accusations, such as labelling a person a "thief" or a "swindler" or "imposter" automatically constitute libel.

Libel per quod : Words that seem perfectly innocent in themselves can become libelous under certain circumstances. Erroneously reporting that Mr. Ashok was seen eating a steak dinner last night may seem harmless unless Mr. Ashok happens to be the President of the Worldwide Vegetarian Society.

In order to win a libel suit brought against the media, the person must prove five things :

1. that he or she has actually been defamed and harmed by the statements,
2. that he or she has been identified (although not necessarily by name),
3. that the defamatory statements have been published,
4. that the media were at fault, and
5. in most instances, that what was published or broadcast was false.

Not every mistake that finds its way into publication is libelous. To report incorrectly that a person died is not libelous because the death, said the courts is no disgrace. Actual harm might be substantiated by showing the defamatory remarks led to physical discomfort, or loss of income or increased differently in performing a job.

To win a libel suit, some degree of fault or carelessness on the part of the media organization must be shown.

Libel Suit Defences : There are three traditional defences against libel–truth, privilege and fair comments and criticism.

The first is truth. Truth is the best defence against libel. However, knowing the truth is one thing, proving it is another. Of what was reported is proven to be true. There is no libel. This defence, however, is rarely used since it is extremely difficult to prove the truth of a statement. The second defence is privilege. There are certain situations in which the courts have held that the public's right to know comes before a person's right to preserve a reputation. Judicial proceedings, arrest warrants, legislative proceedings are some examples of situations that are generally acknowledged to be privileged. If a reporter gives a fair and accurate report of these events, no law sint can result even if what is reported contain a libelous statement. The third defence is fair comment and criticism. Any person who thrusts himself or herself into the public eye or is at a centre of public attention is open to fair criticism. This means that public officials and all those who invite public attention are fair game for comment. This defence applies only to opinion and criticism not to misrepresentation of facts. So, you are protected as long as you do not mis-state any of the facts on which you base your comments or criticism.

Punishment : Section 500 IPC prescribes the punishment for defamation. The section reads as follows :

> "Whoever defames another shall be punished with simple imprisonment for a term which may extend to two years, or with fine, or with both".

Punishment for a journalist may be severe in view of the fact that the defamatory statement gets wide publicity.

Contempt of Courts Act, 1971

The First Press Commission did not suggest any change in the provisions of the Contempt of Courts Act, 1952. The Sanyal Committee set up in 1961 made a comprehensive study of the law relating to contempt. Its recommendations resulted in the enactment of the Contempt of Courts Act, 1971 and the repeal of the 1952 Act.

The Act of 1971, for the first time, gives a complete definition of the expression 'contempt of court' in section 2 by codifying the results of judicial decisions. Clause (a) of Section 2 states that there are two categories of contempt under the Act : (i) Civil contempt and (ii) Criminal contempt.

Wilful disobedience to any judgement, decree, direction, order, writ or other process of a court or wilful breach of an undertaking given to a court constitutes 'civil contempt' under Clause (b) of Section 2.

Any publication which interferes with or undermines the administration of justice or has a tendency to do so constitutes 'criminal contempt' under Clause (c) of Section 2; and this is the category to which the Press generally becomes answerable. The definition in Clause (c) of Section 2 is in the following terms.

Criminal contempt means the publication (whether by words, spoken or written, or by signs, or by visible representations, or otherwise) of any matter or the doing of any other act whatsoever which :

(i) scandalises or tends to scandalise or lowers or tends to lower the authority of any court, or
(ii) prejudices, or interferes or tends to interfere with the due course of any judicial proceedings, or
(iii) interferes or tends to interfere with, or obstructs or tends to obstruct, the administration of justice in any other manner.

Publication of any thing which tends to create in the minds of the people an apprehension about the integrity, ability or fairness of a judge or which tends to deter litigants from complete reliance upon the court's administration of justice, amounts to contempt. Similarly, a publication which is likely to cause embarrassment in the judge's mind to the discharge of his official duty is a contempt of court. But if it is proved that the concerned writing would undermine the prestige or authority of the court or public confidence in the administration of justice by it, then it is contempt even if the vilificatory criticism relates to the judge's non-judicial functions like the functions of an administrative judge. Imputation of improper motives in deciding a case is obviously a contempt of court.

The Press does have the right which is also its professional function, to criticise and advocate. The whole gamut of public affairs including the administration of justice is the domain for fearless and critical comment. But the public function which belongs to the Press makes it an obligation of honour to exercise this function only with the fullest sense of responsibility. Without such a lively sense of responsibility a free Press might readily become a powerful instrument of injustice. The competing claims of the Court to maintain its authority and of the freedom of the Press to comment on matters of public interest must be reconciled. Without a free Press there can be no free society. Freedom of the Press, however, is not an end in itself but a means to an end of a free society. The independence of the judiciary is no less a means to the end of a free society and in fact the proper functioning of an independent judiciary puts the freedom of the Press in its proper perspective. A free Press is not to be preferred to an independent judiciary, nor an independent judiciary to a free Press either. No judge fit to be one is likely to be influenced consciously except by what he sees and hears in court and by what is judicially appropriate for the deliberation. However, judges are human. There is the powerful pull of the unconscious. Since judges, however, stalwart, are human, the delicate task of administering justice ought not to be made unduly difficult by irresponsible publication.

Publication of reports of crime is a regular feature of the news. Such items are clearly matters of public interest. But it is also clear that a trial for the commission of these crimes will probably follow sooner or later. A report of the crime may, however, accurate it attempts to be, contain a statement of fact which is likely to be hotly disputed at trial. It may be a question of identity or of some small detail on which a criminal trial can sometimes turn. In order to compile a report it is usually necessary to interview witnesses who may later be witnesses at the trial. The reporter may be able to obtain a very full account of what occurred and be in a position to publish a considerable amount of what would later become evidence at the trial. But there are dangers in their publication, particularly where the circumstances of a crime seem to lay suspicion upon a particular person. Even the publications of photograph of an accused is a question of extreme delicacy as in many criminal trials identification of an accused person is a vitally important issue. A witness, unable to form a mental picture of the accused might quite honestly derive such a picture of the person whose photograph he has seen in the newspaper. Such a publication may cast doubt on the prosecution's identification evidence or jeopardise the accused. Either way it is undesirable. On the other hand, photographs of wanted men are sometimes published at the request of the police either to assist in their apprehension or to warn the public against them, or both. It must, therefore, necessarily be a question of fact and circumstances whether a publication in any particular case offends against the law.

Journalists sometimes investigate suspected crimes, malpractices and abuses and accumulate evidence. Publication of such material is often in the public interest and also helps in boosting the circulation of the newspaper. The law of contempt does not hinder publication of such accumulated evidence before the accused are arrested and charged. But when once judicial proceedings are set in motion, the Press should not publish the evidence. When a person is being tried for an offence, if the Press has evidence that some other person is guilty of the crime, propriety would demand that the evidence in the possession of the Press be placed before the Court. By adopting such a course it will get the credit for its investigative effort though the advantage of increased circulation through publication exclusively in its columns would be lost.

However, the power to punish for scandalising the court, is to be used sparingly and in deference to the administration of justice only. It cannot be used for vindicating personal insult to the judge. Bonafide criticism that is fair and reasonable criticism of a judicial act in the interest of the public good does not amount to contempt. But if improper motives are attributed to the judges then it ceases to be bonafide. A judgement can be criticised as erroneous but dishonesty on the part of the judge in delivering the judgement cannot be alleged. If a statement is likely to prejudice or interfere with the due course of justice, then the truthfulness of the facts on which it is based, is no defence. Trial by newspapers has been considered by courts as interference with the proper administration of justice in pending cases.

However, punishment can be awarded for interference with the due course of justice only if the interference is substantial. Similarly, a person will not be guilty of contempt of court for innocent publication of distribution during the pendency of civil or criminal proceedings of a matter which would otherwise deem to constitute contempt.

Limitations of Contempt of Court

- Innocent publication and distribution of matter which falls under any of the categories of competent under the Act.
- Fair and accurate report of judicial proceedings; publication of a fair and accurate report of a pending judicial proceedings is protected under section 4 provided it is not prohibited under section 7. Section 7 prohibits such publication where it is prohibited by a statute or by the count on certain grounds, such as security of the State, public order and the like.
- Fair criticism of judicial act, publication of a fair criticism of a judicial act including a judicial decision is also protected under section 5 because the public has an interest in the proper administration of justice. Judges and courts are like to open to criticism and if reasonable argument is offered against any judicial act as contrary to law or public good, such criticism is protected and will not amount to contempt. The plea of fair comment on a judgement cannot be availed of if the comment is made before the case is heard and finally decided. Under explanation (a) to Section 3, a case cannot be said to have been finally decided until the period of limitation for preferring appeal or revision against the decision commented upon has expired or, if appeal or revision has been filed, the appeal and revision, too, has been heard and finally decided.
- Bonafide complaint concerning the presiding officer of any subordinate court is not contempt of court.

Many written words may be both contempt and defamation. To describe a judge in his judicial capacity as a swindler is contempt of court as well as defamation.

Under Section 129 and 215 Criminal Procedure Code, Supreme Court, High Courts and lower courts have been given the powers to punish any institution, an organisation, a person or any government officer for contempt of court.

Punishment

In case of civil contempt, the contemptor cannot be sentenced even to simple imprisonment. He can be detained in a civil prison for not more than six months, normally, a fine would be considered sufficient to meet the ends of justice.

In case of criminal contempt, a contemptor can be punished with simple imprisonment only for a term extending upto six months or with a fine upto two thousand rupees or with both. If he makes a satisfactory apology, the accused may be discharged or the punishment awarded may be remitted.

The time limit for action for contempt of court is one year from the date on which the contempt is alleged to have been committed.

The Working Journalists and Other Newspaper Employees (Conditions of Service) and Miscellaneous Provisions Act, 1955

This Act regulates certain conditions of service of working journalists and other persons employed in newspaper establishments.

The First Press Commission found that the emoluments received by journalists were on the whole unsatisfactory. It could not undertake a detailed investigation for fixing scales of pay for different categories of employees. But it recognised the necessity of fixing a minimum wage for the journalist employees and made recommendations relating to the minimum wages to be paid to them. In 1955, the Working Journalists (Conditions of Service) and Miscellaneous Provisions Act was enacted and the Industrial Disputes Act, 1947 was made applicable to working journalists also. With the successive revisions of the pay scales through Wage Boards, neutralization of the rise in the cost of living and provision of security of service, the terms and conditions of service of newspaper employees have considerably improved. Some important provisions of the Act are :

(i) The provisions applicable to workmen under the Industrial Disputes Act, 1947 shall apply to working journalists.
(ii) The working journalists, who have been in continuous service for at least three years in a newspaper establishment' are entitled for gratuity equivalent to fifteen days average pay for every completed

year of service or any part thereof in excess of six months on termination, retirement, resignation or death as per Section 3.

(iii) No working journalist shall be required to work for more than one hundred and forty-four hours during any period of four consecutive weeks, exclusive of the time for meals. Every working journalist shall be allowed during any period of seven consecutive days rest for a period of not less than 24 hours inclusive of the period between 10 P. M. and 6 A. M.

(iv) Every working journalist shall be entitled to earned leave on full wages for not less than one-eleventh of the period spent on duty and leave on medical certificate on one-half of the wages for not less than one-eighteenth of the period of service.

(v) A Wage Board shall be constituted by the Central Government for fixing and revising rates of wages of working journalists. The Wage Board shall consists of :

   (a) Two representatives of newspaper employees;
   (b) Two representatives of working journalists; and
   (c) Three independent persons, one of whom shall be a person who is or has been a judge of a High Court or the Supreme Court and who shall be appointed by the Government as its Chairman.

The Section 12 of the Act empowers the Central Government to enforce recommendations of the Wage Board and make modifications in the recommendations, if necessary.

(vi) The Central Govt. can fix interim rates of wages in consultation with the Wage Board under Section 13-A.

(vii) A Wage Board shall be constituted by the Central Govt. for fixing or revising rates of wages in respect of non-journalist newspaper employees (Section 13-B). It shall consists of :

   (a) Two representatives of newspaper employees;
   (b) Two representatives of non-journalist newspaper employees;
   (c) Three independent persons one of whom shall be a person who is or has been a judge of a High Court or the Supreme Court and who shall be appointed by the government as its Chairman.

(viii) Provisions of the following Acts shall apply to every newspaper establishment employing twenty or more persons :

(a) Industrial Employment (Standing Orders) Act, 1946.

(b) The Employees Provident Funds Act, 1952.

(ix) If any employer contravenes any of the provisions of this Act, he shall be punishable with fine which may extend to two hundred rupees. If the offence is committed for second time, the fine may extend to five hundred rupees.

Contempt of Legislature

Privileges are certain fundamental rights of each house which are generally accepted as necessary for the exercise of its constitutional functions.

Articles 105 and 194 of the Constitution provide for Parliament and State Legislatures the powers, privilege and immunities they have.

Clause (2) confers immunity to publication of proceedings, papers, etc., of a House only when the publication is made by or under the authority of that House. The implication is that even a true newspaper report of proceedings of a House is not protected under this clause.

Clause (3) as it originally stood stated that in all those respects not covered by these provisions, the powers, privileges and immunities of Parliament and State Legislatures, until defined by law, shall be those of the House of Commons of the Parliament of the United Kingdom as existing at the time of the commencement of the Constitution. The forty-fourth amendment of the Constitution made verbal changes in this clause omitting the reference to the House of Commons, but the substance of the clause remains the same. Thus, the position is that if one were to ask what are the privileges of Parliament and State Legislatures in India other than those specified in Articles 105 and 194, the answer is that they are the same as those of the House of Commons as existing on 26th January 1950.

The First Press Commission recommended that both Parliament and State Legislatures should define by legislation the precise powers, privileges and immunities which they possess in regard to contempt and the procedure for enforcing them. This question has been a matter of public debate over the years and several arguments have been propounded for and against codification of privileges. The main argument against codification of privileges which has weighed with the Parliament and State Legislatures appears to be that once codification is done by a law, such a law would automatically become subject to all the fundamental rights guaranteed in Part III of the Constitution and the matter would become justiciable, conferring powers on the courts to adjudicate on questions of privilege thereby lowering their dignity. It has been said that codification of privileges would expose Parliament and State Legislatures "to an alien body" viz., the judiciary. Second Press Commission stated that the judiciary which is as much a creature of the Constitution as the Parliament or State Legislature is not an alien body under the scheme of our Constitution. In fact, laws enacted by Parliament and State Legislatures are, on occasions, being struck down by the courts when warranted by the constitutional provisions and on that account it cannot be said that the dignity of Parliament or the legislature suffers. Similarly, judges of the highest court in the land are appointed by the executive and for that reason one cannot say that their independence or prestige is affected. They viewed that from the point of view of freedom of the Press it is essential that the privileges of Parliament and State legislatures should be codified as early as possible. A journalist or editor can be punished with imprisonment or administered a warning, admonition or reprimand for the breach of privilege of the House. His privileges like facilities to enter the precincts of the House and cover its proceedings can be withdrawn. He can be asked to publish an apology. However, no fines are imposed.

Contempt has a wider sweep than breach of privilege. Contempt can be committed by an act or utterance which undermines the dignity of the House even without violating any particular privilege of the legislature.

But it is not a breach of privilege to publish without malice a substantially true report of the proceedings of the House even if it is defamatory, seditious or obscene in nature. No civil or criminal proceedings can be launched in a court of law for publication of such a report even if it offends the laws relating to official secrets, defamation, sedition, obscenity or other offences under the IPC.

The legislature in India has not enacted any law codifying its privileges, mainly because any such law will be subject to a judicial review in respect of the citizens, fundamental rights, but the action has been taken in use of inaccurate, distorted, unfair, wilful or mendacious rendering of the proceedings. Now there is a strong demand by the Press.

The Official Secrets Act, 1923

This Act was enacted by the Britishers during the British rule. Some amendments have been made after independence but now there is a strong public opinion by Press Council, Press Commission and Journalistic Associations to revise the whole Act because this Act is very hard and strict. It extends to the whole of India and applies also to government servants and the citizens of India living outside India.

The Official Secrets Act, 1923 is a comprehensive document relating to official secrets and defines a number of offences. The Act is aimed at maintaining the security of the State against leakage of information, sabotage and the like. It consolidates the law relating to official secrets. It deals with two kinds of offence:

(i) Spying (Sections 3 and 4)
(ii) Wrongful communication of any other secret official code or passwords, or any sketch, plan, model, article, note, document or information (Section 5).

Under Section 3 of the Act, it is an offence if any person for any purpose prejudicial to the safety or interests of the State.

(a) approaches, inspects, passes over or in the vicinity of, or enters any prohibited place, or
(b) makes any sketch, plan, model, or note which is calculated to be or might be or is intended to be directly or indirectly useful to enemy; or
(c) obtains, collects, records or publishes or communicates to any other person any sketch, plan, model, article or note or other document or information which is calculated to be or might be or is intended to be directly or indirectly useful to an enemy.

Punishment for spying in relation to the country's defence is upto fourteen years. It is not necessary to show that the accused person was guilty of any particular act tending to show a purpose prejudicial to the safety or interests of the State, and notwithstanding that no such act is proved against him, he may be convicted, if, from the circumstances of the case or his conduct or his known character as proved, it appears that his purpose was a purpose prejudicial to the safety or interests of the State.

Under Section 5 of the Act, it is an offence if any person having in his possession or control any secret official code or pass word or any sketch, plan, model, article, or note, document or information which relates to or is used in a prohibited place or relates to anything is such a place, or which has been made or obtained in contravention of this

Act or which has been entrusted in confidence to him by person holding governmental office, wilfully communicates the same to any person other than a person to whom he is authorised to communicate or it is his duty to communicate. It is also an offence under the same section.

- if any person voluntarily receives any secret information,
- person having in possession or in control any unauthorised information,
- retaining information without authority,
- use of information in possession of government officers to help a foreign power,
- communication with foreign agents,
- if the person fails to take a reasonable care of secret information,
- incitement to commission of offence is also an offence.

Under this Act, it is the duty of every citizen to give information regarding commission of offence by any other person. Every citizen is requested to attend courts to testify. This section prescribes punishment within imprisonment upto five years or fine or both.

Under the provision of this Act any publication by a newspaper of an official secret, whether in the form of a note, document, code or pass word, skecth, plan or model, makes not only the correspondent, editor, printer and publisher liable to punishment but also every director and officer of the company or corporation with whose knowledge and consent the offence was committed becomes guilty of a like offence.

In India, it has been widely demanded that Section 5 of the Official Secrets Act which prohibits free reporting should be done away with Press Commission and the Press Council of India also favoured the same opinion. The Council has asked for the repeal of the Official Secrets Act, 1923 *in toto* and to enact a new legislation which may be called Freedom of Information Act. Exceptions or permissible restrictions to this freedom may be specified in the proposed Act.

The Copyright Act, 1957

Copy right provides the author with protection against unfair appropriation of his or her work. Although its roots go back to the former Copyright Act of 1914. The present act was passed by the Indian Parliament and received the assent of the President in June 1957.

This Act primarily gives proprietary rights (like property) to reproduce, to publish, to perform, to translate, to filmised, to broadcast, to telecast or just to communicate under by-line or without a by-line in respect of the writings, paintings, sculpture, photographs, cartoons performance, etc. These rights rest with the first owner.

Copyright is the right which a person acquires in a work which is the result of his intellectual work/labour. The primary function of the law of copyright is to protect from annexation by other people of the fruits of a man's work, labour skill or test. This Act defines who is the first author, owner, writer or performer. If the writing is done by an employee of an organization or a newspaper as part of the service condition employer will be the owner and not the employee.

The owner has the right to licence (permit) to use his work with or without payment. He has the right to transfer, to sell, to counteract, to bequest (depending on the will), to inherit, to assign to any person. Copyright regarding unpublished work will become effective only when the work is actually published. First owner has the right to relinquish or disclaim the copyright. There is no provision of copyright in the government publications. Hence, journalists make full use of such publications in their articles.

Registration

Registration is optional not compulsory. Registration is not a condition for acquiring copyright. Section 45 of this Act provides for the registration of works for these purposes. It does not lay down that registration is obligatory for acquiring copyright or for availing of the remedies for its protection. Therefore, even when the copyright is not registered, rights remain with the owner. Although a work is copyrighted from the moment it is fixed in tangible form, there is a provision to receive statutory protection through using the symbol C (which means that the copyright remains with the publisher or the author, name of the copyright owner and the year of publication.

Use of Material

Copyright can be used with the permission of the Copyright Board whose Chairman is Registrar, provided a reasonable compensation determined by the Board is paid for.

Period for Copyright

Copyright lasts for the life of the author plus sixty years. Earlier it was fifty years. Copyright for films is twenty years while copyright for broadcasting is twenty-five years.

Infringement of Copyright

Copyright in a work shall be deemed to infringed when any person without a licence granted by the owner of the copyright makes the copies for sale or hire or way of trade displays or offer for sale, distributors either for the purpose of trade, by way of trade exhibits in public. The reproduction of a literary, dramatic, musical or artistic work in the form of a cinematograph film shall be deemed to be an infringing of copy.

Punishment

Under Section 63 of the Act, a person is punishable with imprisonment which may extend to one year or with fine or both if he knowingly infringes the copyright in a work including copies, plates, blocks, etc. can be seized. So, the owner of the copyright is entitled to all such remedies by way of injunction (not to be allowed to produce) forfeited and compensation.

Limitations

It is important to note that copyright protection extends only to copying the work in question. If a person independently creates a similar work, there is copyright violation. As a result one of the things that a person who brings a copyright suit must prove is that the other person had access to the work under consideration.

The law also provides that people can make fair use of copyrighted materials without violating the provisions of the Copyright Act. Fair use means that copies of the protected work can be made for such legitimate activities as teaching, research, new reporting and criticism, without penalty. In determining fair use, following factors are taken into consideration :

1. The purpose of the use (whether for profit or for non-profit motive),
2. The nature of the copyrighted work,
3. The amount reproduced in proportion to the copyrighted work as a whole,

4. The effect of the use on the potential market value of the copyrighted work.

The Press and Registration of Books Act, 1867

This is oldest of the existing press laws. It has been amended a number of times after independence. The provision of Part VA relating to registration of newspapers and the creation of the office of Press Registrar were inserted by the amending Act in 1955.

The word 'newspaper' has been defined in sub-section (1) of Section 1 to mean "any printed periodical work containing public news or comments on public news". Therefore, the definition comprehends not only daily newspapers but also news magazines of all periodicities under one category. The publication of a newspaper commences only after the making of a declaration under Section 5(2) and its authentication under Section 6 as laid down in Section 5(2c). This being so, the Magistrate authenticating the declaration cannot ascertain the contents of the publication to make sure that it falls within the definition of 'newspaper'. However, under Section 8 B(iv), the Press Registrar can make an application before the Magistrate for cancellation of the declaration in respect of a newspaper.

Registration

Under this Act, the intending printer/publisher has to appear in person or through an authorised agent before a specified Magistrate and make a declaration that he is the printer/publication Incharge/Publisher of the newspaper and indicate therein the language and periodicity, the title of the newspaper and also a precise account of the premises where the printing or publication is to be conducted. Then the Magistrate has to write to the Press Registrar to ascertain whether the title proposed for the intended newspaper is free or is the same as or similar to that of any other newspaper published either in the same language or in the same State. The Press Registrar has to give a reply after verification of his records. On receiving clearance from the Press Registrar, the Magistrate has to authenticate the declaration and send copies thereof to the intending printer/publisher and the Press Registrar. After receipt of the authenticated declaration, the Press Registrar has to issue a certificate of Registration. In view of the registration, Second Press Commission recommended that 'there is no need for personal appearance before the magistrate for this purpose. After sending the declaration and the affidavit regarding title the publisher should be free to commence the publication'.

The Parliament Proceedings (Protection of Publication) Act, 1956

This Act is intended to protect the publication of reports of proceedings of Parliament except in newspapers. Section 3 of the Act states that no person shall be liable to any proceedings, civil or criminal in any court, in respect of the publication in a newspaper of a substantially true report of any proceedings of either House of Parliament, unless the publication is proved to have been made with malice.

The Drugs and Magic Remedies (Objectionable Advertisements) Act, 1954

This Act aims at preventing advertisements tending to cause the ignorant and unwary consumers to resort to self-medication with harmful drugs and appliances. Sections (3 and 4) of this Act prohibit the advertisement of certain drugs marketed for the treatment of certain diseases and disorders such as prevention of conception, sexual impotence, menstrual disorders, epilepsy, fits, etc. Advertisements making false claims for the drugs are also prohibited. Section (7) of this Act imposes both civil and criminal liabilities for this contravention of its provision.

Children Act, 1960

The main objective of this Act is to provide for the care, protection, maintenance, welfare, training, education and rehabilitation of neglected or delinquent children. The Act also provides for the trial of delinquent children in the Union territories. The Act prohibits publication of names, etc. of children involved in any proceedings. Under Section 36(l) of this Act no report in any newspaper, magazine or news sheet of any enquiry regarding a child shall disclose the name, address or shall or any other particular calculated to lead to the identification of the child. Further, picture of any such child cannot be published in newspapers. However, such a disclosure can be made with the permission of the authority holding the enquiry, when in its opinion, such disclosure is in the interest of the child. Contravention of this provision leads to punishment with fine which may extend to one thousand rupees under Section 36(2) of this Act.

The Young Persons' (Harmful Publications) Act, 1956

This Act seeks to prohibit the publication in India of such literature as glorifies crime, violence or vice and provides for penalties for contravening its purpose.

The State Govt. is empowered to forfeit harmful publications. The penalty for printing, sale, etc. of harmful publications is imprisonment which may extend to six months with or without fine.

The Delivery of Books and Newspapers (Public Libraries) Act, 1954

This Act provides for delivery of books and newspapers to public libraries. Under Section 3-A of this Act, the publisher of every newspaper is required to deliver at his own expense, one free copy of each of the newspaper as soon as it is published to public libraries as notified by the central government. They are :

1. National Library, Calcutta
2. Connemara Public Library, Madras
3. Central Library, Bombay

The Act further provides that any publisher who contravenes this provision shall be punishable with fine which may be to the extent of rupees fifty only.

The Cigarettes (Regulation of Production, Supply and Distribution) Act, 1975

This Act provides that every advertisement of cigarette should contain the warning–Cigarette Smoking is Injurious to Health—and such warning must be conspicuously, legible and prominent (Section 5). Further, the advertisement should not contain any matter which is inconsistent with the statutory warning (Section 6). Under this Act, any person who advertises or takes part in the advertisement of cigarettes which does not contain this warning shall be punishable for a term of three years or with a fine extending to rupees five thousand or with both.*

---

*Some of these Acts are based on *Newspaper Management in India*, Gulab Kothari; and *Law of the Press*, D. D. Basu.

ETHICS OF JOURNALISM

The subject of ethics, right from the ancient days of Plato to the present, has been a matter of serious preoccupation with philosophers, social reformers, academics and concerned citizens of society. The subject is important not only because it is fundamental to the survival of civilised society, but also because it eludes proper definition in concrete terms.

By general understanding, ethics has to do with conduct—with conduct that is 'right' in view of a given society and time period, with conduct that is good out of a sense of duty or conviction rather than from fear of punishment. By common consent various modes of behaviour and conduct are viewed as 'good' and various others as 'bad', even though in today's society there may be wide individual differences as to the understanding of what is 'good' or what is 'bad'.

In short, ethics are rules of conduct or principles of morality that point us towards the right or best way to act in a situation. Over the years, philosophers have developed a number of general ethical principles that serve as guidelines for evaluating our behaviour. These principles, however, do not contain magic answers to every ethical dilemma. In fact, different ethical principles often suggest different and conflicting courses of action. There is no 'perfect' answer to every problem. Also, these ethical principles are based on western thought. Other cultures may have developed totally different systems. Nonetheless, these principles can provide a framework for analysing what is proper for examining choices and for justifying our actions.

Professional Ethics

There is general recognition of the fact that journalists have responsibilities not only vis-a-vis their own convictions but also towards the public. Summarily, four kinds of responsibility may be defined : (a) contractual responsibility in relation to the media and their internal organisation; (b) a social responsibility entailing obligations towards public opinion and society as a whole; (c) responsibility or liability deriving from the obligation to comply with the law; and (d) responsibility towards the international community, relating to respect of universal values. These four types of responsibilities may in certain respects be contradictory or even conflicting.

The International Commission for the Study of Communication Problems appointed by UNESCO pointed out : Professional ethical norms first began to be codified in all regions of the world. They vary considerably both in their form and scope. In some countries, different codes govern the press, broadcasting and the cinema. These codes are formulated and adopted voluntarily by the professionals and their associations; in other cases, however, they are imposed by the law. Moreover, principles such as objectivity, impartiality, truthfulness and freedom of information are frequently formulated in rather vague and ambiguous terms. Most codes refer to such important concepts as : safeguarding freedom of information; freedom of access to information sources; objectivity, accuracy, truthfulness or the non-misrepresentation of facts; responsibility vis-a-vis the public and its rights and interests and in relation to national, racial and religious communities, the nation, the State and maintenance of peace; unfounded accusations, violation of privacy, right of reply, etc.

Ombudsman

Some newspapers have tried to incorporate an idea from Scandinavia into their operations in order to provide some internal criticism. An individual employed by the paper (called an ombudsperson), is assigned to handle complaints from readers who feel that they have got a raw deal and to criticise in general the performance of the paper's staff. The idea, however, has not made a big splash nationwide, and only a few papers maintain such an institution. In India, *The Times of India* appointed Justice P. B. Bhagwati as the ombudsman.

All these laws, regulations, codes evolved by the government and professional bodies tend to serve the media and society onwards regulating their working in a way so as to have a positive impact and serve the larger societal objectives. To what extent these professional codes actually serve their purpose would largely depend on the journalists and professionals working in the media and the implementation through regulatory mechanism evolved over a period of time.

In India, the Press Council of India (PCI) has been mandated to build up a code of conduct for newspapers, newsagencies and journalists in accordance with high professional standards. The PCI has brought out an updated and succinct compilation of principles of journalistic ethics, sorted out from the adjudications of the Council and the guidelines issued from time to time.

The guidelines framed by PCI for guidance of journalists are given in the Annexure 1 in Section VI.

AINEC Code of Ethics

Some of the professional bodies connected with the Indian press have formulated voluntary codes of conduct as part of their efforts at self-regulation. The Code of Ethics, evolved by the All India Newspapers Editors' Conference (AINEC), which is applicable to the members of that body. This code, though drafted in general terms, emphasises the need for journalists to attach due importance to human and social rights in discharge of their professional obligation, to observe special restraint in reporting or commenting on communal matters (No. 3a) and to promote national unity (No. 3b). The code is essentially persuasive in character; no sanctions have been prescribed for its breach nor any machinery created for its enforcement.

1. As the Press is a primary instrument in the creation of public opinion, journalists should regard their calling as a trust and be eager to serve and guard their public interests.
2. In the discharge of their duties, journalists should attach due value to fundamental, human and social rights and shall hold good faith and fair play in news reports and comments as essential professional obligations.
3. Journalists should observe special restraint in reports and comments dealing with tensions, likely to lead, or leading to civil disorder.
   (a) Journalists shall particularly observe maximum restraint in publishing reports and comments relating to communal tension, incidents, riots, incipient situations likely to lead to communal disturbances. The identification of communities which may lead to chain reactions should be avoided.
   (b) Journalists should endeavour at all times to promote the unity of the country and nation, pride in the country, its people, its achievements and its strength in diversity. Journalists should be most circumspect in dealing with movements and ideas which promote regionalism at the cost of national unity.
   (c) Any reportage on ideas of fresh partition and secessionism must be treated with the greatest caution. Any comment likely to give comfort to the proponents of such ideas and further their interests should be avoided. The integrity of the country and of Indian people must be considered sacrosanct and

beyond question.

4. Journalists should endeavour to ensure that information disseminated is factually accurate. No fact shall be distorted or the essential facts deliberately omitted. No information known to be false shall be published.
5. Responsibility shall be assumed for all information and comments published. If responsibility is disclaimed, this will be explicitly stated.
6. Confidences shall always be respected. Professional secrecy must be preserved.
7. Any report found to be inaccurate and any comment on inaccurate reports shall be voluntarily rectified. It shall be obligatory to give fair publicity to a correction of contradiction when a report published is shown to be false or inaccurate in material particulars.
8 Journalists shall not exploit their status for non-journalistic purposes.
9. Journalists shall not allow personal interest to influence professional conduct.
10. There is nothing so unworthy as the acceptance or demand of a bribe or inducement for the exercise by a journalist of his power to give or deny publicity to news or comments.
11. Freedom in the honest collection and publication of news and facts and the rights of their comments and criticism and principles which every journalist should always defend.
12. Journalists shall be very conscious of their obligation to their fellows in the profession and shall not seek to deprive fellow-journalists of their livelihood by unfair means.
13. The carrying on of personal controversies in the press in which no public interest is involved shall be regarded as derogatory to the dignity of the profession.
14. It is unprofessional to give currency to rumours or loose talk affecting the private life of individuals. Even verifiable news affecting the private life of individuals shall not be published unless the public interest as distinguished from public curiosity demands its publication.
15. The Press shall refrain from publishing matters likely to encourage vice and crime.

Lowering of Ethical Values in Journalism

During the past few years, and more so in the recent past, the lowering of ethical values in the media have been widely reported. The pernicious practice of accepting envelopes containing gift coupons or hard cash by the press reporters in India at the press conferences where new issues are launched has been widely commented upon.

Writing of Business Journalists in *Vidura* (July 1995), Nandini Sahai says : Then there is another class of journalists who are not doing too badly. They call at announcing share-issues. They stand to take home quite a neat sum at the end of the month, mostly in the form of gift coupons and gifts. The *Vidura* issue of June 1994, has Mr. Dilip Cherian saying, "My own personal experience is that in business journalism the chances of becoming corrupt are much higher." It has also succeeded in creating a breed of journalists who boldly 'offer to pay' the newspaper for the privilege of being their financial correspondent.

Not that the phenomenon of journalists getting rich in the course of news gathering is peculiar to India. In China, a lot of Chinese journalists "Write advertisements in the guise of news after receiving various benefits". In April 1994, the Chinese Communist Party launched a drive to root out the spreading phenomenon of paid news coverage (cheque book journalism) in the country's media organs. A circular put out by the Central Committee's propaganda department called for, "unremitting efforts by party organisations to educate journalists on press ethics."

Whereas it is difficult to say how far such efforts in enforcing ethical standards would succeed, the fact remains that professional bodies of working journalists will have to do lot more to enforce codes of conduct evolved by these bodies for their members.

PRESS COMMISSIONS

The Government of India appointed two Press Commissions to make a comprehensive enquiry into the state of press in India and examine issues associated with its working—working conditions of journalists, freedom of the press, machinery for ensuring high standards of journalism, pattern and economics of ownership and ways and means to promote growth of language press and the regional press, etc.

First Press Commission

The First Press Commission was appointed in September 1952 under the chairmanship of Justice Rajadhyaksha. The Commission, which submitted its report in 1954, made several important recommendations which helped in constituting a number of institutions and organising the profession of journalism in a systematic manner. It was the first enquiry of its kind into the working of the press and its report has been a kind of Bible about the Press.

Some of the recommendations and observations of the First Press Commission are as under :

(i) A Press Council be established whose objects should be :

(1) to safeguard the freedom of the press and help the press to maintain its independence;
(2) to censure objectionable types of journalistic conduct and by all other possible means to build up a code in accordance with the highest professional standards;
(3) to keep under review any development likely to restrict the supply and dissemination of news of public interest and importance;
(4) to encourage the growth of a sense of responsibility and of public service among those engaged in the profession of journalism;
(5) to study the developments in the press which may tend towards concentration or monopoly, and if necessary, to suggest remedies therefore;
(6) to publish reports, at least once a year, recording its work and reviewing the performance of the press, its development and factors affecting them; and
(7) to improve methods of recruitment, education and training for the profession by the creation of suitable agencies for the purpose such as a Press Institute.

(ii) *Decline in Editor's Status* : There has been a general decline in the status and independence of the editor and this decline is noticeable particularly in the case of daily newspapers. In the past it was quite usual for the majority of the readers to be both aware and conscious of the role played by the editor in the formulation of the views set out in a paper, and it was quite usual to refer to the paper not merely by its name but by the name of the editor..... The position has changed today and we feel that the bulk of the newspaper readers today may be unaware of who is the editor of their newspaper and indifferent to the name that appears on small print on the last page.

(iii) The news agencies should not merely keep themselves from bias and follow strictly the principles of integrity, objectivity and comprehensiveness in the coverage of news, but it should also appear to the newspapers, and to the public, that the news agencies are maintaining such a course.

(iv) While condemning the practice of giving astrological predictions the Commission said : The spread of the habit of consultation of, and reliance upon, astrological predictions, particularly of the nature and in the manner they are published at present is certain to produce an unsettling effect on the minds of readers. We would describe the practice of publishing such predictions as undesirable.

(v) The Commission found that the emoluments received by the journalists were on the whole unsatisfactory and recommended the appointment of a Wage Board for working journalists.

(vi) The Commission recommended the appointment of Registrar of Newspapers for India (RNI). As a result of this recommendation the office of RNI was created from 1 July 1956. The RNI verifies and regulates the availability of newspapers, registers them, containing detailed information on newspapers. The office also issues Entitlement Certificates to the newspapers/periodicals for the import of newsprint and import of printing machinery and allied materials required by the newspapers.

Second Press Commission

The Second Press Commission was set up in May 1978 with Justice P. C. Goswami as the Chairman; however, Justice Goswami and the members of the Commission resigned in January 1980. The Commission was reconstituted in April 1980 with Justice K. K. Mathew as its Chairman.

The appointment of Second Press Commission became necessary since the press has undergone major changes and had acquired added significance with the continuously expanding readership base.

The Commission redefined the role, status and functioning of the press in a democratic set-up, particularly in view of the experience of the press during the Emergency. The Commission enquired into the growth and the status of the press since the First Press Commission submitted its report in 1954.

The terms of references of the Commission included : (1) role of press in a developing and democratic society; (2) present constitutional guarantee regarding freedom of speech and expression; (3) means of safeguarding the independence of press against economic and political pressures from proprietors and management; (4) role of the press and the responsibilities it should assume in development policies; (5) ownership patterns, management practices and financial structures of the press; (6) chain newspapers; links with industry, their effect on competition and on the readers' right to objective news and free comments; and (7) economics of newspaper industry.

The Commission, which submitted its report in 1982 said : "The role of the press in a developing and democratic society should neither be that of an adversary nor an ally of government. To be a mindless adversary or an unquestioning ally would be to abdicate judgement. A free press in our view should be a constructive critic."

The Commission said : "The press as a medium of communication is a modern phenomenon. It has immense power to advance or thwart the progress of civilisation. Its freedom can be used to create a brave new world or to bring about universal catastrophe."

The Commission made concrete suggestions to curb the influence of foreign money on the press and suggested enactment of necessary changes in laws for the purpose. It recommended the following five step :

1. There should be specific legal provision under which no newspaper undertaking should have any foreign ownership either in the form of shares or in the form of loans,
2. Advertisements as well as printing contracts from foreign sources should be on terms no different from those applicable to similar work done for others,
3. Advertisement rates must be published each year and on every revision, and there should be no discrimination in their application to foreign advertisers,
4. Once a year every newspaper should publish its profit and loss

account with separate information about foreign and Indian sources,

5. Every newspaper undertaking must submit with its annual account the following information to the Press Council.
   (a) Details of revenue obtained from advertisements and printing contracts in respect of foreign sources country-wise, including advertisements and printing contracts received through an Indian agency; and
   (b) Names of the top 100-share holders with their nationality and address and the number and proportion of shares held.

The Commission proposed that the newsagencies in the country explore hitherto untapped areas of news to give reporting a new purpose and unity. The agencies suffer from an urban bias and are preoccupied with political developments in the national and state capitals. The news agencies are hardly in a position to report the social or economic changes taking place or intended changes not taking place—in the countryside. Because of the obsession of the newspapers with the political news, the news agencies spend much of their energy in reporting political events.

There is scope for pooling and countrywide dissemination of the more significant stories of success or failure in rural development. This could form the nucleus of a rural news service which would enable readers, including farmers, administrators and legislators in one part of the country to profit from the experiences in other parts.

The four members of the Commission–Justice Sisir Kumar Mukherjee, Rajinder Mathur, Girilal Jain and H. K. Paranjape opposed the recommendations of the Commission regarding delinking of newspaper ownership from other business. In a 100-page dissenting note expressed the fear that suggestions for the introduction of price-page schedule and fixing the ratio of news and advertisement amounted to abridgement of the freedom of the press.

FREEDOM OF PRESS

To preserve the democratic way of life it is essential that people should have the freedom to express their feelings and to make their views known to the people at large. The press, a powerful medium of mass communication, should be free to play its role in building a strong viable society. Denial of freedom of the press to citizens would necessarily undermine the power to influence public opinion and be counter to democracy.

Freedom of the press is not specifically mentioned in Article 19(l) (a) of the Constitution and what is mentioned there is only freedom of speech and expression. In the Constituent Assembly Debates it was made clear by Dr. Ambedkar, Chairman of the Drafting Committee, that no special mention of the freedom of the press was necessary at all as the press and an individual or a citizen were the same as far as their right of expression was concerned.

The framers of the Indian Constitution considered freedom of the press as an essential part of the freedom of speech and expression as guaranteed in Article 19(l) (a) of the Constitution.

In Ramesh Thapar *Vs.* State of Madras, and Brij Bhushan *Vs.* State of Delhi, the Supreme Court took it for granted the fact that the freedom of the press was an essential part of the right to freedom of speech and expression. It was observed by Patanjali Sastri J. in Ramesh Thapar that freedom of speech and expression included propagation of ideas, and that freedom was ensured by the freedom of circulation.

It is clear that the right to freedom of speech and expression carries with it the right to publish and circulate one's ideast, opinions and other views with complete freedom and by resorting to all available means of publication. The right to freedom of the press includes the right to propagate ideas and views and to publish and circulate them. However, the freedom of the press is not absolute, just as the freedom of expression is not. Public interest has to be safeguarded by Article 19(l)(2) which lays down reasonable limitations to the freedom of expression in matters affecting :

(a) Sovereignty and integrity of the State,
(b) Security of the State,
(c) Friendly relations with foreign countries,
(d) Public order,
(e) Decency and morality,
(f) Contempt of court,
(g) Defamation,
(h) Incitement to an offence.

Freedom of Press Defined

It is an absence of statutory and administrative control on dissemination of information, ideas, knowledge and thoughts.

The freedom of the press and of expression is guarded by the First Amendment to the US Constitution which specifically lays down that this freedom be in no way abridged by laws. It is not that Indian leaders were not aware of the US First Amendment or of Jefferson's famous declaration when he said that "Were it left me to decide whether we should have a government without newspapers or newspapers without a government, I should not hesitate a moment to prefer the latter". Jawahar Lal Nehru echoed similar views "I would rather have a completely free press, with all the dangers involved in the wrong use of that freedom, than a suppressed or regulated press". Voltaire once said, "I do not agree with a word you say but I defend to death your right to say it".

Mrs. Gandhi has never had much faith in the press. Her misgivings about the press were first expressed in her address to the International Press Institute Assembly in New Delhi on November 15, 1966, when she blamed the press for giving wide publicity to student unrest in the country. She said, "How much liberty should the press have in a country like India which is engaged in fighting a war against poverty, backwardness, superstition and ignorance." Mrs. Gandhi would not suggest restrictions that might be imposed on the press but said that it was for the leading editions, and journalists of the country to decide. Nine years later when Mrs. Gandhi declared emergency action was taken against the press immediately and complete censorship was imposed.

Kuldip Nayar, a veteran journalist wrote to Mrs. Gandhi soon after she imposed the emergency, "If newspapers have criticised the government, it is largely because of its sluggish administration, slow progress in the economic field and the gap between promise and performance. My concept of a free press is to ferret out the truth and let the public know."

To preserve the democratic way of life, it is essential that people should have the freedom to express their feelings to make their views known to the people at large. The press, a powerful media of mass communication should be free to play its role in building a strong viable society. Denial of the freedom of press to citizens would necessarily undermine the power to influence public opinion.

An awsome responsibility remarks S. Nihal Singh, "rests on the shoulders of journalists because in the final analysis they are custodians of freedom of the press". If they prefer careerism to standing up for their rights, they are letting down their profession.

Besides the restrictions imposed on the press by the Constitution, there exists various other laws which further curtail press freedom and the right of the citizen to information as well as the right to freedom of speech and expression. They are all in force in the interest of public order of the sovereignty and security of the State.

Yellow Journalism

The degrading kind of journalism is known as yellow journalism. It is a journalism without soul. Facts are distorted or exaggerated. There is very little truth in the stories. Unethical means are adopted to increase the circulation. It is a kind of journalism which lures the readers by any possible means. It makes the high drama of life, a cheap melodrama. Worst of all, instead of giving its readers effective readership, it offers sex and violence.

Joseph Pulitzer, publisher of the *New York World* and William Randolph Hearst who in 1887 became the editor of the *San Francisco Examiner* were the men responsible for the birth of yellow journalism. Hearst's association with the newspaper business came from his father, who was more an aspiring politician than a 'journalist and had originally acquired the *Examiner* for political purposes. William Randolph Hearst ventured east to Harvard where he gained fame more for his pranks than for his studies and was eventually expelled. He did manage to acquire newspaper experience on Pulitzer's *World* and, on his return to San Francisco, took the lessons of sensationalism from the penny press and applied them to big city journalism. (Penny press is a term that describes the mass appeal press of the early nineteenth century in New York. Newspapers were sold for a penny in the streets and they made a profit from advertisers, and were oriented towards less educated, ordinary citizens). With bold, eye-gripping headlines and various escapades to generate or report the news Hearst's *Examiner* began to climb in circulation. The result was that both profit and circulation doubled and then tripled.

Joseph Pulitzer also succeeded in building the circulation of the *Sunday World* in New York to over 300 thousand in the early 1980s. To do this, he combined good reporting with crusades, an emphasis on disasters, melodramatics, sensational photographs and comic strips in colour all to increase reader's interest. Pulitzer crusaded against corrupt officials and for civil service reform and taxes on luxuries, large incomes and inheritances. He pioneered the use of coloured comics in newspapers, which did much to spur the circulation of his Sunday editions. One cartoon in particular made history. It featured a baldheaded, toothless, grinning kid, clad in a yellow sack-like garment.

The 'yellow kid', as the character came to be called, appeared in settings that depicted life in the slums of New York and the cartoon was extremely popular.

It was William Randolph Hearst who mastered the art of attracting readers through appeals to sympathy and anger, the bizarre, and the picturesque. Hearst purchased the New York Journal in 1895, determined to build its flagging circulation to surpass that of Pulitzer's paper. Seeing the popularity of the yellow kid, Hearst simply bought the cartoonist from his rival with a large salary. He added other writing and editorial talent. Then he published more comics, more sensational reports, and more human interest material which led to increased circulation.

Now Pulitzer and Hearst were engaged in a fierce circulation battle as each paper attempted to out sensationalize the other. As one press critic put it, the duel between these two spread "death, dishonour and disaster" all over page one sex, murder, popularized medicine, pseudoscience, self-promotion, and human interest stories filled the two papers. This type of reporting became known as yellow journalism, and whatever its faults, it sold newspapers.

Pulitzer, in ill health, finally withdrew from the battle with Hearst around 1900. Although the period of yellow journalism cannot be said to have been the proudest moment in the history of the American press some positive features did emerge from it. It brought enthusiasm, energy and verve to the practice of journalism. Aggressive reporting and investigative stories were emphasized by the *World* and the *Journal*. It also brought wide exposure to prominent authors and led to some fine examples of contemporary writing. Yellow journalism helped popularize the use of layout and display devices–banner headlines, pictures, colour printing–that would go on to characterize modern journalism.

Entry of Foreign Press

Ever since the economic liberalisation process has set in and multinational companies are dominating the economy of the country, the issue of the entry of foreign papers has been frequently raised.

It would however be pertinent to point out that as early as 1959 the Supreme Court had ruled that a non-citizen running a newspaper is not entitled to lay claim to press freedom as his fundamental right. The apex court ruled that while a corporation or a company was not a citizen and was not guaranteed press freedom, its editors, directors and shareholders could claim that right. So, if a foreign newspaper is run as joint enterprise with an innovating newspaper or a group of newspapers, its Indian directors, shareholders and the editors can seek the protection of the court, while foreign collaborators could sit back and avail of the privilege of freedom of press and enjoy the benefits flowing from the above privilege.

The First Press Commission also did not favour the entry of the foreign media in the country.

Following the recommendations of the First Press Commission, the Central Government had, in 1955, decided that no foreign-owned newspaper or periodical should, in future, be published in India and that foreign newspapers and periodicals, which dealt mainly with news and current affairs, should not be allowed to bring out their editions in India. Another decision taken by the government in 1956 was that communication facilities should be granted to foreign news agencies only where distribution of news within the country would be effected through an Indian news agency owned and managed by Indians, and which would have full and final authority in the selection of foreign news and their distribution and which would also be in a position to supply Indian news to the foreign news agencies.

The Press Council, on a reference from the government of India, communicated its opinion on the subject as follows :

1. The Council generally favours a cautious approach to this very sensitive question of information flow. The dominant view is that direct distribution of foreign news agency copy to Indian subscribers should not be allowed.
2. The Council does not favour publication of foreign papers/journals in India involving equity and management participation.
3. It feels that printing of foreign journals in India is undesirable, though some members have expressed the view that this might be permitted with suitable safeguards pertaining to subject-matters such as national employment and repatriation of profits.
4. A few members feel that there is no reason to bar foreign news agencies from undertaking direct distribution to Indian subscribers.
5. The Council believes that the Government of India will take these views into consideration before arriving at any decision in the matter and reconsider the decision, if already taken, in the matter.

The issue has, however, polarised the media community, overheated the debate on the subject, with both the protagonists and the opponents speaking on the move with almost religious fervour. Those favouring the move consider the step as the logical outcome of the on-going process of liberalisation, whereas those opposing advise caution against going blind folded into an unknown area and cite the 1955 cabinet decision disallowing such entry as sacrosanct.

In an impassioned article, foreign media inside the Indian fourth estate, V. R. Krishna Iyer, says : To commoditise the media and allow their foreign manufacture within the country is fraught with grave risk to our sovereign democracy and nationalist survival. After all, freedom of the press is but a derivative from the fundamental freedom of expression under Article 19. Freedom of speech, and of occupation or business belong only to the Indian citizens and are subject to reasonable restrictions "in the interests of sovereignty of India... friendly relations with foreign states, defamation or incitement to an offence." No 'open seasame' for an outside news heavy weight can be mindlessly granted (*The Hindustan Times*, 11 October 1995).

The Roundtable feature in *Media Asia* 22 (4) carried an illuminating discussion on : Foreign investment in Asian Media—Boon or Bane. In a highly motivated, investment friendly piece, Urban C. Lehner, Editor of *The Asian Wall Street Journal*, argues at length the instance of Singapore making rapid economic headway from 1963-1993, almost a rags-to-rich story, because the key element in its smart economic management was the encouragement of foreign investment. Lehner lists the several advantages of foreign investment in media; infusion of capital and know-how, Asian viewers and readers having more choices at lower prices, foreign investment would lead Asia towards becoming 'information superhighway.' Finally, Lehner condescendingly invokes the Asian governments to recognize that 'foreign investment in Asian media is a boon, not a bane.'

The Chief Editor of *Malayala Manorama* and doyen of the Indian journalists, K. M. Mathew makes out a strong case against foreign investment in print media specially because, whereas laws and conventions in the western democracies place restrictions on foreigners buying stakes in media in their own countries, they would wish India to relax all restrictions and allow anyone and everyone to come to run newspapers in this country.

Those who support entry of foreign investment in media take recourse to the climate of economic liberalisation in the country. If foreign investment is welcome in infrastructure and power industry, why not in print media. Mathew says : We are for liberalisation. I personally and my paper support it. But we want it on our own terms, just as America wants open trade on its own terms. We do not want liberalisation to mean restrictions on our sovereignty and threat to our democratic economy. I am convinced that the entry of all powerful foreign media into India is not in the best interests of Indian media, economy or culture. So, let us be like other democratic countries. Let us not be scapegoats because of our successful democracy. Let us remember that liberalisation in the economic field does not warrant a corresponding action in print media. Liberalisation in newspaper publication is totally different from that of consumer products like edible oil, tooth paste, soft drinks or potato chips. Our media, the sensitive channel of interaction must not be allowed to be swamped by powerful force from outside with no concern for India's interest.

.... Unlike the Indian press, the foreign newspapers are not expected to have any concern for our culture, ethos or tradition. The cultural and moral fallout of the entry of the foreign newspapers would be far more serious than the fallout of the advent of Satellite T.V. in the country where the print media still has greater influence than the electronic media.

Indian Press–On the Threshold of Millennium

The press in India continues to be in a state of buoyancy in terms of growth in circulation, number of newspapers, as also the number of languages in which the newspapers are published. The circulation of newspapers has registered a phenomenal increase. In terms of total newspaper circulation, India is in third place after Japan and USA. An other interesting feature of the Indian press is that newspapers in the country are amongst the lowest priced anywhere in the world. There has been a spurt of activity in the entire Indian language press, resulting in not only vast expansion, but also improvement in quality both editorial and technological.

A country's press reflects the society it lives in, and the excessive space devoted by the newspapers and magazines to politicians and political parties' doings is a mirror of what excites the reader. The newspapers are full of politicians' election speeches and the minute details of elections and electoral politics. The politicians recycle their speeches time without number every day, and the newspapers dutifully publish the same speeches. This excessive preoccupation with politics of the country is a legacy from the freedom movement when the press played an important role in mobilising public opinion against the foreign rule. During the recent years, however, financial reporting and economic policy issues are getting due importance, reflecting in its wake far reaching changes in the business and economic sectors. Economic liberalisation has spawned a new generation of financial journalism with most papers running separate business sections, quite apart from the more specialised economic papers and financial and business journals.

The expansion of language press has resulted in every district having a newspaper and sometimes more than one. This is in addition to the district editions of the big papers and leading dailies published from metropolitan cities, state capitals and other major publication centres. Multiple editions or chains are increasing with easier communications and the introduction of facsimile transmission. Newspapers like *Eenadu* have editions coming out from every district of Andhra Pradesh, *Rajasthan Patrika* has four editions, *Malayala Manorama* has three editions, similarly *Aaj*, *Nai Duniya*, *Amar Ujala* have several editions. *Eenadu* even brings half a dozen editions for different localities in Hyderabad city.

Another interesting aspect of newspaper boom is the Sunday journalism. Several English language newspapers, coming out from metropolitan cities bring out 56-page Sunday edition, including classified section which contains news you can use and 12-page multi-coloured magazine section. Even on week days there are supplements/ pull-outs on Education. Information Technology, etc. Saturday sections for week-end reading offer equally variegated fare on films and fashions, leisure and living styles, music and entertainment. The rich and beautiful, the society gossips, fashion designers and party hoppers constitute Saturday reading in most of these week-end editions.

Of late disquiet has been voiced that the press has been ignoring the issues related to the rural poor and the disadvantaged sections of the society who can't articulate their concerns. As the Nobel laureate economist Amartya Sen, while talking of the efficacy of public action, says : India has not witnessed famines, after independence, because of the democratic polity and the free press. The Chinese government, however, did not wake up to the nature and magnitude of calamity for quite a long time, and disastrous policies were not revised which resulted in death of between 23 and 30 million people during the famines of 1958-61. The informational failure in China was linked to the controlled press.

Since specific issues and situations—poverty, hunger, illiteracy, unemployment and social injustice—have become permanent features of the Indian society and these do not make headline news, unless these lead to riots or crimes; these are generally ignored by the Indian press, except for some coverage by a handful of journalists. Unless the press takes up these issues, the prospect of alleviating the distressing situation would continue to be remote. The press takes note of the subject only at a time when the Human Development Reports, put together by the United Nations, reveal India to be nearly at the bottom of the scale. It is therefore time that the press takes up these issues as a part of its social responsibility so that things in rural India could be ameliorated.

The Malayalam press in Kerala has one outstanding feature to its credit–creative development journalism. *Malayala Manorama* honours the best farmer of Kerala once in two years by awarding the title *Karshaka Sree*, a citation and Rs. 1 lakh. It has won the appreciation of Dr. Norman E. Borlaug, the lone Nobel laureate for his great contributions in eradicating hunger. Another newspaper *Mathrubhoomi* has been sponsoring massive *Kisan melas* to celebrate the anniversary of farm feature every year. These *melas* last five days. The Malayalam dailies have created a golden chapter in the history of creative development journalism by introducing the weekly farm feature page and running it for the last 20 years. Now every year, nearly 100 million pages are made available for farm news by the Malayalam dailies, points out a write up in *Kurukshetra*.

The Indian press enjoys almost complete freedom, subject to certain civil laws–laws of defamation and contempt of court. Freedom of expression is accepted as a core value. Except for the duration of emergency, when pre-censorship was imposed and some of the journalists had to undergo harrowing experience, the Indian press has been able to maintain its freedom. Whenever, there was a threat to freedom of press, legislative or otherwise, the journalists came out as one man and one community to defend challenge to the freedom of expression.

The Press Council of India (PCI) intervenes and adjudicates complaints from the public, mostly against the wrong doings or excesses of individual journalists or the newspapers; but it has only advisory authority. The PCI, has, however, been making efforts to evolve a code of conduct for journalists, and also scrutinise the role of press in a national crisis situation like the demolition of Babri Masjid.

During the nineties the press had to face increasing challenge from the satellite television channels. Several publishing houses established TV divisions, with the *India Today* group becoming quite successful with its news programmes. During mid-1995, TV channels became a growth industry and several senior journalists joined TV journalism, which offered better packages and instant visibility. While TV offered opportunity to give instantaneous news–news as it was breaking, particularly during the Kargil conflict and the recent parliamentary elections; press gave background briefing and analysis to the news events. The press has also started giving greater coverage to subjects like arts, science and technology and law as well as to societal concerns like literacy, education and environment.

The rapid technological changes, which the print media is adapting to survive, has brought about far-reaching changes in the contemporary media scenario. The leading newspapers are taking to on-line journalism in a big way. Commenting on the latest developments in the field, a recent business journal wrote : The onslaught of technology is changing the dynamics of news delivery too. Newspapers, once the medium for breaking news, relinquished that role to television. The internet could take that over. Crudely, the new media ecosystem could look like this : the Net will break news, TV will do follow ups and live coverage and newspapers will end up doing analyses. Some of this may already be happening. At *The Washington Post*, for instance, newspaper reporters file crisp, shorter articles for the web and file bigger articles for the newspaper.

Several print media organisations–*The Hindu*, *Times of India* and *India Today* and others have been developing comprehensive websites of their own, which regularly cover interviews, chat shows, business and economy news, life styles and entertainment. Infact on-line journalism is creating more opportunities of employment and advancement for the print media journalists and the competition to retain the best journalists in the print media is becoming really sharp.

At the present juncture, India, the Indian society and the Indian press are all in transition. The trends that the Indian press is witnessing today are bound to gather strength, while some others are bound to emerge in the wake of rapid technological innovations and developments.

SECTION–III

ELECTRONIC MEDIA

Electronic Media

The contemporary media of communication, based on electronics have set in motion a continuing process of change which has been relentlessly impacting the mind set and attitudes of the present day society.

The electronic media — radio, television, cable television, and now internet have ushered in revolutionary changes in the society as never before. Moreover these changes have developed an accelerated momentum of their own.

In his Patel Memorial Lectures broadcast in 1975 under the title, *The Communication Revolution*, Narayana Menon said :

> In the beginning was the word, but the word was spoken. Then came the invention of writing which froze the spoken word into a visual shape and changed the character and basis of language. next came printing, which gave the written word a mass basis, creating two types of languages—the spoken and the written– and two types of human beings, the illiterate and the literate. And next, broadcasting and the electronic media, making the dissemination of information and ideas, of sound and pictures on a scale so gigantic and global that no one is immune to it. We are still in the middle of it to realise what is happening to us.

Several aspects of electronic media were discussed in the first section of the text book. Here we shall discuss in detail the origin and development, programmes, contents, etc. of radio and television.

RADIO BROADCASTING IN INDIA

Radio broadcasting commenced in India in 1927 with two privately owned transmitters at Bombay and Calcutta. Initiative to undertake experimental transmission and establish broadcasting services had however been underway since 1921 when the Times of India, in collaboration with the Post and Telegraph Department broadcast from its Bombay office a special programme of music at the request of the Governor, Sir George Lloyd who tuned in at Poona.

The government took over the transmitters in 1930 and started operating these under the Indian Broadcasting Company, which took upon itself the pioneering task of starting regular broadcasting in India. The Indian Broadcasting Company went into liquidation after a short life of three years; but by now the taste of broadcasting was firmly established and there was public insistence on its continuance. The service was therefore continued by the liquidator of the company at the expense of the Government of India. A separate office of the Controller of Broadcasting was created in March 1935 and Lionel Fielder of the BBC assumed charge as the first Controller of Broadcasting. The opening of the Delhi station on 1 January 1936 was an important landmark in the history of broadcasting in India. The same year the name of the Indian Broadcasting was changed to All India Radio (AIR).

The development and growth from 1936 onwards was steady but slow. At the time of independence, there were nine AIR stations of which—Delhi, Calcutta, Bombay, Madras, Lucknow and Tiruchi came to India. The Lahore, Peshawar and Dacca stations went to Pakistan.

Gandhiji made what was possibly his only broadcast over Akashvani on 12 November 1947. The All India Radio came to be known as Akashvani from 1957. With the passage of time AIR and Akashvani have become synonym for radio broadcasting in India.

AIR presently has 199 radio stations including 184 full fledged stations, ten relay centres, and three exclusive Vividh Bharati commercial centres. AIR presently has 313 transmitters : 142 medium wave, 55 short wave and 116 FM transmitters and provide radio coverage to a population of 98.8 per cent spread over 90 per cent area of the country. (*India 2001*)

Like any other broadcasting organisation, AIR also defined its basic goals as imparting entertainment, information and education to the people. The proportion of these three elements is left to be decided by the planners at each station within some acceptable norms. The basics of communication requirement are popularly known as LIICCA traits (Language, Information, Interest, Correctness, Credibility and Adaptability). Among all these credibility constitutes the top most requirement for the message to be transmitted in a near faithful manner. AIR, through its various formats, steadily started building up and enjoying credibility, which has enabled it to disseminate the desired and desirable messages. The news and current affairs, and special audience programmes are a real source of information, entertainment and education. These programmes are supplemented by film and folk music and other forms of music and spoken word. The programmes for the children, youth and women as well as rural programmes have developed into store houses of information and have contributed significantly to the development process of the country.

The concept of green revolution and the white revolution could not have been popularised but for the continuous efforts made by the AIR to make these programmes acceptable to its country-wide audience.

The role of stock characters in special audience programmes proved to be potential source of entertainment for the listeners. Loha Singh of Patna, Master Ji and Rounaki Ram of Jalandhar, Alla Rakha and Nikky of Srinagar are some of the names which even today are known to be household names and enjoy respectable status in every family within the broadcast domain of the respective stations. These characters live as the real ones and are better known than the artists performing these roles.

The radio broadcasting, over the years, has expanded not only in terms of number of radio stations and transmitters which has made the reach easier, but also in terms of introduction of programmes to suit the changing socio-economic requirements of a developing nation. The National Channel was introduced as a comprehensive set-up for programmes to be available across the country during those hours when most of other stations were silent. The birth of local radio stations was a new phenomenon in the country which was received very well. These stations were meant to meet the specific requirements of a defined small zone without much of the formal atmosphere of a normal broadcasting station. The broadcasting in India has become a three-tier system.

1. National Broadcasts
2. Regional Broadcasts
3. Local Broadcasts

The National Channel was inaugurated on 18 May 1988 and is located at the Jawaharlal Nehru Stadium, New Delhi. Presently it works as a night service covering over 76 per cent population of the country and provides a judicious blend of information and entertainment. Having the whole of India as its operational zone it draws the best available talent in the country. The programme complexion of the channel has been designed to make it representative of the cultural mosaic and ethos of the nation as a whole. Hourly news-bulletins, alternatively in Hindi and English are broadcast from the National Channel throughout the night.

The capital stations and other major stations look after regional broadcasts. The number of local radio stations is now more than eighty. Local radio station covers the geographical district in which the station is located. Microphones have been made directly available to those people who had by then imagined a radio station to be a prohibited for them. The conditions of 'auditions' and 'approvals' were relaxed for local radio stations. The work of some of the local stations like Nagercoil, Kota and Kurukshetra became virtually better known than many of the major stations.

AM & FM Broadcasting

In radio transmission, a microphone converts sound waves into electromagnetic waves that are then picked up by a receiving aerial and fed to a loudspeaker, which converts them back into sound waves.

There are two main ways of doing this–amplitude modulation (AM) used for long and medium wave broadcasts and the frequency modulation (FM) used for VHF (Very High Frequency) broadcasts. Modulation is the process by which the information to be transmitted is impressed on the radio wave, which serves as a carrier. In AM the strength or intensity of the radio frequency carrier is varied in accordance with the information, while in FM the frequency of the carrier is varied instead of its amplitude.

AM sound needs a band width of 20 kHz, while high quality FM requires a band width of 180 kHz for transmission.

The FM broadcasting is being increasingly adopted as it provides listeners with high quality signals free from interference. FM broadcasting for local services is capable of expansion in a way which relieves much of the burden in the low, medium and high frequency bands and would improve conditions for regional, national and international transmissions. The introduction of FM broadcasting is of special significance to developing countries and particularly to tropical areas affected by solar interference.

FM broadcasting has become popular in India and other foreign countries within a very short time. Its objective is to bring about qualitative improvement in broadcasting. Since FM signals do not interfere beyond a certain area, it is possible to operate several stations on the same frequency. There is hardly any disturbance from other radio stations. Another important feature of FM broadcasting is that it provides paging services alongwith the main channel. Paging is one-way communication which is becoming more and more popular among institutions like banks. Radio Data Service is also available on FM. An other feature of FM broadcasting is that the quality of this broadcast is uniform during the day or night, in hills or deserts and the quality is not disturbed due to extraneous factors.

Ever since the government decided to auction FM channels there has been an upsurge in FM broadcasting. According to newsreports* AIR will earn Rs. 530 crores in the first year from the auction of 108 FM stations in 40 cities with a 15 per cent increase every year. The growth in the FM sector would have a spill over effect and generate employment related to entertainment and electronics. The government is also planning to extend FM to small cities. Over a period of time it is expected that this initiative will result in creation of specialised channels providing value added services like market/traffic information, weather forecasts, local events and other local news.

AIR's Services and Special Audience Programmes

Ever since its inception, AIR has been serving the nation through a vast array of its services and programmes. Its News Services Division is one of the largest radio news organisations of its kind in the world. Likewise the contribution of AIR in popularising classical and folk music, Vividh Bharati and commercial broadcasting service, sports commentaries and programmes like "Forces Requests" or "Sainikon Ke Liye" have endeared the AIR to the vast magnitude of its audience throughout the vast expanse of the country.

We shall briefly discuss some of the important AIR's services and programmes. These services and programmes include :

1. News services.
2. Cultural programmes like songs, music and drama.
3. Extension education programmes like rural broadcasting, educational programmes, programmes for the youth and the family planning programmes.
4. External services directed to foreign countries.

---

* *Times of India*, 25 March 2000.
India Today, 27 March 2000.

The News Services Division disseminates news and comments to the listeners in India and abroad. Interestingly the history of news broadcasting in the country dates back to the period of the Indian Broadcasting Company under whose auspices the first news bulletin went on air from the Bombay station on 23 July 1927. The news wing of the AIR came into existence in August 1937 and by 1939 the news bulletins were being broadcast in five Indian languages—Gujarati, Marathi, Pushto, Tamil and Telugu, besides English, Hindustani and Bengali.

AIR's news network is very extensive—the bulk of news comes from its own correspondents—90 regular correspondents in India besides seven correspondents stationed at Colombo, Dhaka, Dubai, Pretoria, Kathmandu, Singapore and Islamabad. Besides subscribing to the news agencies—UNI, PTI and their corresponding Hindi services—*Univarta* and *Bhasha*, AIR has 246 part time correspondents at important district headquarters. The Central Monitoring Services, which monitor bulletins of major organisations of the world, also constitute another important source of news. Presently AIR puts out 314 bulletins daily with a total duration of 39 hours and 29 minutes. These bulletins are broadcast in the home Services from Delhi; the regional news bulletins and bulletins in the External Services constitute important segments of the AIR news programme.

AIR also broadcasts special bulletins such as sports news, slow-speed bulletins and youth bulletins. 'Comments from the Press' are broadcast every day. A number of news based programmes and commentaries in English and Hindi are also regularly broadcast. During Parliament sessions, commentaries in English and Hindi reviewing the day's proceedings in both the Houses are broadcast.

The External Services Division broadcasts programmes for about 70 hours a day in 25 languages for listeners in different parts of the world. These broadcasts project the Indian point of view on world affairs and acquaint the overseas listeners with developments in India. The target areas of the Division span almost all continents including South East Asia, East Africa, Australia, Europe and the neighbouring countries.

The music programmes constitute 40 per cent of the total programmes broadcast over AIR comprising classical, light, folk and film music. The status and recognition given to classical music, both Hindustani and Karnatic, by AIR could not have been awarded by any other agency in the country. Folk music is also given importance in radio broadcasts. The film music, which enjoys its popularity primarily because of broadcast of gramophone records, audio cassettes, and CDs over the vast network of All Inida Radio. Vividh Bharati is primarily meant to popularise film music in the country.

The AIR broadcasts alive the two prestige programmes—National Programmes of Music (Hindustani and Karnatic) on every Saturday and Sunday. Akashvani Sangeet Sammelan is another annual musical treat for serious classical music listeners and lovers.

Commercials were introduced on Akashvani from 1 November 1967 on Vividh Bharati. Now all the primary channel stations, 30 Vividh Bharati centres, all local radio stations and FM metro channels are taking commercials. Vividh Bharati Service provides entertainment for more than 14 hours a day from 34 centres.

More than 80 AIR stations broadcast plays in various languages. Radio adaptation of outstanding novels, short stories and stage plays are also broadcast. Besides original plays, a large number of radio stations regularly broadcast family drama with a view to creating proper impact on society and help eradicate social evils. The National Programme of Plays is broadcast on every fourth Thursday of the month in Hindi and its regional adaptations are broadcast simultaneously by other stations.

The history of sports in India shall not be complete without specific mention of AIR in promoting sports activities in the country and abroad. Running commentaries have now become a regular feature and millions of listeners stay glued to the transistor sets during football, cricket or hockey matches being played in India or in a foreign country. International events find a prominent place in radio broadcasting in the country.

Movements on social and health care aspects like pulse polio drive and malaria eradication programmes, appeals during natural calamities and disasters have shown effective results through radio broadcasts.

Radio Talks and Discussions

Broadcasting of talks and discussion by a radio station is undertaken according to a plan drawn up after due deliberation and consultation with the subject matter experts. This plan is called the Talk Schedule. This is prepared on a quarterly basis and besides talks, comprises interviews, discussions, symposia, etc. In case of topicality and some other relevant and valuable material being made available, it may not be possible to adhere to a plan drawn up some weeks in advance.

Talks are an important means of education and information; it is therefore essential talks are scheduled according to a plan which would allow certain themes to be properly developed. Selection of subjects for broadcast is made keeping in view the general interest of the audience. There are a number of useful and interesting subjects which cannot be adequately covered by a single talk. In such cases a series of three to four talks are scheduled so as to cover various aspects of a subject.

In this context it will be interesting to mention that the AIR instituted the prestigeous Patel Memorial Lectures, in memory of free India's first Minister for Information and Broadcasting. The series comprises three lectures of about 4000 words each on three days fairly close to each other, the subject as also the language being left to the speaker. The first lecture was delivered by C. Rajagopalachariar on 14 August 1955 in the Convocation Hall of Bombay University and was relayed by all stations. Some of these lectures, which are subsequently published in book form, are remarkable for the range of interests and subjects and the erudition of the speakers who are well known men of letters, leading scholars, scientists, administrators and public men.

Radio and television programmes can be broadly classified in two categories : those aimed at general audience–music, plays, news, features, talks and discussions; and specific programmes which are directed to particular segment to audiences–rural and agricultural development programmes and broadcasts for students, women, tribal people, industrial workers and armed forces.

The transmission of such programmes is among the most important of AIR's activities. Though these programmes vary in content and presentations, they possess distinctive characteristics because of the specific requirement of the audience they address; these broadcasts have certain features in common–particularly broadcasts for school and university students and those for rural listeners. These programmes share certain constructive goals of nation building. Both radio and TV are used for such programmes. Since most of the TV programmes–DD Metro in particular as compared to the National Channel–DD I. and other private channels are increasingly catering to entertainment–serials, soaps, films and film based programmes; it is the radio which is looked upon as a medium for development broadcasting.

Radio Programmes for Rural Audience

Radio broadcasting for rural listeners has been of special significance for a country like India whose economy still continues to be predominantly agriculture based. It is a matter of great interest to know that rural broadcasting in India is older than AIR. An eminent broadcaster, K. S. Mullick in his book, *Tangled Tapes, The Inside Story of Indian Broadcasting*, points out that the local authorities of atleast two places– North-West Frontier Province (now part of Pakistan) and Madras installed a transmitter, and villagers having been provided with battery operated radio sets, rural programmes were introduced. When the two transmitters were eventually taken over by AIR, rural broadcasting was made an integral part of the schedule of every new station that subsequently came up.

The establishment of the Farm and Home units to provide relevant, timely and local specific information areas has proved to be very useful. The emphasis in these farm and home programmes is on a direct method of presentation, dictated by the need to convey hard core scientific and technical information and quick timely guidance. In the broadcast of rural programmes AIR can derive great satisfaction at having gradually won the confidence of the traditionally conservative farmers and helping them through the use of new and improved techniques to diversify crops, achieve higher production with obvious economic advantage to themselves and the country.

Farm and Home units function at various stations of AIR. The average duration of farm and home broadcasts is 60-100 minutes per day from each such unit. The broadcasts also include programmes for rural women and rural children. Broadcast of mother and child care series in collaboration with UNICEF and state governments has been undertaken by many AIR stations. The main thrust has been on issues relating to rights of the child, gender bias and child abuse, etc. Environmental protection programmes receive adequate emphasis in these broadcast to retain ecological balance.

Farm school on air as a method of communicating distant education on farming has been adopted by many AIR stations. Besides imparting technical and other information, the thrust of the broadcasts are : (i) dissemination of information relating to ways and means for increasing production of cereals, oilseeds, pulses, vegetables, fruits, etc.; (ii) diversification of agriculture, social forestry, preservation of environment and farm forestry; (iii) poverty alleviation schemes, health and sanitation, etc.; (iv) adult education programmes and (v) role of panchayats in rural development.

Educational Programmes

In AIR's priorities of utility programmes for specific audiences, school broadcasting came next after programmes for rural listeners. Programmes for schools were started by stations under the Indian Broadcasting Company and have been a regular feature since AIR came into existence. At the initial stage, these broadcasts were intended for students at the secondary school level, subsequently these programmes were extended in support of University Correspondence Courses; and broadcasts for primary schools were also introduced.

The educational programmes on TV are at different levels ranging from basic health education for the not-so-educated to the higher education programmes for university students.

In 1961 India's first School Television Service was commissioned at Delhi for the institutions run by the Delhi Municipal Corporation. At present, regular school TV programmes are produced and telecast from Delhi and Calcutta Kendras. ETV programmes are also telecast from a number of states in different languages covering both formal and informal education. The software for these programmes are produced by the Central Institute for Education Technology in Delhi and state institutes of education technology of different states.

To put quality education within the reach of students in small villages and towns, the University Grants Commission has a countrywide classroom telecast on the National Network. Besides this, syllabus based programmes for the students of Indira Gandhi National Open University are also being telecast on the National Network.

Doordarshan has only recently introduced a knowledge channel–Gyan Darshan–for telecasting educational programmes produced by the Indira Gandhi National Open University (IGNOU). With the channel devoted to exclusively educational programmes, the education sector-basic education, secondary and tertiary level education as well as professional education in business management, computer sciences and other emerging areas, is bound to receive a significant boost.

Family Welfare Programmes

AIR stations broadcast more than 8,500 programmes on Family Welfare every month in all the major languages/dialects of our country. Programmes on AIDS, TB, Dengue, Sexually Transmitted Diseases, water-borne diseases, malaria eradication programme, child survival and safe motherhood programme, sterilization, vasectomy, tubectomy, etc. are broadcast under the title of family welfare programmes. Success stories are also broadcast regularly.

Programmes for the Armed Forces

Programmes for the armed forces were introduced from the Delhi station during World War II when for certain periods entertainment used to be broadcast for British soldiers and serving this country. Now these programmes are broadcast by a number of stations of AIR varying in duration from 30 minutes to 2 hours a day. Apart from providing light fare which is welcome to those in isolated posts without other means of entertainment, these programmes are very useful in giving information sought by officers and men about rules and regulations, family benefits, careers for their children and help in planning their post-retirement years. An interesting feature of these broadcasts is the programme presented by various units using their own musical talent.

Yuva Vani

There are not many broadcasting organizations in the world which could claim a separate channel for the youth as the AIR has. The programme 'Yuva Vani' (The voice of youth) was started from Delhi on 21 July 1969, which, by coincidence, the day on which man first landed on the moon.

The programme caters to the age group 15-30 years which is a spectrum of several sub-groups 15 to 17, 18-20, 21-24 and 25-29 years. Yuva Vani caters to all these groups through their involvement and participation in these programmes.

Besides the above programmes, the programmes for tribals, women, children and industrial workers also. All these programmes provide entertainment, information and education. Since these sectors are so diffused, the programme planners sometimes find it difficult to focus attention on specific objectives.

Radio Plays and Features

Like all other broadcasts a radio play has only two means of creating its effect–sound and silence. It differs from a stage play or a film play, because a radio play cannot appeal to the most dominant of human senses-seeing; it appeals only to aural sense; the success of a radio play depends upon the extent to which a listener can convert sound into pictures. In radio programmes silence is as important as sound. Every pause produces some effect, good or bad.

A practical step towards the encouragement of radio drama was the institution of Akashvani Awards for plays in 1974. In this annual competition any play broadcast from any station in the previous calendar year ending 31 December is eligible.

A feature is a documented programme on a single theme or subject, composed and presented in a radio-dramatic form. Feature has also been defined as 'creative interpretation of reality'. In a feature a theme or idea is projected with an imaginative mixture of music, poetry, narration 'effects', dramatisation and actuality in such a way which creates an impact on listener's mind.

Some of the feature programmes produced by AIR have received awards at the international level, the best known being the programme 'Lali and the Lions of Gir,' by Melville De Mellow, which got the Italia Prize in 1964.

In all radio programmes use of actuality enhances the impact and credibility of the programme. Audio actuality, which is pre- recorded sound is used in newscast. For instance, a radio reporter may do a feature on consumer protection and record an interview with a consumer activist about the implementation of the Consumer Protection Act. He may then select a 20-second portion of the interview in the feature. Use of live actuality or 'sound effects' are regarded as typical of a radio programme. Some of the typically Indian 'sound effects' like spinning wheel, Persian wheel, typical kitchen noises are used in the radio programmes.

Radio which had been, till recently, relegated to a back slot in media priorities has staged a remarkable come back. AIR is even today the most potent medium to carry message to the rural masses. The direction in which current developments are taking place are in the realm of FM radio. The opening up of FM broadcasting to private operators will allow 12 FM channels in the large metros—Delhi, Mumbai, Calcutta and Bangalore and 4-8 channels in 35 other locations. It will be possible to have separate channels for Indian/western classical music, Pop, Rock and other forms of music as well as cinema music channels.

Alongwith contents, technological developments have also contributed to promoting the reach of radio to masses. The use of satellite for radio broadcast, and uplinking and down linking facilities available at various stations have added new dimensions to radio broadcasting in the country. The use of telephone lines and microphone links now within broadcasting organisations, and also of OB van and phone-in facilities are other important features which would enhance the quality of radio programmes. In future the following services will ensure the wider reach and popularity of radio :

1. Radio on demand
2. Auto play back system
3. Unmanned broadcast set-up
4. Expansion of sky radio
5. Mobile radio

The Research and Development Wing of AIR is working some of these concepts. The possibility of introducing these systems, supported by a strong power network, shall make broadcasting more professional and market friendly in the days to come. In near future 100 per cent coverage, both by area and population, will be a reality and narrow casting a true slogan. In the word of video channels, sound broadcasting has its own charm. Radio is certainly not meant to fade away, since it has a direct approach to the listeners on road, a straight call to the farmer in the field and pins hope on rickshawpuller and a solitary reaper alike.

In an interesting debate, Does radio have a place in our lives? It was pointed out that AIR had become like so many other public sector enterprises—mediocre, and that it was fast becoming a museum piece. Some other observations were : Any good programme happens by accident, not by design; AIR has not developed on the lines of BBC which is state funded but not state-run; everything is done by the book, regardless of whether it is the right decision or not.

At the same time it was also pointed out : Radio would continue to prosper because it fulfils a need-contact with the world which can be established inexpensively and instantly; since independence it has been the cultural mouthpiece of the country and that with a little nurturing it can become the most influential mass medium in the country.

Radio certainly has glorious future provided it is given freedom to innovate itself and licences are granted to the private radio stations. It will certainly work better in a competitive environment. The sound broadcaster will have to be more specific on programme contents. The people on the road and patients in hospitals, the distant trekkers in the mountains, the fishermen on the sea will continue to bank on radio broadcast. Smaller and specific listener groups will be the micro-concept of future radio because narrowcasting is bound to emerge as important necessity during the days to come.

Radio has given name and fame to several of the eminent persons associated with its working in the distant past. Some of these are—Nirad Choudhuri, the author who was a talks officer in Akashvani, Delhi; Mark Tully, for many years the Chief of the BBC Delhi Bureau and Melville De Mellow–the eminent news reader and commentator, whose almost ten hour long commentary during the funeral of Mahatma Gandhi is long remembered as a model of excellence in radio broadcasting. The future of such a medium cannot be but promising.

Principles of Writing for Radio and Television

Writing for radio and TV is an art which can be cultivated only after proper practice and due deliberation. While the basic principles of writing for the media are fundamentally the same for print or broadcast media–the presentation has to be different owing to the differing characteristics of the three media–press, radio and television.

Radio and TV are called electronic media because they are electronically operated. In the contemporary society, these two are very important media of mass communication with the clear advantages of their unparalleled reach throughout the country, speed and immediacy.

Radio as the channel between the writer and his audience uses acoustic signals i.e. it addresses itself to one single sense organ at the receiver's end : the ear. Every item of information, all communications which have to reach the public must be made audible, must be converted into speech, into spoken words, just as for example, where writing for a newspaper or a book is concerned, every item of information must be readable, converted into written words.

TV, as a mass media, has registered exponential growth in terms of its reach, range of programmes and number of channels. With the support of satellite technology, TV can reach even the remotest corner of the country. TV is a powerful medium because it is credible medium. One can hear and see an event happening or a news breaking at the same time. Since seeing is believing, things that people may not believe, otherwise, become believable when shown on TV. World events of historical significance–Vietnam War on the American TV screens, or the visuals of students demonstrations at the Tienanman Square in China or the visuals of the Gulf War in your drawing room TV have powerful impact on the viewers. Writing for TV, therefore, involves lot of preparation and planning; it also pre-supposes team work which would mean working with camera and sound team, performers/speakers, graphic artists and several others. The most important consideration in writing for the media for print on the broadcast media is the space. Time is to radio/TV what space is to a newspaper. News items for broadcast media have to be shorter than those for print.

Writing for radio must be precise, brief, properly proportioned should enhance the charm. It is not easy to be simple, direct or brief. You must develop the skills of writing briefly and to the point and resist the temptation of writing prolonged scripts, talks, features or dramas. The time factor is all important. It does not reflect good taste to exceed the scheduled duration, it is in fact a trespass on somebody else's time.

You must begin by making quite sure of your material. You must get hold of the facts. Only once you have done this are you in a position to convey true and correct information to the public. The basic rule of all journalism is simply this : "Never write about anything of which you are not exactly informed." First master the material thoroughly, and then the words to present it will follow.

In order to master the material, you will need to carry out the most thorough research possible. Start by going to the archives or the library of your broadcasting organisation. There, or perhaps also in the municipal or university library, get hold of some literature on your subject. Note down the date of publication and then complement this material by reading magazines and specialist journals. Bring your knowledge up-to-date, because radio is the medium for conveying the here and now. While arranging the material you must ask yourself if you are doing justice to your subject. Is your information complete? Have you not forgotten anything important? Have you answered the questions–Who? What? When? Where? How? and Why?

How to Write for Radio

1. Use right words so that the sentences are not cluttered up. Have a conversational style of writing which is simple and uncomplicated. It helps in easy reading out. Keep sentences short so that a listener can grasp what you are saying. Prefer active voice in writing.
2. Minimise the use of abbreviations in the radio script. Do not use symbols in the script i.e. 10 per cent instead of 10%. Write script legibly.
3. Names of characters and direction for music, sound effects, and so on are all given in capitals and double-spaced, and written in all caps and underlined.

4. Dialogue is written in the double spaced and lower case like typical prose, to differentiate it from instructions. This helps the production people and artists to tell at a glance, what is dialogue and what is not.
5. Add familiarity and humour in the script.
6. Do not repeat what the listeners already know.
7. Do not try to influence your personal likes, dislikes, beliefs, attitudes, etc.
8. Mention time required on the script.

Writing for Television

The essential difference between a TV script is that the visual component is very important in the TV script. Equally essential is the careful blending of both–the audio and video components–so as to leave a harmonious impact on the viewers.

Before scripting for TV programmes, it is essential to research the subject, visit various locations and sites and have a feel of the general environment and atmosphere. This exploration of all aspects including requirement of the crew and duration of their stay, logistics, costs, etc. need to be adequately undertaken. This exercise is called recce. The primary objective of recce enables the writer to develop the outline sufficiently so as to have a proper idea of phases of programme production.

Characteristics of a Good Script

1. Should be simple and clear,
2. Developed logically,
3. Should maintain the overall purpose of the programme,
4. Should reinforce the viewers interest,
5. Should not be too long and too heavily loaded with content,
6. Should be based on proper research inputs (authentic and arbitrary),
7. Should have appropriate pace and rhythm and give occasional respite in the middle of the programme, and
8. The script should allow the visuals to 'breathe' and 'speak for themselves'. Narration should not smother the visuals.

A script writer plays a key role in TV programme production. He works in "the language of the television". He translates the ideas and the content of the subject of presentation into the language of TV i.e. the language of pictures, words, sounds and electronic effects.

1. Definition of objectives in behavioural terms i.e. what a learner of a viewer is expected to accomplish after viewing a programme.
2. Analysis of content and specification of themes and subthemes based on research. The content is arranged in a sequential manner and converted into appropriate visual terms at the stage.
3. Selection of the most suitable format for presentation.
4. Preparation of the story board/camera script/shot division.
5. Specification of content, programme length and characteristics of the target audience.
6. Final layout of the programme by identifying shots and listing the segments and subthemes.
7. Preparation of the content draft.
8. Pretesting and modifying the draft.
9. Finalising the script which becomes the narration.

And here you are as a TV script writer.

Radio and television are the two major components of electronic media. Both these media have become so pervasive that they directly touch our lives and provide us with information, entertainment and education. Whereas radio symbolises the majesty of the spoken word, in television programming both video and audio are equally important. The language used for radio programme should be simple and direct; difficult words and long sentences must be avoided. In television programmes script should allow the visuals to 'breathe' and 'speak' for themselves. Narration should not smother the visuals.

The script for talks is sometimes vetted by the programme staff of the two organisations. The object of vetting is to ensure good taste and the responsibility of the organisation as a public service. The talk should be of right length (about 110 words to a minute), and it should also be lucid, interesting and 'broadcast-worthy.' 'Broadcast-worthy' means that it should be written to suit the medium of broadcasting. A broadcast script is written so that it should be read aloud. Those who write for the broadcast media have therefore to adopt a technique quite different from that required for the printed matter. One can read printed matter at one's own speed but one has to listen to the broadcast talk at the speed of a talker. A printed sentence can be read twice but a listener cannot ask the talker to repeat what he has said or to halt while he grasps what the talker has said or looks up a word in the dictionary.

Each sentence of a broadcast script must, therefore, be clearly understood or the listener will lose the context and will have no means of going back and taking it up where he lost it.

TELEVISION

The invention of television–essentially a twentieth-century phenomenon–was the result of combination of earlier technological developments in the fields of radio-broadcasting, motion pictures, photography and the electronic camera. A Scottish engineer, John Baird, is generally credited with the invention of television, who in 1924, in an improvised laboratory in his lodgings in Hastings, England succeeded in transmitting the form of pictures from one place to another. In April 1927, the American Telephone and Telegraph Company (AT&T) gave public demonstration in which a speech by the US Secretary of Commerce, Herbert Hoover, was broadcast from Washington and watched in New York by an invited audience. The event made front-page headlines in the next day's newspapers.

The BBC, on 2 November 1936, initiated the first regular television service in the world. In May 1937, the BBC televised the Coronation. A couple of months later television cameras went to Wimbledon for the first time. The World War II resulted in six years interruption and TV broadcasting was resumed only in 1946. The United States launched the world's first regular colour broadcasts in 1953. By 1955, the "Eurovision networks" were established linking the West European nations.

The General Conference of UNESCO, which was hosted by India in New Delhi in 1956, made a provision of $ 20,000 to set up a pilot project to study the use of TV as a medium of education, rural uplift and community development. Television was introduced in India in 1959.

Development of television broadcasting proceeded at a very slow pace in the first twenty years of its existence in the country. But right from the very beginning Doordarshan's role as an agent of education and social change was clearly recognised. In 1961, Doordarshan was used as support to middle and higher secondary school education. Its experiments in teaching of science, mathematics and language were proved most successful and received appreciation from many UNESCO experts (Social objectives of Doordarshan given in the Annexure).

It was only in April, 1965 that a general service was started. It was for one hour a day on four days of the week. On 15 August 1965 the service was made daily. It was then, under the guidance of Prime Minister

Indira Gandhi who at that time was also Minister for Information and Broadcasting, that television started making big strides in the country.

'Krishi Darshan' for rural viewers was inaugurated on January 26, 1967, by the Prime Minister, Mrs. Indira Gandhi. It was telecast on Wednesdays and Fridays for 20 minutes each day, and served 80 villages (around Delhi) provided with community sets. This pilot project was initiated by the Department of Atomic Energy, in collaboration with the Ministry of Information and Broadcasting, All India Radio, the Indian Agricultural Research Institute and the Delhi Administration. From July 15, 1970 the duration was increased to 30 minutes, and the programme was also broadcast on Mondays.

The seventies saw major expansion of television. Doordarshan Kendra Bombay was commissioned in October 1972 and Doordarshan Kendra Srinagar in January 1973. Subsequently Doordarshan Kendras were set up at Calcutta, Madras, Lucknow, Amritsar and Jalandhar.

Satellite Instructional Television Experiment (1975)

The SITE was a one-year pilot project in 1975-76, primarily undertaken to experiment with television through satellite communication to broadcast special programmes in six states which included 2400 villages. The experiment aroused wide international interest. India was the developing country in the region to undertake an experiment using space age technology to bring its millions into the mainstream of national development, make them aware of the changing pattern of present day urban life and help them to harness their resources for optimum benefits.

One media analyst evaluated the significance of SITE as : SITE means a lot of things apart from being an experiment. For one thing, it made India TV-conscious and of an advanced style of TV technology. TV is no more confined to the main metropolitan centres. It has suddenly made its presence felt in the villages of Karnataka, Andhra, Orissa, Madhya Pradesh, Bihar and Rajasthan. Hundreds of engineers, technicians and mechanics are acquiring new skills and vast experience. Programmers, broadcasters and telecasters are getting new insights into the medium.

After its termination, a terrestrial service was provided by setting up transmitters at Raipur, Jaipur, Muzaffarpur, Gulbarga, Hyderabad and Sambalpur. In addition, the low-power transmitter installed at Pij by the ISRO was also taken over by the Doordarshan as part of the SITE continuity to serve the Kheda area of Gujarat. The next major development, an organisational one, was the separation of Radio and Television on 1 April 1976. Thus, during just two decades, Doordarshan expanded to cover more and more areas and to put out a varied programme fare in its transmission, including direct telecast of important national and international events.

Doordarshan from 1982 Onwards

The next phase of expansion was undertaken in 1982, just before the Ninth Asian Games in Delhi. It was decided to switch to colour transmission because it was thought that coverage of the Asiad in black and white would embarrass India in the international community.

Then came the great leap forward with the launching of the multipurpose satellite, INSAT-1A. This marked the initiation of the National Programme relayed simultaneously from different centres. The launching of the National Programme also marked the beginning of news networking in Doordarshan. Coupled with the microwave linkage, INSAT helped Doordarshan to bring international events to the homes of the viewers. The INSAT provided the greatest impetus to the expansion and coverage of Doordarshan services. The coverage of 'Asian Games', 'NAM' and 'CHOGM' was made possible by the use of Satellite technology and microwave linkage.

Having attained the skill and expertise to make use of satellite for television programming, Doordarshan started with the operation of its second satellite INSAT-1B, a regular INSAT service in six States of India—Andhra Pradesh, Orissa, Maharashtra, Gujarat, Bihar and Uttar Pradesh.

In 1983, a special plan for television expansion at an outlay of Rs. 68 crore was approved. The plan envisaged establishment of High Power (10 KW) transmitters (HPTs) and Low Power (100 Watt) transmitters (LPTs) in various parts of the country including some important project areas, so as to raise the total number of transmitters in the network to 180 by the end of the Sixth Plan. With the implementation of the Plan, Doordarshan added an unprecedented number of 126 transmitters to its network. Beginning 1 July, 1984 one transmitter was commissioned almost every day for a period of about four months. All these transmitters set up under the special plan, relayed programmes from Doordarshan Kendra, Delhi via INSAT-1B.

Many policy changes started taking place after the ASIAD. First, the government realized that the development of television pivoted around concerns of economics, and one huge source of revenue were the private advertisers. This led to an increasing number of commercial spots on television. The advent of commercials led to the second significant development, namely, an increase in entertainment programmes. The earlier reticence for entertainment was replaced by a 'liberalization' of the policies, and more entertainment programmes began to emerge. The third development was the adoption of sponsored programmes for television, and the government sold time to the advertisers to air these independently produced programmes. This quasi-commercialization saw the advent of a greater number of entertainment programmes of several different kinds, from live sports to serialized soap operas, to extremely powerful serials like *Ramayan* and *Mahabharat*.

During 1984, India's first soap opera '*Hum Log*' was introduced with the aim of promoting women's welfare, family planning, reinforcing positive social values and exposing social evils. This programme became very popular and made a headway for serials like '*Yeh Jo Hai Zindagi*', '*Khandan*', '*Idhar Udhar*', '*Ados Pados*', etc. Since then Doordarshan has been showing sponsored serials in its National Programme. Another serial *'Buniyaad'* was also a big hit. The introduction of the second channel at Delhi and Bombay in 1984 and 1985 added to Doordarshan coverage.

Doordarshan's teletext service known as INTEXT was started in November 1985. It provides the viewers with news, rail and air timings, weather information and other data of common interest with the help of decoders.

In 1984, a second channel was added at Delhi to provide an alternative viewing option to the heterogeneous metropolitan population. Later this facility was extended to viewers in Bombay, Calcutta and Madras. In 1993, these four terrestrial transmitters were linked through satellite to provide more entertainment for the urban audience. This service, known as DD-2 Metro Entertainment Channel, is now available terrestrially in 54 cities. In other parts of the country the programmes could be received using a dish antenna. The Metro Channel caters to the younger generation and has programmes in Hindi and English. News Bulletins produced by established private companies are also telecast on this channel.

To provide additional software in the major languages of the country, many of which are spoken by more than 50 million, Doordarshan started Regional Language Satellite Channels. The programmes on these channels include the regional service, which is available terrestrially in the concerned state and additional programmes which could be received through the use of a dish antenna. As the foot prints of the INSAT Satellite cover the whole country, the Regional Language Programmes are now available for all people in the country, irrespective of their place of residence. At present Doordarshan has 11 regional language satellite channels.

Over the years Doordarshan has emerged as one of the largest television service organisations in the world. There have been far reaching developments in television broadcasting in the country : Doordarshan becoming autonomous after Prasar Bharati Act was notified in November 1997, Supreme Court Judgement on freedom of airwaves, the latest being restructuring of Prasar Bharati Board comprising All India Radio and Doordarshan.

Prasar Bharati (Broadcasting Corporation of India)

The first serious effort to legislate a Comprehensive Broadcast Law was the Draft Akash Bharati Bill, 1978, proposed by the Working Group on Autonomy for Akashvani and Doordarshan, constituted under the chairmanship of Mr. B. G. Verghese. The Draft Bill, intended to be an aid to legislation, provided for a simple statute establishing the National Broadcast Trust, and set out its objectives, scope, powers and basic structure. It was, at that point of time, hoped that the Akash Bharati Act establishing the National Broadcast Trust would come into force from January 1979 and Akashvani and Doordarshan would cease to be the attached offices of the Ministry of Information and Broadcasting. What happened to this initial effort is now a part of history, the Janata party government, which introduced the Bill, with diluted provision for autonomy, was voted out of office before the legislation could be enacted.

Prasar Bharati Act, 1990

It was not for another twelve years, that the Parliament in 1990, enacted the Prasar Bharati (Broadcasting Corporation of India) Act, 1990. The Act provided for establishment of a Broadcasting Corporation of India. A unique feature of the Act was that it enlarged the definition of broadcasting. According to section 2 (c), "Broadcasting means the dissemination of any form of communication like signs, signals, writing, pictures, images and sounds of all kinds by transmission of electromagnetic waves through cables intended to be received by the general public either directly or indirectly through the medium of relay stations and all its grammatical variations and cognate expressions shall be construed accordingly". It is more comprehensive because it takes care of the transmission of electromagnetic waves through space or through cables.

Objectives

The Corporation shall, in the discharge of its functions, be guided by the following objectives, namely :

(a) upholding the unity and integrity of the country and the values enshrined in the Constitution;
(b) safeguarding the citizen's right to be informed freely, truthfully and objectively on all matters of public interest, national or international and presenting a fair and balanced flow of information including contrasting views without advocating any opinion or ideology of its own;
(c) paying special attention to the fields of education and spread of literacy, agriculture, rural development, environment, health and family welfare and science and technology;
(d) providing adequate coverage to the diverse cultures and languages of the various regions of the country by broadcasting appropriate programmes;
(e) providing adequate coverage to sports and games so as to encourage healthy competition and the spirit of sportsmanship;
(f) providing appropriate programmes keeping in view the special needs of the youth;
(g) informing and stimulating the national consciousness in regard to the status and problems of women and paying special attention to the upliftment of women;
(h) promoting social justice and combating exploitation, inequality and such evils as untouchability and advancing the welfare of the weaker sections of the society;
(i) safeguarding the rights of the working classes and advancing their welfare;
(j) serving the rural and weaker sections of the people and those residing in border regions, backward or remote areas;
(k) providing suitable programmes keeping in view the special needs

of the minorities and tribal communities;

(l) taking special steps to protect the interests of children, the blind, the aged, the handicapped and other vulnerable sections of the people;

(m) promoting national integration by broadcasting in a manner that facilitates communication in the languages in India; and facilitating the distribution of regional broadcasting services in every state in the languages of that state;

(n) providing comprehensive broadcast coverage through the choice of appropriate technology and the best utilization of the broadcast frequencies available and ensuring high quality reception;

(o) promoting research and development activities in order to ensure that radio and television broadcast technology are constantly updated; and

(p) expanding broadcasting facilities by establishing additional channels of transmission at various levels.

Broadcasting Council

The Act, in terms of Section 14 (1), also provides for the establishment of the Broadcasting Council, to receive and consider complaints from any person or group of persons alleging that a certain programme or broadcast or the functioning of the Corporation in specific cases or in general is not in accordance with the objectives for which the Corporation is established and to advise the Corporation in the discharge of its functions in accordance with the objectives set out in Section 12.

Parliamentary Committee

13. (1) There shall be constituted a Committee consisting of twenty-two members of Parliament, of whom fifteen from the House of the People to be elected by the Members thereof and seven from the Council of States to be elected by the Members thereof in accordance with the system of proportional representation by means of the single transferable vote, to oversee that the Corporation discharges its functions in accordance with the provisions of this Act and, in particular, the objectives set out in Section 12 and submit a report thereon to Parliament.

13. (2) The Committee shall function in accordance with such rules as may be made by the Speaker of the House of the People.

The Prasar Bharati Bill remained a dead letter with the successive governments, never serious about autonomy for the official electronic media. In fact, the demand for autonomy for AIR and TV dates back to mid-sixties, when the first ever-expert committee (the Chanda Committee) went into the issue. During the past five years, two committees–Paswan Committee on National Media Policy and Nitish Sengupta Committee on AIR and TV–have come up with several suggestions for improvements in the Prasar Bharati Act and bring them in line with present day needs.

The Union Government in 1997 brought about sweeping changes in the revamped Prasar Bharati Act. The amendments, essentially sought to remedy a series of anomalies and flaws in the Act, pointed out by media analysts and underlined in the recommendations of several expert committees. The one provision, which had attracted widespread criticism relating to the constitution of a 22-member Parliamentary Committee to oversee the function of the Corporation, has been scrapped. It had been repeatedly stressed by a number of media critics and legal luminaries that there was no need for the Parliamentary Committee when every Ministry, including the Ministry of Information and Broadcasting, had Standing Committees and Consultative Committees. The Sengupta Committee, appointed to review the implementation of Prasar Bharati Act, also recommended that the Parliamentary Committee to oversee the performance of Prasar Bharati was not really needed.

It was generally feared that the unreasonable clause, instead of helping the Indian electronic media grow wings before it learnt to fly on its own, would place it in the hands of 22 masters to fool around with.

The Ordinance also scrapped the Broadcasting Council envisaged under Section 14. The rationale for doing so was the overlapping functions of the Broadcasting Council and the Broadcasting Authority of India, proposed to be set up under the Broadcasting Bill.

Another significant feature of the amendments relates to public service broadcasting. It would now be the primary duty of the Corporation to "organize and conduct public service broadcasting to inform, educate and entertain the public."

The amended Act clarifies that the Corporation would ensure comprehensive broadcast coverage through the choice of appropriate technology and the best utilization of "broadcast frequencies made available for public service broadcasting", and would also ensure high quality reception. It has also deleted a provision in the earlier Act which aims the central government with powers to determine the maximum limit of broadcast time in respect of advertisements. The Centre would no longer be involved in fixing limits for levy fees and other charges. The amended Act gives full freedom to the Corporation in this respect.

The government has set up a committee to suggest restructuring of Prasar Bharati. The Committee has suggested that Doordarshan should adopt new technology–create a Direct-To-Home (DTH) platform, Internet and broadband multimedia, etc. DD should be a content provider and build synergy with other players in the field. It should follow public service broadcasting model but at the same time maximise its revenue so as to reduce dependence on the government.

Public Service Broadcasting

The role of DD as a public service broadcaster has been repeatedly emphasised. The Sub-committee of the Consultative Committee of the Ministry of Information and Broadcasting, appointed in 1995 to make recommendations about the National Media Policy said : The Sub-committee recognizes that for public broadcasting, adequate funding in the form of state support is necessary. The content of programmes or software is often dictated by the funding and therefore the Sub-committee strongly recommends that the aspect should receive the attention of the government and an institutional system be worked out. The national broadcasters–Akashvani and Doordarshan should bear the responsibility to offer a high quality public service broadcasting that informs, educates and entertains the people. Adequate care should be taken to enable the setting up of non-commercial broadcasting stations to be run by universities, educational institutions, panchayats/local bodies, State Governments, etc.

Freedom of Airwaves–Supreme Court Judgement–February 1995

The Supreme Court of India ruling on airwaves delivered on 9 February 1995 was widely hailed in the following ways : "Public Rules the Air Waves", "Freedom One Step Closer", "Freeing ....." This landmark judgement of the Supreme Court held that the airwaves and frequencies were public property and asked the Central Government to establish an independent, autonomous authority to regulate their use. It lays down important guidelines for Broadcast Law, and also enlarges the scope of Section 19 (1) of the Indian Constitution.

While resolving the litigation between the Cricket Association of Bengal (CAB) and Doordarshan over uplinked self generated signals to a foreign satellite for viewers abroad, the Court in its trend setting verdict delivered by three-judge bench headed by Justice P. B. Sawant (now Chairman, Press Council of India) said that it was the fundamental right of the telecaster to 'educate' the viewers of the game, to watch the telecast was the viewers' sacred right to be entertained. An organiser like the CAB or the BCCI, could not be placed in the same scale as the business organisations wanting to make a large profit by telecasting the series.

The judgement unanimously lays down that monopoly over broadcasting, whether by government or by anybody else, is inconsistent with right to free speech. It is rightly emphasised by Justice Reddy that, "state control really means governmental control, which, in turn means control of the political party or parties in power for the time being. Such control is bound to colour the views, information and opinions conveyed by the media." The unanimous conclusion is that "the broadcasting media should be under the control of the public as distinct from government."

New Information and Communication Technologies

In the contemporary media scenario, broadcasting organisations are becoming more and more technology oriented. Their objective is no longer to be only a programme or content provider—they have to organise themselves to adapt the latest technological innovations. The technology is fast becoming more versatile, sophisticated and cheaper, with the result that access to radio, television, and now even to internet is no longer confined only to a particular section of society. The application of technology to nation building activities—literacy and education, social awareness and information dissemination has been another positive development. We shall discuss some of the important technologies directly related to radio and TV broadcasting.

New Information and Communication Technologies (NICTs) have brought human kind face-to-face with fundamental changes : by abolishing distances they are instrumental in shaping the societies of tomorrow, the most accurate, up-to-date information (in fact information as it is developing) is now available to anyone, anywhere in the world, often in real time and reaches the remotest regions. Some of the NICTs—photocopying, video-recording, facsimile, E-mail, satellite telecommunication and broadcasting, personal computer, etc. are characterised by being cost-effective, cheap, reliable, user-friendly, flexible and having large capacities.

Unlike traditional technologies, newer technologies have special attributes like greater interactivity and knowledge-intensivity. Traditional media like writing and printing, electronic media like radio and television are essentially one-way media and their interactive capabilities are limited. Moreover, the limited interactivity is not live or spontaneous but occurs after a considerable time gap. The emergence of new forms of electronic media like teleconferencing is of particular interest for distance learning because of their interactive capabilities.

Satellite

A satellite is a device that orbits the earth receiving processing and transmitting signals, generating images or data to be transmitted back to earth, such as weather pictures. A communication satellite relays radio or TV signals from one point on the earth's surface to another. A Direct Broadcast Satellite (DBS) broadcasts TV and radio signals over a wide area from an earth station via a satellite to homes (received with a dish aerial). According to Schoenbeck, satellite is really nothing more than a radio relay station, but it offers an advantage that is missing in all other systems–the capacity of a direct line-of-sight path to 98% of the earth's surface. A satellite can 'see' a much wider area than a transmitter on a hill. Remote areas can be served and difficult-terrain will not pose problems in providing direct link with a satellite.

> A satellite system can provide services such as nation-wide television, high speed data transmission, teleconference and computer interworking. International satellites provide clear links for voice, vision and data transfer across continents. The satellites 'assemble' the biggest ever-world audiences for witnessing important events simultaneously.

Satellites have, for the first time, created in the human history a genuinely global communications network. Satellite also transmits television signals; consequently news broadcasting has been most dramatically affected. The first event watched world-wide by the people was the landing of the man on the moon, images of which were beamed from US satellites.

Communication between satellite and the Earth is through microwaves. Transmitters on the ground modulate the message signal and transmit them to the satellite. A satellite contains microwaves receivers and transmitters for bidirectional transmission. The signals from the Earth are received, converted into and intermediate frequency signals and then remodulated on to a different carrier for retransmission back to Earth. This sub-system of the satellite is known as a transponder. A transponder on board a satellite receives signals from the earth, filters it, amplifies it and retransmits it to a different point on earth. A transponder can generally carry 1000 telephone conversations or one colour television.

Optical Fibre

Fine strand of glass or plastic protected by a surrounding material that is used for the convenient transmission of light signals; another simple definition of Optical fibres is : extremely thin and pure glass fibres which are used to guide light waves without loss in transmission.
The important advantages of fibre optics are :

1. Larger channel capacity,
2. Lighter in weight compared to copper cables,
3. No crosstalk between adjacent cables,
4. No interference on account of static or atmospheric electric discharges and, therefore, no noise signals are picked up by the cables,
5. Not affected by extreme environmental conditions, resistant to corrosion,
6. Cheaper than copper cables.
7. A single fibre carries information in both directions (duplex) simultaneously.

Adapted from : *Information Highways*
(CSIR Golden Jubilee Series)

Fibre optics have revolutionized communications. 'Fibre optic' cable can carry potentially hundreds of television channels, telephone and computer services.

Soap Opera

A soap opera is a dramatic serial broadcast mainly intended to entertain. The term was originally used in the United States because the sponsors of these broadcasts were generally soap companies whose advertisements were primarily targetted at an audience of house-wives.

The term 'opera' suggested the melodrama of the high brow musical genre. In the beginning these soap operas were radio serials patronised by soap powder manufacturers like Proctor and Gamble. At that time it was hoped that by sponsoring radio programmes about women, their families and domestic issues, advertisers could reach an audience of house-wives who would add soap powder to their shopping lists. In Latin America, soap operas called *telenovelas* (literally television novels) are one of the most popular genre of television programmes. *Telenovelas* originated in Mexico and Cuba in the 1950s. Britain's longest-running and most popular television soap is *Coronation Street* which started in 1960. The 'best-loved soap' of Britain, described as chronicle of our times, has provided entertainment to huge audiences.

Pro-development soap operas, discussed in the context of *Hum Log* in the *India's Information Revolution* (1989)*, in the third world nations like India are quite different from television soap operas in the United States. A pro-development soap opera, besides entertaining, also subtly conveys an educational theme to promote some aspect of development. The book states : Pro-development soap operas are one bright spot in the generally unfulfilled potential of contemporary Third World Television. They represent a unique combination of education and entertainment–style programming that some call 'enter-education' or 'edu-tainment...' *Hum Log* represents a crucial turning point in the rise of television in India, pointing it toward commercialization and consumerism. Further, India's successful experience with *Hum Log* in the mid-1980s convinced national leaders in other Third World countries to launch pro-development soap operas.

Hum Log began primarily as a family planning soap opera. However, pressure from sponsors and audiences resulted in toning down of the family planning message which was dropped after the first eight episodes to settle into an audience-maximising family drama.

It would, however, be pertinent to point out that *Hum Log* launched the era of commercially-sponsored programmes on Doordarshan. Its commercial success led to the proliferation of domestically produced television serials on Doordarshan; it was also proved that domestically produced TV shows could be enormously attractive to the audience.

Development Programmes

The objectives of the television broadcasting include : to provide

---

* Arvind Singhal and Everett M. Rogers, Sage Publications, New Delhi.

essential information and knowledge in order to stimulate greater agricultural production, to promote and help preserve environmental and ecological balance, to disseminate message of family planning, to promote national integration, to act as a catalyst for social change, etc. Measured against the above stated objectives, Indian television has come no where near achieving these goals. Instead of working as a change agent, TV has ushered in a phase of consumerism that flaunt a highly westernised life style.

Doordarshan's record in popularising development programmes on agriculture, health, consumer protection, distant education has hardly been a success. A sharper thrust, with the greater and direct involvement and participation of the target groups, in the language and milieu familiar to the viewers would go a long way in popularising these programmes. The observations of the Joshi Committee Report in this context would be particularly relevant. The Committee observed: Communication can also help to convert development programmes into a partnership between the experts and the people.... The trouble with many development programmes such as Krishi Darshan is that they are produced within the studio, often with urban men with rural garb. It is often an urban view of rural problems or a view of problems of urbanised villages.

Its potential to promote the extension of new knowledge and practices, as an aid to transfer of technology, extension education and social change remains unexplored. Development oriented culture would certainly have encouraged innovation, diversity of opinions and stimulated national consciousness for the disadvantaged sections of the society.

It is obvious that the objectives for which television was introduced in the country, as a medium for social education, weapon against illiteracy and ignorance, for bringing about awareness among the people of sociological problems, creating sense of participation in India's efforts to usher in a new social order, for playing a vital role in cultivating civic consciousness; remain, by and large, unfulfilled.

Educational Television

Education is an instrument of social transformation and an important input in development effort. In a world based on science and technology, it is education that determines the level of prosperity, welfare and security of the level.

Ever since the inception of television in India in 1959, one major responsibility entrusted to it is to provide support for the education system in the country. School Television (STV) was launched in October 1961 as an organised, systematic and sequential support to formal school instruction. The primary school telecast was undertaken in Delhi in 1975; later on various educational projects were launched to supplement primary education.

Teachers appreciated STV as a tool for teaching (teacher concern) and presentation of content (tele-teacher concern). They were, however, less enthusiastic in accepting STV as a tool of learning for students (student concern) and were quite articulate about the limitations of STV (television concern).

The country-wide classroom (CWCR) of UGC started its telecast from 15 August 1984 with one hour educational programmes.

The establishment of the Indira Gandhi National Open University (IGNOU) on 19 November 1985 represented the government's attempt to provide higher education in India through multi-media distance teaching methods. Since May 1991, the programmes produced by IGNOU, the apex body foı distance education in the country, have provided television support to its registered students for some courses.

During the closing decades of the twentieth century the use of communication technology in distance education has registered an exponential growth in the developing countries of Asia, Africa and Latin America. Some of the latest concepts like virtual university are no longer alien to these countries. It would indeed be instructive to study the contribution of television in promoting education in the country.

Tele-education, Open and Distance Learning

While considering the application of communication technologies to education, tele-education, by all means, has been considered to be a landmark development. The extensive use of television for educational purposes in Asia in the two most populous countries of the region–China and India, the limitations of being one-way medium notwithstanding, is indicated by two important developments : (1) The largest distance teaching institution of the world, the national multimedia distance learning institution in China, is called the Central Radio and Television University (CRTVU), and (2) One of the largest communications experiments in which television programmes were received by local viewers directly from Space-Satellite Instructional Television Experiment (SITE) was conducted in India for a period of one year from 1 August 1975.

China is one of the pioneering countries in the world to have exploited television medium for expansion of education. The CRTVU employs broadcast as the main delivery vehicle and supplements it with print, audio-visual media, tutorials, and computerized instruction. Programmes are broadcast directly to learners at home, in the workplace or the study centres located throughout the country. The CRTVU courses follow a multi-media approach. The input of non-print media varies according to the subject area–science and engineering courses have greater proportion of TV programmes, whereas radio is the chief medium for social science course. TV programmes are transmitted by the Central China Television (CCTV) nationally through the microwave network.

The CRTVU–the apex institute, is backed up by the Provincial Television Universities. Academic programmes are offered in a large number of disciplines including engineering, sciences, economics and management : Academic courses are designed on a nationwide basis, but provincial universities implement the guidelines provided by the CRTVU. Enrolment and examinations are controlled centrally and most eminent writers and presenters are invited to produce TV programmes.

The remarkable aspect of the working of CRTVU is the expansion of its operations in rural areas in order to meet the shortages of technically trained manpower. A vast network has been created to meet the shortage of educational persons in various fields and also to meet the demands of fresh graduates from high schools. Since it is not possible for the provincial universities to meet these demands, the society is looking to the Radio and Television Universities to cater to these demands. During the last eight years these universities have made a tremendous impact on the educational system in the country.

Countrywide Classroom (CWCR)

The Countrywide Classroom (CWCR) project of the University Grants Commission has been the logical outcome of the successful SITE experience. The rapid expansion of television in India during 1984–when one TV transmitter was being installed every day–facilitated the launching of the above programme, aimed primarily for the undergraduate students of colleges located at different places. The contents of CWCR programmes are not linked to any examination, these are neither based on a particular syllabus. Instead these telecasts seek to provide new insights, bring new findings and take the students to various places and laboratories they would rarely see. The project aims at the widest possible utilisation of television potential to improve the quality of university level education. These educational video programmes are telecast twice a day over the Doordarshan network using INSAT Satellite system. The UGC has established a number of media production centres all over the country for producing these programmes. India, in fact, has one of the largest networks for producing quality education software which include Audio-Visual Research Centres (AVRCs) and Educational Media Research Centres (EMRCs)–under the aegis of the UGC. The establishment of the Indira Gandhi National Open University represents the government's attempt to provide higher education through the use of multimedia distance teaching methods. The establishment of the Central Institute of Educational Technology (CIET) in 1984 and also the State Institutes of Education Technology (SIETs), with the objective of utilising educational technology for the improvement and spread of education in the country at the school level, is one majro step towards utilising the media for elementary education. Some of the major concerns at present–qualitative improvement and regular availability of programmes, wider coverage to the users through telecast–have been articulated on different occasions.

Since 20 May 1991, Doordarshan has been telecasting curriculum based video programmes produced by IGNOU, an important component of its educational methodology which aims at making the teaching-learning process interesting both for the student and the teacher. The target audience for these telecasts are primarily IGNOU students spread over throughout the country.

A study conducted by the Communication Division made two important suggestions for strengthening the tele-education programmes of IGNOU :

1. The possibility of telecasting from various regional transmitters with different schedules should be considered in addition to the present nation-wide telecast. Since the mandate of the university is to bring higher education to the large number of citizens, an effort is urgently required to produce programmes in the language the students are adequately conversant with.
2. Close interaction and cooperation among the producers, script writers, faculty members and the production team is required for preparing an effective educational programme.

Educational Teleconferencing

Limitations inherent in tele-education have been pointed out in several discussions on the use of television for teaching and distance education purposes. The most serious limitation, of course, is that television is strictly a one-way communication. The teacher-taught contact, considered all important for any successful educational endeavour is missing in the case of television. The gap between the 'sender' and the 'receiver' is too wide to be easily bridged. A teacher's personal touch and care are not a diminishing commodity subject to the vagaries or showmanship of the medium of television. Hence, TV and teacher should prove to be more of companions than competitors. The problem with television programmes is that these are ephemeral, cannot be reviewed, are uninterruptable and are presented at the same pace for all students. In developing countries, there is, however, the problem of accessibility to television. In India, the vast majority of the students of Open University are not likely to have television in their homes. In such circumstances, they have to use either a community television facility or go to the nearest Study Centre for watching the television programmes.

The emergence of the new forms of electronic media like teleconferencing is of particular interest for distance learning because of their interactive capabilities. The use of electronic media components as an essential part of the multi-media approach to distance learning has always been a dream for those working in developing countries.

Teleconferencing is an interactive electronic communication among two or more locations. The punch word here is interactive and it is indeed this quality of interactivity that really distinguishes teleconferencing from the conventional one-way media like broadcasting or narrowcasting.

Teleconferencing is an already accepted form of technology in advanced countries, especially for business communications. It is only a matter of time for this technology to become popular in developing countries as necessary infrastructure like telephone links and satellite are being made available. Usually, the attraction for adopting teleconferencing is said to be the savings it results in minimizing physical travel. The time-saving involved in this process is also a significant factor. Experience of advanced countries in this process is also a significant factor. Experience of advanced countries in which teleconferencing is in wide usage shows that apart from economy and time saving, this technology improves corporate efficiency and enables participatory management.

The need for communication, staff development, and expert resources makes teleconferencing a particularly appropriate means for distant education institutions. The use of telecommunication to facilitate two-way communication among a number of students located at different venues is the basis of educational teleconferencing. The opportunity for introduction between the experts and the students, which teleconferencing so readily affords, has made it a particularly valuable learning technique.

Teleconferencing–The IGNOU and NOS Experiments

The two apex distant learning institutions in India, IGNOU and the National Open School have, during the recent years, initiated efforts to incorporate teleconferencing as a component of instructional and management methodology.

The teleconferencing experiment of IGNOU, from 4-13 October 1993–essentially a one-way video and two-way audio–was conducted to explore the feasibility of telecommunication based interaction in Distance Education. It was one of the components of the Extended Contact Programme (ECP) of PG Diploma Course of Higher Education. The two major objectives of this experiment were to understand the potential of telecommunication in distance education and to get feed back regarding multimedia approach using talk back system.

The training programme was conducted through live lectures and discussion mode, supplemented by computer-based graphics and charts, audio-visual aid and discussion. During the discussion, the participants used STD telephone facilities for asking question in audio mode. The questions were answered using the audio and video mode.

Open Schooling has evolved as one of the successful experiments in alternate schooling in the last 2-3 decades. Many have remained outside the purview of formal schooling due to socio-economic, geographical and such other reasons. Open Schools adopt distance learning methodologies which include self-learning printing materials and audio-visual cassettes; telecommunication and multimedia approach to teaching with the possibility of learning at one's pace, place and convenience has helped in catering to the individual difference of the learners.

India is one of the pioneers in Open Schooling in the world. The Government, in the Ministry of Human Resource Development, established the National Open School in 1989 for providing an opportunity for schooling to dropouts, young girls, adult women, ex-servicemen and handicapped persons. NOS has a diverse school profile having young and old learners, ranging from 14 years to as old as 89 years, living in different parts of the country. More than two hundred thousand students have so far enrolled in NOS through 800 study centres.

The NOS is confronted with a huge task of training teachers from the traditional system who needed orientation and training to perform effectively in the open learning system. The NOS conducted the training programme for 180 teachers drawn from different districts of Gujarat for three days from 17-19 December 1996. The mode of discussion was through satellite based and telephone-based one-way video and two-way audio conferencing. The interactive network comprised one studio teaching centre at ISRO, Ahmedabad and six receiving centres spread over the state. The experience gained would help NOS to use this technology more effectively in a massive countrywide operational system.

Launching of country's first education TV channel–DD Gyan Darshan–has been another major step to harness the potential of television for educational purposes. The channel was launched on 26 January 2000 in collaboration with the Ministry of Human Resource Development, with DD supplying the hardware and transponder link on satellite. The nodal agency for the new channel is the Indira Gandhi National Open University.

The channel is envisaged as a free-to-air 16-hour channel with eight hours of original programming which will come from various sources : the consortium for education communication, UGC, NCERT, IITs, departments of space, science and technology, etc. The aim of the channel will be to reach different segments of population–pre-school, school, non-formal system learners, teachers, university students, adult learners and others.

In the field of education, the contribution of television–from STV in 1961 to an independent channel DD–Gyan Darshan in 2000 is indeed significant.

Recommendations of Various Committees

Over the years, the Government of India established a number of committees and working groups to study various aspects and issues concerning the electronic media. The UNESCO also established an International Commission for the Study of Communication Problems, popularly known as McBride Commission (1977-79). The reports of these bodies are a valuable contribution to the media literature and constitute precious body of information. Salient features of reports and recommendations of some of the committees are summarised in the discussion below :

1. *Committee on Broadcasting and Information Media (1964)*

This committee, also popularly known as the Chanda Committee, constituted in December 1964, presented the Report on Radio and Television in April 1966. The Committee observed : It is not possible in the Indian context for a creative medium like broadcasting to flourish under a regiment *(sic)* of departmental rules and regulations. It is only by an institutional change that AIR can be liberated from the present rigid financial and administrative procedures of the Government. It recommended that the separate Corporation, set up for Akashvani and Doordarshan, should have the freedom to evolve its own methods of recruitment, regulate scales of pay and conditions of service according to its needs, and devise a financial and accounting system appropriate to its creative activity.

This recommendation was considered by the Cabinet in December 1969, and the Lok Sabha was informed in April 1970 that the present was not an opportune time to consider the conversion of All India Radio into an autonomous Corporation. However, another important recommendation that Akashvani and Doordarshan be separated, was accepted and took effect from April 1, 1976.

Arguing for the grant of autonomy to the two media, the Chanda Committee had said : Theoretically it (AIR) has the freedom of a national newspaper to present objectively topics of current interest but in practice it has failed to do so mainly for two reasons. First, successive ministers usurped the policy making functions of the Director General and started interfering even in matters of programme planning and presentation, and second, the selection of the directing staff was so made as to ensure unquestioning compliance. As a result the public image of AIR has become tarnished, its objectivity destroyed and its initiative gradually whittled away.

2. *Working Group on Autonomy for Akashvani and Doordarshan (1977)*

The committee, also popularly known as Verghese Committee, appointed in August 1977 submitted its Report to the Government in February 1978. The report is a landmark document on the aspect of granting autonomy to the electronic media. Its major recommendations were :

(i) An autonomous national trust should be established under which Akashvani and Doordarshan would function. It gave a name to the proposed authority–Akash Bharati : the National Broadcast Trust;

(ii) Radio and TV should work for the public purpose. They should function within the framework of a broad perspective of national communication policy;

(iii) The proposed autonomous broadcasting trust authority should be owned by the nation and be accountable to the Parliament;

(iv) The priority of broadcasting has to change from "urban elitist moorings to the rural and semi-urban areas and to the urban poor." The quality of programmes would have to improve. It should also work towards filling the rural-urban and tradition modernity gaps;

(v) The idea of one autonomous corporation each for All India Radio and Doordarshan did not find support from the Working Group. It opted for one autonomous national trust for both of the broadcast media–radio and television. It also rejected the concept of autonomous regional corporations, but it envisaged decentralization of national broadcasting authority; and

(vi) The autonomy of the authority and independence from control of the government should be guaranteed by the Constitution.

The Government introduced a Bill in May 1979 which envisaged setting up of an autonomous corporation known as Prasar Bharati. Since the Government went out of office, the Bill lapsed and the successor government headed by Mrs. Indira Gandhi decided not to set up an autonomous body.

The government later on introduced the Prasar Bharati (Broadcasting Corporation of India), Act 1990 in September 1990. However, the continued foot dragging on the implementation of the Prasar Bharati Act and the yawning gap between the government's rhetoric and its practice, clearly shows that autonomy for the electronic media is as distant a dream as ever.

3. *International Commission for the Study of Communication Problems (1977)*

The Commission, also popularly known as MacBride Commission, was established by UNESCO to study among other issues such as increasing importance attached to communication as a social phenomenon and the consequent interest shown in the development of communication media; the growing impact and repercussions of technological progress in the field, etc. The President of the Commission, Sean MacBride, transmitted the Final Report to the Director General, UNESCO in February 1980. Some of the important recommendations of the Commission are :

(i) Communication be no longer regarded merely as an incidental service and its development left to chance. Recognition of its potential warrants the formulation by all nations, and particularly developing countries, of comprehensive communication policies linked to overall social, cultural, economic and political goals. Such policies should be based on inter-ministrial and inter-disciplinary consultations with broad public participation;

(ii) Within the framework of national development policies, each country will have to work out its own set of priorities, bearing in mind that it will not be possible to move in all directions at the same time. But, as far as resources allow, communication policies should aim at stimulating and encouraging all means of communication;

(iii) The communication component in all development projects should receive adequate financing. So-called "development support communications" are essential for mobilizing initiatives and providing information required for action in all fields of development–agriculture, health and family planning, education, religion, industry and so on. Essential communication needs to be met include the extension of basic postal services and telecommunication networks through small rural electronic exchanges; and

(iv) Development strategies should incorporate communication policies as an integral part in the diagnosis of needs and in the design and implementation of selected priorities. In this respect communication should be considered a major development resource, a vehicle to ensure real political participation in decision making, a central information base for defining policy options, and an instrument for creating awareness of national priorities.

4. *Working Group on Software Planning for Doordarshan (1983)*

The Working Group, also popularly known as the Joshi Committee, was established to make recommendations regarding programming in Indian television. It submitted its report in April 1984, sub-titled as 'An Indian Personality for Television'. The report was formally laid on the table of Lok Sabha in 1985. Even though the Working Group was formed to make recommendations regarding Doordarshan, its report underlines the overall communication approach and policy concerning other sectors of mass media.

The Working Group Report made several recommendations on creating appropriate environment for the development of creative software for Doordarshan. In the first place, the Working Group was convinced that such an environment did not exist within the present structure of the organization. It was also convinced that whatever the claims of the Government, Doordarshan did not enjoy 'functional freedom' and the lack of such freedom is having a detrimental effect on the planning and quality of its programmes. It recommended the setting up of a National Doordarshan Council which would have three roles to perform : to review and guide the organisation's performance, as a guardian of Doordarshan's functional and professional autonomy, and as a counterpart of the Press Council for examining complaints of inaccuracy or bias in the reporting of news and comment on current affairs. The Report emphasized that a developing country like India is exposed to the danger of erosion of its national cultural identity, and the need is to resist the cultural invasion from outside through restriction of imported programmes and 'positive software planning'. It discerned a credibility gap created by the growing hiatus between profession and practice, between official policy pronouncements emphasising use of television for development and education, and the increasing drift and departure from them in actual programming. It, therefore, urged the exploitation of the 'development potential' of television, of using communication technology for 'leapfrogging into growth and development'. It endorsed the Nehru and Sarabhai approach of tapping the communication revolution in general and television in particular as a major weapon in the fight against poverty and illiteracy.

Elaborating on the theme of generating relevant software suited to the country, Dr. Joshi in his Sardar Patel Memorial Lectures, 1985 on 'Communication and Nation Building : Perspective and Policy', observed:

> Relevant software suited to the country can be generated with joint efforts of scientists and media men to introduce the people to the world view of the scientific age and to its fruits which help in solving the age-old and new problems of human life. Equally important is to draw upon the rich software on scientific education from developed countries and to adapt it to the country's needs.

CABLE TELEVISION

With the sudden and spectacular growth of satellite and cable television network since 1991, the most dramatic revolution on the TV screen got underway, when India ended decades of isolation from the rest of the world. Cable television promised multiple channels and multiple choices for the viewer. Its introduction had profound effects on the broadcasting situation–programming, advertising and innovating formats to attract the attention of viewers.

Liberalisation of airwaves has resulted in a proliferation of satellite channels in India. Doordarshan began telecast on as many as 13 channels on Independence Day, 1994. Some other channels available in 1994 included CNN, BBC, Star Plus, Prime Sports, V, Zee, Jain, Sun, Asianet and ATN.

The advertisement code of Doordarshan and All India Radio was amended in March 1994 allowing advertisements relating to jewellery, precious stones, approved mutual funds, foreign banks, including financial services, matrimonial agencies, astrologists and manufacturers of hair-dye.

Cable Television (Regulation Bill)

The Government on 29 September 1994 promulgated the Cable Television (Regulation) Ordinance which was later passed as the Law, legitimizing the cable business and making the operators more accountable. The Bill made it mandatory for cable operators to be citizens of the country and restricted foreign equity in such networks to 49 per cent.

The Bill also provided for compulsory transmission of two Doordarshan satellite channels, and empowered the competent authority to prohibit transmission of certain programmes in the public interest. The Bill provided for registration of the existing cable operators within 90 days, and made the operation of non-registered cable networks an offence. It provided for the cable operators adhering to the prescribed programme and advertisement code and maintaining a register.

The advent of satellite and cable television has led to proliferation of television channels–mostly in private sector. The main concern of television industry is to earn as much revenue as possible through commercial advertising which is directly related to the size of its audience. The private channel operators know that the easiest and quickest way to build up viewership is by providing just entertainment which essentially means–heavy reliance on films and film-based programmes, tele-serials, soaps, chat-shows, etc. The film industry provides substantial proportion of such channels' programming. The key to success for the private TV channels is–entertainment, more entertainment and more entertainment. These channels hardly provide useful information and education for the development of the society.

In the wake of proliferation of cable channel network, it has been observed that television, which was generally regarded as a serious business of ideas and creativity, has largely become a business of pure economics. TV was shaping up as a vehicle for entertainment, which is aimed at garnering maximum advertising. At the same time, advertising should not offend morality, decency, aesthetics and ignore societal concerns.

The rapid television expansion–an ongoing process since 1984–is gathering speed in the wake of cable and satellite television invasion. Television in India is no longer an urban phenomenon. It is fast penetrating into mofussil and rural areas of the country. The major cable and satellite television companies in the world view India as one of the top five TV markets in the 21st century. Alongwith this rapid and unchartered expansion of TV in India are tied a host of related socio-cultural issues–cultural alienation, accessibility, credibility, violence and vulgarity, encouragement to the forces of commercialisation and consumerism in the society.

In a feature, Can Japan Catch the Wave, *Time*, 27 February 1995, makes an interesting observation regarding the Japanese women not wanting cable television in their homes. The President of Titus Communications—a cable-TV joint venture involving Itochu, Toshiba, Time Warner and US West, Minoru Akimoto says : In Japan where housewives have final say on financial matters they won't like it. They will say, "You want me to buy a service that gets my husband to watch more TV? He hardly talks to me as it is. And you want me to pay more for that?"

There has been pervasive concern about the impact of TV viewing on various segments of society–women, children and the general standards of social norms and behaviour. An independent survey conducted by a leading newspaper in the metropolitan areas revealed that cinema and soap operas have currently become an addiction with the teen agers with an upper middle class background. Their famous heroes turn out to be the ones famous for their propensity for militant action. The Media Task Force set up by the US Administration expressing rising concern about juvenile delinquency, crime and general unrest. An eminent media analyst says : TV enters the living room directly, its images have greater impact on the very young who cannot distinguish fact from fiction. Children and teenagers cannot be banned from watching when their elders do so. It is not only sex and violence that affect them, they are dazzled by the attractive portrayal of western cultures and lose respect for their own. They are also sensitised to the culture of the commercials that follow programmes. The overall result is that children are becoming more demanding and alienated from the traditional norms and culture.

Presently cable and satellite (C & S) is going through very rapid growth because other options like Direct to Home (DTH) are not available. According to one estimate there would be about 70-75 million C & S households in five years compared to the present number of about 30 million. There will also be further growth in terms of the variety of channels (although we may continue to have 50-60 channels as at present) which will cover a wider range of subjects and languages. The channels will get more specific in audience in content and audience segmentation. Depending upon the commercial viability, there would be specialised channels to meet specific needs of different interest groups.

Another development is the provision for the permission and possible introduction of DTH in the Broadcasting Bill. DTH means that the programme/channel reaches the viewer directly from the satellite without going through the intermediary stage of a cable operator or a TV station. It is technologically feasible to get even 200 TV channels through DTH. The benefit to the viewers to wider choice, better quality and receiving (and therefore paying) only for those channels that one is interested in watching. Although DTH would be costlier than the cable operator, it would be particularly useful to those areas that do not have the facilities of cable TV operations particularly rural and remote areas.

The deep concern and anguish about issues such as portrayal of women on TV, explosion of crime, violence and sex has been repeatedly expressed through several media seminars, women organisations and NGOs. A well known Delhi-based organisation, working in the area of consumer protection, public interest litigation and other important matters concerning improvement in civic life in a recent write up stated :

> TV is no longer just a means for informing news, disseminating information and building opinion. It is also for providing entertainment. The unfortunate development is that it has

increasingly become the instrument for projecting crime, thrillers, horrors, vulgarity and obscenity. Scenes of sex, crime and violence capture the imagination of large sections of viewers, especially children. And these create a disturbing impact on them.

Specialists have identified as many as 60 types of violence projected on TV, both audio and visual. These include slapping, threats, screaming, shooting, assaulting, abusing, pushing, stabbing, mental torture, eerie sound tracks and threatening music. Most of the violence is explicit and graphic and noticeably lengthy.

Children admire superheroes such as *Shaktiman* who is capable of extraordinary physical feats; they tend to imbibe the exploits of such superheroes. In one such serial, as many as 17 acts of violence were found in one episode of 25 minutes. These included assaulting, slapping, plunging, shooting, strangulating, burning, stabbing, grotesque representations, bodily transformations and supernatural occurrences. Family drama serials also often depict conflicts which involve violence. These carry scenes of domestic violence, often involving children. There is an obvious tendency to glorify violence.

These circumstances need to be urgently considered by governmental authorities as well as social activists so that measures can be devised and adopted for mitigating the situation. These include persuading channels to adopt self-regulating measures, imbibing in producers norms and guidelines and dealing with defaulters. They should also be forced to fix time, not earlier than 10 p.m., in which serials and programmes containing scenes of sex and violence can be telecast. They should avoid repeated these shows at an earlier time, and also put across a written or verbal warning before such a programme begins. Child-specific programmes should be developed and telecast by all channels.

It is necessary that people should raise voice against the growing tendency of depicting scenes of crime and violence on TV programmes serials; these can prove disastrous to the society and its future build-up. Ways and means must be devised for avoidance of the slide towards social disaster.

Credibility and Objectivity

Credibility and objectivity of electronic media are the two basic ingredients essential for building up values of trust and reliability between the media and its users. It is more so when the power and reach of the electronic media has increased phenomenally. In order to enforce the values of objectivity and impartiality, various guidelines and codes–The Broadcast Code governing AIR and Guidelines for News Policy for Broadcast Media have been made applicable to the AIR and Doordarshan. However, there has been a visible hiatus between what has been prescribed and what is implemented in practice.

Emphasising the importance of objective and impartial presentation of news, the Verghese Committee observed : The principles of fairness, balance, accuracy and well-rounded objectivity apply not only to news but to all current affairs programmes including commentaries, discussions, news, analyses, documentaries, newsreels and magazine features. Balance, however, does not imply a mechanical balancing of views in each programme, but rather an overall balance achieved over a series of programmes. This is what Akashvani and Doordarshan owe to their audience and this is what the Indian people must always expect of them.

Over the years, due to multiplicity of channels, as also because of opening up of DD II to independent producers–all of them with their news and current affairs programmes, the situation has been mitigated to a large extent. One has only to remember, that under previous dispensation how heads rolled when the name of the daughter-in-law of the Prime Minister got mentioned in the news bulletin in the case of illegal allotment of petrol pump pending before the Delhi High Court. Earlier a full fledged enquiry was ordered as to how a visual of the dozing Prime Minister was included in the news. It appears that Prime Minister and members of his family–their names and visuals–are beyond the pale of normal practice of news production.

ELECTRONIC MEDIA AND DEVELOPMENT

The objectives of television broadcasting include: To provide essential information and knowledge in order to stimulate greater agricultural production, to promote and help preserve environmental and ecological balance, to disseminate message of family planning as a measure of population control and family welfare, to promote national integration to act as a catalyst for social change, etc.

Ever since the process of planned development was ushered in the country, with the launching of the First Five Year Plan in 1951, the role of communication in support of development was recognised.

In the spread of information facilities however the imbalance in favour of urban concentrations and prosperous areas continues. There is need for sustained attempt to inform the people in the rural areas and particulary those in backward regions, about the specific schemes in agriculture, forestry, road construction, marketing, the supply of credit and other inputs so that the benefits of these programmes are more widely spread.

From the Sixth Five Year Plan onwards, funds allocation for electronic media, and particularly for television progressively increased. The Sixth Plan period (1980-85) saw massive expansion of Indian television.

Measured against the above stated objectives, Indian television has come no where near achieving these goals. Instead of working as a change agent, TV has ushered in a phase of consumerism that flaunt a highly westernised life style. A sharper thrust, with the greater and direct involvement and participation of the target groups, in the language and milieu familiar to viewers would go a long way in popularising these programmes.

This promising medium has not been able to develop the characteristics of the national broadcasting service, predominantly Indian in content and character. Various factors have been responsible for the medium being not closer to the minds and hearts of the people. Its potential to promote the extension of new knowledge and practices, as an aid to transfer of technology, extension education and social change remains unexplored.

BROADCAST BILL

Work on a comprehensive Broadcasting Bill had begun in 1995 shortly after the Supreme Court Judgement on freedom of airwaves. The Bill, which was introduced in Parliament in May 1997 as Bill No. 71 of 1997, expressed concern over portrayal of violence and sexual conduct and stressed the need to lay down standards of taste and decency, to promote values of national integration, national harmony, scientific temper and Indian culture. The Bill took note of the Supreme Court Judgement, the Cable Television Networks (Regulation) Act, the report of the Working Group (1983) and the Sengupta Committee's observations for reviewing the provisions of Prasar Bharati (1996) which had recommended the setting up of Radio and Television Authority of India (an independent body which is not a part of Prasar Bharati). Several security and national integrity concerns reflected in the Bill particularly in the conditions for giving or cancelling licenses. These concerns include : broadcasting should not incite crime, lead to disorder, be offensive to the public feeling and news should be impartial and accurate. The Statement of Objects and Reasons, laid in the House by the Minister for Information and Broadcasting on 12 May 1997, recapitulated the changing broadcasting scenario.

Statement of Objects and Reasons

The broadcasting scenario, especially in the realm of satellite broadcasting, has undergone a revolution during the last few years. A large number of satellite television channels have been beaming their programmes through the Indian skies to our people. All these channels are foreign entities and their programmes are uplinked from outside the country without any regulation through the law of our land, while Indian entrepreneurs and Indian companies are not at present permitted to own either Radio or Television stations.

2. Concern has been voiced both inside Parliament and outside about the implications of these unregulated television programmes and the denial of level playing field to Indian entities. The only legal instrument available is the Indian Telegraph Act, 1885, which is considered totally inadequate to govern modern broadcasting media. All leading democratic countries have enacted laws specifically regulating broadcasting media. The introduction of the Broadcasting Bill is a step in this direction.

3. It is felt that the public service broadcaster alone will not be able to meet the needs and urges of the people in terms of variety and plurality of programmes required in different regions by different sections of society in our vast country. Keeping in view our great democratic traditions, it is imperative that our citizens are well informed and given wider choice in matters of information, education and entertainment. This can be provided by facilitating private broadcasting in the country.

4. The Bill seeks to establish an autonomous Broadcasting Authority for the purpose of facilitating and regulating broadcasting services in India so that they become competitive in terms of quality of services, cost of service and use of new technologies, apart from becoming a catalyst for social change, promotion of values of Indian culture and shaping of a modern vision. It will also curb monopolistic trends in this sensitive field, so that people are provided with a wide range of news and views.

Following its introduction, the Bill was referred to a Joint Select

Committee of Parliament which was supposed to study its implications and make recommendations. When the Parliament met in November 1997, it was widely expected that the Joint Select Committee would present its recommendations to Parliament and a discussion on the Bill would be taken up.

The rapid changes in the governments and the stewardship of the Ministry of Information and Broadcasting have delayed the passing of the Broadcast Bill. Since the Bill will incorporate provisions on several sensitive issues–restriction on cross media ownership, foreign equity component, changes in cable law and approval of DTH broadcasting, efforts are being made to obtain expert opinion and consultation from as wide cross-section as feasible. The group of ministers is looking at the host of issues emerging from historical changes in the broadcasting environment as also technological issues concerning convergence of broadcasting, internet and digital technology.

The review of the working and structuring of Prasar Bharati Board and the passage of the Broadcasting Bill will determine the future of electronic media in the country. Equally important would be the role of advertising and the market forces which largely determine the contents of broadcasting in private sector. In any case AIR and Doordarshan would continue to dominate the working of electronic media in the country. It is fascinating to refer to the following excerpt from the *Doordarshan 99*, brought out by Broadcasting Corporation of India.

The eight weeks from mid-May to mid-July 1999, when the Indian Army fought in Kargil, was a defining period in the fifty years history of Independent India. Kargil emotionally integrated the country as never before. People saw officers and Jawans from Kerala and Nagaland and from Rajasthan and Bihar fighting hand in hand to defend the Himalayan peaks. They understood the hardships faced by the fighting men, they lauded the bravery of the Jawans, and wept with the bereaved families. Television brought to the living rooms, in not only the big cities but also in small towns and tiny villages, various images from the theatre of war–some inspiring and some poignant.

When India was last engaged in a similar conflict in 1971, television was limited to Delhi only where there were just forty-five thousand television sets. In contrast, in 1999 television reaches an estimated 69 million homes. In 1971, people heard and read about the war but in 1999 people witnessed, and in a way participated in the action. This power of the visual medium has been reflected in reports of enthusiasm of the young people to join the armed forces, the large gatherings of people paying homage to the martyrs and the donations which poured into the various relief funds, etc.

ANNEXURE

SOCIAL OBJECTIVES OF DOORDARSHAN

- To act as a catalyst for social change.
- To promote National Integration.
- To stimulate a scientific temper in the minds of the people.
- To disseminate the message of family planning as a means of population control and family welfare.
- To provide essential information and knowledge in order to stimulate greater agricultural production.
- To promote and help preserve environmental and ecological balance.
- To highlight the need for social welfare measures, including welfare of women, children and the less privileged.
- To promote interest in games and sports.
- To create values of appraisal of art and cultural heritage.

Doordarshan Code

Doordarshan has adopted the All India Radio Broadcasting Code, which states : "Broadcast on All India Radio by individuals will not permit :

1. Criticism of friendly countries;
2. Attack on religion or communities;
3. Anything obscene or defamatory;
4. Incitement to violence or anything against maintenance of law and order;
5. Anything amounting to contempt of Court;
6. Aspersions against the integrity of the President, Governors and Judiciary;
7. Attack on a political party by name;
8. Hostile criticism of any State or the Centre; or
9. Anything showing disrespect to the Constitution or advocating

change in the Constitution by violence; but advocating changes in a constitutional way should not be debarred."

Conventions

The following are some of the conventions observed by All India Radio :

1. Appeals for funds are disallowed except in national emergencies;
2. Exclusion of trade names in broadcasts which amounts to advertising directly (except in commercial service); and
3. Direct publicity is not permitted for or on behalf of an individual or an organisation which is likely to benefit only that individual or organisation.

SECTION–IV

MEDIA MANAGEMENT

Media Management

PRINCIPLES OF MANAGEMENT

Management is the most important function in every organisation. It provides an invigorating force that brings life in an organisation. It is a distinct process consisting of activities of planning, organising, staffing, directing, controlling and co-ordinating the activities. Lundy described "management is principally a task of planning, co-ordinating, motivating and controlling the efforts of others towards a specific objective" (It covers major three functions of management, viz. planning, implementing and controlling). Henry Fayol says "to manage is to forecast, to plan, to organise, to command, to co-ordinate and to control". It attempts to describe management in terms of what a manager does and not what management is. In every organisation, managers have to design and maintain an environment in which individuals work in groups to achieve selected missions and objectives. Managers direct the effort and activities of other people toward common objectives. Appley viewed "management as the development of people and not the direction of things." He says "management is essentially personnel management. Human resources have unlimited potential hence special importance to the development of human resources should be given. He further remarked that management is the art of getting things done through and with informally organised groups". This concept can easily reflect almost all aspects of modern management. In the words of W. Newman, "a manager is a leader, who gets things done by working with people (willingly) and other resources in an organised manner. In order to reach an objective, he co-ordinates the activities of others rather than perform operations himself". Management is the fine art of getting the employee to want to do his prescribed work as per plan willingly and with voluntary co-operation. In short management must recognize that people are more important than things and management must be employee-oriented and not merely job-oriented. If management practices good human relations, getting things done or productivity can be automatically assured.

F. W. Taylor, Father of Scientific Management say: it was not prefer to just find a way of doing something. A manager had to find one right way. They used time and motion study for developing a right way. According to Taylor, Gantt and others analysis, planning and control of work should be separated from the execution of work and management should be responsible for detailed analysis, investigation and planning of work in advance, whereas workers should be responsible for the performance of the work as per plans. The basic theme of Taylor was that the managers should study work scientifically in order to identify by "one best way" to get the things done.

Taylor codified his idea in terms of certain principles which are as follow :

1. All jobs can be observed and analysed in order to determine the one best way of accomplishing them. Management must use scientific method rather than rule of thumb method.
2. The best man for the job can be scientifically selected and trained.
3. One best way is followed by paying the man on incentive basis – tying his wage or salary to how much he produces.
4. Harmonious organisation can be obtained by assigning the appropriate man to each set of operations. This will prevent any discord.
5. Management has to choose the best means of economical production. Specialization of workers is essential to increase efficiency of production.
6. Co-operation between the labour and management can be achieved. This will ensure maximum output in place of restricted output by workers.
7. A striving for enterprise and the development of each man to his greatest efficiency and prosperity must be accomplished.
8. Workers must be inspired or trained to use the scientific methods developed through time and motion study.
9. Management must organise in such a way that it can properly manage and carry out its duties.

Scientific management assumed the industrial efficiency can be improved through the application of the methods of science and the movement of high wages for higher productivity. It advocates that standardisation of working conditions, work methods, time study, motion study, standardisation of work, planning of daily tasks, etc. can promote industrial efficiency. Taylor emphasized five concepts on which management theory and practice could be based. These are : Research, standards, planning, control and co-operation. Including above principles of management, principles suggested by Henry Fayol, the great French writer on management are also briefly discussed below :

1. *Principle of Objective*

This principle requires that every member of the newspaper organisation should be familiar with its basic goals and objectives, and every activity of the newspaper organisation should be directed and should result in the accomplishment of these objectives.

2. *Principle of Specialisation*

Also known as the principle of Division of Labour, the principle of Specialisation implies that the work of every person in the newspaper organisation should be limited as far as possible.

He should concentrate his efforts on a single line of endeavour which permits him to have better acquiantance with the subject matter and a better utilisation of time.

3. *Principle of Span of Control*

This principle states that no superior should have more than a specific and limited number of subordinates. The principle of span of control makes the newspaper executives aware of the fact that on account of the limitation of time and ability there is a limit on the number of subordinates that they can effectively supervise.

4. *Principle of Authority and Responsibility*

According to this principle, authority and responsibility should go side by side in the newspaper organisation. It implies that a person working in the newspaper organisation should be held responsible for carrying out an activity in so far as he has authority over that activity. Authority should not be conceived apart form responsibility.

5. *Principle of Unity of Command*

The principle of unity of command is the most widely recognised principle of management. It states that each subordinate should have only one superior. Ernest Dale states this principle as follows : "Each person should receive orders from only one superior and be accountable to him". The principle of unity of command is based on the sound reason that if a person receives orders from more than one superior, it would lead to confusion and chaos.

6. *Principle of Unity of Direction or Order-giving*

This principle states that orders concerning a particular operation should be received directly from one person only. It was stated by Fayol as "one head and one plan for a group of activities having the same objectives". The principle of unity of direction is largely meant to ensure co-ordination.

7. *The Exception Principle*

The exception principle means that every manager at every level should take all decisions within the scope of authority and only matters beyond the scope of his authority should be referred to his superior for decision. It means that decisions which recur frequently should be reduced to a routine and delegated to subordinates while the supervisors should concentrate their energy and time on unusual matters of exceptional character. This principle will enable the top executive to devote his time to policy matters and his energies will not be frittered away on matters of routine.

8. *Scalar Principle*

This principle means that authority and responsibility should flow in a clear unbroken line from the highest executive to the lowest operative. According to Fayol, "The scalar chain is the chain of superiors ranging from the ultimate authority to the lowest ranks." This principle envisages that in every undertaking some kind of hierarchy involving superior-subordinate relationship should be established and that direct authority should flow from superior to subordinate throughout the entire organisation.

9. *Principle of Balance*

This principle implies that the various parts of an organisation should be in balance and that none of the functions should be given undue emphasis at the cost of others.

10. *Principle of Discipline*

Fayol considered discipline as a general principle of management. He stresses discipline as "respect for agreements which are directed at achieving obedience, application, energy, and outward marks of respect". According to Terry, "Self-imposed discipline is the most effective type of discipline, it is encouraged by proper managerial actuating efforts".

11. *Subordination of Individual Interest to General Interest*

This principle states that in a business the interest of one employee or groups of employees should not prevail over that of the concern. To ensure this the Fayol suggested (1) firmness and good example on the part of superiors, (2) agreement as fair as possible, and (3) constant supervision.

12. *Remuneration of Personnel*

This principle of Fayol states that remuneration should be fair which gives satisfaction both to personnel and firm (employee and employer).

13. *Order*

By order Fayol meant a place of every one and every one in his place, the right man in the right place. He believed that this order demanded precise knowledge of the human requirements and resources of the concern and constant balance between their requirements and resources.

14. *Equity*

This principle of Fayol states that the managers must treat employees with "kindness". Desire for equity and equality of treatment are aspirations to be taken into account in dealing with employees.

15. ***Stability of Tenure of Personnel***

Fayol pointed out that instability of tenure is at one and the same time cause and effect of bad running. He asserted that generally the managerial personnel of prosperous concerns is stable, that of unsuccessful ones is unstable.

16. ***Initiative***

This principle of Fayol enjoins managers to sacrifice some "personal vanity" in order to permit the subordinates to keep up their zeal and initiative.

17. ***Esprit-de-Corps***

This principle states that "union is strength". Fayol exhorts managers to encourage cohesiveness and Esprit-de-Corps among his subordinates.

NEWSPAPER OWNERSHIP

The Indian press has been a private commercial enterprise from the days of Hickey, the pioneer of journalism. The trend towards individual ownership and later concentration of ownership was already discernible in pre-independent India. There was a time when all the newspapers were local and most were individual enterprises. The earliest colonial newspaper was owned and operated by a printer as a supplement to his job printing. Today individual own the largest number of newspapers. Nearly 70 per cent of the total newspaper circulation is in the hands of a few families or units and although their number may be limited, their circulation and influence is much more than what their numbers are. This is exactly the grievance against the Indian press that although it is published in several languages, and is spread over the length and breadth of a vast country like India, the virtual control of the press is in a few hands. The newspapers are also brought out by co-operatives, religious and political groups or by journalists themselves. Some of the Government departments at the centre or in the states also bring out publications.

Concentration of ownership or monopolies in the sphere of newspaper and magazine publishing takes the form of industrial houses bringing out multiple publications such as morning and evening papers and dailies for the general readers, specialist dailies for businessmen and professionals as well as science journals, comics, business weeklies, women's magazines and children's periodicals. The Times of India is the largest publishing house bringing out regularly all types of publications. The Indian Express Group, its closest competitor, is owned by the Goenka industrial house and publishes its daily from as many as nineteen major cities. The Anand Bazar Group and the Hindustan Times Group (owned by Birlas) are the other contenders. In Kerala the Malayalam Manorama Group rules the roost.

Ownership of newspapers is thus concentrated in the hands of few groups which as a result wield much power. The concentration of ownership is a major threat to a free press, for it considerably narrows the range of opinions and the field of debate.

The First Press Commission had focussed the following forms of ownership of newspapers and periodicals prevalent in 1954.

1. Individual,
2. Partnership,
3. Joint Stock Company, Public or Private,
4. Trust,
5. Society registered under various Acts, and
6. Cooperative ownership.

Though the concentration of newspapers are mostly in the few hands but other types of newspaper ownership management and operation are also developed. There are :

1. Individual Ownership
2. Partnership
3. Corporation
4. Group or Chain Ownership
5. Employee Ownership
6. Vertical Ownership
7. Joint operation.

Now we will discuss the advantages and disadvantages of all these ownerships.

1. Individual Ownership

This type of ownership is more common among weekly newspapers. The owner usually is the editor, printer, publisher and manager, etc. He does the entire work himself and when necessary serves in almost any position in the plant.

Advantages

1. The owner makes all decisions related to business and editorial policies.
2. He is given absolute control of newspaper.
3. He receives all profits and bears losses whatever occur.
4. He keeps intimate connection with the newspaper.
5. He maintains secrecy in operations.
6. He makes quick decisions.

Disadvantages

1. The owner is liable for the newspaper's entire debt.
2. Unlimited liability is placed on the individual owner.
3. Individual ownership is not adaptable to an expanding business.
4. In case of owner's death decline in business is evident.
5. Long-term loans may be difficult to obtain, since creditors must consider the life expectancy of the proprietor.
6. Success of the newspaper depends heavily on the ability and credit status of the owner.

2. Partnership

According to the Indian Partnership Act, 1932, partnership is "the relationship between persons who have agreed to share profits of a business carried on by all or any of them acting for all". In a partnership firm there should be at least two partners, the maximum number can be raised to twenty. In partnership persons make an ownership agreement, either orally or in written for the purpose of establishing, purchasing or operating a newspaper. To avoid legal problems it can be registered with the Registrar of Firms. A partnership deed containing name of business, amount of capital, name of place of operation of business, duties and powers of partners, appropriation of profits, etc. should be signed.

Types of Partnership

It may be of two types.

a. General
b. Limited.

General Partnership : This type of partnership is based on an agreement between two or more persons to establish or purchase a newspaper and engage in publishing it. It is more common form of partnership but each partner is liable to an unlimited degree. Each partner is a general agent for the newspaper and in any business matter one partner may act for both.

Limited Partnership : A limited partner is responsible for the debt of the newspaper only to the amount agreed upon as an investment and has no right to contract for the newspaper and on control of its assets.

Advantages

1. Responsibilities of newspapers are divided, thereby lessening the workload on each partner.
2. Judgement of more than one mind is brought into business operation.
3. Persons of different capabilities and financial standings are permitted to pool their talent and money.
4. Maintenance and operation costs are divided.
5. Partnership is easy to form.
6. Quick decisions are possible.
7. Larger resources are also possible.

Disadvantages

1. Each partner runs the risk of becoming liable for an usually large debt incurred by any one of other partners.
2. Partnership may be discontinued at any time by death or withdrawal of a partner.
3. Each partner is liable for the newspaper's entire debt.
4. Each person is privileged to obligate the newspaper.
5. Long-term credit is sometimes hard to obtain.
6. A partner who is irresponsible may jeopardize the interest of the other partner or partners.

7. Lack of harmony among partners also creates problems sometimes.
8. Partnership also has a lack of public confidence.

3. Corporation

This is the most common form for daily newspaper because it is more adaptable to problems of expansion, centralisation or transfer of fractional ownership.

Advantages

1. The personal liability of investors in case of law suit, it is limited to their share of interest in the corporation.
2. The business of the newspaper is not readily affected by changes in stock ownership.
3. Transfer of control is flexible.
4. Operations can be expanded easily by increasing capital.
5. A publisher who owns 51 per cent of the shares in the newspaper and whose powers are defined in the articles of the corporation may control the policies and obtain from outside sources 49 per cent of the capital needed for operation.

Disadvantages

1. Profits distributed to stock holders are first taxed as income to the corporation and again as dividends to the shareholders.
2. Corporation taxes are imposed.

4. Group or Chain Ownership

Group comprises two or more newspapers published by a single establishment from the same centre.

Chain ownership applies to more than one newspaper published by the same establishment from more than one centre.

Newspaper chains take various forms depending on the point of operation at which cooperation is dominant. In some cases a holding company controls at least 51 per cent of the shares in each newspaper. The holding company may have supervision over editorial policies of individual newspapers or the company may allow each to formulate its own. Major materials such as newsprint. machinery and other equipments and supplies usually are brought through general headquarters.

Newspaper groups are formed without a common holding company but with a chain of command from an elected set of officers and directors. Publishers in the organisation have the controlling interest in the newspapers they publish and also may have an interest in the other newspapers. They manage their own newspapers and formulate their own policies with the advice and council of the officer.

Advantages

1. Supplies may be purchased through a control office with discounts for quantity.
2. Advertising space may be sold nationally with a single organisation representing all newspapers in the group.
3. Certain details of book keeping and other office procedure may be centered in a common office for all newspapers.
4. A large group owner could afford to improve news coverage by having correspondents and news bureaus in the state capital and foreign cities. This arrangement is too expensive for a small owner to maintain.
5. The chains are also better able to afford the latest technical equipment thereby making newspaper production more efficient.
6. Chains have the resources to provide more elaborate training and public service programmes than do individually owned papers, the validity of each of these agreements depends in great measure on the particular group owner involved. As Earnest Hynds concluded in his book 'American Newspapers in the 1980s', "some group-owned newspapers are among the nation's best ; some newspapers belonging to groups are at best mediocre".*

Disadvantages

1. Managers or publishers might not feel compelled to promote the local community to the same degree that they would if the newspapers were owned by them or by a local corporation or partnership.
2. Permanence of management is more in question than when the

* Earnest Hynds, "American Newspapers in the 1980s", New York : Hastings House, 1980, p. 144

newspaper is entirely locally owned.

3. Subscribers sometimes feel that the newspaper is managed by remote control and they are not as close to the editor as they would like to be.

5. Employee Ownership

Employee ownership usually develops where a publisher has held the controlling interest and upon retirement or death wants the paper continued under its established policies in the hands of associates. Furthermore, the publisher appreciates the interest and the ability of employees and desires to recognise their loyalty in this way. This type of ownership allows employees to buy shares in the newspaper corporation. In some cases the employees own a majority of the shares and control the policies of the newspaper.

Advantages

1. Employees are given an incentive to protect the best interest of the newspaper.
2. Very few changes are made in personnel.
3. Sense of ownership on the part of employees, helps to create high morale.
4. Questions pertaining to wages, hours and other production matters are understood better and are more easily handled.
5. Interdepartmental barriers are more easily broken.

Disadvantages

1. Opportunities for bringing new people into the organisation are fewer.
2. Sale of property is difficult, even if it should appear beneficial to the newspaper.
3. Length of employee service is likely to be given greater consideration than production abilities.

6. Vertical Ownership

A newspaper may also operate under a vertical ownership plan, meaning that the newspaper and the enterprises serving it are under common ownership. A corporation owning and operating a large city daily, for example, also may own and operate other media, news and advertising syndicates, a paper mill and a transportation system etc. These allied institutions contribute to the success of the newspaper.

Advantages

1. It helps to reduce general expenses of newspaper operation.
2. It provides practical investment of newspaper profits.
3. It assures the newspaper of certain services and materials needed for its successful operation.

Disadvantages

1. It widens the publisher's interests and responsibilities to the extent of a possible lessening of attention in the newspaper.
2. Capital that could be used for improvement of the newspaper might be drawn into financing of other jointly owned enterprises.

7. Joint Operation

It is a system of co-operative operation between two or more newspapers of different ownership within the same premises. This system is sometimes used to reduce maintenance and operation costs. The newspapers are produced in the same plant, but each has separate news and business offices and its own reporters and editors, advertising sales people and circulation employees. Each newspaper formulates its own policy. For a joint publishing operation, an agreement is drawn up setting forth the financial obligations of each newspaper, or a corporation is formed representing capital from both ownership.

Advantages

1. Maintenance and operation costs are reduced.
2. Production hours in the plant are increased.
3. Attention of publishers and owners is focussed more on the community than on competitions.
4. Publishers may give more unified and complete newspaper service to their public.
5. Pleasant relations are developed among newspapers in a competitive field.

6. Advertisers usually are permitted to buy space either in all newspapers at combination rate or in separate ones at the individual newspaper's standard rate.
7. Joint handling of some advertising and perhaps some news copy permits reduction of personnel in the news and advertising sections as well as in the mechanical department.

Disadvantages

1. With reduced competition, publishers might strive for greater projects than their newspaper service deserves.
2. Use of common production facilities may lead to standardisation, resulting in loss of newspaper individuality.
3. With competition partly eliminated efforts towards specific improvements might be lessened.

It is well known that there does exist a concentration of newspaper ownership, call it a monopoly or oligopoly. The Press Commission came to the conclusion that even if the concentration of ownership might not be controlled there should be diffusion of ownership which would minimize the effects of monopoly control.

It suggested, therefore, "that in view of this difficulty we recommend that diffusion be brought about by gradual distribution of shares to the employees and to a small extent to the public, both in existing undertakings and in those to be started in future. Such transfer will guard against control of undertaking passing to strangers, and to the employees sharing in the success which they help to create would have an interest in securing in continuance of the undertaking which provides them with employment.

EDITORIAL DEPARTMENT

The role and responsibilities of members of a newspaper editorial department depend on its administrative structure. This, in turn, is determined by the number of staff members employed. Newspapers and magazines have different structures. Since a newspaper has to be produced every day, it calls for speedy work with lots of persons working in it than the magazine which may be weekly, fortnightly or monthly. In publication houses which bring out a group of newspapers and magazines, the chief editor is the one who is responsible for the total policy of the publishing house. Though individual editors are free to express their opinions and to adopt attitudes, the chief editor has to bring in a community of approach to avoid direct personnel criticism by editors of one another. He is the link between the management and editorial departments. The term Chief Editor has come into vogue only recently in India. In west, editor-in-chief is often known simply as the editor. In cases where newspapers are published from different centres, the chief editor is one who has a number of resident editors each incharge of the edition coming out from that particular city. *The Indian Express, The Times of India, The Statesman, The Hindustan Times* all are chain newspapers with resident editors of particular edition.

Working of Editorial Department

The editor holds the key position in the newspaper organisation. He is responsible for the editorial content of the newspapers including everything from comics to news stories to editorials. Baskette and Sissors have succinctly remarked that "the editor is a diamond cutter who refines and polishes, removes the flaws and shapes a stone into a gem. He searches for ills in copy and meticulously scans the product for flaws and inaccuracy, ever searching for the maximum power of words".* Unless somebody works as a reporter, he will have little contact with the editor. The editor's influence is exerted through those who report directly to that editor usually the managing editor and the editorial page editor.

The main functions of the editorial department are :

- Gathering of news
- Macro and micro selection of news and features
- Editing of news and features
- Interpretation of news
- Selection of lead articles
- Editorial writings

The editor of the newspaper alone cannot handle the editing work and is, therefore, assisted by a number of persons as shown in Figs. 1 and 2, chief correspondents, resident editors, managing editors,

---

* Floyed K. Baskette and Jack Z. Sissors, *The Art of Editing*, New York; MacMillan Publishing Co. Inc, 1977, p. 4.

assistant editors, news editors, sub-editors, stringers, staffers and other functionaries like photographers cartoonists, feature writers and reviewers, etc. In fact, the editor is the captain of the team. He guides those working under him and is aware of their talents and makes the best use of their abilities. His main concern is to get material from the assistant editors in order to fill up the editorial page.

A good editor of a newspaper is aware of the scope and interpretation of news. He takes keen interest in the presentation of news and is aware of the details of important happenings. He keeps track of the readers' requirements. He influences people to strive willingly for mutual objectives. The editor gauges the public mind to give his ideas and opinions on current issues to maintain cordial public relations.

He is also responsible for day-to-day review of the newspaper. Such a review is done in meeting which is held every day by the editor. It is during those meetings that a decision is taken on editorials, comments, standard of news, its presentation and placement, news in competing papers, allotment of work, arrangement of photographs, correction and denial of news etc.

In a modern newspaper organisation, the editors have to work in accordance with the views and established preferences of newspaper managements. His views on particular subjects or issues, and his policies are also reflected in the editorials. Denis states, "Reporters may then deliberately or unwittingly slant their stories to fit those policies. Failure to do so might slow promotion, or even put a journalist on the unemployment line. The extent to which formal and informal controls can influence the individual's work varies with the structure of the organisation. Often the debate between news and business values hinges on the belief that when news organisations worry too much about profits, they court consensus in their communities and avoid controversy, which is the essence of news". Bailey bristled at "the growing tendency to encourage, in fact, to require, editors to become businessmen to be part of a 'management team' to concentrate on things that involve business rather than journalism".*

---

* Charles W. Bailey, *Exit Lines from a Minnesota Editor*, Washington Journalism Review, February 1983, pp.14-15.

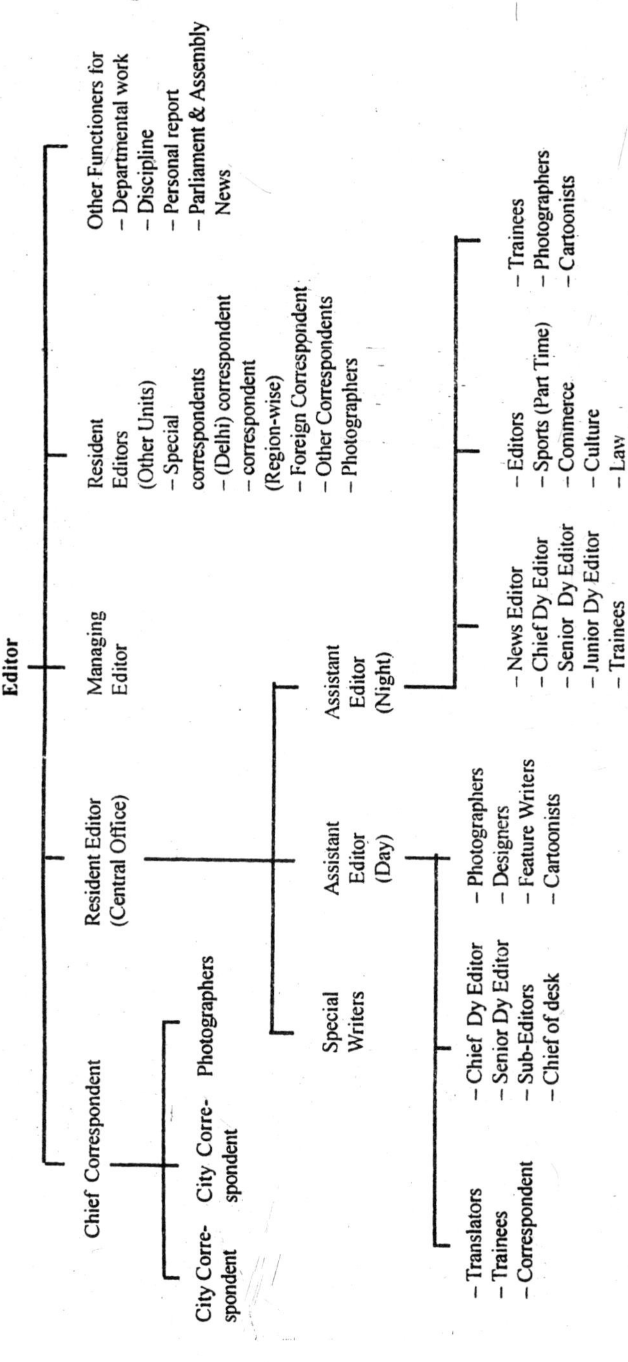

Fig. 1. Organisational structure in editorial department.
Source : Kothari, Gulab, Newspaper Management in India, Netherlands : Intercultural Open University, 1995.

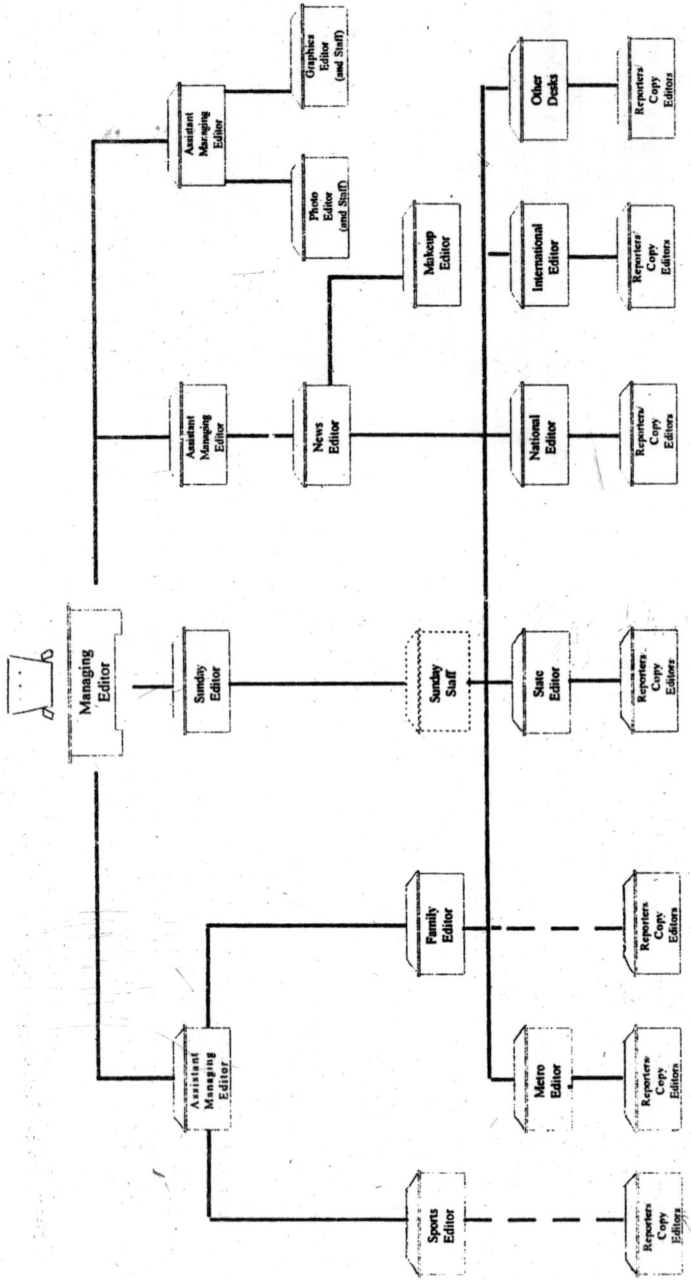

Fig. 2. Typical news room organization of the metropolitan daily newspaper.

Source : Brooks, Brian, S. *et al.*, 'News Reporting and Writing, New York : St. Martin's Press, 1988.

ADVERTISING DEPARTMENT

Newspapers derive their revenue from two sources : advertising and circulation. Advertising provides 75-80 per cent of the total revenue while circulation accounts for about 20-25 per cent. Hence advertising department is the most important department of a newspaper industry. As circulation promotes sales, advertising promotes space. As such, the work of collection and publication of advertisements becomes crucial in a newspaper organisation. This department must constantly strive to improve the advertising service and increase the advertising volume because rising costs of newsprint, competition among newspapers and the threat from satellite television have greatly affected the financial status of the newspaper industry.
Advertising revenue comes mainly from three sources :

(i) Display advertising
(ii) Local or casual advertising
(iii) Classified advertising.

1. *Display advertising* : Display advertisements may have few words, much blank space and often an illustration of the product.

They draw strong attention value and high legibility because of the conspicuous arrangement of contents–large or bold face type, attractive illustrations, colour and other devices. Display advertisements are charged is terms of column centimetre on page. Extra rates are charged for the use of colour. While an open rate is charged for single insertion, usually lower rates are offered to advertisers who plan to run a series of advertisements is the newspaper over a period on contract basis.

Newspaper advertising is usually sold by the publisher on a run-of paper (ROP) basis. ROP means the advertisement will be placed in the position in the paper that is most suitable and satisfactory to the publisher. Thus the newspaper does not make a commitment as to the exact placement of the advertisement. However, certain advertisers prefer 'special position' of their advertisements in the newspaper. Newspapers charge extra for preferred positions. Newspapers also charge extra for split-run service. The split run is the process by which alternate copies of the same newspaper are printed with different advertisements for the same product.

2. *Local or Casual Advertising :* Local advertising originates from local or regional advertisers on an irregular basis to announce some special event such as a sale, opening a branch, starting a new business or introducing a new service or product in the area. Casual advertising may also come in response to special supplements a newspaper or some other organisations initiate.

Newspaper advertising departments often help casual advertisers in writing or preparing copy and designing advertisements. These advertisers are often charged on individual basis.

3. *Classified Advertising :* Classified advertisements are published without any conspicuous display on specific pages of newspapers. With the passage of time, it becomes a convention for each newspaper to publish classified advertisements in a particular section. Classified advertisements are grouped by contents and contain diverse elements. They are set in small point size type. Headings and sub heads are set slightly in larger type sizes. They come from many sources and cover an extreme range of products and services. As the name implies, classified advertisements are categorised under small heads for instance, advertisements such as 'Property wanted', 'Plot for sale', 'Accommodation wanted', 'Accommodation Available', 'Lost and found', 'Tuitions', 'Matrimonials', and many more. These advertisements are small and often require editing or rewriting since people who provide the advertisement matter are sometimes unable to state their requirements clearly.

The rates of these advertisements are quoted per word, per column, per line, or per column centimetre. The newspapers normally require such advertisements to be paid for in advance. Public notices, tenders and other statutory publicity by Government departments are usually published in the classified section to conserve space and minimise cost. Public notices and legal advertising are legally required to be published in newspapers and other media. They convey information to the public which is essential for the democratic functioning of Government and sound conduct of its business.

Functions of Advertising Department

1. Designing and Production

The general purpose of advertising is to attract attention, create an interest in the product or service advertised. It should create desirability to use among the users. Advertisements obtained from agencies cause no problem to the advertising department. However, for local and directly released advertisements, the department offers its services and expertise in preparing copy and layouts to produce the desired impact. In case advertisements do not produce the results advertisers expect, the newspaper will be blamed for lacking advertising potential and the advertisements released in it will be considered a waste.

2. Billing and Collection

Preparation of bills and collection of payments from advertisers is an important function of the advertising department. Payments for classified advertisements are usually received in advance. Payments for those released by agencies accredited to INS become due only after 75 days. In some newspapers, billing and collection may be an integral function of the department, while in others this may be left to the accounts department. In either case the advertising department should be aware of the credit worthiness of its clients.

3. Dummy Preparation

To prepare a dummy edition means to plan a blueprint of an advertising and/or editorial contents of a publication. Elements are only sketched or miniature layouts are prepared. No proofs or pasting are involved. Dummy preparation, which finally ends in giving the ratio between editorial contents and advertising space also begins with the determination of approximate space to be allocated to the two elements. While a newspaper is supposed to be the first of all a vehicle for conveying news, how much news and the number of pages to be published in an edition are normally decided by the volume of advertisements rather than the amount of news available. After the advertising department has made its claim, the editorial department is notified of the number of pages planned and the size of the newshole available to it.

For advertising department, dummy preparation provides a way by which it can blueprint the exact location of every advertisement instead of leaving that important function to the composing department. By doing this work itself, the department is able to rotate the page positioning of advertisers in a planned way. It guarantees that advertisements of competing advertisers will not appear on facing pages. The dummy system places responsibility on the editorial department for the choice and positioning of all reading matter directly in the hands of editorial staff. Hence dummy system provides a means of planning an edition in a controlled and orderly fashion.

CIRCULATION DEPARTMENT

Circulation means the number of newspaper copies sold and paid for. It is the foundation of a newspaper's success : it is the basis of all revenue. It is true that newspaper sales account for less revenue than advertising, but circulation is the force that makes the advertising pay. More the circulation more will be the advertising. Without it, there would be no advertising. Circulation also is a measure of the newspaper's service. Greater circulation gives the evidence that the newspaper is fulfilling its obligations to the community. Frank Thayer has rightly stated, "Circulation is a channel through which the results of essential newspaper objectives are tested : circulation is a gauge to measure newspaper effectiveness. When circulation is impaired, publishing hazards tend to be multiplied and intensified".

Variable Factors in Determining Circulation

No department of a newspaper runs more risk of getting off balance in its work flow than the circulation department. The paper must be delivered at homes at regular hours each day and it must be in good order. Circulation volume must rise continually or at least remain stabilized at a profitable level.

The following factors have a great bearing on circulation.

1. *Population*

No doubt more the population more will be the circulation, but the size of the population does not always determine the volume of circulation. Some communities with small population have newspapers with large circulation, and some communities with large populations prove to be poor newspaper receivers. This can only mean that internal population conditions as well as population numbers have a strong bearing on circulation.

2. *Education*

The enrolment of students in institutions of higher learning has increased. The opening of new fields of learning, rapid advances in all phases of science, better methods of teaching, and greater expenditure on education have all contributed to greater eagerness for information and wider and more intensive reading of newspapers.

3. *Social Conditions*

Shifting tides of urban renewal, population mobility, suburban flight and other sociological factors directly affect circulation. Whether such conditions are localized or national in scope, newspaper management is obviously challenged to cope in ways that call for resourceful and innovative approaches to the problem at hand.

Functions of Circulation Department

Circulation department of a newspaper establishment is akin to the marketing department of a business or industrial establishment. Its activities may be classified as follows :

1. *Packing and Dispatch*

As the newspapers come out of the press, arrangements must be made to pack them as quickly as possible in packets for dispatch to sales agents. In packing care has to be taken that they reach the agents without damage or delay. Mistakes in counting papers or addressing packets would result in inconvenience to both agents and readers and also mean some extra costs for the organisation.

2. *Transportation and Distribution*

Since the newspaper has a very short life, the speed with which it can be distributed becomes critically important. The circulation manager has to co-ordinate various modes of transportation so that the daily could reach the readers in the shortest possible time. Public transportation system is not dependable. Depending on the geographical area to be covered, and the number of agents to be served, each newspaper has to work out its own transportation network in determining the distribution in the minimum possible time.

3. *Relationship with Agents*

The agents are the most important persons for circulation department because they come in direct contact with the readers and are aware of the likes and dislikes of the readers. They also know about the position of other competing newspapers because they are in direct touch with the readers. They can be extremely helpful to know the response of the readers about contents of the newspapers, price of paper, timely supply of newspaper etc. Gulab Kothari suggested it, therefore, becomes important to motivate the agents and hawkers through higher commission, conveyance facilities and many more.

4. *Subscriptions*

This section usually deals with the distribution of newspapers sent by mail. Some subscription copies may also be distributed through agents. The subscription section receives advance payment for a newspaper for a definite period. Posts and telegraphs department provides concessional rates for dispatching the newspapers to any part of the country or to a destination beyond its borders. Trilok Sindhwani states, "the cost of distribution of newspapers rises progressively because of increased cost of freight and incidentals. Sometimes it is only through a subscription service that a newspaper can be supplied economically to readers far from the centre of publication.

5. *Collection of Sales*

The main responsibilities of the circulation department are selling newspaper, delivering it timely and collecting its revenue. Although these functions are distinct and separate, they are closely related. Efficient collection is one of the key factors in building a list of permanent subscribers. If the paper is delivered by independent contractor, its proceed is collected on dual system. The contractor collects it from the customers and the newspaper collects it from the contractor. Circulation revenue therefore, forms a vital component of the cash flow and total revenue recoveries.

6. *Print Order*

The number of copies to be printed of each edition is usually determined by the circulation department. This department prepares print order for each edition on the basis of supply requirements of agents, hawkers, subscribers, advertising voucher copies, complimentary copies and other requirements. This is a time bound operation and to a large extent establishes deadlines for other departments.

7. *Supply of Information to RNI and ABC*

To supply information to the Registrar of Newspapers of India (RNI) and to the Audit Bureau of Circulation (ABC) is a statutory obligation. These are the accounting organisations which audits and accredits circulation of daily and periodical newspapers.

8. *Promoting Circulation*

Building, maintaining and promoting circulation are the primary functions of the circulation department. Without it, advertising would suffer, thus loss of revenue. Circulation can be promoted by giving inducements to the new subscribers, distributing free supplements, reducing advertising rates and by prize winning contests, etc. Quick and timely supply of the paper at the desired place also helpd in building circulation.

PRODUCTION DEPARTMENT

As the term implies, this department is responsible for transforming the creative work of reporters, editors and advertising people into the finished product of the newspaper. This department is headed by General Manager who runs a battery of technical personnel to look after different aspects of production – typesetting, art studio, platemaking and printing. Since most dailies are now printed by offset printing, the arrangement of this department has changed markedly over the last few years. Before we go for the latest method of producing the newspaper, let us have a look at the old method of bringing out newspapers.

Earlier method of producing a newspaper–In the earlier days the letters were assembled for producing a newspaper through hot-metal typesetting. It was so called because molten metal at the temperature of 750° F was used. Typesetting techniques were : *Hand composing* (where single letters were picked up by hand from pigeon-hole cases, assembled into words, justified into columns and then used for printing); *Linotype* (where slug which means full solid line was cast on machine); *Monotype* (which casts and assembles single characters with the help of two machines); and *Ludlow* (which was used to cast headlines). These typesetting methods had merits and demerits. For example, hand composing was easy to learn, easy to carry out corrections but was slow. Linotype was fast but corrections were expensive as even for one mistake one had to cast a fresh line. Monotype was also fast and corrections were easy to carry out but co-ordination of two machines were a problem. Ludlow also cast fresh line but it was slow process.

Special typewriters were also used for typesetting. Their names were Justowriters and varityper. The main characteristics of these typewriters were that justification of the lines on both sides was possible, and different type designs could also be obtained. But these typewriters also did not suit to new technology because the speed was slow and also uneconomical.

After typesetting the full page was assembled in the galley and was locked up in the chase which was ready for printing. Printing was done with the help of letterpress process in which printing area was in relief and the non-printing area below. Ink was applied on the printing area. Paper was placed over the printing area and the pressure was applied which resulted into the printing of the paper (Fig. 3).

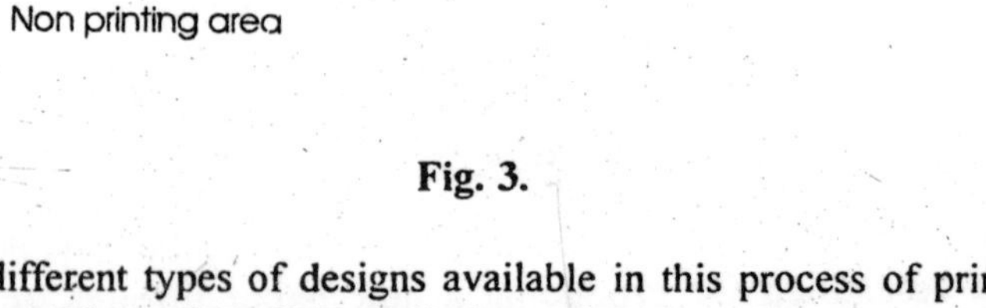

Fig. 3.

Three different types of designs available in this process of printing. These are Platen (treadle), Cylinder and Rotary. Plater press is the simplest press as it requires very little skill. In this machine forme of type is placed in a vertical position. The paper is positioned against the platen, which closes in clamshell fashion to press it against the inked forme. When the platen swings open to receive another sheet of paper, the forme is reinked. Platen presses are limited in size and are consequently used primarily for printing letterheads, cards, forms and other small jobs. Cylinder machines are bigger in size. They can print one page of a daily newspaper, or two pages of a tabloid or four pages of a magazine. Cylinder machines are quite slow because they require two revolutions for one impression. In the first revolution the impression is made, in the second the cylinder rises to allow the paper to be removed. A production speed of 3,500 to 4,000 impressions per hour is typical.

Rotary process do not print direct from flat formes as in the case of cylinder machines. Printing in this operation is done from a curved surface (curved surface was made by casting hot lead against a fibre mat). The unit consists of two kinds of cylinders, one that contains the printing plate and another that serves to press the paper against the plate. Rotary machine can produce as many as 70,000 copies of newspapers in an hour including folding and cutting, etc.

In nutshell, small printing presses use platen machines because skill is easily available and these are economical. Cylinder machines are used for book work but rotary is very rarely used. All these machines are becoming outdated because colour work is very-very expensive in letterpress process.

Latest method of producing a newspaper–Now computers are used for typesetting. This method in also called cold typesetting because molten metal is not used ; rather reporters type their stories at Video Display Terminals (VDT) which place the stories in a computer's memory. These stories are "called up by copy editors, who trim and make changes in the stories and code them for use in the paper. If upon further reflection, the managing editor decides that the story is not newsworthy enough for inclusion, the story can be purged from the machine. The managing editor can also instruct the computer to store the copy for future use. The newsworthy stories are then sent back to the computer for processing. Decisions about page make-up and the amount of space to be devoted to a story are made as the deadline for publication approaches. Photographs and other art work are selected for inclusion; space is cleared for late breaking stories and updates are inserted.

In the composing room high speed computerized photo composition machines take electronic impulses and translate them into images and words. The stories are printed on strips of photographic paper. These strips then go to the make-up room where alongwith advertisements, photos, artwork, and headlines, they are pasted up into full newspaper pages (computers are now being developed to do this job). This pasted up page looks and reads just like the final printed page. This paste-up is taken to the camera room, where a photograph is made of the whole page. This results in a negative, which is sent to the plate-making section. An offset plate is prepared which is ready for printing.

Newspaper technology is now almost all computer-driven, and most publishers continue to automate their operations as new technology becomes available. Electronic page make up of display advertisements with graphics has become a reality. It has eliminated typesetting on photo sensitive paper, paste-up of mechanicals and many other steps.

Computerised typesetting is a very neat and clean process of typesetting. It has eliminated many operations as proof-reading and sub-editing, etc. It does not require scarce and expensive metal as it was in the earlier method. Type size can be increased or decreased even fractionally through magnification and reduction control. The range of type sizes is infinite. It is a very fast method of typesetting but this is very highly sophisticated method and requires skilled manpower.

After the pages are made up on the screen, an offset plate is made by placing the negative between glass and a sheet of photosensitive metal and exposing the plate to bright light. The finished product is a plate with two areas : those parts that were exposed to light and the rest of the plate. Some newspapers use plastic instead of metal plates for direct printing. Printing area and non-printing area are on the same level in the offset process unlike letter press process where printing area was raised and the non-printing area was recessed. Ink is applied on the plate. Printing area receives and non-printing rejects ink because offset works on the principle that water and oil do not mix but they repel each other (Fig. 4).

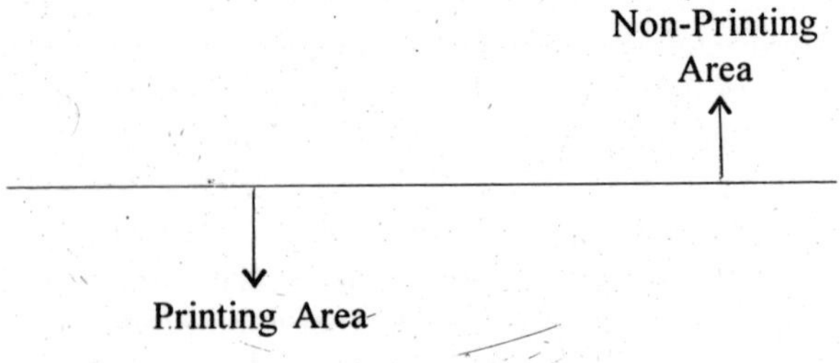

Fig. 4.

This is the indirect method of printing as printing is not directly done from plate cylinder rather impression from plate cylinder goes to rubber blanket and from rubber blanket to impression cylinder (Fig. 5).

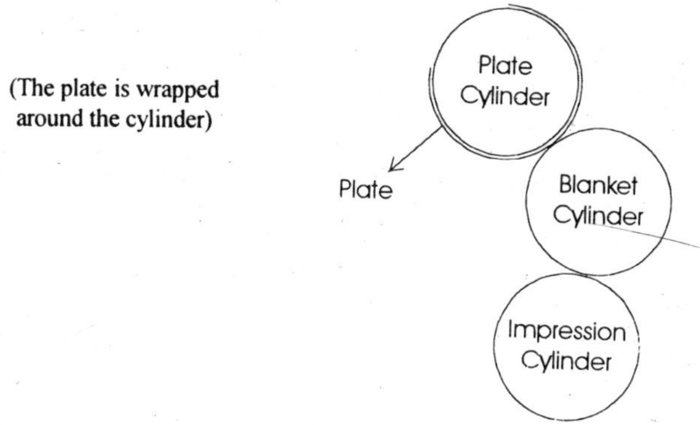

Fig. 5.

A thin coating of water is placed over the entire printing area and the water adheres only to the non-image area. Ink is applied to the entire printing area, and adheres only where there is no water. The ink readily transfers to the paper pressed to the image. A small amount of water also transfers to the paper but is not noticed to the naked eye.

In the printing section both sheet-fed and web-fed offset rotaries are used. In sheet-fed offset, single sheet is fed into the machine. Paper goes into the machine automatically at a break-neck speed. In web-fed offset huge rolls of newsprint are threaded into the presses. Finished and folded papers in multi-colours emerge from the press and are sent, by conveyor belt to the distribution areas. The distribution staff counts and bundles the newspapers and then hands them over to the circulation truck drivers, who then deliver them to newsstands and carriers.

Offset printing is very cheap for colour productions. Anything that can be photographed can be used as composed type. Even the typed copy can be used for offset process. Line drawings, charts, diagrams, and similar other illustrations add absolutely no cost to a job printed by offset. Rough paper can be used for fine printing. As plates are plain the process is suitable for Hindi newspapers having short vowels, half and joint letters, etc. The printing plate is inexpensive and can easily be curved around the cylinder. Four colour printing is often possible at lower costs. Though it has many advantages it has some disadvantages also as it is impossible to remove the effect of water in this process. The colours appear slightly washed out on account of the effect of water. Printing is expensive for small runs. Anyhow the increased use of offset in publishing newspapers and magazines has greatly increased the use of these presses.

SECTION–V

PUBLIC RELATIONS AND ADVERTISING

Public Relations and Advertising

Public Relations, Meaning and Definition

Public, for the purpose of discussion of public relations, is a group of people with some kind of common interest with which we are concerned.

By general public we mean the entire population–the rich and the poor and the middle class, men and women, young and old, educated and uneducated, all the racial, ethnic and religious groups. Incidentally, although the term public relations is plural, it is used in the singular. It would be seen clearly that the relations of the corporation, university, trade union or any other organisation to the public is what it is meant to be. It would become clear that "Public means every group of segment with which the institution has relations...... employees, customers, suppliers, governments, communities and academics". Public relations is used in the following ways :

1. Relationships with individuals or groups which comprise an institution's publics ?
2. The ways and means used to achieve favourable relationship with these sub-publics ?
3. The quality or status of an institution relationship.

The purpose of public relations practice is to establish a two-way communication to resolve conflicts of interest by seeking common ground or areas of mutual interest and to establish understanding based on truth, knowledge and full information.

The scale of activity to promote good public relations may vary considerably according to size and nature of the interested parties but the philosophy, strategy and the methods will be very similar, whether the public relations programme is designed to influence the international understanding or to improve relations between the company and its customers, agents and employees.

In a family or a small closely knit community, there are few obstacles to mutual discussion and the communication of ideas. Even here there are plenty of opportunities or misunderstanding. In public and commercial life, however, the family circle is usually widely dispersed and the absence of personal contacts makes co-operation and understanding difficult. People skilled in public relations practice use modern methods of communication and persuasion to bridge the gap and to establish mutual understanding.

Public relations is a two-way persuasive communication process which is used as an instrument of generating goodwill, co-operation, understanding, etc. between an organisation on the one hand and its public on the other. Public relations can never be aggressive, it is always persuasive.

It is the persuasive communication process. Accordingly the public relations exercise will depend on truth, honesty, courtesy, social interaction and use of convincing power and logic, instead of intimidation or dominance. Information should not be partial but total and sincere.

In public relations exercise long term objectives are achieved. Hence, it will be a continuing exercise.

Organisation will mean all type of institutions, factories, companies, offices, etc.

Public include all those persons who are carried with a particular organisation in one form or other. Each organisation will have different publics.

Short Hand Definitions

According to the British Institute of Public Relations, "Public relations is the deliberate, planned and sustained effort to establish and maintain mutual understanding between an organisation and its publics". To others, Public Relations is :

- the art and science of developing reciprocal understanding and goodwill,
- the behavioural science concerned with the study of behaviours and attitudes of the management of the organisation as well as the employees and other publics of the organisation,
- the technology of making other people agree to your proposal,

- the persuasive communication designed to influence specific publics, and
- doing good and getting credit for it.

It is an instrument of filling communication gap particularly between its organisation and its publics.

It has been observed by Cutlip and Center : Public relations is a management function which evaluates the public attitude and identifies the policies and programmes in co-operation with the publics. Baldeo Sahai in his book : *Public Relations–A Scientific Approach*, explains, "Public relations is the behavioural science which seeks to serve an organisation and its publics by bridging their communication gap between the two so as to foster the mutual trust and goodwill".

It is the behavioural science and like any other empirical science should follow the scientific methods. This includes laying down objectives, preparing a plan of action, collecting relevant facts, choosing tools to implement the plan, examining the alternatives, exhibiting the plan and finally evaluating the results. The entire exercise is based on fact and truth.

The service of the organisation lies in bridging the communication gap between the organisation and publics and building an image of liability, efficiency and public services.

The communication gap also includes feed back–that is information about reaction of the publics to the activities of the organisation.

Bernays says, "Public relations is two-way street". PRO is not only the spokesman of organisation, he is also its eyes and ears.

To foster trust and goodwill is the ultimate object of all P. R. programmes. Trust cannot be earned by overplaying and underplaying facts, not by presenting a distorted picture. Trust can be created only on the basis of truth.

Man is a social animal. He has to adjust himself in a society according to the norms of the society. It will include all type of workers, children and all other innocent people. We should be very considerate to all these persons. Concept of adjustment tells us the legitimacy of P. R. Hence, the process of understanding the norms of society will be called P. R.

People are interdependent. This interdependence is due to social security, necessity or may be economical. This needs public relationing.

Man is a very complex entity. On the one side, he behaves rationally and on the other emotionally. Hence, it is very difficult to take out work from him because of different characteristics. Therefore, some technique should be there that is P. R.

Every physical action of human being will create positive as well as negative reaction. To decrease this reaction, one should be very sweet and courteous. Hence, P. R. serves as an earthling process.

P. R. is not unpaid advertisement. It has the beauty of art and the techniques of science. The substance of public relations is to develop understanding among different constituents which deal with the organization. The objective of a PR programme is to promote mutual understanding between an organisation and all those with whom it comes into contact both within and outside the organization to project its image and to eliminate all sources of misunderstanding. *The PR effort should be to earn goodwill, project correct public image and motivate publics in favour of the organization's policy programmes, products or services. The PR programme should, therefore, not comprise stunts and gimmicks but be based on purposeful dissemination of information about the objectives and activities of the organisation.*

Essentials of Public Relations

Sam Black has given ten essentials of Public Relations in his book, *Practical Public Relations (p.199).*

1. The practice of public relations is a profession, an art applied to a science. The public interest, not pecuniary motivation, is the primary consideration in its practice. The profession has its literature, its voluntary associations and its educational curricula–all criteria of a profession.
2. Public relations concerns itself with the relations of a unit, an organisation or an individual with the public on which it depends for its viability. Public relations advice covers adjustment to the public, information to the public and persuasion to the public to accept a service or product.
3. The need for the public relations practitioner as a societal technician has been brought about by the revolution in transportation and recommunication, more widespread literacy, the increasingly complex network of communications, and the resultant greater participation by the public in the shaping of all institutions.
4. Effective public relations establishes a meeting point to the highest degree of adjustment between an organisation and the public on which it depends.

5. Effective public relations is based on reality not on images, whether true or false. Deeds and action that serve the public interest are the basis of sound public relations.
6. An organisation seeks public approval and support on the basis of the public interest. The public interest is the criterion by which a public relations professional accepts a client. He rejects the client who does not serve the public interest.
7. The public relations man first evaluates by scientific public opinion research, the concords and discords between his client and his public. He advises his client on the modification of attitudes and actions which are indicated. He advises on information needed by the public to provide a basis for understanding and support. He advises on method of persuasion necessary to gain public support.
8. Professional public relations practice depends on the application of the social sciences (Psychology, sociology, social psychology, public opinion, communication study and semantics) to the problem at hand.
9. The public relations professional plays an important role in preparing the various segments of the society for coming developments in order to prevent 'future shock'.
10. The professional public relations man is remunerated on the principle of quantum merit which sets the pattern in other professions.

Principle of Public Relations

As the specialist who cutivates the tree is equally concerned with its individual parts, the root scheme on which its prosperity depends, so with public relations. Its practice spreads, it accommodates itself with its environment, and the environment accepts. But the under lying principles from which it derives sustenance are of prime importance to the practitioner and to those whom its activities affect. An appraisal of public relations is bound to be determined by the way its practitioners approach their work– their philosophy, attitude, ethical standards and knowledge of technical skills.

Their philosophy is summed up in the concept that public relations is an essential function of the management of any enterprise. This is true whether the organisation engages in governmental, social or economic activity. Their attitude is defined by a conviction that service in the public interest is the ultimate criterion by which a man or a policy must be judged. Their ethical standards agree with these regulations, stated and unstated that govern our culture as to equity and morality. Their technical skills are developed through aptitude, training and performance of such competence that the results they work to achieve are reasonably predictable. Public relations success is based on optimism, a wellspring of ideas and much thoughtful planning. A public relations administrator is judged instantly by the words of his mouth but ultimately by the meditations of his heart. This is a practice in which a person of normal endowments gets along better than a magician.

Public relations practice has spread from industry to education, government and other social and economic institutions. With it has spread increasing awareness.

The term 'corporate image' gained greater popularity in the 1960s. It was almost universally misused and misunderstood. Its novelty died away, perhaps because of over use. A clever and handy phrase defining the goal of efforts to project a company's identity, it was harmless as long as it remained advertising and public relations jargon. But the catch phrase soon passed into the common language and became a 'concept'. It is not surprising that the public came to view the image as a slick process and tagged it with a bad name. It is now too late to eradicate, the 'corporate image' from the language, it is too firmly rooted. But public relations people can get back to fundamentals avoiding the use of phrase and emphasizing that a corporate identity must stem from what a company actually is and that corporate reputation must be earned with solid policy and action.

Till very recently, it was believed that the essence of mass persuasion was exposure of an idea, a brand, a name, a product of the target audience. The success of communication was measured in terms of the number of people reached and the number of exposures. Today we know that not only do individuals respond differently to the same stimuli, but the response to a communication is also very selective. The PR professionals, therefore, need to evolve a new set of principles to guide their efforts. Their efforts should be involved in modifying or altering the attitude of an individual towards a particular object, idea, person or institution. Secondly, their efforts should also be towards systematic scanning, monitoring and interpretation of the relevant social environment, and how these impinge on the performance of the organization.

(1) *Trust in integrity* : The first and foremost principle is that he should be trustworthy. This is the key to his acceptance in the chain of communication. He is required to be what he represents himself to be, an advocate. His integrity must go even further. Everything he writes

or says, or causes others to write or say in the interest of his employer should be in the public interest. This is an obligation imposed on few other hired men. An attorney does his full duty in serving his client though he may not believe in his power to help his client win. But the publicity man is in a different fix. If his employer is engaged in indefensible practices affecting the public, which he refuses to change, the publicity worker, weighing his responsibilities to employer and to public, may have to make a decision as to which he shall serve. He does not have the protection of ancient custom as does the lawyer. He is obliged to put the public interest first, even of that means to serve his business connection. If this seems to demand a harsh application of self-discipline, the publicity worker should nevertheless be prepared to make it. The occasions will be few in which such a choice is forced upon him. But to make it is to guard his future as a respected member of a profession. Blatantly insincere PR efforts are not ineffective but build up resistance to the acceptance of any future persuasive efforts.

(2) *Sound moral base :* Good public relations implies a sound moral base. However, the practice can long endure only when it is dynamic. Harmless conduct is not enough. Action is required. This may be expressed as striving for three objectives :

(a) To attract attention.
(b) To win belief.
(c) To impart understanding.

These steps are taken to reach a goal : to convince people that they should adopt a certain attitude or pursue a certain course of action.

To perform this feat, public relations must begin at the heart of the organization it serves. It must find the answer to three questions :

What is the message management wants to impart.
To whom ?
How ?
Purpose ?

One should not have public relations for fun's sake. Without knowing what, to whom, how and why a public relations programme has no purpose. To get at the answers may require considerable time and effort. They may raise more questions. They may raise doubt. But once answered they should enable management to :

(a) understand the organization's nature and purposes thoroughly,
(b) communicate this understanding to others, and
(c) observe and evaluate the effect.

As a consequence of public relations activity on this sound base, management can gain the opportunity, both in detail and in the large, to make such internal changes in organization, product, service or method as will enable it to survive and prosper in a public climate of goodwill.

This is the self-aware, the wide-awake way to go about public relations practice. This is the way that leads to full self-realization by management.

(3) *Appropriate dealing :* To be effective, public relations should deal differently with different groups depending upon their mental make up and background. As such, it has to take note of the heritage, history, culture, philosophy, psychology, mythology and social conventions of the society it seeks to serve. What is effective in U. K. may not make a dent in Australia. In a vast country like India an approach which may appeal to educated urbanites may go over the heads of many inhabitants of rural regions.

(4) *Solving information overload :* The mass media message output being phenomenal, the mass audience suffers from what has come to be known as 'information overload' i. e. communication being targeted by different interest groups from all sides to the same audience. It is necessary, therefore, for the PR practitioner to be careful in 'positioning' his PR messages. Instead of directly sending persuasive messages, one can adopt a strategy of injecting ideas and information into that broad stream of communication , for example, a newspaper which flows incessantly to the target public. These may be picked up alongwith all other ideas and information, and subtly help become part of a receiver's thinking, which moulds his attitude. This requires tact, and comes with experience.

(5) *Elasticity and adjustment :* We are living in a dynamic age. PR practitioner has to keep in mind the international trends. Whatever science achieved over the past 100 years seems insignificant in relation to the revolution brought by it over the last ten years, and whatever changes it may bring about by the turn of the century may put to shame all the changes introduced so far. In a situation of rapid flux, elasticity and adjustment to change will form an essential part of PR practices.

(6) *Choice of tools* : The growing visibility of events, through the mass media, has led to higher public reaction levels. Therefore, as a principle, the PR professionals need to know all that could be made to capture the imagination by becoming real forces in people's minds actions, emotion, stirring speeches, films, events, dramatizations, displays, exhibitions or symbols, have a chance to capture to public attention, and win public support.

(7) *Awareness of international changes* : The international scenario is noted for at least four important developments, which are of special concern to PR anywhere, particularly in the developing countries. These lie in the fields of communication technology, political awareness, economic interdependence and social equality. Technically, a stage has been reached when whatever happens in any part of the globe can be heard and seen instantaneously. Almost all countries of the world have attained independence and are engaged in improving the living standards of their people.

(8) *Knowledge of new technologies* : For those in public relations dealing directly with dissemination of information, the new technologies are of the utmost importance for several reasons. First, they have to integrate these techniques in the system of their thinking and keep on increasing their fund of information continuously. Secondly, they have to learn to apply these tools wisely for the good of the community. New tools will be what man makes of them. Thirdly, they have to take note of developments these techniques have spawned and accelerated in other areas.

(9) *Social upsurge* : In the social field, communication technology, political freedom and economic prosperity are being used to improve the lot of the illiterate and the poor. The PR practitioners should help free governments to ameliorate the condition of these people. With radio, television and communication satellites, basic information about available opportunities and modern production methods is reaching far flung areas. As backward people in developing countries acquire new skills, their living standards are bound to rise. When prosperity increases and huge human masses join the national mainstream these people will have to be approached, informed, cultivated and motivated into desired activity.

(10) *Ensuring receptivity* : For the PR to be effective, the basic principle that always needs to be kept in mind in that the target public must be in a 'posture of receptivity'. This is of critical importance in PR. It is a recognized fact that the favourable inclination of an individual towards

all messages from a given source is the result of his total experience with that source. The character of an organization is exemplified by its actions and the sincerity of its previous attempts and efforts. On this depends the acceptance or rejection with which the organization's communication is met. Rross, Editor of *Saturday Review*, explained why PR people usually remain in the background :

> "The principle of anonymity evolves from a very simple philosophy of our work : When things go wrong for a corporation in the public relations area it is the management of the corporation that takes the bumps. We believe that when things go right they deserve the credit and it should not be synthetic".

Good practice certainly must be based on principles that are understood. Yet in public relations the discovery and recognition of workable principles have been empirical. Only since the early 1950s has the academic world taken public relations seriously enough to undertake theoretical studies. One authority, Prof. John E. Marston of Michigan State University, has prepared a set of principles of communication as applied in public relations. He points out that a completely exhaustive list of such principles of effective communication has not yet been made and is not likely soon to be made, for social scientists are continually discovering and refining them. His list comprises the following principle :

Humanization, suiting the message and the means of communication to the audience, speaking the receiver's language, timeliness, dramatization, two-way communication, reaching your own people first, facing the facts, performing a needed service, stressing positive benefits, repetition, overcoming refusal to pay attention, using leaders of opinion, preconditioning the audience, and keeping all communications in harmony.

These principles are always in flux, and if they are to live and prosper they must continuously change and grow. The ambition of public relations practitioners is not so much to be credited and recognized as to deserve general acceptance. Their work is largely anonymous. They help to set the stage, to coach management, to interpret the audience to management and sometimes to write the script. Other persons are more visible and vocal. Public relations does not create or project a more corporate image. It presents, and reveals reality, the warm and human personalities of the institutions it serves.

Methods of Public Relations (Tools)

Once the facts are collected, plan prepared, information has to be communicated to the people to achieve the desired objectives. A PRO is, therefore, called upon to communicate to a heterogeneous population who has a vast variety of tools at his disposal. There are two aspects of communication. One, the physical transmission of a message and two to bring about a change in the prevailing attitudes of people. In dealing with various public, a PRO must, therefore, first understand the mental pictures of a particular group and employ appropriate tools to modify these pictures. The success of an individual, an industry, an organisation or a government depends upon the ability about appropriate attitudinal changes to communicate effectively. PRO practitioner should analyse a situation carefully, lay down objectives choose the proper tools and utilise them individually or in combination to achieve effective communication at the desired end. Tools do not make a man but man makes tools work. Only those who know the strength and weakness of each of the following tools can effectively use them.

Tools

1. Written Word

(a) Newspapers and periodicals
  - (i) Press releases
  - (ii) Press conferences

(b) House journals

(c) Advertising

2. Audio-visual
  - (a) Radio
  - (b) Television
  - (c) Films

3. Other Media

(a) Photographs

(b) Folk media

(c) Exhibitions

(a) *Oral communication* : Oral communication is personal communication. It is persuasive communication. A person can word his message differently for different people. He can have a free and frank discussion and work around the listener's biases. The talk between two persons is based on trust and mutual goodwill. Either they arrive at an agreement or they agree to differ and continue the discussion later. Mahatma Gandhi and Jawahar Lal Nehru were no great orators but they spoke from their heart and their words, like bullets hit the bull's eye. They practised what they preached and were the heroes of the Indian people.

How to be Effective

A PRO must be master in oral communication. He does not push out press releases all the time but talks most of the time to his colleagues within the organisation or with representatives of the press. Occasionally he is also called upon to deliver formal speeches or organise group discussions and seminars. The preparation of speeches is often the task of the public relations department. Orators are born not made but it is possible for most people to achieve a good standard of public speaking if they are prepared to take some trouble. A short speech, delivered with feeling, will always carry more weight than a long address read carefully from a prepared script. One has to weigh his words before speaking and cultivate the art of conducting conversation. Here is a list of few points for oral communication given by Baldeo Sahai in his book, *Public Relations–A Scientific Approach.*

1. Sincerity of purpose is the secret of being a good conversationalist and a successful public relations officer. While collecting information from a senior executive the objective is to publicise the activities of his department and build up a better image of the organisation.
2. In his dealings, with press representatives, public men or office colleagues it is necessary to retain their confidence. Whatever has been told to him in confidence should never be divulged. Official secrets should never be disclosed. A secret is a secret. It is not to be told even to the most friendly correspondent.
3. Between management and workers, a PRO should try to carve out a place so as to enjoy the confidence of both. In talking to workers he should find out what is nagging them most and convey their genuine grievances to the right quarters. He may put across management's

point of view before the workers in a friendly manner. In this way he can bring about better management-labour relations.

4. Like a journalist, a PRO is supposed to know everything of something and something of everything. A PRO who has wide-ranging interests and can talk intelligently on many topics will be more successful in his profession.
5. One salutary principle of a good conversationalist is never to talk ill of anybody. Always talk about the good point of a person and be liberal in your praise. Don't discuss a person's defects. Worldly wisdom dictates that it is not helpful to talk ill of people.
6. To be a good talker, it is necessary to be a good listener. A verse in Urdu says that one should speak once after listening twice because God has given us only one tongue and two ears. If one talks less and listens more he will kill two birds in one shot.
7. PRO may also be called upon to organise group discussions, seminars or symposia. He should maintain a list of authoritative speakers on various topics. At times it may be necessary to have a mass meeting to put across certain ideas or policies where necessary. The press may be invited to cover such functions and adequate arrangements made for proper seats and supply of background material.

Guidelines for PRO

1. A PRO should first decide what he wants to say and put down his ideas lucidly and briefly.
2. It is better to get in touch with the Deputy Director General at the Centre or the Station Director of the region for arranging talk, discussion or an interview, etc. Give him all the relevant information, including if possible the names of authorities who can speak on the subject with intimate knowledge.
3. Programmes beamed for the ruralites should not be confined to subjects of rural interest. The objective should be to keep village people informed generally on all important developments in a country. The tool is to be pressed into service to transform their 'inner pictures' and change their outlook from the bullock cart to the jet-age stage. It is, therefore, necessary in the national interest, to include news about all types of developmental activities in rural programmes.

4. Women constitute almost half of the population. As with the rural population, the information level of women has to be raised. Here it is not an event but a process which has to be projected. For that, a special feature story or a skit about the activities of the organisation can work wonders if presented in an interesting form. If necessary, the PRO may commission professional literatures to help him.
5. Recast your material to suit the mental level of your listeners. An eye must be kept on the possibility of utilizing other special audience programmes like those for industrial workers and youth.
6. Try to sponsor a radio feature on special occasions like completing a decade, a silver or golden jubilee, launching a new venture, achieving a breakthrough in research and development, exports or import substitution.
7. In case of organisations which provide farm inputs like seeds, fertilizers and pesticides, it would be far more effective if the programmes based on interviews with producers and users are produced. The management representative will explain the merits of his product and the right way of its use. The actual user will then give his name and place and relate his own experience and explain the difficulties if any which will be answered by the producer. A composite programme like this based on recorded interviews will go down much better on regional radio stations than straight talks, or even discussions. A PRO may first discuss programme pattern with the station director and take a recording team with him. Sometimes he may himself record the items as suggested by the station director and pass on the recordings to the radio station. Similar programmes can be prepared for urban people also. After all the objectives of the PRO, and that of the AIR producers are identical to produce effective programmes which will motivate the people in the national development effort.
8. When organising a programme on radio, try to avoid a straight talk, even though it may be from the chief executive. The PRO is concerned with the success of the programme. It should make an impact, stimulate thinking, invite comments, people should talk about it. Better have a group discussion, or at least an interesting interview.

House Journal

A house journal is a periodical publication which tries to establish regular communication between an organisation and its employees and other public. It is an outcome of large organisations and management complexities. In the small organisation the owner calls his employees together and communicates to them whatever he has to, face to face. In the bigger organisation, direct communication becomes difficult and messages are conveyed through cyclostyled circulars. These grew into news letters and finally into house journals. A house journal creates a sense of belongingness among its employees. It makes him feel that he is not alone, that he is safe and secure, that there is somebody to take care of him and his family. It is a medium of communication intended to project the image of the organisation both within and outside of the organisation. The purpose is to improve the morale of the employees, create favourable climate for the working of the organisation and promote and provide opportunities for creative expression. This is a unique opportunity, and the journal conveys the message regularly.

A PRO should examine whether his organisation really needs a house journal. A company may be small, but its public may spill over several countries. The commodity it manufactures may be in international demand. It would be necessary for the company to keep in constant touch with its clients and inform them about its latest product. Such a concern, though employing only a handful of workers, would need an external house journal. There may be other organisations employing a few thousand persons and serving millions like a telephone exchange, an electricity department with workers on the job spread all over. In such cases a house journal may not serve much useful purpose. The point to be stressed is that a house journal is not a status symbol that every PR department should have. The activities, objectives and size of the organisation should be taken into account to decide whether a house journal is necessary. Therefore, the management should take a deliberate decision whether a house journal is to be brought out by the organisation. If yes, what objectives it is supposed to fulfil and the objective of a house journal will differ from organisation to organisation depending upon its activities.

Advertising

Advertising is also very effective medium for communicating public relations purposes. Traditionally, organizations have used advertising to sell products but lately, firms use advertisements for purposes other than product promotion. This unique type of advertising became known as institutional advertising, image advertising, public service advertising and public relations advertising.

Where promotional advertising was hard sell, public relations advertising was softer. Public relations advertising focused on the general image of the company wished to convey and the public issues it wished to confront.

Audio-Visual Media

(a) Radio

Radio is primarily a medium of news and entertainment with commentaries, talk shows and debate. Its use as a public relations tool must be approached within this context. The following are the ways to reach rural audience :

1. through news and informational programmes;
2. through entertainment programmes;
3. through the feature programmes.

(b) Television

Television has impact and realism, is welcomed everywhere, and is readily available as a publicity medium for practitioners who will take the time and trouble to learn how to use it. An increasingly larger portion of TV time is being given to news broadcasts and to the news documentary, social issue and action coverage. These programmes offer many opportunities to the alert publicist.

On using TV as a public relations tool, Sydney H. Eiges offers the following counsel.

Networks have the glamour, the star appeal and the high budget programme but in public relations thinking television should also be considered as a service provided in hundreds of communities by individual stations. Each of these stations is essentially concerned with its own community. Identifying a story with that of the community at large arouses the interest of the local station and wins its co-operation planning a campaign on a local basis can often be more productive than aiming only at networks which are if necessary more difficult to crack. Materials and ideas should be aimed specifically at individual communities or regions. Stations should be approached individually and personally.

Following are some of the tips for the practitioners seeking time on TV :

1. Approach the right person in the station.
2. Have a definite plan to discuss.
3. Have an idea with audience appeal, so that the station won't lose its viewers while the programme is on the air.
4. Programme idea must be within the station capabilities.

(c) Films

The film is a very powerful medium of public relations, and its use dates back to the increasing popularity of the documentary film in the decade before the war. The function of documentaries has been taken over to a great extent by television, but there is still a very important place for film in public relations as a medium of communication, instruction, education, entertainment, marketing, research, etc. It brings the audience in direct contact with facts and ideas through sight, hearing and emotions. It thus makes a direct impact on the captive audience.

The motion picture offers a number of advantages as PR medium. These are :

(i) greater impact because of its powerful appeal to eye, ear and senses;
(ii) effective learning aid on account of auditory and visual qualities;
(iii) accurate reproduction of objects and events;
(iv) clarity;
(v) long life-span; and
(vi) measurability of circulation and effectiveness statistically, etc.

To sum up, the film is an appropriate medium of PR but the organization has to have necessary resources for this expensive medium. Also, the decision to use film as PR medium should be made in relation to costs and relative effect of other media available to PR.

Other Media

(a) Photographs

Photographs and illustrations are an important aid to public relations. The first point to appreciate is that photographs always lend authenticity.

Everyone knows that photographs can be as misleading as statistics, but nevertheless they are generally accepted as authentic proof of facts or events. They add to interest in the story, and at times have a compelling appeal that is absent from printed matter, however well laid out and displayed.

Photographs reduce boredom. It has definitely edge over the printed matter. A picture can be worth a thousand words. It enhances the meaning of a news story or a feature or an article. It is more effective. The hurried reader may miss a news story but he would hardly miss a picture. He absorbs the message at a glance.

It has news worthiness even for the illiterates. An illiterate person who cannot go for reading, photographs are of immense importance. He can immediately judge what the photographs is about.

(b) Traditional Media

The traditional media have played a very important role in solving several emotional problems and channelizing the destructive forces into constructive ones. In India too, music, dance and drama have always played an important role in combating destructive elements and in harmonizing emotional outbursts relating to caste, creed, religion and language issues. Several folk forms of entertainment prevalent in different parts of India were powerful media of public instruction and a unifying force for emotional integrity. They brought the poor and the rich together. Thousands of people suffering from domestic and psychological problems used to witness them as a relief to their perplexed life. Such healthy entertainment did dissuade the human beings from destructive activities.

The use of traditional medium for communication according to modern needs is a very delicate affair. The PR man can make clever use of traditional media for his campaigns, particularly in the rural areas. Dr. Karan Singh, then Minister for Health and Family Planning, asserted : "Folk media has credibility with the masses which no sophisticated mass media can hope to achieve. He considered folk media to be much more effective than electronic media. Traditional folk forms constitute the genes of a country's culture. They contain its artistic information in the most subtle form and carry it forward from generation to generation. The expression is informal, spontaneous and intimate, encouraging audience participation and often involving the entire village or community".

In the developing countries where illiteracy is wide-spread and communications scanty, the folk media assume greater importance. They emerge from local soil and form an integral part of the life of the people.

Public relations practitioners should dig into the wealth and adapt these media with the help of modern techniques, in the desired forms.

(c) PR through Exhibitions

Exhibitions are an important medium to project an organization's materials processes, products, or its activities, services, ideas to the public.

The aim is to either boost up sales or to project the activities or the corporate image to the organisation or to develop contacts with similar other bodies in the country and abroad in the specialized field or to earn the goodwill of the people or of a section of the community.

Once the objectives are decided, efforts must be made to achieve them as effectively and economically as possible. Arrangements will have to be made in tune with the prevalent standards. The general idea of participation is to attract attention, to make an impact, to earn goodwill, and to motivate viewers.

It offers an excellent opportunity for personal contact with prospective consumers, customers or dealers. Most of their queries can be answered on the spot, and others noted for follow up action.

Before organising an exhibition PRO should bear in mind the following basic points as produced by Baldeo Sahai in his book (*PR–A Scientific Approach*) :

1. What does the exhibition expect to achieve ?
2. What ideas are intended to be implanted in the mind of the visitors ?
3. On what lines would he like to motivate them ?

The PRO may like to use the exhibition.

(i) to create or strengthen awareness about the existence of his organization;
(ii) to explain its activities to visitors with the help of pictures, models and other display media;
(iii) to take them round the exhibits and show them actual products and photographs as seeing is believing;
(iv) to meet the existing and potential customers;
(v) to invite business inquiries and adequately answer them;
(vi) to make a mental note of the doubts or apprehensions expressed by visitors about the products or services for future follow-up;
(vii) to aid and supplement market surveys and longrange research;

(viii) to back the effort of local dealers and retailers; and
(ix) to take orders and pass them on to the sales department.

4. The PRO would like visitors to his stall to carry away with them the impression that :

(i) the organisation renders useful service to the community;
(ii) it spends substantial sums on research to improve the quality of its products;
(iii) customers are treated respectfully and offered satisfactory after-sale service;
(iv) it is manned and managed by honest, reliable, energetic persons;
(v) it looks after its workers and is a good employer; and
(vi) all in all it is an efficient organisation quite dependable in its dealings.

5. He would like to motivate visitors :

(i) to prefer relation with his organisation as a consumer or a dealer; and
(ii) to think well, speak well and write well about the organisation.

PRESS RELEASE

The usual way of issuing information to the press is by writing a press release. A press release is official, authorised statement about the policies and activities of an organisation. As the company or the government has to stand by it, the press release must be factual, correct and project the policy clearly and without ambiguity. It should leave no scope for misreporting. This is then sent by post or by hand to various newspapers and periodicals and to radio and television news offices. It should also be communicated to the news agencies, who have direct teleprinter contact with the main newspaper offices in the country. The news agencies edit the release and do not send it out in its entirety, so it is always worthwhile sending out the full release as widely as possible. The PRO should give adequate information on all points of public interest. If he examines the material critically from the view point of a press reporter and the public, he will immediately discover certain areas where further light or classification is necessary.

The press release should be written in journalistic style. It should follow the principles of news reporting. The introduction or lead should be in a summary format. It should answer the five W's and one H as it is in a news story. The second and the subsequent paragraphs should elucidate and elaborate the points. It should provide facts or information of interest to the readers and should attempt to cover all aspects of a specific subject. The release should not be generally lengthy. It should be concise and to the point. The release is a piece of clear writing without any ambiguity, without any effort towards colour or ornamentation. As far as possible each story should be complete in itself. Public memory is short and people are not likely to remember what had been said on the subject a couple of months ago, or even the previous fortnight. Moreover, repetitive publicity is the essence of selling an idea.

It should have a consistent format. Generally, the name of the agency from where the release emanates is given on the top. The date and place are indicated on the top right side. The release should have a title or sub-title also, if necessary.In the case of releases from non-official organizations, it is desirable also to mention the designation of the person issuing the release and his telephone number.

Types of press release covering Government news :

1. Press Communiques
2. Press notes
3. Handouts
4. Unofficial stories or unofficial handouts

Press communiques are issued when some important government decisions or announcements are made such as cabinet appointments, conclusion of the foreign dignitaries visits, etc. The press communique is formal character. It carries the name of ministry or department and the place and date at the bottom left hand corner of the release. Generally, the press is expected to reproduce the press communique without any substantial change. No heading or sub-heading is given on press communiques.

Press notes are less formal in character. They are issued on important matters. They also carry the name of the ministry/department and the place at the bottom left hand corners. Headings or sub-headings are given in press notes.

Handouts are issued on a variety of subjects and on day-to-day activities of the ministry/department, VIP speeches, questions and answers in Parliaments, etc. The handout is a less formal type of release and not issued under the government's formal authority. It bears the name of the PIB or other releasing agency on the top without any mention of the ministry/department to which the release pertains. The place and date are indicated on top at the right hand side. One of the most important common categories of handouts relate to the speeches of ministers or other high officials. The handout is released only when the speech is connected with governmental activity. No official handout is issued if the minister has spoken in his personal capacity as a member of a political organization. The speech when released to the press in the form of handout is summarised and properly edited. Formal, introductory and concluding remarks are omitted and redundant and repetitive material taken out. A proper title and sub-title are given. The important aspects which are to be stressed are included in the beginning paragraph or in the lead. The full text of the speech is not released unless the subject is of very great importance.

Unofficial handouts are issued on the subject where the government would not like to assume official responsibility in the matter but feels that there may be positive advantages in making information public unofficially. These handouts are supplements to oral briefings. The unofficial handouts do not have the imprint of the PIB or of other releasing agencies. The date and place are indicated at bottom left hand corner.

Timing of releases is very important. All releases should so far as possible reach the desk by 6 or 7 p. m. The PRO should finalise history at least one hour in advance of the official delivery time.

Non News Releases

These are such releases which do not cover news but give information in an indirect way and help in building the image of the government. More widely known releases of this type are back grounders, biographical sketches, contradictions, articles and features, newsletters, releases on reports, broadcast talks, etc. The releasing agency's name is given at the top. The place and date are indicated on the top right hand side. Title and sub-title are also given.

Press Conferences

The holding of the press conference has become an accepted means of issuing information to the press. A press conference should never be called merely to handout a development or information which could be covered equally well by a press release. The main justification for holding a press conference is that the subject is an important one likely to elicit plenty of questions from the journalists present.

A press conference should never be held as a routine affair. It should be held to announce all major policy decisions and important announcements. Press conferences can also be arranged for other officers on specific subjects if they are authorised to communicate with the press.

The invitees to the government press conference are normally all accredited correspondents including foreign correspondents, accredited cameramen and representatives from radio and T.V., etc. In the case of private organization all correspondents who normally cover the organization are invited to the press conference. Official invitees to the press conference should be reduced to the minimum. The information officer or public relations officer should brief the speaker in advance about the correspondents and the nature of questions likely to be asked. Where business houses have public relations officer, they should fully brief the subject-matter so that the executive can speak with informality and ease. Before the press conference begins they should also gave a proper but brief introduction of the speaker and the subject. Invitations to the press conference should be sent well in advance indicating the date, day, time, subject and venue of the conference. The name of the person holding the press conference his designation or status should be mentioned.

It is advisable to hold the press conference in the forenoon or early afternoon so as to catch the dak editions also of newspapers.

In case of important press conference it is necessary to tape-record the proceedings. Discussion on individual and personal cases should be avoided. Generally not more than half a dozen questions are to be allowed on any one aspect of the subject.

It is necessary to prepare a comprehensive note on the subject of the press conference. This note should be distributed a little before the press conference is scheduled to start. This will help in many ways, particularly in checking facts and statistics.

Tea, coffee or light refreshment can be served at the press conference. The press conference arrangements should be well thought out. Transport can be provided both ways if the press conference is held at some distance or out of the way place. Give equal treatment to all newspaper representatives. The publicist should treat them on equal basis. Under no circumstances should any press representative be excluded from the press conference on this account.

PUBLIC RELATIONS IN DIFFERENT SECTORS

Public Relations in Government Sector

Public relations in the government sector is very important at the same time difficult and demanding. It is important because people should understand how they are being governed. Once they appreciate this, government will find it easier to secure their support for and participation in implementing its policies and programmes, thus ensuring quicker national development.

This is difficult in the sense that communication between the Government and its public has increased, sometimes creating a wide gap. This distance is not only physical, but social, cultural and also emotional. Whatever is decided in the Parliament has to be explained to each group in its language.

Therefore, it becomes pertinent that the parctitioner should be fully conversant with the philosophy, history, culture and social attitude of his people. He should know the problems of the government in its entirety and must have a clear concept of the country's socio-economic development, economic plans, and an overall view of the different sectors, their long and short-term perspectives.

Public relations in a government department has two main functions. The first and foremost is, to give regular information on policy plans and achievement of the department and second is, to inform and educate the public on legislation, regulations and all matters that affect the daily lives of citizens.

In the government section, PRO speaks on behalf of the government. Whatsoever he says or releases to the press are comments of the government. He must, therefore, be accurate and should understand policies thoroughly because his job is to elaborate and clarify. This is possible only when he himself is quite clear about policy implications.

Public relations is the responsibility of every one in an organisation. It is not the sole prerogative of the public relations staff. The minister and indeed every civil servant has his own contacts with the people and with authorities who are able to give him evidence of what people are doing and saying. The public relations officer can supply supplementary intelligence, and it is an important part of his duties to keep the rest of his departments promptly informed on what is appearing in the press and what is being said and shown on radio and television.

PR man should also guard against VIP publicity. He should avoid issuing long handouts particularly when they relate to personal achievements or speeches of VIPs.

PRO should be a professional journalist. He has to maintain high ethical and moral standards. His conduct reflects the conduct of the government. Feedback is yet another important duty of the PR man. Government should be well informed about what has been said in the different media about the particular policy programme.

PR man should create an atmosphere in which press people are automatically attracted to him as a source of information.

Whenever a press conference is to be held it is the duty of the information officer that he should decide in advance about the date and the time of the conference.

There is general lack of understanding about what PR is supposed to do or can do. Most PR people are drawn from the press, or are supposed to have very good relations with newsmen. Some government officials think that whenever information is passed on to a PRO, he should immediately get it published. They should, therefore, be kept at arm's length and told only what needs to be told. PROs must do some internal PR with the authorities and educate them about the actual position.

Sometimes PROs do not do their homework properly. If they are not well informed, if they cannot secure proper publicity for the activities of their ministry if they have not been giving proper advice to the authorities on public relations, nobody can help them get a better status. PROs have to work hard and with greater care, to maintain freedom of expression and credibility of what they release to the public through various media.

PR in the Public Sector

In the case of the public sector in India, the PR man will not be able to conduct a purposeful campaign unless he is aware of the following :

- the magnitude of operations of the public sector as a whole;
- the concept, the culture, and the philosophy of the public sector in our economy and in democratic framework; and
- the inherent difficulties of PR work in the public sector in the context of the coexistent competition and hostility of the private sector.

Public sector includes the following undertakings :

- wholly owned and managed by government;
- wholly owned by government but managed privately under the overall

supervision of government; and

where majority of ownership and controlling interest is in the hands of government.

Features of the Public Sector

1. The public sector exists on no profit basis.
2. It belongs to the people and is financed by the involuntary savings of the people. Therefore, unlike the private sector, where the share-holders alone are financially interested in the undertaking, the public sector has to be responsive to the financial interests of the public at large.
3. The public sector has tc be responsive to the public opinion, while the private sector need worry only of the share-holders.
4. The public sector is concerned with basic industries such as steel and coal involving huge investments, long gestation period, initial losses, and lesser return to the capital.
5. It looks after the employees welfare and offers maximum employment.
6. It generally reduces the regional and economic imbalance while reflecting the site of industries.
7. The public sector takes over 'sick industries'.

Since public sector employs a very large force, a positive PR approach is therefore needed to deal with a large number of people. The PR man is required to create a feeling of identity and of common purpose among the workers. Greater sharing of information in a participative manner with the workers is necessary to establish cordial relations. With proper PR, the management decisions such as new work methods, employment of workmen, etc. can be implemented without confrontation with the workers.

The public sector PR effort has to be directed to remove the distortions of one-sided publicity that prevails at present. This task needs to be performed by public undertakings collectively and not by any undertaking in isolation.

Since public and private sectors are complementary to each other and both compete for scarce resources–capital, foreign exchange, skilled manpower, etc. The PR man in the public sector, however, should not run down the private sector but should explain and highlight the pioneering work assigned to the public sector.

PR man should not only be well versed in publicity techniques but should have a clear grasp of the basic objectives for which the public sector was created.

PR effort should not be used for non-productive purposes. PR man should be associated with the decision making processes in the enterprise. He should be deeply involved in its affairs. Only then will he be able to provide a bridge of understanding between the enterprise and the public.

He should have direct access to the primary sources of information in the organisation. He should be provided with functional facilities such as transport, telephone and entertainment expenses, etc.

He should try to improve his professional competence and establish his usefulness to the organisation. PRO should be more alert and alive than other managers. It is not enough for them to adjust themselves to changing situations. They have to anticipate and shape situations to suit their requirements.

Functioning of the public relations in public sector bristles with difficulties. Neither the objectives of the public sector as a whole nor those of individual enterprises have been clearly laid down. Many public sector organisations do not choose their PROs on the basis of competence, rather non-competent persons are employed on such posts.

Most of the time PR man does not have access to sources of information and does not always attend meetings where policies are formulated. After such a meeting, he is often handed a press release and asked to get on with the job. He is often used as a fire-fighting service, summoned by the top brass only at a time of crises. There is little appreciation that PR is a continuous process and relations with the media or with workers are built brick by brick over years.

Public relations is generally treated as the poor relation of the organization and does not enjoy a status conducive to efficient performance. There are few facilities available to train newly recruited PROs or to improve the professional competence of existing PROs. Today, when technological developments are fast increasing and PROs are not up-to-date, they cannot function effectively.

Sadly, the profession of public relations is not very well recognised. An organisation cannot do without accountant, but anybody is considered competent to handle PR.

Public Relations in Private Sector

Public relations plays a very important role in the private sector. It has two main objectives to fulfil :

(a) to establish contact with three important sections of the public–its customers, its stockholders and its employees. Securing the mutual understanding and co-operation of these groups is essential to success.

(b) To promote the company's services and product in a highly competitive market.

Customer Relations

Relations with customers depend very much on quality, price and delivery time, but also very directly on the reputation of the company. Public relations can play a vital part in safeguarding a reputation or in building up a new '*public image*'. It can also do valuable work in improving methods of communication with existing and potential customers.

PR is an aid to marketing all along the line, right from the stage of planning of a new product to its effective selling. The PR man can evaluate to customer's attitude towards a product and provide valuable lines to the marketing department so as to enable it to take corrective action and to decide about the continuation, modification or dropping of a particular product or service. The objective of PR is to win the customers' goodwill on a long term basis.

The PR department should be also fully alive to the customers' complaints. Though the individual complaints are normally handled by the complaints department, but the PR man has to be closely involved in this work as it affects the image of the organization. The PR man should also initiate prompt action in the complaints voiced in the media. He should reply to all the complaints. Even in the case of groundless and frivolous complaints, the PR man should write a polite letter to the customer. If the complaint is true, it is advisable to tender an apology and replace or repair the product.

It is necessary to the PR man to make a concerted effort in co-operation with the production and marketing departments to project a new product or a new service. This can be done through features in house journals, by bringing out folder, brochure, etc.

Stockholder Relations

The goodwill and support of shareholders is of vital importance to the existence to a success of any business concern. Public relations effort should be to attract the affluent rich sections from the rural areas and motivate them to invest in the industrial concerns. For this purpose, techniques of communication, relevant to this new class, have to be employed.

The public relations in private concern normally does not have any direct responsibility for the preparation of the annual report, the balance sheet, audit reports, etc. The PR man, can, however, help a great deal in projecting the organisation's image with the shareholders by advising the management on the overall approach in the annual report.

The branch of public relations can yield good results by helping the companies through keeping in touch with their shareholders e.g. by inviting them to film shows, tea parties, sending them copies of house journals and by arranging annual general meetings. Meetings can be held in different cities if a majority of stockholders live outside the capital. Alternatively some meetings of the board can be held outside the capital, followed by receptions for shareholders living in the locality. Any thing that can bring stockholders into closer touch with the Board must serve to strengthen the company.

Employee Relations

Internal public relations is an extremely wide field. It embraces almost everything, other than salary which encourages employees to make their maximum contribution to productivity and the prosperity of the company. The purpose of PR's internal communication is twofold : to convey management decisions, policies and programmes to the employees at different levels and to feedback the management with the reactions of the employees.

The correct policy should be to disseminate more and more information and establish management's credibility with the employees. Only that information should be withheld which may lead to speculative activity or may create problems for the company with its other public. When information is given out it has to be ensured that the message is not distorted. It is better if the message is given in the mother tongue of the workers.

The PR man can also make an excellent impact on employer-employee relations if he organizes the celebration of religious festivals and other community functions.

Public relations cannot guarantee, to prevent strikes, but a well conceived public relations programme can play a useful part in eliminating misunderstanding and lack of information.

Public Relations in Support of Sales

The second objective of public relations in private sector is to promote the company's services and products in highly competitive world. In other words, the ultimate aim of most companies or organisations is to sell their product or service at home and overseas. With other methods of communicating with existing and potential customers in which public relations assists sales promotion, press relations is of prime importance.

PUBLIC OPINION

To understand the nature of the public opinion it is appropriate to divide the term into two components and examine, separately the nature of "public" the character of "opinion" and then the combined functioning in the public opinion process. Public is a group of people with similar interests who have a common opinion on a particular subject. The group may be small, a large or it may be a majority group. The concept of a "public" was introduced by John Dewey in his book *The Public and its Problems* and has defined a public as a group of individuals who together are affected by a particular action or idea. Thus, each issue or problem creates its own public. A group of students confronted with the controversial question of whether to strike is a public with a similar interest to hold elections involved in the process of forming public opinion. On the other hand, the same group of students standing at summerhill chowk and unanimously agreeing on the perfect weather is not involved in public opinion formation since no controversial question confronts the group.

Every person is identified with several policies, each of which may be involved in the process of opinion formation on one or more controversial subjects. A public involved in the opinion forming process may be numerically limited, consisting of three or four persons employed in a small office; or it may number in the millions in the case of ethnic, religious, or political groups. Public involved in opinion formation may be concentrated in one place or distributed widely in many countries throughout the world.

Public have common interests that unify the individual members, creating a similarity of view points and leading to unanimity of opinion on controversial subjects. According to Carroll Clark, former chairman of the Department of Sociology, University of Kansas, unanimity in group opinion can be achieved by the following factors :

(a) underlying common interests strong enough to override sharply opposed interests and sentiments;

(b) a common discourse in terms of which an exchange of views may be affected;

(c) access through communication media to information on an issue;

(d) tolerance of opposing views and willingness to discuss the issue; and

(e) utilizing informal social mechanisms or formal political machinery for reaching a collective decision and taking collective action.

An opinion is simply the expression of an attitude on a controversial issue. Opinion implies controversy and dispute, whereas fact implies general acceptance. According to Webster's New Collegiate Dictionary, "Opinion is a view, judgement, or appraisal formed in the mind about a particular matter". An opinion is stronger than an impression and weaker than positive knowledge. It "implies a conclusion thought out yet open to dispute. A more or less settled opinion is a "sentiment" and if held firmly, a "conviction". A "view is" an opinion more or less coloured by bias".

Public opinion is the aggregate result of individual opinions on public matters. Public matters are those of people affected by the same affairs. Publics cannot have and do not have opinion, because a public is not an entity in itself. Public opinion is the sum of accumulated individual opinions on an issue in public debate and affecting a group of people. In other words, it is an expression of a belief held in common by members of a group or public on a controversial issue of general importance. Public opinion is usually expressed after controversy, dispute, and debate over some controversial question that concerns the welfare doctrines and value system of a group. For public opinion to be aroused, there must exist a contemporary issue or question of some concern about which members of the groups are likely to be in disagreement.

Public opinion is not simply the opinion of the majority of a group. On each issue the interested public will divide itself into two or more differing points of view, which will not necessarily be contradictory or mutually exclusive. The opinion must be representative of the group as a whole. Hennessy (1981) says in his complete and concise definition "Public opinion is the complex of beliefs expressed by a significant number of persons on an issue of general importance".

Attitudes in Opinion Formation

The basic objective of public relations is to measure, analyze, and influence public opinion, which develops from the attitudes of individuals comprising the public. Therefore, it is important to understand the meaning of attitudes. An attitude in the feeling or mood of an individual for or against some person, organization, issue or object. It represents the predisposition of an individual to evaluate controversial questions in a favourable or unfavourable manner. Simply started, an attitude is a way of looking at situations. An expressed attitude is an opinion.

Attitudes that express feelings of like or dislike are a product of numerous physical and mental influences. Body processes affect attitudes. Good health contributes to favourable attitudes, while illness fosters negative ones. Cultural, racial and religious backgrounds often determine a person's attitudes. Customs and habits influence attitudes. A person who is in the habit of going temple regularly has a favourable attitude toward religion.

Kinds of Attitudes

There can be of three types–positive, passive and negative.

Positive : A positive attitude induces a person to react favourably toward another person, an issue, a policy or an organisation.

Passive : An individual will have a passive attitude toward an issue a person, or an organisation when he does not give any opinion on issues affecting the group. A worker who has a passive attitude toward labour unions will have no opinions on controversial questions involving union policy or activities.

Negative : Attitudes also may be negative, giving the individual an unfavourable opinion of a person, issue or organisation. A negative attitude is usually accompanied by feelings of unpleasantness or dissatisfaction.

The intensity of an attitude is the strength of the belief or feeling of a person toward a person, object or group. An attitude may be specific or general, simple or complex. A complex attitude may have numerous beliefs and considerable knowledge supporting it. A simple attitude, based on a single belief is much easier to change.

Arousing Attitudes

The objective of public relations is to determine and analyse attitudes of people in order to understand and perhaps, to anticipate public opinion on controversial problems. In influencing public opinion, public relations has the two-fold problem. One is lessening antagonistic attitudes and the two is persuading people with favourable attitudes to adopt a more positive attitude and to express task of public relations in influencing public opinion is to arouse the passive attitude of the majority of the group on controversial questions.

To arouse an attitude in an individual who is passive toward a controversial question depends upon the stimulation of a need created by an event or communication. The public relations practitioner may have no control over the need for change or the conditions conducive to change but nevertheless can magnify or minimize the importance of the need many people continue to have attitudes acquired in the past, and good communication can arouse these old attitudes. A felt need or dissatisfaction with prevailing conditions is essential to arousing existing attitudes to create a positive attitude, the public relations practitioner appeals to a need that may not be recognized, or points and that an indifferent or neutral attitude does not provide the satisfaction that the individual desires, and so creates dissatisfaction with prevailing conditions change in existing attitudes changes in attitude occur when an existing attitude no longer provides a person with satisfaction or when the aspirations of the person are raised. Changes in attitude are also brought about when an individual experiences problems, frustrations or dissatisfaction with cherished beliefs, self-image economic status, value system and other circumstances. Appeals to the physical, social and economic needs for people are most effective in changing their attitudes. Attitude change is directly related to the immediacy of the issue to the individual. An issue directly affecting the satisfaction or personal welfare of a person is likely to cause a change from a passive attitude to either a positive or a negative opinion.

Events Change Attitudes

Events play an important part in changing attitudes and opinions. Particularly, happenings or occurrences of direct significance to a member of a group are a major determinant of attitude and opinions. Events provide information that often induces a change of attitude. Events may transform passive attitudes into positive opinions. A gas leakage in the industrial plant arouses the latent attitudes of people about the danger of hazardous manufacturing in a residential neighbourhood. This event may arouse public opinion against the owner of the plant and bring about safety legislation to protect the community against a recurrence of the disaster, events make a stronger impact on attitudes and public opinion than do simple communications. Because events speak louder than words, public relations practitioners recognize the importance of events in transforming passive attitudes into positive opinions on controversial issues. It should be recognized, however, that communication events may, themselves, be highly significant.

Transferring Attitudes to Opinions

Opinions are the public expression in response to motivation arising from the needs, preferences, and interests of individuals composing the public. The principle motives inducing persons to express their attitudes in the form of opinions are their desire for comfort and convenience, safety and protection, gain satisfaction of pride, or satisfaction of affection.

The opinions of individuals are activated by their attitudes which are motivated by mental and physical forces that induce them to express opinions. People usually are not aware of the motives impelling them to express attitudes in the form of opinions. The intensity of one's motives varies from time to time as the urgency of a need increases or diminishes with circumstances. Public relations practitioners should understand the motives that cause people to express their opinions so that public relations communications can appeal to the needs and motives of the public.

Process of Opinion Formation

Public opinion is a composite opinion resulting from the interaction of the individual opinions of members of a group. It has been defined as the expression of all members of a group who are giving attention in any way to a given issue. Fine process stands with an interaction of individual attitudes, mind sets, and beliefs concerning an issue. It is essentially the product of a collective mental life, which, in a democracy, includes the expression of the majority, if there be a majority, and the minority at any given time. Public opinion involves a transformation of individual opinion into group opinion, brought about by the influence exerted by members of a group on the individual's opinion.

The process of opinion formation goes something like this :

(1) A number of people recognize a situation as being problematic and

decide that something ought to be done about it. They explore possible solutions and do some fact finding.

(2) Alternative proposals for solving the problem emerge, and these are discussed back and forth.

(3) A policy or a situation is agreed upon as best meeting the situation recognized as problematic. Agreement and a decision to promote its acceptance lead to group consciousness.

(4) A programme of action is undertaken, and this is pressed until the requisite action is obtained.

Basis of Public Opinion

Today public opinion is based more on rational thinking done to education and improved communication. While the opinions of elemental groups are influenced by appeals to their emotions, intelligence and comprehension play an important part in formation of public opinion of advanced groups. More persons are weighing and considering information on controversial issues, suspending their judgement's until they have the facts, and evaluating the information they receive from various sources. Rational, advanced groups are composed of persons who possess the facts about an issue that affects the group. The quality of public opinion is basically dependent upon the quantity and quality of information. The group that has the most reliable and complete information about controversial issue is likely to exhibit the most enlightened opinion. Uniformed public are more easily swayed by instinct and emotion to accept the falsehoods of propaganda. Employees who do not know the facts about their company operations often become tools for a demagogue.

Methodology to Gauge Public Opinion

Some "Laws" of public opinion as given by Handley Cantrill in his book *'Gauging Public Opinion'* and reproduced by Cutlip and Center in their book *'Effective Public Relations*', p. 203, are as follows :

1. Personal contacts, by telephone or mail or with persons you know.
2. Advisory committees or panels.
3. Analysis or an organisation's incoming mail.
4. Evaluation by field agents or salesmen on opinions held about the organization
5. Press clippings and radio and TV monitoring of what has been said

on a particular subject.
6. Study of national public opinion polls to gain sense of opinion, climate and trends.
7. Sales records
8. Speeches and writings of recognized opinion leaders.
9. Study of voting which reflects public opinion on certain issues.
10. Conference of those involved in a particular problem or situation.

These informal methods can be helpful but they lack representativeness and objectivity. Still such methods can provide vital and significant clues to opinion trends and reveal sources of things people like and do not like.

More Reliable Methods to Measure Public Opinion

Talking to each and every one is not possible. Instead social scientists and market researchers have developed the technique of talking to a small but representative group in each public. This is the sample survey. Sampling is a great money saver and is accurate when the sample is representative. By asking precise understandable question of truly accurate miniature of a whole, public opinion can by measured with a high degree of accuracy. These survey tools offer an effective means of facilitating an inflow of information and opinion.

Types

1. *Cross-Section Surveys* : Under this method a set of questions is asked of a cross-section sample of a given public. The questionnaire builds a bridge between an organization and members of the public.

1. *Methods to Draw Sample*

(i) *Probability sample* : In this system people to be interviewed are chosen at random by some mechanical formula, such as evry 7th in the list.
(ii) *Area sample* : This is a form of probability sample in which geographical areas are listed, cities for example, then units to be surveyed are chosen at random.
(iii) *Quota sample* : In this method demographical characteristics sex, age, residence, occupation, income level of the population in question are studied then interviews are assigned by quota in the same proportions as these characteristics exist in the whole population.

All these methods involve a degree of sampling error, which usually can by kept within tolerable limits. The results obtained through cross-section survey are more qunatitative than qualitative in nature. They often fail to reflect the depth and intensity of opinions expressed by respondents.

2. *Survey Panels*

Under this method, a panel of people is selected and is interviewed several times over a period of time. The selection of participants is determined on a cross-section basis. Panels are used to learn what happens to people under varying conditions over a span of time. It is an effective device for controlled experiments. This method suffers from several weaknesses as panels are difficult to administer, and it is hard to keep all members interested over a long stretch.

3. *Depth Interview*

This is a qualitative instrument of measuring public opinion. It is an informal kind of interview. The respondent is encouraged to talk fully and freely. Elmo Roper says, "Because of the informal nature of this technique and the fact that the most productive depth interviews are those which give respondent the widest range of latitude for responding, one major problem in its use is how to evaluate its meaning." He thinks the really qualified depth interviewer is rare.

4. *Content Analysis*

This is a method of systematically coding and classifying the content of one or all of the mass media. This method can tell an organisation what is being published about it and in what context it is talked about. Media content can be measured as to how much is descriptive, how much is favourable, how much is critical. Content analysis also can be useful in periodically assessing content of informational output against stated objectives.

5. *Mail Questionnaires*

This is economical method but danger is that there is no assurance the respondents will be representative of the whole population. This method lacks the flexibility and the interpretations possible in personal interviews.

It is difficult to get an adequate response to many mail questionnaires. This economical device can be useful when used with due caution. It is most effective in soliciting opinions of homogeneous groups where the cleavage of opinion is decisive. This method can be helpful in uncovering sources of criticism and praise. Space should be provided for additional comment at the end.

PROPAGANDA

The word propaganda was born in the seventeenth century, when the catholic church set up its College of Propaganda to propagate the faith. But during World War II Goebbels used propaganda as an instrument of politics, a power for social control. The function of propaganda is not essentially to convert, rather its function is to attract followers and to keep them in line.

The task of propaganda, given suitable avenues, is to blanket every area of human activity so that the environment of the individual is changed to absorb the (Nazi) movement's world views. According to him, in propaganda one was forced to distort facts or even to falsify them to achieve one's purpose. This view has stuck on and propaganda has come to mean any publicity which is not necessarily related to realities.

According to the Institute for Propaganda Analysis, propaganda is an expression of opinion, by individuals and groups, which is deliberately designed to influence opinion or action by other individuals or groups with reference to predetermined ends. Propaganda influences public opinion. In its broadest sense, propaganda is honest and forthright communication intended to advance a cause through enlightenment, persuasion, or a dedicated sense of mission. It is currently employed by religious, charitable, political and social service institutions to influence the thoughts and actions of others for their best interest. In this sense, propaganda is legitimate permission.

However, propaganda as practised by some governments and organisations, has come to be accepted widely as a subversive activity that appeals to bigotry and intolerance, hate and fear, by suppressing facts and publishing false and misleading information in a vicious and reprehensible manipulation of public opinion.

Frederick E. Lumley wrote "Propaganda of every kind awakens passion by confusing the issues; it makes the insignificant seem weighty; it makes the important seem trifling; it makes the channels of communication full of exciting stuff; it keeps people battling in a fog".

In nutshell propaganda is an organized effort to propagate a doctrine, an idea or a cause. Propaganda may have an ethical content. It is persuasion based on self-interest.

Propaganda has come to be known as an evil force through its wide spread use in creating hate and fear in time of war by means of atrocity stories, brainwashing, brutality, and barbarism. Today propaganda is a major instrument of international conflict; it is employed in television and radio broadcasts, magazines, and newspapers to influence public opinion throughout the world.

Propaganda vis-a-vis Advertising and Public Relations

The notice of the advertiser is clearly to persuade a customer to buy some product or service. There is no concealment or hidden purpose in the appeal of the honest advertiser. Beyond the principle of ethics and morality, it is essential to the honest advertiser that the public accept his advertising claims as aboveboard and as an honest effort of persuasion.

Public relations is sometimes referred to as propaganda. Since they are deliberately designed to influence public opinion. Public relations programmes may be considered as propaganda in the best sense of the word. Most public relations programmes are honest and straight forward efforts to influence public opinion. However, as the word "propaganda" is commonly understood today, public relations is not propaganda, it is not a subversive activity that suppresses relevant facts, publishes false and misleading information, distorts the truth, and attempts to manipulate public opinion. Critics of public relations often refer to it as propaganda with the implication that it is an evil force that seeks to subvert public opinion.

Techniques of Propaganda

Subversive propaganda employs various following techniques to manipulate public opinion.

Evasion of truth : This is the worst characteristic of propaganda. Deliberate falsehoods are fabricated with intent to deceive the public. Propagandists use variations of the "big lie", they employ words with double meanings, omit significant facts and resort to gross exaggerations to convince the public that it should accept the propagandists' views.

Name-calling : This is a common strategy to include the public to condemn or reject a group or idea without considering the facts. A propagandist often employs scapegoats, who are blamed for the evils suffered by the public : communists are accused of creating racial strife and civic corruption; capitalists are referred to as "reactionary pigs". All forms of name calling are designed to simplify issues and appeal to the prejudices of the public.

An appeal to humility : This is the characteristic of some propaganda. The propagandist identifies his leaders or party with persons of humble origin in order to gain the support of people of similar circumstances. For example, Shri Vivekanand Swami is the symbol of humble beginning with appeal to the masses.

Use of testimonials : These are frequently used by propagandists to further their causes. Quotations from the statements of well-known politicians, actors, athletes are used in support of various causes. Such persons may be misquoted, their remarks taken out of context or distorted in order to influence public opinion.

Provocation : It is a technique of propaganda in which the propagandist provokes violence in hopes that the opposition will be blamed for it. Violence may be provoked by an employer during a labour strike in order to create unfavourable public opinion of the strikers. To divert public attention from a major issue a minor situation may be created to cast discredit an opponent.

Delaying strategy : An intentional delaying strategy is sometimes employed by propagandists to defeat opposition on an issue. Although professing to favour certain legislation, a propagandist may achieve his real purpose of defeating it by deliberate delaying tactics, such as offering amendments, asking for further investigation, on pleading that the time is not ripe for its adoption. The objective of this strategy is to weaken public interest and support for an issue and will ultimately be forgotten or defeated.

The favourable argument strategy : It involves presenting only those arguments that support the viewpoint of the propagandist and ignoring all conflicting facts. The public, getting information on only one side of the question, accordingly has a biased and distorted viewpoint.

These propaganda techniques are designed to confuse the issue, evade the truth, make the insignificant seem important, and distort the facts by appealing to passion and prejudice.

PUBLICITY

Good public relations start with good performance as viewed by the public. The function of publicity is to reflect the performance and get public acknowledgement and appreciation for it. Publicity that does not reflect good performance is likely merely to destroy credibility. It is a communication tool which is concerned with dissemination of information about an organization to attract attention or to gain recognition, to build image, and to win the approval of the target public. Cutlip and Center in their book, '*Effective Public Relations*' define publicity as, the dissemination of information making matters public from the point of view of one who wishes to inform others also systematic distribution of information about an institution or an individual. Excerpts from the book, *The Practice of Public Relations*, by Fraster P. Seitel, p. 303.

> No matter if you work for the largest manufacturing company, the poorest politician, or the tiniest non-profit organisation, chances are if you are engaged in public relations work, attracting positive publicity will be among your primary responsibilities.
> Securing publicity is perhaps the most well-known aspect of public relations work. Clearly it is the function most associated with public relations. In most people's minds publicity is public relations.
> Publicity through news releases and other methods is designed to broaden knowledge and to generate positive recognition about an organisation, its personnel and its activities. Publicity is most often gained by dealing directly with the media, either in reacting to enquiries or in initiating the communication.

Selecting Publicity Media

Proper selection of the mass media is essential in preparing and placing news releases. The common practice of indiscriminate mailing of releases and articles to media without knowledge of their editorial content, audiences, and editorial policy is wasteful. A flood of worthless releases is inundating the desk of editors and overflowing their wastebaskets. Since the average cost of preparing a news release, including time spent in gathering data, writing, editing, processing and photography is very high, the preparation and distribution of publicity must be given greater attention by publicity departments.

To ensure that news releases receive favourable consideration publicity media should be subjected to the same scrutiny by public relations practitioners. A record should be continuously maintained for individual newspapers, magazines, and radio and television stations, indicating whether they use new product news, personnel news, financial news, or general news–with or without pictures.

Newspapers and magazines should be read and broadcasts audited to determine the publicity they use. Editors may be asked for sample copies of their publications for review, and for information about pending special issues. Records should be maintained of all periodicals sent.

Publicity Media

Newspapers, magazines, radio and television are the media used for publicity.

Newspapers

Newspapers are the major medium of publicity. They are read by a number of people who influence public opinion. Newspapers appeal to the special interests of women, sports enthusiasts, business executives career seekers and others through special sections providing opportunities for product publicity on these subjects. The large number of newspapers provide an opportunity for corporations and associations to secure valuable publicity.

Magazines

Magazines are an important medium for product news, feature stories and pictorial publicity. They tend to be read thoroughly and leisurely. The typical issue will be read by several persons and will likely be preserved for future reference. Magazines, which afford space to till a complete story, are particularly suitable for service or educational publicity articles. The attractive appearance, good paper, and fine colour reproduction of magazines make them ideal for picture publicity.

Radio and Television

Radio and television publicity has developed rapidly in the country. Radio covers 95 per cent of the geographical area while the TV covers nearly 80 per cent of the geographical area. There are about twenty-five crore radio sets and TV sets in the country. Television is becoming the most effective medium for publicity because of its audio visual characteristics.

Types of Publicity

The important types of publicity are news releases, business feature articles, service feature articles, financial publicity, product publicity, pictorial publicity and emergency publicity.

1. ***News***

The most common type of publicity is news of local, regional or national interest. There are two types of news publicity–spontaneous news and planned news.

Spontaneous News

This type of publicity originates from an unplanned event, such as a strike, major accident, fire, explosion, flood or drought, etc. News media are notified, and they may send reporters, photographers and camera crew to the news source.

Planned News

Planned news publicity originates in the day-to-day developments and occurrences within organization which may be of news value and public interest. News releases are prepared and distributed by public relations staff at the headquarters. Subjects of news releases would include, for example, plant expansion, changes in personnel, production figures, special events, major appointments, plant openings, anniversaries, speeches by executives and interviews by executives, etc.

2. ***Business Feature Articles***

Business feature articles, also known as case histories on trade press stories, are an important type of publicity published by business, trade and technical media and prepared by industrial firms to support their marketing objectives. A business feature defines problems common to an industry and describes solutions to these problems by a particular concern that uses, the product of the company preparing the publicity. A business feature may be developed from speeches discussing product applications. Many business features are prepared by independent, or free lance, writers and photographers, whose work is co-ordinated by a member of the public relations staff.

3. ***Service Feature Articles***

Service feature articles are written to provide newspaper and magazine readers with information, advices and suggestions on home, fashion, health, food, beauty and care, etc. Service publicity is produced by the publicity staff and counsellors of manufactures of consumer products.

4. ***Financial Publicity***

Many of the news releases and feature articles which appear on the financial pages of daily newspapers and financial magazines are kind of financial publicity. For example, financial news releases feature, dividend declarations meagres, annual and quarterly reports, annual meetings, new products and other financial news. These are prepared by the publicity staff with the cooperation of investment houses, bank and insurance companies, etc.

5. ***Product Publicity***

News of new products, product improvements, new product applications, and product performance are subjects of product publicity released by publicity staffs of manufacturers to editors of industrial magazines and consumer periodicals. Product publicity gives consumers information about complex technical equipment, drugs, and scientific products to enable them to choose intelligently from the wide variety of products on the market.

6. ***Pictorial Publicity***

At present, there is a growing demand for newsworthy, in conventional or original still photographs by newspapers and magazines. Many companies maintain staff cameramen for continuous photographing of special events, new facilities, interviews and local news features. Freelance photographers are also employed to supplement their work. Newspaper photograph editors will assign a staff photographer to cover a special event if it is of quite importance.

7. *Emergency Publicity*

To ensure proper handling of media relations during an emergency, the public relations department should prepare, in advance a carefully considered emergency publicity programme. Foremen and supervisors should be instructed, before an accident occurs, how to deal with the media in times of emergency.

One person with authority in each facility should be designated to speak for the company, to give information to the media, and to answer questions of reporters. Unfavourable news should not be concealed. Favourable facts should be given to the press, such as prompt and brave action that minimized a more serious situation.

Terminology used in describing an emergency to the press should not be inflammatory, as for example, "I thought for sure it was the end". And accident should be described as a "failure" not an "explosion", an "emergency" rather than a "disaster".

The media should be notified immediately when an emergency occurs. The news personnel arriving at the scene should not be ignored. Guards and receptionists should be instructed to honour press cards. Reporters should not be greeted with such statements as "no comment" or "I do not have time to talk now". The public relations staff should be at the scene to cover the happening, prepare news releases, and scenepictures, which would be made available to the media.

COMMUNICATION WITH THE MEDIA

Good relationships with editors, editorial writers, publishers, columnists, and news broadcasters are vitally important to secure publicity. An understanding of the job requirements and viewpoints of newspeople is essential in getting their cooperation in fair and accurate reporting of the affairs of an organisation. The primary objective of a reporter is to get the facts for a news story and get it in his or her paper or in the air at the earliest possible time and before it appears in completing media. This means that a reporter is always working to meet deadlines. Good relations with the press can further be developed by observing a few simple principles which are as follows :

- Don't be evasive, be frank and honest.
- Always be available to the press.
- Don't overplay the company or colour the facts.
- Always assure that you will be quoted so be careful and accurate when making statements.

Avoid "off the record" statements but, if necessary, clearly label them as "not for publication".

- Don't complain of errors.
- Don't mislead a reporter.
- Don't condemn the editor when a story is left out of the paper.
- Don't go over a reporter's head to his superior with a complaint.
- Anticipate a newsman's interest and have the facts ready.

Methods of Communication

1. *Personal Contacts*

The principal method of communicating with the media is by calling on editors, publishers, and feature writers of newspapers, magazines, news agencies, feature syndicates, and news directors of radio and television stations. Through such personal contacts, publicity staff members determine the needs of editors and news directors and become acquainted with the programmes and columns which require feature material.

2. *Press Conferences*

On rare occasions, press conferences are arranged by public relations directors. The purpose is to obtain publicity in connection with vitally important news, such as the introduction of a new product, settlement of a labour dispute, change in management, plant expansion, etc. A press conference should not be called unless the importance of the news clearly indicates doing so, and then it should be timed so that the news will secure the widest coverage.

3. *Mailing of News Releases*

News releases are usually distributed by mail. Since the editorial requirement of each medium varies publicity should be sent only to those editors who are likely to use them. A list should be prepared and classified according to the type of material each will use. The list may be compiled on punch cards showing the name and address of the news organisation, deadlines, telephone numbers, names of editors and a code classification number so that specific media may be sorted out for special releases.

4. *Media Previews*

Previews to which the media are invited are desirable for securing cooperation when introducing new models or opening new plants and facilities. The day before the official public showing, the media are given a preview; company official welcomes newspeople and answers their questions. News releases, photographs and media kits giving complete information about the new product are distributed.

5. *Media Management Luncheons*

Luncheons are arranged at which media representatives have an opportunity to meet management. These luncheons may be arranged before annual or regional share holders' meetings. Business and financial writers, editors, publishers and local correspondents of business magazines are invited to hear about corporate performance and financial status. Company officials speak after the luncheon. Questions are answered, and a motion feature featuring the company's operations may be shown.

6. *Media Kits*

Media kits containing mimeographed news releases, photographs, biographies and background material are prepared by public relations departments and distributed to the media at special events, such as anniversaries, plant openings, new product announcements, and press luncheons.

Evaluation of Publicity

The usual method of evaluating the effectiveness of the publicity of a company is to measure the number of column inches of company news published by newspapers and trade, technical and business magazines. The number of inches of published publicity, how is not conclusive evidence of effectiveness of press publicity mere appearance of a news at or feature in a periodical assurance that the story was seen or read in whole or in neither is there evidence as such the number of readers of a particular news story. The only positive knowledge derived from clippings that a story was printed. A more conclusive measurement of the effectiveness of publicity is essential, and surveys of publicity readerships, similar to those employed in appraising the readership of advertising, are needed to give more conclusive evidence of the impact of publicity on public opinion.

ADVERTISING

The history of advertising goes back to ancient Greece and Rome, signs were used to carry information for advertising goods and services. These signs consisted of illustrations of symbols of the products advertised. Afterwards printing signs were replaced by written words and advertising began appearing in newspapers. Now advertising is drawing attention to a commodity or service with the aim of selling it. Modern advertising is a child of production for profit. People in tribal or feudal societies produced goods for themselves or for neighbours whose needs they know. Barter system was in existence and each man with something to sell in exchange is his own advertiser. Organized advertising becomes necessary only when production passes from an individual to an industrial level that is, when production is organized by businessmen who raise capital and hire labour with it. The larger industries become, and the further they allowance toward mass production the more dependent they become on advertising to help sell their products. Hence, advertising is one of the means of mass communication alongwith other means as publicity, sales promotion and public relations indeed, without its services in communicating with the public, many industrial and business firms would be forced to shut up, their employers would be thrown out of work, and on economy would collapse defining advertising. John. E. Kennedy a copy writer has defined advertising as a salesmanship in print; which indicates that the ultimate objective of advertising is to sell.

According to Concise Oxford Dictionary, the word *to advertise* means to make generally or publicly known, describe publicly with a view to increasing sales. The word *Advertising* is drawn from advertise which means to make it known. According to London School of Practitioner and Advertising, "Advertising presents the moot persuasive possible selling message at the lowest cost".

Frank Jefkin in his book '*Advertising Today*', "Advertising is the dissemination of information concerning an idea, service or product to compel action in accordance with the interest of the advertiser".

Professor J. K. Galbraith in his book '*The Affluent Society*' says : Advertising is an industry which lends itself to competitive frauds.

John Burns says "The tragedy of the working man is the poverty of his desires". By stimulating those desires and by creating new ones, advertising has changed all that. It has transferred what were once considered luxuries. Advertising has changed our personal and social habits. Advertising depends absolutely on its power to communicate and to persuade".

Actually advertisement is a promotional message and advertising is a selling on idea. Firm develops a product to satisfy market demand. For maximum exposure to his product advertiser needs large contact and it is possible only through mass communication. Hence, advertising is one of the means, of mass communication alongwith other means as publicity, sales promotion and public relations.

In 1948, the American Marketing Association developed a definition which is widely quoted : "Advertising is any paid form of *non-personal* presentation and promotion of ideas, goods, or services by an identified sponsor".

There are three key words in this definition. First, advertising is *non-personal*; which means that advertising is directed toward a large group of anonymous people. Even direct-mail advertising, which may be addressed to a specific person, is prepared by a computer and is signed by a machine. Second, advertising typically is *paid for*. This fact differentiates advertising from publicity, which is not usually purchased. Sponsors such as Coke and Britannia pay for the time and the space they use to get their message across (But the organizations such as the Red Cross, Public Relations Department, etc. advertise but do not pay for because they give the social advertisements for the welfare of the people which is called publicity). Broadcast stations, newspapers, and magazines run these advertisements free as a public service. Third, for obvious reasons, the sponsor of the advertisement is identified. In fact, in most instances identifying the sponsor is the prime purpose behind the advertisement otherwise, who advertise? Perhaps the only situation in which the identity of the advertiser may not be self-evident is political advertising. Because of this, broadcasters and publishers will not accept a political advertisement unless there is a statement identifying those responsible for it.

Functions of Advertising

Advertising fulfils the following basic functions in society :

(1) *Marketing function* : It serves a marketing function by helping companies that provide products or services sell their products. Personal selling, sales promotions, and advertising blend together to help market the product.

(2) *Education function* : People learn about new products and services or improvements in existing ones through advertising.

(3) *Economic function* : Advertising plays an economic role. The ability to advertise allows new competitors to enter the business arena, competition, in turn, encourages product improvements and can lead to lower prices. Moreover, advertising reaches a mass audience, thus greatly reducing the cost of personal selling and distribution.

(4) *Social function* : Finally, advertising performs a definite social function. By vividly displaying the material and cultural opportunities available in a society, advertising helps increase productivity and raises the standard of living.

Types of Advertising

Advertising is accepted as an important part of any social system, and a large majority of the population feels that it creates better products and services for society. Advertising messages continuously surround us. Our value structures, attitudes, and basic needs affect how one perceives these messages. The most common types of advertising are standard advertising and public service advertising. In addition, contemporary social issues and governmental regulations have induced new types of advertising. Among these are social responsibility advertising, counter advertising, advocacy advertising and image advertising. Let's examine the different types of advertising in brief.

1. Standard Advertising

Standard advertising attempts to persuade us to purchase certain products and services. They appear in all media and are financed by the company or organization that has products to sell or services to render. The motive is to sell and to create in the consumer a feeling of need and desire for a product or service. Decisions as to the type of message the advertising will use, in what media they will be placed, and how often they will appear in the media are usually made by the manufacturer or distributor, sometimes in conjunction with an advertising agency. Once these decisions are made, time or space is purchased, and a contract is signed specifying such things as the number of times the advertising will appear, when it will appear, and in the case of hoardings, at what location.

2. Public Service Advertising

Public service advertisings are those devised by non-profit organizations to answer a public need. Time or space for this type of advertising is provided free as a service to the public by the print or broadcast media. Most broadcasting stations provide a certain amount of broadcast media time for public service programming. Public service announcements run a regular schedule with the commercial. They usually last anywhere from a few seconds to five minutes, the most common lengths being 30 or 60 seconds.

3. Social Responsibility Advertising

Social responsibility advertising seeks to warn against the dangers inherent in the excessive use of some product or service. The safe driving, alcohol consumption and other advertisements that admonish us to act responsibly belong to social responsibility advertising. These advertisings are sometimes sponsored by either a non-profit organization or special public relations organizations representing a particular industry. There are many other types of social responsibility advertising besides the two we have already mentioned. Significant campaigns to use natural resources responsibly have become common and fire prevention and wildlife management are other examples. Energy conservation has also received wide exposure in advertising sponsored by non-profit industries and in some cases the energy companies themselves.

4. Counter- Advertising

Counter-advertising concentrates on warning consumers about alleged fraud or misrepresentation in advertising. These types of advertisings are diverted against a product or service. Advocates of counter advertising claim that standard advertising does not sufficiently inform the public to enable consumers to make intelligent buying decisions; counter advertisings are, therefore, necessary to counteract some of the allegedly unwarranted claims found in standard advertising. Some familiar counter advertisings are those that warn against abusive collection practices by credit agencies,.the dangers of air and water pollution and cigarette smoking.

5. Advocacy Advertising

Closely related to counter-advertising is advocacy advertising. Whereas counter-advertising is normally directed at a particular objectionable product, a company producing such a product, or an industry responsible for creating a societal ill, advocacy advertising champions preventive action against conditions affecting the public welfare. Advertising raising our awareness of heroin addiction, the rising crime rate are all examples of advocacy advertising. In most cases advocacy advertising is sponsored and paid for by an organization that wants to be associated with community involvement. Advocacy advertising is finding more and more sponsors as companies and organizations want to gain the added benefit of directing a message against a common fault of society while at the same time keeping their name visible to the public.

6. Image Advertising

Image advertising is a team primarily applied to messages sponsored by corporations to improve their corporate images.

Leading National Advertisers (LNA), a group charged with reading and tabulating ads in America's top magazines and select newspapers have a standard definition, "To truly be labelled 'corporate' the end must deal with the company's policies, functions, facilities, objectives, ideas, and standards, build favourable opinions of the company's management skills, technology, or social contributions, enhance the investment qualities or financial structure of the company or promote it as a good place to work".

Parts or Elements of Advertising

Every product, corporation, or non-profit institution eventually takes on a personality by means of which people visualize it, remember it, and describe it to either people. Creative people must, therefore, understand the process of putting the different elements in an infinite number of ways. When they start putting their creative strategy in action, they must know, which part of the advertising should come first, the headline, slogan, picture, brand name and so on. Let us discuss these elements in turn.

1. Slogan

It is a phrase or a sentence that describes either the benefit derived from the product or one of the product's most important attributes. It consists of a single phrase by which an advertiser conveys an important idea which will presumably lead readers to remember and think favourably of his company. It may play either a principal or a subsidiary role.

Slogan has two most common purposes : One, to provide continuity for a campaign, perhaps for a year or for many years. Two, to crystallize in a few memorable words the key idea or theme one wants to associate with a product.

An advertiser is most likely to use a slogan when he has some basic idea or theme he wants to establish and continue for a long time. For example, 'Toothpaste that promises glowing skin'. There may be political slogans, like – 'The leader you can trust. In war, In peace, Similarly, there can be social as well as religious slogan also.

Types of Slogans

To be effective, a slogan should be consistent with the purpose of the advertisement. Therefore, if there is a drastic change in a campaign's purpose, it is usually wise to change the slogan also. Mainly there are two types of slogans, one that emphasises a product, two that emphasises action to be taken.

Slogan that emphasises product or reward : Every product has some reward to offer consumers. It may have some hidden quality that differentiates a product from the competition's. The trick, then, is to find some way of dramatizing in effective words a particular product's advantage. For example, 'Toothpaste that promises glowing skin'.

Slogans that emphsize action to be taken : The slogan might urge directly that you use the product or service for example. Bright spare for your bright ideas.

Characteristics of Slogan

(i) Slogan should be brief, well balanced and easy to say.

(ii) It should be built on one idea.
(iii) Easy to remember.
(iv) Make it help differentiate the product.
(v) Make it provoke curiosity, if possible.
(vi) Make sure it highlights either a product, reward or an action.
(vii) Use rhythm and rhyme.
(viii) Make sure the slogan is not likely to confuse the consumer.

2. Headlines

Group of words used to attract the attention of customers is called headline. John Caples described that the headline is the most important element in most advertisements.

Functions

(i) The prime function of the headline is to gain immediate attention sometimes the headline is expected to do this job alone; more often it works hand in hand with the illustration or other visual elements.
(ii) A second function of most headlines is to lure readers into the text. Not only does the headline attract and select but it invites the readers to step in and stay a while. Instead of telling the whole story, it tells just enough to arouse interest.

Characteristics

(i) Headings should have an immediate impact on the readers.
(ii) It should include some promise of reward either direct or indirect.
(iii) It should be understandable at a glance because people will not spend time trying to figure out what you are saying.
(iv) Headlines should be specific and to the point. It should not be general and applicable to any product.
(v) It should be co-ordinated with other element of the advertisement.

There is no rule saying that you have to include a headline in every advertisement. If some other element can fulfil its functions more effectively, by all means omit the head.

Classifications of Headlines

(i) *Direct headlines :* Direct headlines are straight forward and informative. It tells people whether the message is in line with their predispositions. If the features of the product are strong and can arouse the interest, stimulate sales response, direct headline is better. It can state the fact, but it could not explain the method.

(ii) *Indirect headlines :* If the appeal of the product is not very strong, use indirect headlines.

(iii) *Combination headlines :* Combination headlines seek to combine the virtues of direct and indirect headlines.

(iv) *News headlines :* These types of headlines can be most effective of all where the product or service has something new to provide for the consumers.

(v) *"How to" headlines :* It can be either direct or indirect. In this type of headline the words "how to" can be implied as well as spelled out.

(vi) *Question headlines :* When a writer frames a headline as a question, he expects to make his audience seek the answer in the text. A question headline will be more provocative if it carries some interesting information or a stimulating idea.

(vii) *Command headlines :* A command headline politely "orders" the reader to do something.

Headline Length

There is no ideal length for a headline. It should use the words necessary to accomplish its job–no more, no less.

3. Subheads

Very often, advertisements have only one headline. Some have several, of these, one is usually the main headline, and the others subordinate. Subheads serve several purposes. For example, a writer who expresses a provocative thought in his main headline may want to expand on that thought in a subhead directly following.

4. Illustrations

An illustration in an advertisement is only one step behind from the real product or service advertised. It is, therefore, closer to reality than the written language. Illustrations are usually the most important visual element in any print advertisement.

Functions

(i) They attract the attention of the desired target audience.
(ii) They communicate a relevant idea quickly and effectively.
(iii) They interest the audience in the headlines and copy.
(iv) They help make the advertisement more believable.

To make an illustration selective, you must make sure it has some relevance to your product or to the copy. This should be clear to the readers when they first note the advertisement or when they read the copy.

Characteristics

(i) The best illustrations usually have a simplicity that makes it easy for the reader to get the point.
(ii) It should be chosen with singleness of purpose and the readers should get the point almost as soon as they see the page.
(iii) The most interesting picture will be the one readers can identify with themselves or their own problems and needs. It must tell first enough to what the reader's desire to find out the details of the product, the situation, or the image you are trying to communicate.
(iv) The illustrations should be believable, so that the readers accept the rest of the advertisement. Readers will be critical of anything that strikes them as illogical.

Kinds of Illustrations

Illustrations are commonly classified both on the basis of their subject matter and on the basis of the technique used to portray the picture.

Subject-wise Classification

The illustrations can be classified subject-wise in the following way :

(i) The product itself.

(ii) Part of the product.
(iii) The product ready for use.
(iv) The product in use.
(v) The product being tested.
(vi) Differentiating features of the product.
(vii) Consumer reward as a result of using the product.
(viii) Effect on the consumer of not using the product.
(ix) Testimonial for the product.

Technique-wise Classification

The two basic illustrative techniques available to the advertiser are photographs and art-work.

(i) Photographs

Our society has become picture oriented. Watching television has made it expect to see and watch news event, and to see products in use. It is appropriate that a new product be announced by a photograph, we associate realism and authenticity with photographs. Photographs are used extensively in industrial and trade publications so that the technicians who read them will learn what the products look like and how they will perform.

(ii) Artwork

Original art work is often used to create a desired mood. If some product feature is to be exaggerated or if a mood of warmth or coolness or sophistication is sought, a skilful artist is engaged. Artwork tends to cost more than photography. Artwork helps to make cartoons and diagrams-cartoons represent a quality of homour.

Diagram : It is another useful form of artwork, especially in illustrating complicated products.

5. Copy

Copy is the written portion of an advertisement. The basic idea of an advertisement is to motivate people. It is the main body of words or the textual matter of an advertisement. The copy, regardless of medium, is basically an amplication of the headline theme. If you have a headline, body text should explain it.

Before writing any actual copy, a copy writer can wisely draw up a copy policy. "A copy policy is a diagram or blueprint of a number of pieces of copy that are to be written". It should explain the following :

(i) To whom the copy is addressed any why?
(ii) What media are being used?
(iii) The exact purpose of this piece of copy.
(iv) The points that are to be made and the sequence in which they are to be made.

Functions

(i) The copy must arouse interest.
(ii) It must provide believable information that is easy to understand and likely to what desire to own the product.
(iii) It must compel the readers to see the product and to try it out or at least accept the image the writer has presented.

Rules for Copy Writing

(i) Gain a thorough understanding of the consumers to whom the message is to be addressed.
(ii) State what consumers want to hear.
(iii) Know the language of the reader and talk to him in his own language.
(iv) Stress on one appeal preferably.
(v) Do not talk too many things.
(vi) Employ the present tense.
(vii) Be specific.
(viii) Avoid fine writing, write simply.
(ix) Make sure that the copy is readily understandable to consumers at the first instance.
(x) Break the copy into paragraphs, not only for the purpose of conveying the message properly but for easy reading also.
(xi) Make no untrue statements or statements which are likely to be doubted by readers.

(xii) Brevity is the best gift of copy.

(xiii) Say maximum in the minimum space.

(xiv) Thoughts should be conveyed properly.

(xv) Make the copy interesting which will lead the readers to read rest of the body text.

(xvi) Use short rather than long words wherever possible, but do not discard the long word if it reflects your meaning more exactly.

(xvii) Copy should be timely, relevant, crispy and juicy.

Classifications of Copy

(i) *Reason Why Copy*

Any copy that features a reward in the headline or illustration and explains why it is true is called reason why copy. Advertising should always give consumers a reason to buy the product.

The reason why approach is more common in print than in broadcast advertising. In print, readers can proceed at their own speed from headline to copy. In the broadcast media, the speed is controlled by the sender, and a less-than-attentive listener or viewer is likely to miss the reasons why an opening lead is true.

(ii) *Humorous Copy*

Advertisement can be made more appealing by a touch of humour. According to television consultant Harry Wayne McMohan, the number of television commercials that use humour in communicating their message is increasing. Humorous copy may have the following generalizations :

(a) Humorous messages attract attention.

(b) Humorous messages may detrimentally affect comprehension.

(c) Humour may distract the audience, yielding a reduction in counter-argumentation.

(d) Humour tends to enhance source credibility.

(e) Humour should be related to the target audience.

(f) A humorous context may increase liking for the source and create a positive mood.

(iii) *Descriptive Copy*

When copy includes description of the product or service and the description becomes the major focus of the advertisement, the copy is called descriptive. This happens when the appearance of the product or reward it promises needs strong emphasis in the copy to make it clear to prospective buyers.

(iv) *Testimonial Copy*

Advertisers tend to prefer celebrities who are widely known, easily recognized, well liked, and who have not endorsed a wide variety of products. The principal advantage of using celebrities is their ability to attract immediate attention. For example, Hemamalini is shown using Lux or Kapil is drinking Maltova and so on.

(v) *Straight Copy*

Straight copy has a very straight message. It identifies the needs of the people you call it in simple words, "Warm in Dhaliwal Shawl".

(vi) *Dialogue Copy*

When two or more persons are shown communicating with one another and solving their problems is called a dialogue copy. But the dialogue should be well written, should be interesting, convincing and persuasive. Poor dialogue is dull and unnatural dialogue is unconvincing.

(vii) *Narrative Copy*

The story is the main in the narrative copy. Almost everyone likes to hear an interesting story. The story is one of the oldest forms of literature and is a reliable approach to communicating an advertising point. Among the common forms of narrative copy are the short story, the picture and caption, and the comic strip.

6. Product

It is a model or shape of the product. If you have a multiproduct company, your product must be related to your other products also. Product's strong points must be highlighted while the weak points minimized. While designing product, you must answer the following :

- What is the product made of?
- How is the product used?
- What are the competitive advantages and disadvantages of the product.
- How the product packaged?
- How is the product designed?
- Where is the product sold?

7. Trademark

The term trademark includes any word, name, symbol, or device or any combination thereof adopted and used by a manufacturer or merchant to identify his goods and distinguish them from those manufactured or sold by others. Under this concept we have three main types identification marks : (i) Brand names, (ii) Corporate or store names, and (iii) Identifying symbols for brands or companies.

(i) *Brand names :* A brand name may come from almost any source. It may come from company name as Nestley company use 'Nescafe' or from personal name as 'Vimal' sarees or Jindal Strips Ltd., etc.

Sometimes, a word that has no relevance to the product advertised may be used effectively as a brand name. For example "Arrow" for shirts is a familiar example.

(ii) *Corporate or store name :* Some companies use the firm name throughout the product line. For example, 'Lakme' lipstick and cream manufactured by Lakme company.

(iii) *Visual symbols :* Visual symbols have long been used to identify goods and services.

Although brand names, firm names, and other identifying trade symbols differ in format, certain principles apply in the creation of all of them. Some of these stem from certain legal requirements, some from the principles of effective communication. A mark should not be confusingly similar to an existing one in sound, appearance, or generally accepted meaning. It will not do simply to alter the spelling; obviously some people may only hear the name and never see it at all. The name should be pronounced quite differently from an existing one, but the consumer may pronounce it the way it looks, not necessarily the way you propose.

Importance of trademarks

- It gives the legal protection to the manufacturers.
- It increases the credibility of the firm because the buyer buys the product only after looking at the brand name.
- Registration of trademarks prohibits duplication.

Selection of an Advertising Media

An advertiser wants to reach as many good prospects he can, as frequently as he should, with the most effective selling message at the lowest possible cost. Having decided what he wants to say and to whom he wants to say it, he turns his attention to the question of where to say it.

Different media are available for conveying the message. His difficult job is to pick up the right type of media and the specific media within each type which will serve him best.

For most advertisers, no one type of medium or individual medium within a type alone suffices to communicate the advertising message. Two or more are necessary to attain desired objectives. The largest advertisers use several types of media and consider them complementary rather competitive. Media selection is one of the more important decisions to be made in the formulation and tactics of an advertising campaign.

Some of the media convey their messages through eye, some through ear and some through eye and ear simultaneously.

Problems in Media Selection

In media selection one of the first problems involved concerns the *matching up of the product* or service to be advertised with one medium class rather than another. A second problem involves which *medium* or *mix of media,* offers the best promise of achieving an objective. A third problem concerns the size of an advertising appropriation and how the appropriation can be allocated among different media. A fourth problem involves a *comparison of available media,* in terms of cost in relation to popular acceptance. A final problem involves contracting with the various media.

Different types of media reach either different audiences or similar audiences under different conditions of receptivity. They provide different ways of conveying the selling messages. To determine which types will prove most serviceable poses a real problem for an advertiser. Each type of medium has something of value to offer under certain conditions, varying with the product, the market, the objective, the time, the appropriation and so on.

Many factors may exert an influence in the selection process. They can conveniently be classified into two groups.

1. Creative factors
2. Mechanical factors

Creative Factors

The "creative" factors have to do with the nature of the message the advertiser wants to deliver. One such factor is the visual versus oral requirements of the message as a beautiful complexion can be portrayed better by pictures than by voice. Media permitting good colour work are therefore desirable where this sort of "appearance" appeal is to be emphasized. Such an appeal is more difficult to make successfully in radio advertising. Likewise, if a new package or some particular feature of the product is to be stressed in advertising, a visual representation may be more effective than a verbal description. On the other hand, piano lessons may be profitably advertised over the radio because the listener can be given an excellent idea of the skill he can acquire after taking a certain number of lessons.

Another creative factor is the mood of the message the advertiser wants to deliver. If he intends to introduce a new product with circus like "hoorah" he is sure to give serious consideration to outdoor advertisements. If the copy has a strong news slant, newspapers and radio have advantages over other media.

Mechanical Factors

Among the "mechanical" factors which may influence the choice of types of media are :

1. *Advertising objectives :* Different advertising objectives demand different types of media. If we want to attain intensive distribution

within a short period then newspapers and radio 'spots' are better.

2. *Flexibility as to budget control :* Choice of advertisers regarding media becomes limited who are skeptical about the advertising budget because some of the media may not permit cancellation at the last minute.

3. *Competitor's media :* Competitor's media should not be adopted blindly. If competitor's media is not effective, choose another media otherwise the same.

4. *Cost :* Cost is always a major factor in the selection of types of media. One cannot choose television with a limited budget.

5. *Availability of desirable facilities :* An advertiser must consider whether the various types of media can be used in the way that circumstances demand the must give attention to such factors as the availability of radio or TV, or the desirable magazine or newspapers facility.

6. *Geographical distribution and consumption pattern :* A product distributed only in Punjab should not be advertised in national newspaper or magazine. Per capita consumption may vary from one State to another. An advertiser may very well raise consumption in the poor States (where the product is used less) by using the media of that State.

7. *Coverage of cities of various sizes :* The choice of media is affected when to cover the cities of various sizes. A company whose sales are confined to city areas may buy space in newspapers which circulate largely within the city limits. On the other hand, a company manufacturing a produce such as farm machinery is more likely to be interested in rural district.

8. *Selection of coverage :* Media selection may be influenced by the nature of the groups to be reached for example, age, sex, and special interests. For youngsters, children's magazine, radio and TV are the best media. For women, advertisements can be given in women's magazines or in day time in radio and television. Because in day time, they are mostly free.

9. *Flexibility as to copy :* Types of media vary with respect to the opportunity they affect the advertiser to prepare his copy close to the

time it comes to the attention of customers. This is particularly important for the product whose sale hinges on the weather or on events of one sort or another.

10. *Length of copy necessary :* For a new product whose purchase can be induced by a sales message of considerable length, outdoor posters and radio are deficient as primary media. They may effectively supplement magazine.

11. *Need for supplementary coverage :* Some types of media are chosen to supplement other types. Any deficiency in the circulation of national magazines may be offset by using newspapers in larger cities.

12. *Life of advertisement :* Some media like radio and television offer just one opportunity to deliver each advertising message to prospective buyers. If the buyer does not see or hear the message on that one occasion, the only way is by running another advertisement. But magazine and outdoor advertisement give the advertiser an opportunity to expose his message to customers for days and weeks.

13. *Prestige value :* Prestigious products can be given in prestige magazines like 'India Today', 'Front Line', 'Femina', etc. because it increases the value of the product advertised.

14. *Consumer friendliness :* Television is such a medium because of the influence of the personalities who can be seen and heard. Newspapers and magazines undoubtedly have some of these qualities.

15. *Merchandising value :* Important to many advertisers is the degree of opportunity a medium offers for impressing distributors, dealers and salesmen. The more "local' a medium is or seems to be, the more likely are advertisements in it to win the interest and co-operation of these groups.

16. *Product interest :* Some products are interesting to large number of consumers and their advertising almost automatically attracts considerable attention and interest. Other products lack fundamental interest and it is difficult to draw the attention of people to advertisement of them and to hold that attention. For this latter type of product, media which reach a "captive audience" motion pictures may have something to offer.

ADVERTISING MEDIA

Advertising is a powerful communication force and a vital marketing tool–helping to sell goods, services, images and ideas through channels of information and persuasion. To an advertiser, however, the media are vehicles that carry messages to large groups of prospects and thereby aid in closing the gap between producer and consumer. Once a medium has established itself and has built a significant audience, it is in a position to attract advertisers who are willing to pay for the privilege of reaching that audience with their advertising messages. Some media, such as outdoor signs, direct mail or the posters we see in retail stores, offer consumers only the information contained in the advertising itself. They provide advertisers, however, with a channel through which they can reach potential buyers at the ideal place and time to stimulate sales.

To a media buyer, there is seemingly endless variety of advertising media, ranging from skywriting and banners to television networks and magazines. Each media category consists of hundreds or even thousands of competing business. The money any advertiser appropriates for buying media space or time is limited, and media sellers work to convince buyers that the media they represent well media advertiser needs more efficiently and more effectively than any other medium.

Classification of Media

An advertiser wants his message or information to reach prospective consumer. So, different media of advertising are a means of delivering a sales message or such other information. In the business world of today, every producer is trying his level best to attract the attention of consumers toward his product. Hence, number of media are available to him which can be classified as follows :

(i) Print Media
(ii) Audio Visual Media
(iii) Outdoor Media
(iv) Indoor Media

I. Print Media

It includes newspapers, magazines and direct mail. These are the most significant of today's print media. The newspaper and magazine vehicles deliver messages, in combination with news, entertainment, or other editorial material to measurable groups of readers. The degree of a reader's interest in the advertising content of a publication varies from person to person, from vehicle to vehicle, and from advertisement to advertisement. Normally, however, the reader's primary focus is on the articles or stories. Thus, a publication's editorial content provides an atmosphere of acceptance for advertisements. In many cases, it attracts the exact audience an advertiser seeks.

A newspaper is typically either a daily or weekly publication that is regarded, with some exceptions, as a local advertising medium. In fact, one of its primary advantages to an advertiser is the intense local coverage or penetration it provides. The word "coverage" in this context describes a medium's ability to reach a certain percentage of homes or prospects in a given area. Newspapers normally select their news, features and editorial subjects with an eye to the wants and needs of people within a particular community. They are geographically selective.

Magazines, on the other hand, are qualitatively selective. They are edited to appeal to the special interests of certain types of people regardless of where they live. Even multimillion circulation magazines with editorial appeal for both sexes such as Reader's Digest are more selective qualitatively than newspaper in terms of average income and educational levels.

Classification of Newspapers

Newspapers can be classified broadly in the following categories :

(a) *Size :* In terms of size, newspapers are divided into standard and tabloid types. The standard newspaper is approximately 22 inches deep by 8 columns wide, with each column about 2 inches in width. The term "standard", therefore simply refers to a large page paper as "*The Hindustan Times*", "*The Times of India*", "*The Tribune*", etc. whereas "Tabloid" papers are only about half that size of a daily newspaper.

(b) *Frequency :* By frequency of publication, newspapers fall into two broad groups, dailies and weeklies. However, a daily is published seven days a week, whereas a weekly is published once a week.

(c) *Audience :* Newspapers may also be distinguished on the basis of the audience they attract. Thus, in addition to general interest newspapers we have many that cater to special groups such as business.

(d) *Language :* Newspapers can also be classified on the basis of language. Some may be in English, Hindi, Urdu, Bengali and Punjabi, etc.

Advantages of Newspapers

Newspapers offer a number of advantages to the advertisers :

(a) Newspapers provide territorial flexibility than other media do. With newspapers the advertiser can place the advertisement where the potential market looks best.

(b) It is possible to convey the sales message rapidly and quickly.

(c) Newspapers reach diverse sections of people. Customers of a particular group can be selected by placing the advertisement in a special interest section.

(d) Sales message can be changed or modified to suit the target group.

(e) Repetition of the message with variation can impress the message with greater certainty.

(f) Newspapers provide community prestige. Readers feel emotionally attached with the newspapers they read. They believe in the advertisements appearing in such newspapers.

(g) The cost of advertising message per reader is lower than any other medium.

(h) Newspapers are portable. The messages can be read anywhere while sitting in a bus or a car.

(i) They are the private medium though they are widely circulated. The message can be read totally in privacy.

Limitations

Despite their advantages newspapers have several limitations.

1. Newspapers have a short life. There is nothing quite so stale as a newspaper a few days old. The chances that advertising will have any impact beyond the day of publication are therefore very low. On the other hand, potential buyers know that each day's production is a fresh one.

2. Most studies indicate that the average reader spends between 15 to 20 minutes on a paper. This means the advertisement has to make its impression quickly or not at all.
3. Poor reproduction reduces the impact of advertisements on readers. Even though reproduction has improved substantially, the newspaper still rates well below magazines in this respect. If appearance is important in the sale of a product, the product is likely to suffer when its picture is reproduced in the newspapers.

Types of Advertising

Newspaper advertising can be divided into several types. Most generally, we distinguish among :

(a) Display Advertising

(b) Classified Advertising

(c) Special Advertising (for example, public notices, political and government reports).

(a) Display advertising : Such type of advertising is placed on news and feature pages throughout the paper. It has strong attention value because of the illustrations, the arrangement of headings and body text, the white space, colour or other visual devices.

(b) Classified advertising : As the name implies, such advertisements are placed in a special page of the paper and are arranged under subheads according to the product advertised or the want the advertisement is supposed to satisfy. Classified display allows more flexibility or arrangement than regular classified in that borders, larger type, white space and photos may be used.

(c) Special advertising : Such type of advertising is mostly given by the government and the political parties.

Rate Structure in Newspapers

Most newspapers quote different for display and classified advertisements. The basic unit of space is the column inch, an area one column wide by one inch deep. The black and white advertisements and the position of the advertisement at the convenience of the publisher carry less rates than the coloured advertisements and special position advertisements.

In some markets where two papers are owned by the same publisher, the advertiser may buy space in both at a single combination rate.

MAGAZINES – A MEDIUM OF ADVERTISING : ITS MERITS AND LIMITATIONS

Magazines, the second form of print publication advertising, offer the advertiser advantages which in many respects are the opposites of those offered by newspapers. The newspaper appeals to all people in a particular community; the magazine appeals to particular people in all kinds of communities. The life of a daily newspaper advertisement is short–rarely more than a day. A magazine advertisement continues to live and produce result for a week, a month, or longer, as the periodical is read and reread not only by those who buy it, but by others who come in contact with it.

Although newspapers are limited in the quality of reproduction, most magazines offer high quality paper and printing. The deadline for newspaper insertions is usually two or three days in advance of publication, but such flexibility is impossible with a magazine advertisement; few magazine deadlines are as short as three weeks prior to publication date, and some may be as long as two months. The newspaper is primarily a local medium, and the magazine is mainly national.

Classification of Magazines

Like newspapers, magazines can also be classified in the following categories :

(a) *Size :* Some magazines are printed in the standard sizes but some of them in small or bigger sizes.

(b) *Frequency :* Another way to classify magazines is by frequency of publication : weekly, biweekly, monthly, bimonthly, quarterly or semiannually. But monthly magazines outnumber all other types.

(c) *Audience :* The magazines can also be classified on the basis of the audience to which they are directed. On the basis of the audience served, there are three broad types of magazines.

(i) Consumer Magazines

These are edited for the people who buy products for their own consumption. A common division of consumer magazines separates them into general appeal and special interest appeal. The former type offers readers a diversified editorial content, whereas the latter focuses on more restricted subject. For example, Reader's Digest appeals to both men and women and to many levels of age, occupation, income and education.

Special interest magazines are flourishing these days as people have become more educated and their tastes grow more sophisticated. But the effectiveness of magazines as advertising media does not rest entirely on their ability to deliver selective audiences. Editorial content influences readers' mood and their receptivity to advertisements.

(ii) Farm Magazines

These are circulated to farms and their families. Farm magazines may be general or specialized, nation-wide or regional.

(iii) Business Magazines

A business publication appeals to an occupational group or a particular industry. They fall into three subgroups : (1) Trade magazines–addressed to retailers, wholesalers, and other distributors, (2) Industrial magazines–addressed to business people engaged in all phases of manufacturing, and (3) Professional magazines–directed at physicians, lawyers, engineers, architects and other professional people.

Rate Structure in Magazines

Magazines advertising rates are quoted in units of pages, partial pages and full pages. Most rates include a commission to advertising agencies. Compared with newspapers, magazines are relatively of small size, and they enjoy longer audience reading time. With a few exceptions, therefore, neither the placement of advertisements on a page nor the location of specified advertisement pages within a publication is a great importance to the magazine advertiser. Because of its extra exposure, the outer cover of a magazine is always considered a preferred or premium position and commands a higher rate than inside pages.

DIRECT MAIL ADVERTISING

When a company enters business, its first advertising communications are on a person to person basis. Later as it grows, it sends letters or cards through the mail to the prospective customers. Finally, if it continues to prosper, the company branches out into using mass-media with the pre-selected audience these media provide. Nevertheless, the firm probably continues to use direct mail. Although direct mail is not truly a mass medium, it is an important one. It would be hard to find a business firm that did not at some time use direct-mail advertising.

It is a way of delivering sales message to prospects through the medium of post. Effective direct mail advertising is based on an efficient postal system. In this type of advertising the appeal is made to particular individuals directly. Distribution of pamphlets to pedestrians is called direct advertising. But when the message is sent by post it is called direct mail advertising.

Types of Direct Mail

(1) *Sales letters :* These are the most frequently used form of direct mail– normally the first form any business firm will use. They may be individually typed, multigraphed, or reproduced by some other duplicating process.

(2) *Post cards :* Reply cards are often used to encourage a direct reply from the receiver of a mailing piece. These are usually attached to a folder or booklet or fastened by a seal to another card. The advertiser pays the postage on these when they are returned. He must first secure a permit from his postmaster and print its number on the card.

(3) *Leaflets :* A leaflet is usually a single printed sheet. It is often used in conjunction with a letter to explain an offer or idea more fully. It is normally folded once or twice.

(4) *Folders :* Folders are larger than leaflets and are usually printed on heavier material. The larger size holds more of the sales story and permits use of more visual material. Folders can often be handled economically as self-mailers with the name and address stenciled on an open area of the cover.

(5) *Broadsides :* A broadside, as the term implies, is often larger than a folder. It should be so large that its size helps to impress the receiver with the importance of the offer. Some broadsides are sent to dealers for display in the store as posters or print of the sale promotion pieces. Others are designed for the ultimate reader. When folded, a broadside should be suitable for the mailbag.

(6) *Booklets :* A leaflet that contains several pages is more properly called a booklet. If the sales story is complicated and considerable

information is needed, a leaflet is not enough it is better to use a booklet. Information about product manufacturing and various models is often included in a booklet.

(7) *Catalogues :* Like a booklet, a catalogue has many pages. But its main function is to serve as a reference book. These are buying guides. It has a list of goods properly arranged and illustrated with prices.

(8) *Gift novelties :* Gifts are offered to the customers with the aim of winning the hearts of customers and building the image of the selling house. These gifts may be in the form of calendars, diaries, cigarette cases, thermometers, memo pads, ash-trays, pens, pencil, glasses, stickers and bottle openers, etc. All these gift novelties have either the name of the product or of the selling house imprinted to them. These gifts go on reminding the customers about the product or the selling house. They provide the customer the opportunity of testing the products and of good, deciding to buy the product.

(9) *House organs :* House organs are publications issued periodically by business or other organizations. Some house organs are 'internal' in that their circulation is for employees or organizations members. Some are 'external' in that they go to dealers, customers and others.

Advantages

Direct mail offers advertiser many advantages :

(1) *Selectivity :* Probably the outstanding advantage to direct mail advertising is its extreme selectivity. It reflects its ability to deliver messages to selected prospects who are difficult to reach economically through other media.

(2) *Elasticity :* The advertiser is free to add or delete names in his mailing list. If he does not have much finances he may decrease the number of persons to whom the sales message is to be posted, and if his budget permits, he may increase their number.

(3) *Intensive coverage :* If you want to reach all your dealers once every few days for several weeks, through direct mail, you can make the coverage as intensive as you like.

(4) *Personal :* Direct mail advertising is personal as compared to press advertising which is impersonal. A person who receives the sales message through post is better impressed than in case of other advertising.

(5) *Speed:* Because direct mail can be moved quickly, it can take advantage of timely or seasonal appeals.

(6) *Flexibility of format :* An other important advantage of direct advertising is its flexibility–in format in size, in colour and in cost. Unlike the mass media, where we are bound by certain physical rules, direct mail involves no physical limitations– except our budget.

(7) *Complete information :* If the product or the situation demands it, direct mail can furnish a great deal of information. Long copy, illustrations, diagrams or any other device that will provide useful stimulus to the sale can be included.

Limitations

Direct mail also has certain disadvantages.

(1) *High cost per reader :* Even the cheapest mailing piece has a high cost per reader.

(2) *Mailing list :* Much of the success of any direct-mail campaign depends on the quality of the mailing list. In many instances, it is hard to get a list of high quality.

(3) *Customer resistance :* Ordinarily direct mail advertisements contain no editorial or entertainment material to soften the impact of the advertising message. Consequently direct mail advertising must evoke its own attention, arouse its own interest in what is said.

(4) *Recurring cost-time consuming :* It is time taxing and requires regular investment in stationery, printing and posting. Medium or small sized concerns cannot afford it.

II. Audio-Visual Media

In this type of advertising, we shall discuss the following medium.

(a) Radio
(b) Television
(c) Film

(a) Radio

Radio is really a major and a healthy medium of communication and advertising. It covers 97.3% population and 90% geographical area. It has 187 broadcasting centres, whereas 32 Vivid Bharati and commercial broadcasting stations operating in the country. Radio is a time oriented rather than space oriented medium.

Advantages

Radio offers advertisers a number of advantages :

(1) *Immediacy :* It is very timely medium. It transmits instantaneously advertising messages.

(2) *Low cost :* Radio is relatively low cost advertising medium, even when commercials are run many times a day in markets across the country.

(3) *Flexibility :* Any communication that can be adapted to sound can be used on radio. Alterations in the sales message are possible even at the last minute. Programmes can be made to suit season, day and even hour.

(4) *Audience selection :* Unlike television , radio provides a practical, low- cost vehicle for reaching a specialized audience. If you want to reach children, house wives, farmers or any other particular groups, there are sure to be a variety of stations around the country.

(5) *Human appeal :* This medium has human appeal. Sales messages are alive, animated and dramatic. They can be made as interesting as human appeal.

(6) *Medium of the ear :* It requires very little effort and concentration on the part of the listener. As the ears are less selective than eyes, listeners can engage themselves in other works while listening to radio programmes.

Limitations

Radio has some limitations also which reduces its effectiveness :

(1) *Lack of pictorial presentation :* The greatest drawback of this medium is that there is no pictorial presentation of the product.

(2) *Fleeting :* The message is fleeting. A radio programme once missed is missed for long. The message is not available for reference or for re-reading.

(3) *Lack of demonstration effect* : This medium is not suitable for those products which need demonstration. The characteristics of the product cannot be shown, these can only be heard.

Types of Radio Advertising

Radio is unique in that sound alone must accomplish the communications job. Once a mass medium, it is more likely these days to talk to an audience fragmented by several stations, most of them catering to a particular segment of the audience. The following types of commercials appear on radio.

(1) *Singing* : The singing commercial or jingle, is usually based on a catchy or compelling tune–perhaps original, perhaps borrowed from a popular song of today or yesterday. This is one of the oldest form of advertising.

(2) *Narrative* : The narrative commercial is widely used in spite of the problems of telling a story in 60 seconds or less. Many depend on humour of the development of the characters and of the plot.

(3) *Straight* : This type of commercial is delivered by one person and is much like straight line copy in the print media. No special devices are used to disguise the message. It is simple to produce and adaptable to almost any product or situation.

Tariffs of Radio Commercial

Advertising rates in radio depend on the day and time. Higher rates are changed for prime time and for holidays. They vary from station to station. Rates also vary from programme to programme. Those programmes which are listened by several people carry more rates than those programmes which are not vary popular among people. Advertisements appearing in slots (Slot is a group of advertisement appearing together and are also called jingles) carry less tariffs than the advertisements coming in sponsored programmes.

(b) Television

TV is only about 38 years old but it has proven itself capable of reaching and holding large audiences comprising many different demographic groups. TV's realistic communication potential, a combination of sound , motion and emotion, make it deal for product demonstration, nearly 90 per cent of the nation's leading advertisers place advertisers in TV than in any other medium.

Advantages

The following are some of the advantages that serve as a guide in placing the advertisements in TV.

(1) *Impact :* Used wisely, television has almost unbelievable impact. Television brings into the viewer's living room a combination of moving picture and the speaking voice. It is thus almost the equivalent of a door-to-door sales who can deliver advertising message very effectively.
(2) *Mass coverage :* Theoretically one can reach almost everyone with a combination of newspapers, or even of magazines. But television reaches with considerable impact a large number of persons not effectively reached by the print media.
(3) *Repetition :* Consistent reiteration of your sales message helps make people feel that they know you whether or not they like you. Television makes it possible to repeat your messages as often as you can afford.
(4) *Prestige :* Television is a very prestigious medium of communication. Only prestigious products are advertised in TV.

Limitations

Television advertising involves several unique problems.

(1) *Fleeting messages :* On television advertising messages come and go quickly. If people have their sets on but are not watching or listening they cannot return later (unless of course they have a video tape recorder), and when commercials are bunched together, a viewer might use the time to get a snack.
(2) *Costs :* It is the costliest medium. It is beyond the reach of medium and small sized concerns. In addition to the changes for air time, advertisers incur heavy costs for art work and art material, for talent, music, sound effects, scripting, camera and so forth. A one minute filmed or taped commercial is costly and it becomes less expensive only if it can be used many times and can reach a sizeable audience.
(3) *Distrust :* The printed word carries a stamp of authenticity that broadcasts can never attain. People tend to believe something if they see it in print.

(4) *Lack of selectivity* : Many advertisers need a special audience but television can be a handicap due to its mass coverage. This limitation, through, is becoming less pronounced. Mass audiences are becoming more fragmented because of multiple sets in a home and access to different channels.

Kinds of Television Commercials

Some television experts divide commercials into three simple categories–live, film and tape. Some classify them on the basis of time. Some use the presentation format. Some talk of commercials in terms of production techniques. This confusion testifies to the dynamic nature of modern television. We will examine some of he common formats here.

(1) *Straight announcement* : This is the basic format for many commercials and consists primarily of someone looking at the camera and delivering a sales talk, perhaps pointing at or holding up the product during the talk. The economy of the straight announcement is obvious when the story is a dramatic or newsworthy one. One good television salesperson and a simple set can carry the message. But to be effective it has to compete with a host of dramatic and entertaining commercials for the viewer's attention.

(2) *Demonstration* : Demonstration is so important in television that it should be considered as a possibility for every commercial. Because people are interested in what products will do for them, demonstration is usually good communication. In a large per cent of commercials demonstration of the product or service is the dominant theme. Demonstration commercials are usually filmed or taped because the best of products occasionally fail to operate correctly.

(3) *Dramatization* : In a dramatized commercial, the point is presented through a story that can be told briefly, even in thirty seconds–the most popular television time segment. The theme is sometimes presented as a contrast–'before using the product' versus 'after'. Dramatization of a product's is uniqueness is often made more memorable if a touch of humour or a bit of exaggeration is added. Because the time frame for a television commercial is so short, the plot must be simple. If possible, all three of television's elements–sight, sound and motion–should play an integral part in telling the story.

(4) *Documentary* : Sometimes a dramatized commercial will be adapted to the documentary.

(5) *Dialogue :* Any commercial in which two or more people are talking could properly be called a dialogue commercial. It may include two well known actors. The basic advantage of the dialogue commercial is its ability to involve viewers and encourage them to participate activity in the dialogue.

Advertising Tariffs

Advertising rates vary according to the particular time period as well as according to the programme being broadcast. Higher rates are charged on holidays than on working days. Prime time advertisements are the most expensive.

Films–A Medium of Advertising and its Classification

It is an excellent medium of advertisements. Though the medium is older than television, the messages are similar to TV commercials in format and style. It combines sound, motion, sight and timeliness. Many business houses get commercial films made to boost their sales. This publicity can be done with the help of cinema slides, quickies or filmlets, solus films, and magazines type. Slides are stills which are shown before and during intermission where feature films are being screened in cinema halls. They tell us about local dealers and other services. Quickies or filmlets are silent and run approximately for 15 seconds. Solus films are sound films which have duration of two to five minutes. Magazines films last upto five minutes. They combine entertainment with sales message. India's film industry is the largest in the world with approximately 12,000 cinema houses.

Merits

Cinema screen advertising has the following advantages :

(1) Larger screen and better projection equipment present a more powerful message to the viewer.
(2) It is impossible for theatre advertising to approach the potential coverage of TV, so film advertising is most effective in area where the impact of television has not been great.
(3) It provides the advertiser captive audience. Audience, even if not willing to look or listen to the sales message gets some part of the message. For such persons it can have a reminder value.

Limitations

This medium has also the following disadvantages :

(1) It is considered a priced medium. Movie goers may feel that they pay their money for entertainment and do not want to be part of a captive audience for advertising.
(2) It is not possible for common manufacturers to get films produced for specific purpose of advertising because it involves a lot of expenditure. In today's business world there is cut throat competition in advertising. Every advertiser comes out with more attractive publicity to mar the image of the first advertiser. So, one advertisement cannot last long. It has got to be replaced by a new and more attractive advertisement which entails a lot of expenditure again.
(3) Film-goers feel that they have come for the feature film not for the advertisement. Under such circumstances no sales message can be as much effective as in other media.

Tariffs

Advertising rates vary from cinema to cinema houses. They also vary for the type of commercials. In some cinema houses weekly and monthly rates are charged. Evening shows also carry higher rates than the morning shows.

III. Outdoor Advertising

Outdoor advertising is among the most important of all media where the number of media is limited or where the rate of literacy is low. Outdoor advertising means advertising which people come across when they are out of doors. These advertisements are so designed and placed as to catch the attention of the people within a split of second time. Their aim is to stamp the brand image on the minds of readers or viewers who happen to look at them.

Advantages

Key characteristics of a typical outdoor advertisement are :

(a) In outdoor advertising it is easy to identify advertiser or product name.

(b) Short, simple and legible copy makes easy to comprehend the message.

(c) Advertiser through colour, art and short copy generate a quick feeling or association that will contribute to their brand image.

(d) Repetition is another quality that appeals to many advertisers. If your product or service is advertised at busy cross roads, audiences will see the advertisement again and again. Retention of an idea is essential in order to induce action. The more often the idea is repeated, the more likely it is to be retained. Even though the audience is limited to a specified area, the sheer weight of constant repetition is likely to produce results.

Limitations

Outdoor advertising has also built-in limitations :

(a) One obvious limitation is brevity. How much can you tell consumers about your product on a poster? There is no chance for consumers to browse leisurely, as they do with the newspapers or magazine, or to see the product demonstrated, as they do on television.

(b) Another limitation is the public fear that outdoor advertisers are despoiling the landscape.

Classification of Outdoor Advertising

(a) *Hoardings :* Hoardings are also called billboards. Hoardings are metal boards, large in size, fixed on a frame and installed along the roads and streets. The advertising message is painted on these boards and the boards are installed in such positions as command maximum OTS (opportunity to see) and OTR (opportunity to read). These are very effective for rural areas as these are big in size and each element can be given the best possible treatment. But in hoardings cost of fabrication and maintenance is very high. It creates boredom and monotony by seeing it daily.

(b) *Wall paintings :* These are much bigger than hoardings. As the name implies, the blank space on the side of a building is used for painting or designing a product. Because of the size they enjoy all points of immensity treatment. But it is obviously impossible to standardize painted walls because the shape and the area vary according to the size and shape of the building where space is available. Scratches also spoil the paintings. Moreover the position of the wall cannot be changed as the walls are not constructed for the purpose of advertising.

(c) *Posters :* These are placards displayed in public places. They are displayed on the walls, building tops or street corners, railway stations, bus stops and market places. These are generally on a sheet of paper and are posted either on cardboard or metallic sheet supported by a wooden or metal frame. Layout, location and position of the poster are important things. These are the most flexible of all outdoor media. The advertiser can frequently change the posters to make them timely and seasonable.

(d) *Banners and streamers :* Banner is small in size and is carried by one person, whereas the streamer is carried by two persons and is big in size. These are made of cloth or rexin or plastic. These are generally painted or paper letters are pasted on it. Banners and streamers are very cheap. Cost of fabrication and installation is also very low. But this is very temporary medium of advertising. Very little content can be printed on it. It is also not durable because it can be spoilt by rain or wind.

(e) *Balloons :* This is very novel medium of advertising. A balloon of mammoth size is filled with hydrogen gas and is made to stay at a certain height in the sky. Brand name is impressed on the balloon for the viewers to read. It has a very high OTS (opportunity to see). But this is an expensive medium and very few contents can be written on it.

(f) *Electricity and telephone polls :* This is very impressive and attention catching medium of advertising. Generally posters are pasted in a frame. Cinemas make very good use of it. But this causes disturbance to the traffic.

(g) *Electric signs, neon signs and glow signs :* They have the reminder value and are supplementary medium of publicity for they follow the press advertisements or commercial broadcasts or commercial telecasts. Normally brand names or names of manufacturers are made to attract attention against the dark background of night. They are very common on the main thoroughfares and at important bus and train terminus in big cities. Brightness and use of different colour combinations make them alluring. They are very powerful reminders.

Neons are actually gas tubes moulded in the format of letters or graphics. The tubes are filled with neon gas and a suitable pigment.

These tubes are illuminated by electric current. Neons are colourful, glamorous and attractive. They catch the attention immediately. They are very effective, prestigious and appealing medium of advertising. But these can be used only in the evenings and in the cloudy days. They contain very brief message and carry very high fabrication and maintenance costs.

(h) *Signs or sign boards :* These are the plates or boards in which the name of the company or product is advertised. These boards can be illuminated internally or externally. But its effectiveness is local. OTS and OTR are limited because these are stable at one place. Fabrication and maintenance costs are also moderate. These are used for spot advertising.

(i) *Travelling displays or transist advertising :* Pieces of display like posters, signs and painted bulletins are affixed in and outside the vehicles like buses, trucks, taxis and van, etc. Such pieces when they are fixed inside the vehicles are called car cards and are meant for the commuters. They have a fairly wide circulation and can be read like press advertisements. Such pieces which are fixed outside the vehicles are not effective as car cards. People hardly look at these.

(j) *Aerial advertising or sky writing :* It is a kind of publicity in which pilots through their aeroplanes, write the brand name or the name of the selling house with sodium vapour or by illumination at a height of some fifteen thousand feet. This message is visible over a radius of 25 to 30 miles. This type of publicity is done at sea beaches or such other places where a lot of people gather. It is a supplementary form of publicity.

IV. Indoor Advertising

A manufacturer or dealer has to display his goods in order to attract customers. The word display implies arranging something for view or in view. It means a systematic arrangement of products to attract the attention of customers. Nothing can be said about the first display of the product in the words, but today it is the most practical and powerful medium of publicity and sales promotion.

Display can be solus, semi-solus or related. In case of solus display only one article is displayed. Here, the aim is to bring into prominence one article only. In semi-solus display one prominent article may be displayed alongwith several less important but related articles. In related display articles which are related to one another are displayed e. g. shirt, trousers, neck ties, handkerchiefs, etc. This display brings into prominence the connection between the articles and improves the sales prospect of the displayed atricles.

Classification of Indoor Advertising

(a) *Kiosk :* These are generally seen in exhibitions, fairs, platforms, bus-stands, cinema lobbies, show rooms, shops and godowns, etc. Kiosk is basically an almirah or a rack or a stand which is prestigiously illuminated and glazed of any shape or size. In these kiosks the products are displayed artistically.

Kiosks are very attractive, prestigious and glamorous medium of advertising. Display creates temptation and credibility. But OTS and OTR are very limited and are confined to that area only. Fabrication cost depends upon the type of display. On-lookers can be converted into buyers.

(b) *Window display :* These are similar to kiosk but are permanently fixed and always at the outdoor wall. These are more prestigious even than kiosk because these can be seen from outside. Dummy models are used.

Window display aims at attracting customers into the shop by arousing their interest. They serve as an introduction of seller to buyer and stamp the first impression on him. It costs a great deal but in the long run they justify their cost.

Tastefully decorated windows are great attention getters. They goad the customers to get into the shop and buy. In this way, they have, get in effect, on the customers which increases sales. It provides adequate space to demonstrate the beauty and utility of a product with the help of life size models. Customers get a chance to see things in their real shape, size and colour. Window is the face of the shop. It tells customers what sort of products are sold by a certain shop and thus saves their time and energy. Customers judge the value of a shop by its window. Any shortcomings in the interior display are excused by the customers if the exterior display is good and attractive. Window display helps to raise the reputation and prestige of the shop. They attempt to slow the pace of passing consumers long enough to entice them into the store to look further, thus, the windows, which are in fact advertisement, should be both striking and timely.

(c) *Counters :* Counters are also seen in show rooms, shops, exhibitions, fairs, etc. Counters are at a lower height. Its purpose is not only to display the product, but to provide a counter on which the transactions can be made. Counters are also glazed and can be used as tables. Its effectiveness and format is like kiosk. This is used for spot advertising.

Point-of-Purchase Advertising

Point-of-purchase advertising is used to build brand and corporate images. It may help to associate a scientific background with a product. Occasionally, it may help the product to appear luxurious or antique or very modern. In fact point-of-purchase is used as a collective term to describe a wide range of advertising devices. It consists of promotional materials situated in, on or immediately adjacent to retail distribution points.

Displays may help secure a better location in a store by raising the product closer to eye level by increasing the amount of shelf space devoted to it, or by moving it nearer a choice spot like the check-out counter.

Point-of-purchase advertising is also not free from limitations. Manufacturer's sales can't check to see that all point-of-purchase advertising is installed in every possible outlet. A display may be removed very soon because another manufacturer agrees to pay a higher price for the space. Only a binding contract for a specified time period, accompanied by close policing on the premises, will prevent such actions.

Organisation of Advertising Industry

There are three main components of advertising industry.

1. Advertisers
2. Advertising Agencies
3. Media

Advertisers

Advertising is an important part of the overall marketing plan of almost every organisation that provides a product or a service to the public. There are mainly two types of advertisers–National advertisers and retail advertisers.

(a) *National advertisers :* National advertisers sell their product or service to customers all across the country. The emphasis in national advertising is on the product or service and not so much on the place where the product or service is sold. For example, the cocacola company is interested in selling soft drinks. It does not matter to the company if you buy their product at the local market, from a store or from a vendor; as long as you buy their product, the company will be happy.

(b) *Retail advertisers :* These are also called local advertisers. Retail advertisers are companies such as local restaurants, car dealerships, TV repair shops and other merchants and service organisations that have customers in only one city or trading area. The retail advertiser wants to attract customers to a specific store or place of business.

The way organisations handle their advertising depends on their size. Some companies have their own advertising departments; a small retail store might have one person who is responsible for advertising and marketing and who may also have other job functions. Large or small, there are several basic functions that must be attended to by all advertisers. These include planning the advertisement and deciding where they will appear, setting aside a certain amount of money for the advertising budget, co-ordinating the advertising with other departments in the organisation and if necessary supervising the work of an outside agency or company that produces the advertising. In addition, some large advertisers have departments that can create and prepare all the advertising materials, purchase the space and airtime for the advertisements, and check to see if the advertisements were effective in achieving their goals.

No matter how the advertising is handled, it is likely that quite a few people in the organisation are really part of the advertising business. In some companies, the president or chief executive becomes actively involved. Moreover, sales and marketing personnel keep a close watch on the type of advertising that is planned and where the advertising is to appear. Even the people in the design and production departments are often asked to contribute ideas to the company's advertisements. In short, it could be said that almost every one in the company feels that he or she is involved with the company's advertisements because the advertising represents them in some way.

Advertising Agencies

The increased importance of advertising in the marketing process led to the birth of the Advertising Agency. It is an organisation that specializes in providing advertising services to its clients. According to the American

Association of Advertising Agencies, an agency is an independent business organisation composed of creative and business people, who develop, prepare, and place advertising in advertising media for sellers seeking to find customers for their goods and services. The roots of the modern day agency can be traced to Volney B, Palmer of Philadelphia. In 1842, Palmer bought large amount of space in various newspapers at a discount and then resold the space at higher rates to advertisers. The act of advertising the copy, layout, and artwork was still prepared by the company wishing to advertise; in effect, Palmer was a space broker, that situation changed in the late nineteenth century when the advertising agency of N.W. Ayer and Son was founded. Ayer and Son offered to plan, create and execute a complete advertising campaign for their customers. By 1900 the advertising agency became the focal point of creative planning, and advertising was firmly established as a profession. D. Dattaram and Co. was the first Indian agency to start its advertising business in 1905.

Classification of Advertising Agencies

Agencies can be classified by the range of services that they offer. In general terms, there are three main types :

(i) Full service agencies
(ii) Media buying services
(iii) Creative boutiques

(i) *Full service agency :* As the name implies, a full service agency is one that handles all phases of the advertising process for its clients; it plans, creates, produces and places advertisement for its clients. In addition, it might also provide other marketing services such as sales promotions, trade show exhibits, news letters and annual reports. In theory, at least, there is no need for the client to deal with any other company for help on promoting their product.

(ii) *Media buying service :* It is an organisation that specializes in buying radio and the television time and reselling it to advertisers and advertising agencies. The service sells time to the advertiser, orders the spots on the various stations involved, and monitors the stations to see if the ads actually run.

(iii) *Creative boutique :* It is an organisation that specializes in the actual creation of advertisement. In general, boutiques create imaginative and interesting advertising themes and produce innovative and original advertisements. A company that uses a creative boutique would have to employ another agency to perform the planning, buying and administrative functions connected with advertising.

Full service advertising agency studies the product or service and determines its marketable characteristic and how it relates to the competition. At the same time the agency studies the potential market, possible distribution plans, and likely advertising media. Following this the agency makes a formal presentation to the client detailings, its findings about the product and its recommendations for an advertising strategy. If the client agrees, the agency then launches the execution phase. This phase entails writing and producing the advertisement buying time in various media delivering the advertisement to the appropriate media, and verifying that all advertisements actually appeared. Finally, the agency will work closely with the client's sales people to make sure that they get the greatest possible benefit from the advertisement.

Functions of Advertising Agency

Today advertising agencies are found in virtually every major city in the world, and their role in stimulating economic growth is solidly established. To understand advertising, we need to examine the functions an ad agency performs.

1. *Talent :* The basic function of an advertising agency is providing talent. The creative efforts of the out director, the detailed analysis of the research director, and the political understanding of the campaign director are just a few examples of the many abilities advertising agency personnel have to offer. A business organisation, or person will contract the services of an advertising agency to help market a product. The product may be soap, the corporate image of a company, a political figure, or a non-profit organisation.
2. *Research :* The second function of an advertising agency is research. In order to distribute the message to the public successfully, the agency must first know all that it can about the product. The company wants to develop an advertising campaign for a new product. It is

your job to plan the advertising campaign.

One of the first job is to research the product and the company, you must learn everything you possibly can about both, your research must even take you close to the heart of the firm's inner operations. Occasionally, research may reveal certain questionable business operations, dealings that may force your agency to withdraw from handling the campaign. Handling a disreputable firm's advertising may leave your agency with the problem of collective money for your services.

Second type of research is the market research. It aims at finding the potential market for the new product you will need to know if there are other products on the market that can successfully complete with your client's product, you will want to know where the customers for the product can be found, you will want to know the characteristics of your potential customers.

3. *Distribution* : The third important function of an agency is distribution, there you will decide what type of message you are going to create for the company and what media will be most helpful in sending this message to the public. Let us assume your research into the company's background gives it a clean chit and that you decide to continue with the account. You have learned that the bark chips make a good beding to place around strawberry. Next, you conduct further research into a possible name for the bark chips your research strikes a positive note on the name "Barke"! The name is catchy, is easily remembered and carries the substance of the product into the name.

Now comes the decision on how to the tell "Barko" story to the public. It is the time to call a meeting of the agency's department heads; for example, Account Executive, Research Director, General Manager, Art Director, Production Director, Photographer, copy writer and so on. The ideas obtained from these functionaries would help in planning an advertising campaign.

4. *Monitoring feedback* : This is the fourth function of an agency perhaps retailers receive complaints about "Barkos"! Perhaps there is a rival product, and the public is confusing your product with its competition. By monitoring consumer feedback, a decision on whether to revise the message, the medium, the target audience or all of them can be made.

As the business of reaching the public with information about new products becomes increasingly complex the work of ad agencies becomes more and more important, complex multimedia buying decisions, the psychology of attitudes toward styles and colour combinations, and the ability to coordinate advertising messages across many different media all demand talent based on the ad agency's years of expertise.

If an advertising campaign has the backing of effective talent research, distribution, and feedback, it has the best chance of succeeding. Today more and more specialized advertising is developing, demanding new creativity by advertising personnel. Celebrities are increasingly being used in âdvertisements, and not only the creative talents of an advertising agency but legal talents are required to understand the regulations of complex contracts between stairs and the products and agencies with which they are associated.

Advertising agencies are developing to reach to the target audience. Some of the most effective advertising includes advertisement written in their native language. All of these specialized campaigns are creating new demands on agencies and are requiring new talents for people who work in advertising.

Organisation Chart of an Advertising Agency

President

Creative Services	Account Services	Marketing Services	Administration
Writers	Account Executive	Media Planning	Personnel
Art Directors		Research	Office Management
Print Production		Sales Promotion	Clerical
TV and Radio Production			Accounting

Source : Joseph R. Dominick : The Dynamics of Mass Communication.

Media

The last part of the advertising industry consists of the mass media. Media serve as a link between the company that has a service or product to sell and the customers who wish to buy it. The media that are available for advertising include radio, television, newspapers, magazines and others that are not so obvious, such as direct mail, hoardings, point of purchase displays, etc. Even the slickest and most imaginative advertising message will fail if it is delivered to the wrong people. To make sure that this catastrophe does not happen, advertisers employ highly skilled media planners to help them place and schedule their advertisements. With the numerous mass media that are available to deliver the message and the hundreds of individual media outlets to choose from, it is necessary to study closely what each of the various media can offer.

When advertising specialists look at the various media, they tend to evaluate them along four dimensions.

(a) *Reach* – How many people get the message?
(b) *Frequency* – How often will the message be received?
(c) *Selectivity* – Does the medium actually reach potential customers?
(d) *Efficiency* – How much does it cost to reach a certain number of people?

Newspapers have good reach. Many newspapers are published daily, which means that advertisers can present their messages to the audience with a high degree of frequency.

Magazines tend to have a more limited reach than newspapers. Further, most magazines come out once per month, which means that the potential for frequent presentations of an advertisement is not high. On the other hand, magazines offer a tremendous degree of selectivity for the advertisers. If an advertiser wanted to reach housewives, he could choose among several publications designed for that audience segment. The cost of magazine advertising tends to be relatively high, but this cost must be evaluated against its efficiency in reaching a target group.

Radio has excellent reach and allows advertisers to present their messages with great frequency. Moreover, the cost of radio advertising is low and presents, a good value to advertisers.

Television has almost universal appeal and allows for frequent repetition of messages. The potential of selectivity of TV increases with the widespread growth of cable TV channels, MTV, for example, mainly of fifteen to twenty year old. On the cost dimension, the cost of advertising on television is very high. It is so expensive that many smaller companies simply cannot afford it.

Hoardings, billboards and other outdoor advertising media score high in terms of reach and frequency dimensions. With proper positioning and lighting outdoor advertising can be seen twenty-four hours a day all year long. Its selectivity is limited; however, since its audience will be composed of all people who happen to pass a certain point. Outdoor advertising also tends to be a relatively expensive way to advertise.

Direct advertising, especially direct mail, has the potential for widespread reach. It also has the potential for frequent delivery of the message. Direct advertising is probably the most selective of all advertising media. Special mailing lists allow the advertiser to focus on his or her particular target audience. Direct mail advertising has its disadvantage of being highly expensive. It has become more expensive with the recent increases in postal rates.

Finally, of course, in addition to the above considerations, advertisers have to take into account many other factors before deciding on what medium to use. An important part of any decision involves considering the creative limitations imposed by the physical properties of each medium. Television, for example, allows the advertiser to show the product in action. On the other hand, TV advertisements are short and cannot be used to present a great deal of technical information. A magazine advertisement can be in full colour and can present a large amount of data, but it might not have the same impact as a television advertising. In nutshell, choosing what media to use in the final advertising mix is a difficult decision.

Producing Advertisements

Large companies have their own advertising departments in the overall corporate organisation. Mainly there are four major departments in an organisation for producing advertisements.

1. Creative Department
2. Account Services Department
3. Marketing Services Department
4. Administration

1. *Creative Department* : As the name implies, it actually produces the advertisement. People in this department write the advertising copy, choose the illustrations, prepare artwork and supervise the scripting and production of radio and TV commercials.

2. *Account Services Department* : This department is responsible for the relationship between the agency and the client. Advertising agency appoints account executive (AE) to promote communication and understanding between client and agency. The AE must represent the viewpoint of the agency to the client but at the same time must keep abreast of the needs of the advertiser. Needless to say since the AE tends to be the person in the middle, his or her job is an important one of the agency.

3. *Marketing Services Department* . This department is responsible for advising the client as to what media to use for his or her messages. Typically, this department makes use of the data collected by the Audit Bureau of Circulation (ABC). This department is also in charge of any sales promotions that are done in connection with the advertising. These may include such things as coupons, premiums and other aids to dealers.

4. *Administration :* Finally, like any other business, advertising agency also takes care of the day-to-day administration of the agency and prepares the advertising for its clients.

Formulation of an Advertising Campaign

Some people define a campaign as a series of advertisements with an identical or similar message placed in one or more of the advertising media over a particular period of time. But this definition of an advertising campaign is narrow because it tends to focus on the finished advertisements or commercials. A campaign must involve more than the creation of a series of related advertisements that are disseminated via advertising media. A broader definition is : an advertising campaign consists of an analysis of the marketing and communication situations in order to make sound strategic decisions that can be carried out by designing a series of advertisements and commercials and placing them in the various advertising media.

One of the first and most critical things advertising planners must do is to analyse the marketing framework within which advertising decisions are made. The successful advertising campaign evolves from a clear understanding of the firm's marketing mix. By marketing mix we mean the choice of ingredients that a company combines in order to satisfy the needs or wants of a particular group of customers. We consider here four major ingredients.

1. The *product* to be marketed,
2. The *price* of the product,
3. The *channels of distribution* through which the product is sold, and
4. The *promotion* used for advertising and selling the product.

1. *Product :* As an ingredient of the marketing mix, the term "product" is used in a broad sense to mean several types of marketing decisions as follows :

   (a) *Development and planning of the product :* Will this be a product that appeals to a large number of consumers or will it have a narrow appeal? If have a multiproduct company, how does this particular product will relate to other products? A company must decide the extent to which it wants to change existing products to convey a feeling of 'newness'.

(b) *Packaging :* It is another aspect of product policy that bears directly on marketing mix. In many industries, the package is a powerful selling force because it constantly competes with other packages for the customer's attention in self-service and self-selection situations. For a few products the package costs more and is frequently more important than the product itself in inducing potential customers to buy often the physical appearance of the package directly affects advertising decisions.

(c) *Brand name :* To what extent will the brand name be distinctive and easily remembered? Will it 'sound right' in broadcast commercials and 'look right' in private advertisements? Does the brand name convey the product image we seek to convey?

2. *Price :* The setting of price and its importance in the marketing mix are indeed complex. They depend partly on the appraisal of consumer behaviour toward possible prices. The price that is charged for a product usually relates to product quality, which in turn relates to the type of consumers who are sought to buy the product.

From an advertising stand point the price charged for a brand affects several decisions. For example, price often relates to the size of the advertising budget. If a product's price allows a generous margin of gross profit, increased advertising may be feasible. The media that are chosen also may relate to pricing policy. A brand priced at the high end of the price range may require media selections that convey this message. Generally high priced brands more consistently advertised in publications that appeal to upper income, higher-educated segments of the population. And, of course, the type of message we use in advertising will be affected by pricing strategy.

3. *Channels of distribution :* The marketer has a choice of several methods of distribution. Selling can be direct to consumers. Or the channel may consist of manufacturers, wholesalers and retailers, or it may involve only manufacturers and retailers. Regardless of the channel of distribution used, the marketer must blend this ingredient of the mix with the other elements. Thus, a brand marketed by a company that seeks to establish high prestige through its product, pricing and advertising policies must follow suit by selecting retail

outlet that match the total strategy. Certain types of discount stores, which focus heavily on low price and minimum service, would not be a good channel outlet.

4. *Promotion :* The promotion ingredient of the marketing mix generally consists of three specific areas : advertising, personal selling and sales promotion. We will limit our discussion here to personal selling and sales promotion as advertising will be discussed in the planning of advertising. The degree to which personal selling is a major or minor ingredient in the marketing mix depends on a number of factors. Complexity is one factor to consider. For many industrial goods, the prospective buyer needs technical explanations of how they work, and personal selling often is the dominant promotional tool in such cases. Among goods sold at the retail level, those with hidden qualities and complicated features benefit from personal sales effort. As in the case of other mix ingredients the type and extent of personal selling affects advertising decisions. Because advertising and personal selling are both forms of promotion the need for coordination is critical. In many cases advertising material is used by sales people when they call on a customer.

Sales promotion denotes activities that supplement advertising and personal selling. The most common of these are premiums, contests, coupons, special price offers, dealer incentives, point of purchase displays, etc. Sales promotion is included in the marketing mix when advertising and personal selling cannot alone do an effective job. Many channel members and ultimate consumers enjoy the excitement that sales promotion devices generate.

The Planning of Advertising

Having examined the market mix as a basic input to the advertising campaign, we now focus more directly on advertising decision elements. The major planning categories–research inputs, strategic decisions, and so on appear in the order as follows as the most planners follow. Only when these factors are analysed and co-ordinated with each other as well as with the elements of the marketing mix, can a plan be considered complete.

Research Inputs

The planner of an advertising campaign should begin with research.

Research, when done properly, minimizes guess work and allows the decision maker to develop a plan as scientifically as possible. There are, of course, mainly four types of research.

(a) *Consumer research :* Most of the practitioners stress the need for consumer information. Consumer research can give guidance in a number of planning areas like—setting objectives, defining target markets and developing message and media strategies. Suppose our company is planning to introduce a new and advanced washing machine. We might do consumer research to determine how certain people feel about new washing machine; their knowledge of the product, their feelings about washing, their fears of using such a product. Our research may help greatly in deciding who our best prospects are, what types of advertising will appeal to them, and even which media they use the most.

(b) *Product research :* It is a special kind of consumer research that concentrates on consumer opinions and preconceptions about the product service, or idea that is being advertised. To make a product successfully, we probably have to learn not only people's attitudes towards it, but how these are symbolized in a brand or corporate image. We must decide what the product's strong points are and capitalize on them in the advertising campaign. Most successful campaigns emphasize product strengths and minimize product weaknesses.

The most important questions in product research are :

1. What is the product made of?
2. How important is product quality (in relation to price)?
3. How is the product used?
4. What are the competitive advantages and disadvantages of the product?
5. How is the product packaged?
6. How is the product designed?
7. Where is the product sold?

(c) *Market analysis :* This type of research helps locate markets for a particular brand. It involves finding those variables that indicate who your best prospects are and where they are. Market analysis provides the raw data from which a planner can decide on target market. Target market can be defined in any number of ways, for example, by the demographic characteristics of consumers, by geographic locations, by socio-psychological groupings or by degree of product usage.

(d) *Competitive situation :* In developing and advertising campaign, it is wise to monitor what our competitors are doing, for example, one of the first thing a planner often wants to know before developing the campaign is how well various brands are doing in terms of market share.

Strategic Decisions

Having developed a number of research inputs, the decision maker next is likely to make a number of important strategic judgements. The specific decisions will, of course, vary greatly with the situations–the kind of product, service or idea involved, the competition, the company's organisation and so on. Nevertheless, most advertising plans should include the following elements.

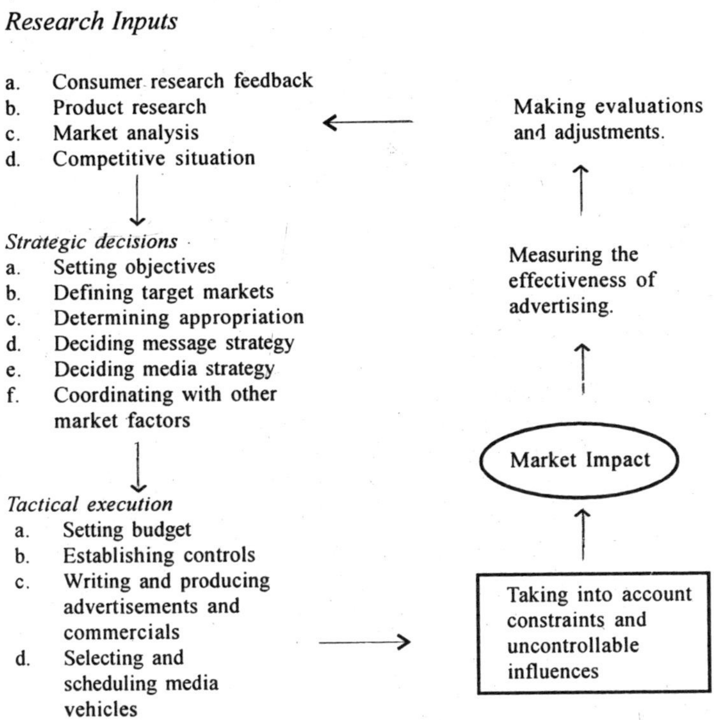

Source : S. Watson Dunn and Arnold M. Barban's Advertising and its Role in Marketing.

(a) *Setting objectives :* Clear, precise objectives should be established so that the results of the campaign can be determined. And not only must general campaign objectives be set; objectives for several strategy areas must likewise be stated with equal precision.

(b) *Defining target markets :* Ideally, research done at the outset of the campaign planning will greatly assist the planner in deciding which target markets to emphasize. Target markets can be segmented along a number of lines–demographics, psychographics and product usage. Suppose you want to advertise soft drinks you would like to know which segment of the total market represents your best potential–teenagers or lower-middle class. You would also like to know the importance of these markets and how they can best be reached by your promotional campaign.

How you define your target markets has a substantial influence on other strategic decisions. Certainly whom you decide to appeal to has an immediate effect on your message and media strategies.

(c) *Determining the advertising appropriation :* Decisions about advertising appropriations involve top level consideration. Infact, in many cases the advertising planner does not determine the appropriation, rather, it is established by the top marketing executive or even the top operations official of the company.

(d) *Deciding message and media strategies :* Deciding the appeal of the advertising message and the media of dissemination is the 'heart' of campaign planning. Once these strategies are executed with advertisements appearing in specific media, the campaign assumes tangible form. Market analysis, through helping to pinpoint the target, can assist in deciding which media to use. Message and media decisions are critical in the development of an advertising campaign.

(e) *Coordinating with other marketing factors :* Advertising does not function in a vacuum. Rather, it operates in concert with a number of other marketing variables. The advertising campaign must be coordinated with these marketing variables.

Tactical Execution

Once the key strategic decisions are made, the planner then must decide how to execute them. An excellent set of strategies poorly carried out typically results in an unsuccessful campaign. Thus, it is critical to execute the plan effectively and efficiently.

For the most part, tactics involve implementation of the message and media strategies. Messages must be developed verbally through specific pieces of copy and graphically through layout designs, television story boards, artwork and typography. All this must be done within a specific time period.

The media strategy also must be implemented in a number of tactical ways. Specific vehicles must be chosen. A strategic decision to use radio spots be taken. The planner would also have to decide the size and appearance of each advertisement and the length of each broadcast commercial. And the planner would draw up a media schedule to assure continuity of effort. Finally, media strategies must be coordinated with message strategies for effective execution.

Another important tactical aspect of the campaign is the control of the advertising appropriation. This is achieved by setting up a budget and establishing controls to make sure it is followed.

Constraints and Uncontrollable Influences

A campaign planner cannot control all the variables that enter into the decision-making process. Many factors that can influence an advertising campaign are beyond the control or even the influence of the planner, yet they must nevertheless be taken into account. Some of the typical constraints are as follows :

(a) *Ethical environment :* Advertising campaigns must conform to existing law. Cigarettes cannot be advertised on radio or television.

(b) *Social and cultural environment :* The advertising planner must often consider social and cultural factors not codified in laws. For example, there are wide cultural variations in our country, and different social classes have different patterns of consumption.

(c) *Economic environment :* Economic conditions affect advertising decisions in both tangible and intangible ways. In times of economic recession, the amount of money appropriated for advertising often is cut. Less tangible is the reduced influence of advertising in motivating consumers during periods of economic uncertainty. Economic conditions are also likely to affect media prices, obviously a factor in campaign planning.

(d) *Physical environment* : Weather conditions can sometimes affect advertising plans, for example, an advertiser who is calling for cooler advertisements will have to change his plans if rains start.

Plan in Action

After essential background information has been gathered through research, and strategy and tactics have been developed with regard to influential constraints, the plan is put into action. It may cover the entire market area under consideration, or it amy be tested in only a few selected markets. Testing of the compaign, or parts of it, might even be limited to a representative sampling of consumers. In any event, putting the plan into action will produce a market impact and that impact could be positive, negative, or neutral depending upon the plan's objectives.

Measurement : The measurement of this market impact brings us almost full circle in terms of our conceptualization of the compaign planning process. That is, the effectiveness of the advertising must be determined. The following answers are needed here :

(a) How well does the campaign accomplish stated objectives?
(b) To what extent have we covered our target markets with the compaign?
(c) How effective are our advertisements and commercials in communicating the campaign theme?
(d) which media do the best job?

Feedback : The result of measuring the effectiveness of advertising is to provide the planner with feedback on the total process. And this feedback then logically srves as a research input for the next stage of the campaign. Thus, each successive campaign plan should benefit from its predecessor.

Evaluations and adjustments : Once a compaign has been planned and executed, and the market impact has been measured the planner must conduct a post mortem analysis : What actions were successful? Why? If we had done certain things differently, would results have been drastically changed? If so, why? After evaluating the campaign, the planner should make whatever adjustments in thinking are necessary to overcome deficiencies in the next campaign.

Layouts, Design and Qualities

Layout is a fairly rough working drawing showing how an advertisement is to look. This drawing can be presented to management for approval. Several types of layouts are used to accomplish the laboratory workings.

The advertising layout has basically two functions to perform. One is mechanical and the other is symbolic function.

Mechanically, the layout is the plan that indicates where the component parts of the advertisement, for example, headline, slogan, illustrations, text and so on are to be placed for most effective communication. The layout guides the copywriter in planning copy and in estimating costs.

Symbolic function : The final layout, when transformed into the finished advertisement, gives the audience its first impression of the company that is sponsoring the advertisement. A very formal layout gives the impression that the advertiser is probably stable, conservative and solid. A modernistic layout gives the impression that the company is probably dynamic. A layout with crowded element gives the impression that the store caters strongly to bargain hunters. Conversely, a layout with a considerable amount of white space projects an image of exclusiveness.

Preparing Layout

The layout artist most often has to work within certain space limitations. In newspapers and magazines he is limited to certain standard sizes and shapes, type faces and so on. If he is using postcards, his advertisement must fit the confines of card. In designing outdoor posters, he is limited by standard poster sizes.

The layout artist can do a better job if he expresses the advertising idea in the most effective visual form. He has to go through the various stages in preparing layout.

Thumbnail layout : A thumbnail layout is a miniature sketch of a proposed print advertisement. Several sketches of possible layouts are prepared. These sketches are one-eighth to one-fourth the size of the final product. A thumbnail sketch offers the artist an opportunity to try out a variety of ideas; later he can select the most promising ones and blow them upto actual size.

Rough layout : Out of the several thumbnail layouts, one of the thumbnail layouts is selected for further development. Rough layout will be the exact size of the final advertisement. It is an experimental but very important one. Change can be made at this stage. In a rough layout, the picture will be drawn, however, crudely, the headline will be spelled out, the text unit will be more rigidly located by rough pencil and the logo-type placed precisely.

Semi-comprehensive or finished layout : A rough layout may be used for presentation of a proposed print advertisement to management for approval, and used as a guide for advertising production, but normally not. Instead a semi-comprehensive layout is employed for these purposes.

The semi-comprehensive is the first in a hierarchy of layout means to allow good communication of a proposed idea for the theme of an advertising campaign. A picture is drawn in more refinement, a headline lettered to indicate typographic design, a text unit will be indicated to permit typesetting of its content, and a logotype placed even more precisely. For almost every proposed print advertisement, the semi-comprehensive layout serves all purposes of a layout in every respect.

Comprehensive layout : Comprehensive or "comp" is a facsimile of the finished advertisement. In other words, this type of layout represents a singular advertisement by appearing almost exactly like that which will be finally published. The picture in the comp layout likely will be in finished form, and all the words of a headline and text and logotype may be typographically set and a proof of it is pasted on the layout. The comp is the ultimate of all layout types to present an idea for a proposed print advertisement to management for approval. Some comprehensives are so painstakingly put together that they look better than the final advertisement.

Types of Layouts

Layouts tend to fall into certain standard classifications according to the format they follow. The seven basic layouts are suggested by Hafer and White.

(1) *Standard layout :* This consists of a dominant illustration, headline, body copy and logotype-generally in that order.

(2) *Editorial layout :* This type of advertisement resembles editorial material in a publication.

(3) *Poster layout :* In this type of layout almost total emphasis is put on the visual.

(4) *Cartoon layout :* This type of layout includes cartoon at the beginning to attract attention.

(5) *Comic strip layout :* This type of layout includes cartoon drawings following the format of the comic strip.

(6) *Picture caption layout :* In this type of layout pictures and captions are used to show the many facets of the product or service advertised.

(7) *Picture-cluster layout :* This layout uses a single dominant element made up of a set or cluster of items.

Actualities of Effective Layouts

Certain qualities of effective layouts differentials from the ineffective ones. Some of these important qualities can be discussed as below :

1. *Composition*

The following guidelines will be helpful in making the good composition of an advertisement. Ideally, the picture should occupy slightly more than one-half of the entire space. If there are several, the total area of all of them combined should occupy that amount of space.

As a general rule, it is best to place the headline directly above the body text. A text that has a headline gets higher reading than a text without a headline. If a layout indicates that the main head should go above the illustration, it may be helpful to put a subhead under the illustration to lead the reader into the text.

Unless the name of the product is prominently displayed in the headline or shown in the illustration, the logotype should be emphasized and put in a prominent setting size, counterart or isolation may be used to emphasize a logotype or illustration of the package.

Typographical consistency reassures readers that they are looking at one advertisement, not several.

– Repetition of the same motifs helps unify an advertising layout.

or

– Borders are useful to keep readers from wantering away readers from wandering away from the advertisement, especially in newspaper advertisements.

2. *Balance*

Balance is of two types : Symmetrical or formal balance and Asymmetrical or informal balance.

Symmetrical balance : This type of balance is used most where dignity or stability is dominant. An advertisement is balanced when it looks balanced. The optical centre of an advertisement is at a point about fine-eighths of the way up the page.

Asymmetrical balance : Asymmetrical or informal balance can be created by bringing heavy elements near to the centre and light elements away from the centre. If one side of the advertisement seems too light, one can add "weight" in several ways.

Informal balance usually generates more excitement and is used in the majority of print advertisement.

3. *Movement*

Every advertisement should move naturally from one element to the next. Readers are likely to start off somewhere above and to the life of the centre and then roam around the page. But their eye movements can be controlled by skilful manipulation of the elements.

Size : Most people are attracted by the largest and most dominant matter on the page.

Cartoons or pictures and captions : The reader must start at the beginning and follow the sequence to get the point.

Gutters of white space : The contract between white and dark backgrounds directs eye movement.

4. *Proportion*

Two areas are more pleasing to the eye if one is slightly larger than the other. It is more appealing to have masses of space in such proportions as three to five or two to three. These are less monotonous than equal masses.

5. *Contrast*

One way to emphasize a particular element in a headline is by contrast.

Dark masses stand out against a light background. Contrast between headline, types and colours, etc. reduces monotony. One should not, however, sacrifice legibility for the sake of contrast.

6. *Simplicity*

A layout is simplified when we keep down the number of different type faces and make sure the illustrations are harmonious. We should avoid decorations. The temptation to overload an advertisement should be avoided as too many elements make an advertisement far too complex. Each element must communicate a message. If it does not eliminate that element.

7. *Clarity of Presentation*

Layout artist should make sure that the visual and verbal elements should be skilfully blended to give the reader a unified impression. It is particularly difficult for the artist to present ideas clearly when he has a number of elements. One possibility is the classic layout based on characteristic patterns developed over the ages by great artists.

8. *Judicious Use of White Space*

Artists and copy writers sometimes disagree on how much white space should be included in an advertisement. The artist often prefers a great deal of white space to set off the illustration and give its focus. Copy writers, however, sometimes fight to use as much space as possible for their body text. Actually, white space can sometimes communicate as effectively as the text or illustrations if you want to tell people that you have a prestige product, it is wise to use plenty of white space so that the layout will convey this impression.

Advertising vis-a-vis PR and Marketing

Advertising is drawing attention by public announcement to a commodity or service with the aim of selling it. Modern advertising is a child of production for profit. People in tribal or feudal societies produce goods for themselves or for neighbours whose needs they know. What trade there is, is mainly in the form of barter, and each man with something to sell or exchange is his own advertiser. Organized advertising becomes necessary only when production passes from an individual or communal to an industrial level, that is, when production is organized by businessmen who raise capital and hire labour with it. The larger industries become and the further they advance toward mass production, the more dependent they become on advertising to help sell their products. Indeed, without its services in communicating with the public, many industrial and business firms would be forced to shut up shop, their employees would be thrown out of work, and our kind of economy would collapse. Advertising depends absolutely on its power to communicate and to persuade.

When modern advertising was in its infancy, the advertising agent was simply a space salesman for newspapers and periodicals. He persuaded people with something to sell, to advertise in the papers he represented. In return he received a commission from the newspaper owners on the cost of the space booked. Agents are still paid in this way, although around the 1880's they began to prepare their clients' advertisements, and to advise them to where to place them to get the best value for money.

One of the first needs of advertisers was to find out how many copies were sold of the papers in which he bought space, since in those days circulation figures were closely guarded secrets. The right to know a paper's circulation having been established, a great deal of research was still needed before advertisers could feel confident that they were using the best media for the products they were trying to sell. They wanted to know how many people on average read each copy of a particular newspaper or magazine, because this figure may differ considerably from one paper to another. They also wanted to know what sort of people the readers were– their sex, age, social class, educational background, profession, average income, hopes, hobbies and habits, etc.

Advertising is powerful communications force and a vital marketing tool helping to sell goods, services, images and ideas through channels of information and persuasion. John E. Kennedy– a copy writer has defined advertising as Salesmanship in Print, which indicates that the ultimate objective of advertising is to sell. In 1948, the American Marketing Association developed a definition which is widely quoted "Advertising is any paid form of non-personal presentation and promotion of ideas, goods or services by an identified sponsor".

The key words are presentation and promotion. Presentation refers to an offering whereas promotion involves communication and persuasion, therefore, advertising is designed to offer people ideas, goods or services and persuade them to benefits, utility and desirability.

The terms non-personal, paid form and identified sponsor point out what advertising is not. Advertising is non-personal selling, for it does not use individual, face to face communication. Similarly, a word of mouth is also not advertising since this too suggests use of human agency. Advertising is not publicity, since unlike publicity, it is paid for and identifies the sponsor of the message.

Who Advertises?

Both individuals and groups can originate messages. A departmental store might want to let public know about the 30% sale at its store, the National AIDS society may want to communicate to the public at large facts about the sexually transmitted disease. These sources are designated by the function of their advertising as either commercial advertisers or non-commercial advertisers.

The nature of advertising and the use of mass-media as its methods of transmission suggests that audiences are generally large groups or masses of people. However, the choice of medium can serve to widen or to reduce their market selected for a specific advertisement. For example, television and radio give vast coverage, whereas direct mail advertising can limit receipt of the message to a smaller selected group of people. The basic target groups in advertising are most frequently classified geographically–national and local–or according to their primary characteristics–consumer, business.

Functions of Advertising

(a) *Business function* : Advertising performs a business function. More precisely advertising is one alternative among various promotional tools.

(b) *Communication function* : This function of advertising is accomplished through the selection of the target market and the choice of appropriate mass media for sending messages to these target groups. An effective communication process requires creativity–which is not only originality but the ability to achieve results–and a means for evaluating these results.

In short, advertising is a means to a desired goal and not an end in itself.

Present Day Advertising

Modern day advertising is designated as media decade. This designation is in response to the development of new electronic information technologies that provide many ways to disseminate messages on both television or home terminal seasons. These techniques include cable subscription television, communication satellites, direct broadcast satellites, teletext, videotext, video cassettes and video discs, telephone and interactive view data systems which link the viewer's television set to a control data bank via telephone lines. The changing nature of media has brought about a resurgence of creativity and emotional appeals.

Advertising vis-a-vis Marketing

The marketing concept and the advertising concept both provide useful ways of deciding how to choose among many alternatives. Marketing is a broad concept directed primarily at the long range goals of sales. Advertising is directed more to short range goals and particularly to the satisfactory transfer of meaning from advertiser to audience.

The emphasis in marketing is given on sales, for example, to increase the share in market from 6 to 10 per cent in two years, whereas the emphasis in advertising is given on the transmission of a message that may contribute to sales, for example, to convey the audience that a particular cream will keep the skin soft for a longer time than competing creams.

Actually marketing is "all business activities involved in the flow of goods and services from physical production to consumption." According to Philip Kotler, "Marketing management is the analysis, planning, implementation and control of programmes designed to bring about desired exchanges with target audiences for the purpose of personal or mutual gain. It relies heavily on the adaptation and coordination of product, price, promotion and place for achieving effective response".

Although the ultimate purpose of most advertising is to make a sale its immediate purpose is to communicate, specifically to communicate a message to a particular target audience. In communicating this message, there may be several important objectives, such as creating awareness, creating a favourable image, and soliciting requests for information.

Communications objectives should be both specific and measurable, so those who work out the campaign and those who appraise it have a goal to guide them. Russell Colley illustrates this effectively by dividing advertising objectives into four stages of commercial communication.

(a) *Awareness* : Consumers must be made aware of the existence of a brand or company.
(b) *Comprehension* : They must comprehend what the product is and what it will do for them.
(c) *Conviction* : They must become convinced to buy the product.
(d) *Action* : Finally, they must take action.

Advertising and Marketing Mix

An efficient business adjusts its internal capabilities to its changing environment by developing and administering a marketing mix that meets the needs and wants of particular markets at a particular period of time. While the mix can contain numerous elements, the basic ingredients have been designated as the four Ps—what PRODUCT to be sold at what PRICE in what PLACE (channels of distribution), and its method of PROMOTION. The product mix includes name, packages and design, the price mix covers discounts and terms of sale, the place (or distribution mix) decides about channels of distribution outlets, and promotion mix encompasses advertising, personal selling, publicity and sales promotion.

In summary, a marketing mix is combination of procedures used by a firm to achieve its marketing objectives. Advertising is only one ingredient in this mix, but its performance is closely related to the other elements of product decisions, pricing decisions, the channels of distribution selected by the firm, and all forms of promotion. A product covers besides its tangible characteristics, a cluster of satisfaction such as name, package and colour. Advertising helps promote these satisfactions, product development strategies such as market segmentation, product differentiation and product positioning frequently require advertising support. Pricing the product is a major marketing decision, and the determination of how heavily the product should be advertised is an important factor in the selection of the ultimate price. Advertising and publicity are forms of mass communication, personal selling offers an exchange, and sales promotion activities supplement and support these other efforts. All these ingredients can be incorporated into a promotional/ communication network through which a firm may provide information and/or persuasion to facilitate the sale of a good or service or the acceptance of an idea.

Advertising Process in the Market

Once we have taken a decision to advertise the product in the market we will have to answer five W's and one 'H'. These are what, when, where, who, why and how. With these five W's we shall have to answer measurement and budget. These five 'W's are arranged depending upon their priority in the market.

First of all we will have to answer WHY 'I am communicating.' This means setting our objectives and making sure that everything in the advertising plan is related to those objectives.

Secondly, **Who** do I want to reach? This means careful analysis of the target group.

Thirdly, **Where** will I communicate my advertisement message? This means selecting the media for our use.

Fourthly, **What** do I want to say? This determines the communication messages.

Fifthly, **How** will I say it? This becomes our strategy supported by a series of action oriented programmes.

Sixthly, **When** will I communicate? This becomes the time table. Timing can mean success or failure of a programme. The time table disciplines the entire plan.

Whether it is a simple one time message or a full blown, long range plan, we will not go wrong if we carefully answer those six questions. Two additional elements i. e. measurement and budget are needed to complete the plan.

Measurement will enable us to evaluate our results against our objectives.

Budget is the most important ingredient of the whole process. The crucial question is how much a company should spend on advertising and how to allocate these expenditures. In nutshell, advertising is a business function and as such requires efficient management. In preparation for its advertising effort the firm must design appropriate managerial framework.

Advertising vis-a-vis Public Relations

As we have already discussed advertising is paid, non-personal communication through various media by business firms, non-profit organisations and individuals who are in some way identified in the advertising message and who hope to inform or persuade members of a particular audience. Public relations on the other hand is a deliberate, planned and sustained effort to establish and maintain mutual understanding between an organisation and its public. To one counsellor, "Public relations is communicating truth-good works well told." In short public relations is doing good and getting credit for it.

Advertising generally aims to sell products through paid means, whereas public relations attempts to "sell" the organisation itself. Good public relations cannot be bought, it must be earned. The credibility derived from sound public relations work may far exceed that gained through paid advertising. Public relations requires a firm base of theoretical knowledge, a strong sense of judgement, solid communication skills, and, most of all, an uncompromising attitude of professionalism.

Public relations use advertising publicity, or any other tool that might be appropriate to build good relations with various sectors of the public. For Andrew S. Edson, "Advertising is what you pay for and Public relations is what you pray for".

In the 1980s, most companies realized that public relations could play an expanded role in marketing products. In the past, marketers treated pubic relations as an ancillary part of the promotional element in the marketing mix. They were concerned primarily with making sure their products met the needs and desires of customers, were priced competitively, distributed widely and promoted heavily through advertising. Gradually, however, these traditional nations among marketers began to change for several reasons. The net impact of all this was that, while a company's products were still important, customers also began to consider a firm's policies and practices on everything. Beyond these social concerns, the effectiveness of advertising itself began to be questioned. The increased number of advertisements in newspapers and on the airwaves caused "clutter" and posed a significant burden on advertisers to make the public aware of their products.

Basically, public relations can play a critical role in "positioning" a product appropriately in the market. A product's position is the image the product conveys in the public mind. Companies spend millions of rupees trying to position their products in the public mind. Public relations offers a practical and inexpensive device for conveying product messages and helping position a firm's products. About eight of ten new products fail to catch on. The cost of these annual failures has been estimated in the billions of rupees. Public relations, then, should be involved early and integrated fully into the marketing plan. Whether in helping market a new product or in enhancing the staying power of an old one, public relations can make a telling difference in product success. In light of the difficulty today in raising advertising awareness above the "noise" of so many competitive messages, marketers are turning increasingly to product publicity as an important adjunct to advertising.

Although the public is generally unaware of it, a great deal of what it knows and believes about a wide variety of products comes through press coverage. Traditional product publicity–whether it introduces a new product or promotes a long standing one–focuses on some feature of the product that appeals to the public. More recently, companies have begun to link products or brands to event or issues that help publicize the product while positioning it in the public mind. Such an approach has been named by public relations counsellor Art Stevens as "brandstanding".

Public Relations Advertising

Traditionally, organisations have used advertising to sell products. Only occasionally did firms use advertisements for purposes other than product promotion. This unique type of advertising, the marketing of an image rather than a product– became known variously as institutional advertising, image advertising, public service advertising and public relations advertising. Where promotional advertising was hard sell, public relations advertising was softer. Where promotional advertising talked about the particular virtues of using specific products, public relations advertising focussed on the general image the company wished to convey and the public issues it wished to confront. While promotional advertising sought purchasing action for its products, public relations advertising sought support for its positions. Such advertisements typically were used to announce name changes, management changes, merger plans or other information that promoted the company in general rather than its products in particular.

Objectives of Public Relations Advertising

The objectives of public relations advertising fall into two general categories : image building and action inducing. Many companies find in their research that the public holds a distorted image; they then turn to advertising to help correct it. Producing action is, of course, related to image building.

Purposes of Public Relations Advertising

Traditional public relations or non-product advertising–as opposed to image or issue positioning–is still very much in practice for specific purposes. Such advertising can be appropriate for a number of mutually supportive activities.

1. *Mergers and diversifications :* When a company merges with another, the public needs to be told about the new business lines. Such advertising provides a quick and effective way to convey this message.
2. *Personal changes :* A firm's greatest asset is usually its managers, its sales people and its employees. If any change is made among them, the public is informed.
3. *Organization resources :* A firm's investment in research and development implies that the organization is concerned about meeting the future intelligently, an asset that should be advertised.
4. *Manufacturing and service capabilities :* The ability to deliver quality goods on time is something customers cherish. A firm that can deliver should advertise this capability.
5. *Financial strength and stability :* A picture of economic strength and stability is one that all companies like to project. Advertisements that highlight the company's financial position earn confidence of everyone.
6. *Growth history :* People want to deal with the growing company. It is also the kind of firm for which people will want to work.
7. *Company customers :* Customers can serve as a marketing tool, too. Well known personalities who use a certain product may be enough to win additional customers.
8. *Organization name change :* Occasionally, firms change their names. To stick in people's minds, a name change must be well promoted and well advertised. Only through constant repetition will people become familiar with the new identity.
9. *Trademark protection :* The companies, whose products are household names, are legitimately concerned about the improper generic use of their trademarks in the public domain. Such companies run periodic advertisements to remind people of the proper status of their marks.
10. *Corporate emergencies :* Occasionally, an emergency situation erupts– a labour strike, plant disaster or a service interruption. One

quick way to explain the firm's position and procedures without fear of distortion or misinterpretation by editors or reporters is to buy advertising space. This tactic permits a full explanation of the reasons behind the problem and the steps the company plans to take to resolve the dilemma.

Problems in Public Relations Advertising

The problems involved in public relations advertising are too numerous to be discussed. First, public relations advertising involves dangers unknown in product advertising. If you advertise your jelly as having great flavour and taste, some people will still prefer one of the competing brands. Some of them may like it but some of them may not like it. Either way, you are bound to have a certain reaction from people who disagree, perhaps violently, with your point of view.

Second, issues involved in public advertising are more complex than those involved in the purchase of a product. Frequently, however, a particular product offers one dominant reward, and the advertising can concentrate on this point. Issues such as inflation, free trade and many others covered in public relations advertising are extremely complex, and it is difficult to distill them into a few sentences of copy.

Third, it is difficult to chart any cause and effect between a particular campaign and the formation of particular opinions or attitudes.

Fourth, business executives seem both to mistrust and to misunderstand public relations advertising. One public relations specialist claims that advertising is the most misunderstood of the public relations tools, mainly because even the practitioners do not understand how it really works or how to sell it even when they do understand it.

How to Prepare Effective Public Relations Advertising?

1. Tell your story directly to an individual in his own language.
2. Be frank, fair and honest.
3. Do not talk up or down to anyone.
4. Use simple, unvarnished words and facts.
5. Tell one story at a time.

In summary, advertising can be a very important tool of a corporation's or industry's public relations programme. It cannot, however, convince the public that a certain firm or industry is something, it is not. But it may capitalize on good deeds and communicate them to the public.

Publicity, like advertising can be used as part of the public relations programme. But success in getting a specific item accepted by an editor will be determined primarily by its news value. Industries, like companies have public relations problems and can often use advertising to help alleviate them.

POLITICAL ADVERTISING

The Press in India, since its very inception in 1780s, has been intimately concerned with politics and political developments. The newspapers seem to he inordinately concerned with political trivia. Since a country's press feflects the society it lives in, sometimes it appears that the excessive space devoted in newspapers and magazines to politicians and political parties doing, is a mirror of what excites the readers.

In his paper, Press System in India, the Director of the Indian Institute of Mass Communication, Dr. J. S. Yadava has pointed out: The press on the whole today is more concerned with political developments, event and personalities, than economic, social and cultural issues. Many systematic studies have confirmed this notion. The coverage of socio-economic and development issues is usually not more than 5-10 per cent of the total new space. Her further adds :The press instead of remaining a stimulant of social awakening has increasingly become largely a source of news about political events and politicians. The salience to politics to the extent of being obsessed is the dominant feature of the Indian press today.

Likewise, the widely read columnist and the former Director of the Press Institute of India, S. Nihal Singh says : The newspapers are full of politicians' election speeches and the minutiae of electoral politics. The politicians recycle their speeches times without number everyday, and the newspapers dutifully publish the same speeches day after day under big headings.

This intimate association of the Indian Press with politics is legecy from the freedom movement. The press played a significant role in carrying the news and messages about all aspects of freedom struggle throughout the pre-independence period. In fact most of the eminent leaders of freedom movement- Mahatma Gandhi, Jawarlal Nehru, Lok Manya Bal Gangadhar Tilak, Annie Besant, C.R. Das and others were themselves eminent journalists. This emphasis on political reporting continued even after independence. Commenting on the above aspect, B. Kuppuswamy says: One of the chief defects of Indian press is the continuing emphasis on political events and political speeches, and the neglect of reporting and analysis of the development activities in the country. The lengthy reports on political defections and details regarding 'toppling game' make not only depressing reading but also give a distorted picture of the events in the country. the immediate need in the country is a reduction in the emphasis in political reporting and an increase in development reporting.

The reporting of public affairs in the pre-independence era, and for several years even after independent had a distinct difference. The reporter wanted to reach the reader with reader with a message, which was chiefly concerned with the nationalist aspirations of the people, about the news of the struggle and progress of the independence movement and even about social and political issues like separate electorate reforms, communal harmony, swadeshi, non-cooperation movement, etc. political reporting had elements of political advertisement, but the purpose and focus was different. Political advertisement espoused noble cause. Politics itself was considered to the public service. Besides the news element, political reporting took the shape of campaigns, and reports about the progress of the campaigns launched by the nationalists leaders, like Quit movement and the release of political prisoners, etc.

It would be of interest to observe that Mahatma Gandhi- himself a great communicator by all means – considered advertisement to be totally unnecessary and even undesirable for meeting the expenses of running a newspaper. An expect from the Indian Opinion, 14 September 1912 says: We have also come to the conclusion that, consistent with our ideals, we could not accept advertisements for paying our way. We believe that the system of advertisement is bad in itself, in that it sets up insidious competition, to which we are opposed, and often lends itself to misrepresentation on a large scale; and that, if we may not use this journal for the purpose of supporting us early, we have no right to cater for and use our time in setting up advertisements. We have always used our discrimination and rejected many advertisements which we could not conscientiously take. Our friends and well-wishers, who have hitherto extend their support to us, will not, we hope, take it amiss if we discontinue the practice of inserting advertisements.

Political advertisement generally takes the shape of political propaganda. Propaganda is an organised effort to propagate a doctrine, a concept or a campaign. It does not generally have ethical content. It is persuasion based primarily on self-interest. Whereas advertising is paid for directly political advertisement is more akin to political campaigning or publicity. Ever since electoral politics has assumed prominence, political advertisement has come into its own. Political advertisement seeks to project the image of the party in a way which appeals to the largest segment of the electorate. The party manifestos–with best possible postulates including Social Justice, Fighting Communalism, Rural Development, Health, Education, in short issues which would go down well with the electorate, are publicised through various means–press conferences, distribution through organised outlets throughout the country and election speeches. The spokespersons of political parties make use of radio and television–made available to all recognised political parties through Election Commission, for getting across their point of view. This takes the shape of unpaid political advertisement.

The power of mass media in winning elections is perceived to be decisive. In Germany there is greater mutual dependence of politicians on publicists for "Publicistic advertising success". The impact of publicity on gaining power is clear from the following excerpt :

> "The people" is perceived as a media-guided opinion unto. Legislators and government of West Germany are characterised as being put in place as a result of electoral majorities produced by the media. There was no popular will building up "from bottom to top", only publicity-guided opinion. "The politic" today had to be perceived as a gaining of power by publicity; rule came about through publicity "from the top to the bottom".

Political Consultants and Media-Image Makers

In USA, political campaigning and the impact of TV appearance by the leading presidential candidates, has always been a matter of deep interest. Since 1960s, a group of 'political consultants' has emerged which also serves as media image makers. The emergence of television has affected the political behaviour of politicians and the political campaigns in the following respects :

1. Nominating conventions are now planned with television in mind. They are designed not so much to select a candidate as to make a favourable impression on public opinion.
2. Television has increased the cost of campaigning.
3. Television has become the medium around which most campaigns are organised.
4. Campaign staffs now typically include one or more television

consultants whose job it is to advise the candidate on his or her television image.

The above trend is also fact containing on in India. The advertisements for election campaigns run into mind bogging figures. Several political parties make use of the services of well established advertising agencies for planning and executing their electoral campaigns. Massive public meetings are organised, and special arrangements are made for press coverage. Political parties via with each other in spending on extensive press coverage which is subsequently used as a barometer for indicating public support.

Video and Political Advertisements

With the appearance of video, election campaigning in India took an entirely new turn. The potential of video for rousing the masses and for political campaigning was first demonstrated in India during the Andhra Pradesh Assembly elections in 1983. Video was also used on a large scale for political electioneering in the eighth Lok Sabha elections in 1984. About 5,000 view prints of a 20-minute video film, entitled Ma, based on Indira Gandhi's life, were extensively shown in the villages. It was believed to be one of the major factors behind the sweeping victory of Congress (I). But it was only during the ninth Lok Sabha elections in 1989 that the full impact of the video as a medium of mass communication was first realised by most of the leading national parties.

Subsequently there has been no looking back. There was an intense competition amongst political parties in commissioning video films and video raths. In Delhi the Jain TV specialized in preparing video films on political parties and their leaders. Such films were screened in villages and in public meetings which certainly helped in creating a receptive and conducive environment for electoral conducive environment for electoral success.

Posters, large scale hoardings, buying advertisement space in newspapers, public meetings, press conferences, door to door convassing and interpersonal contacts–all constitute important ingredients of political advertisement.

Political Advertising and Public Relations

Political advertising makes full use of the concept of public relations and its techniques. The three short hand definitions of Public Relations are reproduced below :

According to the British Institute of Public Relations, "Public relations is the deliberate, planned and sustained effort to establish and maintain mutual understanding between an organisation and its publics".

Public Relations is the persuasive communication designed to influence specific publics.

It is an instrument of filling communication gap particularly between its organisation and its publics.

Political advertising involved all the elements of above definitions. It is a planned and deliberate effort to persuade and convince the people, may be large population of the country, electorate or the voters living in a specified area or a constituency. Political advertising does not sell a product but aims at influencing specific publics. It also seeks to fill communication gap between the political party, its workers and supporters. Since political parties in countries like India have to cater to its 'publics' which runs into millions, interpersonal contacts for its leaders can work only to a limited extent. That communication gap can be filled in only through public relations techniques, which have been spelt out in detail in several other chapters of the course.

During the 1998 elections to the 12th Lok Sabha, political advertising in India came of age. Several political parties–BJP and the Congress in particular engaged consultants and ad. agencies and pulled out all stops to project their leaders and programmes and perspectives. The BJP with a number of advertisements in the print media–"The moment I decided" projecting Atal Behari Vajpayee as the future Prime Minister of India excelled in using advertising with maximum impact. And as the result showed, the BJP did succeed in selling its slogan of "Stable Government, Able Leader". It was political advertising at its very best with all the resources, efforts and talent geared to reach even the remotest corner of the country. Every party had its media–savvy and articulate senior functionaries as the spokespersons for representing the party's point of view.

Television in 1996 played a fairly major role in presenting different political perspectives before viewers, but it was inhibited because of strict controls by the Election Commission presided over by the over-powering and dominating personality of T. N. Seshan which maintained a hawk like watch over what was put out from the television. This time Doordarshan–both DD 1 and DD 2 did a creditable job in presenting a variety of programmes on the elections. The real breakthrough, however, has been

24 hours channel launched by STAR TV. In the beginning there was scepticism about the ability of TV channels in keeping the programmes going, but to every body's surprise, the programmes went on fairly satisfactorily not only on STAR TV, but on others as well–TVI; Home TV and Sony also had their interesting and informative election programmes.

All this underscores the point that television is now going to play a very crucial role in all the elections. It was not only for publicity and propaganda purposes alone that media had been employed. Equally noteworthy were other programmes of news and analysis of events. Every channel curtailed its normal programmes for the duration of elections. However, as a result of proliferation of channels, there was a surfeit of the same key politicians and party spokespersons rushing from one studio to another, repeating the same thing over and over again. There was also too much of the sameness pervading all the election channels. Whereas STAR News did exceptionally well, Prannoy Roy's coverage catered primarily to English speaking elite viewership. In terms of visuals STAR News was far superior. DD 1 and DD 2 had the advantage of an array of OB Vans and field reporters. It had some of the best known anchors and programme producers including Rahul Dev, Karan Thapar, Swapan Dasgupta, Yogendra Yadav, Madhu Trehan, who were highly knowledgeable about politics and current trends. The programme, 'India Decides' was indeed a delight to watch.

With the "Sonia factor", suddenly all over the screens of television channels, allegations of bias flew thick and fast. The election coverage and the 72-hour TV programme was dramatic, exciting, thrilling and delightful to watch. With this political advertising and Indian Television have successfully crossed an other significant milestone in its journey towards covering public affairs.

Advertising Codes and Ethics

The advertising industry has made rapid strides specially since the early nineties. The policy of economic liberalisation and growth of economy have largely been contributory factors, apart from technological advances.

The advertising industry has been frequently criticised for putting out misleading or exaggerated claims in respect of products, goods and services advertised. It has also been perceived as guilty of glorifying certain habits or tendencies regarded as undesirable, and encouraging consumerist culture. This has quite often led to demands for stricter legal controls. The industry, on the other hand, promises to meet the situation through a system of self-regulation.

The one general difficulty about self-regulating measures or industry codes is the enforcement of such regulations. In this context, K. S. Venkateswaran, in his book, *Mass Media Laws and Regulations in India*, says : Exaggerated claims, appalling bad taste, economy of truth in providing information about products and services, and a general lack of concern for consumer's interest have given the industry a bad side to its reputation which it could do without.

Industry Codes and Monitoring Mechanism

Most of the countries have a number of institutions and professional bodies designed to perform a self-regulatory role. Their performance has been some times termed as 'media accountability system'–which is meant to increase the social responsibility of media. Such bodies evolve codes for self-regulation and monitor their implementation. They have also been called media monitors.

Media monitors also perform another useful function. They provide a valuable forum to the users of the media to express their criticisms or opinions concerning the performance of the media. In the case of newspapers, for example, an effective press council can ensure that the reader is not short-charged by unscrupulous or shoddy journalistic practices. The council can give him a platform from which to ventilate his grievances against biased, inaccurate or inadequate reporting on matters of legitimate public interest. Similarly, a good broadcasting standards council can go a long way in ensuring that the general public is protected from the evils of gratuitous violence or sex on radio and television without having to suffer the harsher alternative of statutory censorship.

In the field of advertising, the Advertising Standards Council of India (ASCI) an umbrella trade body of advertising agencies in the country, drew up a Code of Self-Regulation in 1985 which seeks *inter alia* : to ensure the truthfulness and honesty of representations and claims made in advertisements and to safeguard against misleading advertisements; to ensure that advertisements are not offensive to generally accepted standards of public decency; to safeguard against the indiscriminate use of advertising for the promotion of hazardous or otherwise unacceptable products; and to ensure that advertisements observe fairness in competition. The Code is administered by a Consumer Complaints Council of the ASCI consisting of 14 members, eight of whom are from professions or backgrounds unrelated to advertising. Complaints can be brought to the Council by anyone alleging a breach of the code and they are investigated by the Council. If after proper enquiry the Council comes to the conclusion, by a simple majority, that a complaint is justified, it would make a report to the Board of Governors of the ASCI who will then proceed to implement it as expeditiously as possible.

The Advertising Agencies Association of India (AAAI) is an other representative body of the advertising agency profession. With a view to maintaining high standard of advertising, the AAAI has adopted a code of standards of advertising practice, which covers advertising ethics *vis-a-vis* the customers and advertisers.

Code of Ethics for Advertising in India

Some excerpts from the Code of Ethics for Advertising in India, issued by the Advertising Council of India are reproduced below. The excerpts include general rules of conduct in advertising, instructions to avoid vulgarity and indecency and use of National Emblems.

Introduction

Alongwith the development of a very complex distribution system, the requirements of a market economy, faced with the need for ensuring a regular flow of mass production, have given rise to the development of new techniques of sales promotion.

Of these, advertising has proved itself to be of inestimable value for producers and distributors as well as for consumers. It enables the former to maintain contact with customers who are widely scattered and often unknown, and it assists the latter in choosing those goods and services that are the best suited to their particular requirements.

Advertising has become an important social and economic force in the world of today. It is, therefore, essential that any unfair advertising practice likely to alienate public confidence should be eliminated. Hence, the need for rules of conduct drawn up for the purpose of preventing possible abuses and of promoting an increasing sense of responsibility towards the consumer on the part of the advertisers, advertising agencies and media owners and suppliers.

Recognising that the legitimate function of advertising is the advocacy of the merits of particular products or services this code is intended to be applied in the spirit as well as in the letter and should be taken to set out the minimum standards to be observed by the parties concerned. This Code does override all ethical standards in advertising laid down by individual organizations, but it does not supersede the standards of practice laid down by individual organizations as incumbent upon their own members and applying to their own particular trade or industry.

General Rules of Conduct in Advertising

1. Advertising should be so designed as to conform not only to the laws but also the moral, aesthetic and religious sentiments of the country in which it is published.
2. No advertising likely to bring advertising into contempt or disrepute should be permitted. Advertising should not take advantage of the superstition or ignorance of the general public.
3. No advertisements of talismans, charms and character reading from photographs or such other matter as well trade on the superstition of the general public shall be permitted.
4. Advertising should be truthful, avoid distorting facts and misleading the public by means of implications and omissions. For instance, it should not mislead the consumer by false statements as to :
   (a) the character of the merchandise i.e. its utility, materials, ingredients, origin, etc.
   (b) the price of the merchandise, its value, its suitability or terms of purchase.
   (c) the services accompanying purchase, including delivery, exchange, return, upkeep, etc.
   (d) personal recommendations of the article or service. Testimonials which are fictitious and/or fraudulent or the originals of which cannot be produced must not be used. Anyone using testimonials in advertisements is as responsible for the statements made in them as he would be if he had made them himself.
   (e) the quality of the value of competing goods or the trustworthiness of statements made by others.
5. No advertisement should be permitted to contain any claim so exaggerated as to lead inevitably to disappointment in the mind of the public. Special care is called for in the following cases :
   (a) Advertisements addressed to those suffering from illness. (In

this respect the Code of Standards of Advertising in relation to medicine must be adhered to).

(b) Advertisements inviting the public to invest money. Such advertisements should not contain statements which may mislead the public in respect of the security offered, rates of return, or terms of amortisation.

(c) Advertisements inviting the public to take part in lotteries or competitions such as are permitted by law or which hold out the prospect of gifts. Such advertisements should state clearly all the conditions for the lottery or competition or the conditions for the distribution of the gifts.

(d) The publication of employment notices requiring fees for application forms, prospectus, etc. and security deposits should be forbidden except when such advertisement emanate from Governmental or quasi-Governmental sources.

6. Methods of advertising designed to create confusion in the mind of the consumer as between goods by one maker and another maker are unfair and should not be used. Such methods may consist in :

   (a) the imitation of the trademark or name of the competitor or the packaging or labelling of goods; or

   (b) the imitation of advertising devices, copy, layouts or slogans.

7. Advertising should endeavour to gain the goodwill of the public on the basis of the merits of the goods or services advertised. Direct comparison with competing goods or firms and disparaging references are in no circumstances permitted.

8. Indecent, vulgar, suggestive, repulsive or offensive themes or treatment should be avoided in all advertisements. This also applies to such advertisements which in themselves are not objectionable as defined above, but which advertise objectionable books, photographs or other matter and thereby lead to their sale and circulation.

9. No advertisement should offer to refund money paid.

10. The use of National Emblems is prohibited by law in advertisements, trademarks, etc. except by Governments or Governmental agencies. Also the use of the picture of Mahatma Gandhi, the President, the Vice-President and the Prime Minister of India is forbidden in such advertisements, trademarks, etc. except by previous permission. This rule does not apply to advertising of books, films or other items in which these personages form the chief subject.

Consumer Redressal Forums

Having recognised the need to protect consumers from unfair treatment at the hands of suppliers of goods and services, including advertisers, the Government passed a law in 1986–the 'Consumer Protection Act'. The Act affords a legally enforceable right and offers remedies against misleading or false representation. Under this Act, any consumer who feels that he has suffered harm or damage as a result of such advertisements can lodge a complaint with a Consumer Redressal Forum at district, state or national level. It will, however, be important to note that Code of Ethics would not be effective, unless there is a strong mechanism to oversee its implementation. The ASCI also will have to decentralize its functioning so that even a lay man becomes aware as to where and to whom the complaints could be addressed. At present there is a long road ahead in India for the advertising industry to adopt these ethical practices.

SECTION–VI

ANNEXURES

GLOSSARY

ANNEXURES

ANNEXURE I

PCI GUIDELINES

Norms of Journalistic Conduct

The fundamental objective of journalism is to serve the people with news, views, comments and information on matters of public interest in a fair, accurate, unbiased, sober and decent manner. Towards this end, the Press is expected to conduct itself in keeping with certain norms of professionalism universally recognised. The norms enunciated below and other specific guidelines appended thereafter, when applied with due discernment and adaptation to the varying circumstances of each case, will help the journalist to self-regulate his or her conduct.

Accuracy and Fairness

(1) The Press shall eschew publication of inaccurate, baseless graceless, misleading or distorted material. All sides of the core issue or subject should be reported. Unjustified rumours and surmises should not be set forth as facts.

Pre-publication Verification

(2) On receipt of a report or article of public interest and benefit containing imputations or comments against a citizen, the editor should check with due care and attention its factual accuracy-apart from other authentic sources with the person or the organization concerned to elicit his/her or its version, comments or reaction and publish the same with due amendments in the report where necessary. In the event of lack or absence of response, a footnote to that effect should be appended to the report.

Caution against Defamatory Writings

(3) Newspaper should not publish anything which is manifestly defamatory or libellous against any individual or organisation

unless after due care and checking, they have sufficient reason to believe that it is true and its publication will be for public good.

(4) Truth is no defence for publishing derogatory, scurrilous and defamatory material against a private citizen where no public interest is involved.

(5) No personal remarks which may be considered or construed to be derogatory in nature against a dead person should be published except in rare cases of public interest, as the dead person cannot possibly contradict or deny those remarks.

(6) The Press shall not rely on objectionable past behaviour of a citizen for basing the scathing comments with reference to fresh action of that person. If public good requires such reference, the Press should make pre-publication enquiries from the authorities concerned about the follow up action, if any, in regard to those adverse actions.

(7) The Press has a duty, discretion and right to serve the public interest by drawing reader's attention to citizens of doubtful antecedents and of questionable character but as responsible journalists they should observe due restraint and caution in hazarding their own opinion or conclusion in branding these persons as 'cheats' or 'killers' etc. The cardinal principle being that the guilt of a person should be established by proof of facts alleged and not by proof of the bad character of the accused. In its zest to expose, the Press should not exceed the limits of ethical caution and fair comments.

(8) Where the impunged publications are manifestly injurious to the reputation of the complainant, the onus shall be on the respondent to show that they were true or to establish that they constituted for comment made in good faith and for public good.

Parameters of the Right of the Press to Comment on the Acts and Conduct of Public Officials

(9) So far as the Government, local authority and other organs/ institutions exercising governmental power are concerned, they cannot maintain a suit for damages for acts and conduct relevant to the discharge of their official duties unless the official establishes that the publication was made with reckless disregard for truth. However, judiciary which is protected by the power to punish for contempt of court and the Parliament and Legislatures, protected

as their privileges are by Articles 105 and 194 respectively, of the Constitution of India, represent exception to this rule.

(10) Publication of news or comments/information on public officials conducting investigations should not have a tendency to help the commission of offences or to impede the prevention or detection of offences or prosecution of the guilty. The investigating agency is also under a corresponding obligation not to leak out or disclose such information or indulge in disinformation.

(11) The Official Secrets Act, 1923 or any similar enactment or provision having the force of law equally bind the Press or media though there is no law empowering the state or its officials to prohibit, or to impose a prior restraint upon the Press/media.

(12) Cartoons and caricatures in depicting good humour are to be placed in a special category of news that enjoy more liberal attitude.

Right to Privacy

(13) The Press shall not intrude upon or invade the privacy of an individual unless outweighed by genuine overriding public interest, not being a prurient or morbid curiosity. So, however, that once a matter becomes a matter of public record, the right to privacy no longer subsists and it becomes a legitimate subject for comment by Press and media among others.

Explanation: Things concerning a person's home, family, religion, health, sexuality, personal life and private affairs are covered by the concept of PRIVACY excepting where any of these impinges upon the public or public interest.

(14) Caution against identification : While reporting crime involving rape, abduction or kidnap of women/females or sexual assault on children, or raising doubts and questions touching the chastity, personal character and privacy of women, the names, photographs of the victims or other particulars leading to their identity shall not be published.

(15) Minor children and infants who are the offspring of sexual abuse or 'forcible marriage' or illicit sexual union shall not be identified or photographed.

Recording Interviews and Phone Conversation

(16) The Press shall not tape-record anyone's conversation without that person's knowledge or consent, except where the recording is necessary to protect the journalist in a legal action, or for other compelling good reason.

(17) The Press shall, prior to publication, delete offensive epithets used by an interviewer in conversation with the Press person.

(18) Intrusion through photography into moments of personal grief shall be avoided. However, photography of victims of accidents or natural calamity may be in larger public interest.

Conjecture, Comment and Fact

(19) Newspapers should not pass on or elevate conjecture, speculation or comment as a statement of fact. All these categories should be distinctly stated.

Newspapers to Eschew Suggestive Guilt

(20) Newspapers should eschew suggestive guilt by association. They should not name or identify the family or relatives or associates of a person convicted or accused of a crime, when they are totally innocent and a reference to them is not relevant to the matter reported.

(21) It is contrary to the norms of journalism for a paper to identify itself with and project the case of any one party in the case of any controversy/dispute.

Corrections

(22) When any factual error or mistake is detected or confirmed, the newspaper should publish the correction promptly with due prominence and with apology or expression of regrets in a case of serious lapse.

Right of Reply

(23) The newspaper should promptly and with due prominence, publish either in full or with due editing, free of cost, at the instance of the person affected or feeling aggrieved/or concerned by the impunged

publication, a contradiction/reply/clarification or rejoinder sent to the editor in the form of a letter or note. If the editor doubts the truth or factual accuracy of the contradiction/reply/clarification or rejoinder, he shall be at liberty to add separately at the end a brief editorial comment doubting its veracity, but only when this doubt is reasonably founded on unimpeachable documentary or other evidential material in his/her possession. This is a concession which has to be availed of sparingly with due discretion and caution in appropriate cases.

(24) However, where the reply/contraction or rejoinder is being published in compliance with the discretion of the Press Council, it is permissible to append a brief editorial note to that effect.

(25) Right of rejoinder cannot be claimed through the medium of Press Conference, as publication of a news of a conference is within the discretionary powers of an editor.

(26) Freedom of the Press involves the reader's right to know all sides of an issue of public interest. An editor, therefore, shall not refuse to publish the reply or rejoinder merely on the ground that in his opinion the story published in the newspaper was true. That is an issue to be left to the judgment of the readers. It also does not behove an editor to show contempt towards a reader.

Letters to Editor

(27) An editor who decides to open his columns for letters on a controversial subject, is not obliged to publish all the letters received in regard to that subject. He is entitled to select and publish only some of them either in entirety or the gist thereof. However, in exercising this discretion, he must make an honest endeavour to ensure that what is published is not one-sided but represents a fair balance between the views for and against with respect to the principal issue in controversy.

(28) In the event of rejoinder upon rejoinder being sent by two parties on a controversial subject, the editor has the discretion to decide at which stage to close the continuing column.

Obscenity and Vulgarity to be Eschewed

(29) Newspapers/journalists shall not publish anything which is obscene, vulgar or offensive to publish good taste.

(30) Newspapers shall not display advertisements which are vulgar or which, through depiction of a woman in nude or lewd posture, provoke lecherous attention of males as if she herself was a commercial commodity for sale.

(31) Whether a picture is obscene or not, is to be judged in relation to three tests, namely :

(i) Is it vulgar and indecent?

(ii) Is it a piece of mere pornography?

(iii) Is its publication meant merely to make money by titallating the sex feelings of adolescents and among whom it is intended to circulate? In other words, does it constitute an unwholesome exploitation for commercial gain.

Other relevant considerations are whether the picture is relevant to the subject matter of the magazine. That is to say, whether its publication serves any preponderating social or public purpose, in relation to art, painting, medicine, research or reform of sex.

Violence not to be Glorified

(32) Newspapers/journalists shall avoid presenting acts of violence, armed robberies and terrorist activities in a manner that glorifies the perpetrators acts, declarations or death in the eyes of the public.

Glorification/Encouragement of Social Evils to be Eschewed

(33) Newspapers shall not allow their columns to be misused for writings which have a tendency to encourage or glorify social evils like Sati Pratha or ostentatious celebrations.

Covering Communal Disputes/Clashes

(34) News, views or comments relating to communal or religious disputes/clashes shall be published after proper verification of facts and presented with due caution and restraint in a manner which is conducive to the creation of an atmosphere congenial to communal harmony, amity and peace. Sensational, provocative and alarming headlines are to be avoided. Acts of communal violence or vandalism shall be reported in a manner as may not undermine the people's confidence in the law and order machinery of the State. Giving community-wise figures of the victims of communal riot, or writing about the incident in a style which is likely to inflame

passions, aggravate the tension, or accentuate the strained relations between the communities/religious groups concerned, or which has a potential to exacerbate the trouble, shall be avoided.

Headings not to be Sensational/Provocative and must Justify the Matter Printed under them

(35) In general and particularly in the context of communal disputes or clashes :
   (a) Provocative and sensational headlines are to be avoided;
   (b) Headings must reflect and justify the matter printed under them;
   (c) Headings containing allegations made in statements should either identify the body or the source making it or at least carry quotation marks.

Caste, Religion or Community References

(36) In general, the caste identification of a person or a particular class should be avoided, particularly when in the context it conveys a sense or attributes a conduct or practice derogatory to that caste.

(37) Newspapers are advised against the use of word 'Scheduled Caste' or 'Harijan' which has been objected to by some persons.

(38) An accused or a victim shall not be described by his caste or community when the same does not have anything to do with the offence or the crime and plays no part either in the identification of any accused or proceeding, if there be any.

(39) Newspapers should not publish any fictional literature distorting and portraying the religious characters in an adverse light transgression of the norms of literary taste and offending the religious susceptibilities of large sections of society who hold those characters in high esteem, invested with attributes of the virtuous and lofty.

(40) Commercial exploitation of the name of prophets, seers or deities is repugnant to journalistic ethics and good taste.

Reporting on Natural Calamities

(41) Facts and data relating to spread of epidemics or natural calamities shall be checked up thoroughly from authentic sources and then

published with due restraint in a manner bereft of sensationalism, exaggeration, surmises or unverified facts.

Paramount National Interest

(42) Newspapers shall, as a matter of self-regulation, exercise due restraint and caution in presenting any news, comment or information which is likely to jeopardise, endanger or harm the paramount interests of the State and society, or the rights of individuals with respect to which reasonable restrictions may be imposed by law on the right to freedom of speech and expression under clause (2) of Article 19 of the Constitution of India.

(43) Publication of wrong/incorrect map is a very serious offence, whatever the reason, as it adversely affects the territorial integrity of the country and warrants prompt and prominent retraction with regrets.

Newspapers may Expose Misuse of Diplomatic Immunity

(44) The media shall make every possible effort to build bridges of co-operation, friendly relations and better understanding between India and foreign States. At the same time, it is the duty of a newspaper to expose any misuse or undue advantage of the diplomatic immunities.

Investigative Journalism, its Norms and Parameters

(45) Investigative reporting has three basic elements.

(a) It has to be the work of the reporter, not of other he is reporting;

(b) The subject should be of public importance for the reader to know;

(c) An attempt is being made to hide the truth from the people.

(i) The first norm follows as a necessary corollary from (a) that the investigative reporter should, as a rule, base his story on facts investigated, detected and verified by himself and not on hearsay or on derivative evidence collected by a third party, not checked up from direct, authentic sources by the reporter himself.

(ii) There being a conflict between the factors which require openness and those which necessitate secrecy, the investigative journalist should strike and maintain in his report a proper balance between openness on the one hand and secrecy on the other, placing the public good above everything.

(iii) The investigative journalist should resist the temptation of quickies or quick gains conjured up from half-baked, incomplete, doubtful facts, not fully checked up and verified from authentic sources by the reporter himself.

(iv) Imaginary facts, or ferreting out or conjecturing the non-existent should be scrupulously avoided. Facts, facts and yet more facts are vital and they should be checked and cross-checked whenever possible until the moment the paper goes to Press.

(v) The newspaper must adopt strict standards of fairness and accuracy of facts. Findings should be presented in an objective manner, without exaggerating or distorting, that would stand up in a court of law, if necessary.

(vi) The reporter must not approach the matter or the issue under investigation, in a manner as though he were the prosecutor or counsel for the prosecution. The reporter's approach should be fair, accurate and balanced. All facts properly checked up, both for and against the core issues, should be distinctly and separately stated, free from any one-sided inferences or unfair comments. The tone and tenor of the report and its language should be sober, decent and dignified, and not needlessly offensive, barbed, derisive or castigatory, particularly while commenting on the version of the person whose alleged activity or misconduct is being investigated. Nor should the investigative reporter conduct the proceedings and pronounce his verdict of guilt or innocence against the person whose alleged criminal acts and conduct were investigated, in a manner as if he were a court trying the accused.

(vii) In all proceedings including the investigation, presentation and publication of the report, the investigative journalist/newspaper should be guided by the paramount principle of criminal jurisprudence, that a person is innocent unless the offence alleged against him is proved beyond doubt by independent, reliable evidence.

(viii) The private life, even of a public figure, is his own. Exposition or invasion of his personal privacy or private life is not permissible unless there is clear evidence that the wrong doings in question have a reasonable nexus with the misuse of his public position or power and has an adverse impact on public interest.

(ix) Though the legal provisions of Criminal Procedure do not in terms, apply to investigating proceedings by a journalist, the fundamental principles underlying them can be adopted as a guide on grounds of equity, ethics and good conscience.

Confidence to be Respected

(46) If information is received from a confidential source, the confidence should be respected. The journalist cannot be compelled by the Press Council to disclose such source; but it shall not be regarded as a breach of journalistic ethics if the source is voluntarily disclosed in proceedings before the Council by the journalist who considers it necessary to repel effectively a charge against him/her. This rule requiring a newspaper not to publish matters disclosed to it in confidence, is not applicable where :

(a) Consent of the source is subsequently obtained; or

(b) The editor clarified by way of an appropriate foot-note that since the publication of certain matters were in the public interest, the information in question was being published although it had been made 'off the record'.

Caution in Criticizing Judicial Acts

(47) Excepting where the court sits 'in-camera' or directs otherwise, it is open to a newspaper to report pending judicial proceedings, in a fair, accurate and reasonable manner. But it shall not publish anything :

– which, in its direct and immediate effect, creates a substantial risk of obstructing, impeding or prejudicing seriously the due administration of justice; or

– is in the nature of running commentary or debate, or records the paper's own findings, conjectures, reflection or comments on issues, *sub judice* and which may amount to arrogation to the newspaper the functions of the court; or

– regarding the personal character of the accused standing trial on a charge of committing a crime.

Newspaper shall not as a matter of caution, publish or comment on evidence collected as a result of investigative journalism, when, after the accused is arrested and charged, the court becomes seized of the case : Nor should they reveal, comment upon or evaluate a confession allegedly made by the accused.

(48) While newspapers may, in the public interest, make reasonable criticism of a judicial act or the judgment of a court for public good; they shall not cast scurrilous aspersions on, or impute improper motives, or personal bias to the judge. Nor shall they scandalise the court or the judiciary as a whole, or make personal allegations of lack of ability or integrity against a judge.

(49) Newspaper shall, as a matter of caution, avoid unfair and unwarranted criticism which, by *innuendo*, attributes to a judge extraneous consideration for performing an act in due course of his/her judicial functions, even if such criticism does not strictly amount to criminal Contempt of Court.

Newspapers to Avoid Crass Commercialism

(50) While newspapers are entitled to ensure, improve or strengthen their financial viability by all legitimate means, the Press shall not engage in crass commercialism or unseemly cut-throat commercial competition with their rivals in a manner repugnant to high professional standards and good taste.

(51) Predatory price wars/trade competition among newspapers, laced with tones disparaging the products of each other, initiated and carried on in print, assume the colour of unfair 'trade' practice, repugnant to journalistic ethics. The question as to when it assumes such an unethical character, is one of the facts depending on the circumstances of each case.

Plagiarism

(52) Using or passing off the writings or ideas of another as one's own, without crediting the source, is an offence against the ethics of journalism.

Unauthorised Lifting of News

(53) The practice of lifting news from other newspapers and publishing them subsequently as their own, ill-comports with the high standards of journalism. To remove its unethicality, the 'lifting' newspaper must duly acknowledge the source of the report. The position of features articles is different from 'news': Feature articles shall not be lifted without permission/proper acknowledgement.

(54) The Press shall not reproduce in any form offending portions or excerpts from a proscribed book.

Non-return of Unsolicited Material

(55) A paper is not bound to return unsolicited material sent for consideration of publication. However, when the same is accompanied by stamped envelope, the paper should make all efforts to return it.

Advertisements

(56) Commercial advertisements are information as much as social, economic or political information. What is more, advertisements shape attitude and ways of life at least as much as other kinds of information and comment. Journalistic propriety demands that advertisements must be clearly distinguishable from editorial matters carried in the newspaper.

(57) Newspaper shall not publish anything which has a tendency to malign wholesale or hurt the religious sentiments of any community or section of society.

(58) Advertisements which offend the provisions of the Drugs and Magical Remedies (Objectionable Advertisement) Act, 1954, should be rejected.

(59) Newspaper should not publish an advertisement containing anything which is unlawful or illegal, or is contrary to good taste or to journalistic ethics or properties.

(60) Newspapers while publishing advertisements, shall specify the amount received by them. The rationale behind this is that advertisements should be charged at rates usually chargeable by a newspaper since payment of more than the normal rates would amount to a subsidy to the paper.

(61) Publication of dummy advertisements that have neither been paid for, nor authorised by the advertisers, constitute breach of journalistic ethics.

(62) Deliberate failure to publish an advertisement in all the copies of a newspaper offends against the standards of journalistic ethics and constitutes gross professional misconduct.

(63) There should be no lack of vigilance or a communication gap between the advertisement department and the editorial department of a newspaper in the matter of considering the propriety or otherwise of an advertisement received for publication.

(64) The editors should insist on their right to have the final say in the acceptance or rejection of advertisements, specially those which border on or cross the line between decency and obscenity.

(65) An editor shall be responsible for all matters, including advertisements published in the newspaper. If responsibility is disclaimed, this shall be explicitly stated beforehand.

ANNEXURE II

I. GUIDELINES FOR THE STATE GOVERNMENTS AND THE MEDIA IN RELATION TO COMMUNAL DISTURBANCES 1991

(i) The State Government should take upon themselves the responsibility of keeping a close watch on the communal writings that might spark off tension, destruction and death, and bring them to the notice of the Council;

(ii) The Government may have occasion to take action against erring papers or editors. But it must do so within the bounds of law. If newsmen are arrested, or search and seizure operations become necessary, it would be healthy convention if such developments could be reported to the Press Council within 24 to 48 hours followed by a detailed note within a week;

(iii) Under no circumstances must have authorities resort to vindictive measures like cut in advertisements, cancellation of accreditation, cut in newsprint quota and other facilities;

(iv) Provocative and sensational headlines should be avoided by the Press;

(v) Headings must reflect and justify and matter printed under them;

(vi) Figures of casualties given in headlines should preferably be on the lower side in case or doubt about their exactness and where the numbers reported by various sources differ widely;

(vii) Headings containing allegations made in statements should either identify the person/body making the allegation or, at least, should carry quotation marks;

(viii) News reports should be devoid of comments and value judgement;

(ix) Presentation of news should not be motivated or guided by partisan feelings, nor should it appear to be so;

(x) Language employed in writing the news should be temperate and such as may foster feelings or amity among communities and groups;

(xi) Corrections should be promptly published with due prominence and regrets expressed in serious cases; and

(xii) It will help a great deal if in-service training is given to journalists for inculcation of all these principles.

II. GUIDELINES TO THE PRESS ON RAM JANAMBHOOMI-BABRI MASJID DISPUTE (21-22 JAN., 1993)

Guidelines for guarding against the commission of the following journalistic improprieties and unethicalities :

1. Distortion or exaggeration of facts or incidents in relation to communal matters or giving currency to unverified rumours, suspicions or inferences as if they were facts and base their comments on them.
2. Employment of intemperate or unrestrained language in the presentation of news or views, even as a piece of literary flourish or for the purpose of rhetoric or emphasis.
3. Encouraging or condoning violence even in the face of provocation as a means of obtaining redress of grievance whether the same be genuine or not.
4. While it is the legitimate function of the Press to draw attention to the genuine and legitimate grievances of any community with a view to having the same redressed by all peaceful, legal and legitimate means, it is improper and a breach of journalistic ethics to invent grievances, or to exaggerate real grievances, as these tend to promote communal ill-feeling and accentuate discord.
5. Scurrilous and untrue attacks on communities, or individuals, particularly when this is accompanied by charges attributing misconduct to them as due to their being members of a particular community or caste.
6. Falsely giving a communal colour to incidents which might occur in which members of different communities happen to be involved.
7. Emphasising matters that are apt to produce communal hatred or ill-will, or fostering feelings of distrust between communities.
8. Publishing alarming news which are in substance untrue or make provocative comments on such news or even otherwise calculated

to embitter relations between different communities or regional or linguistic groups.

9. Exaggerating actual happenings to achieve sensationalism and publication of news which adversely affect communal harmony with banner headlines or distinctive types.
10. Making disrespectful, derogatory or insulting remarks on or reference to the different religions or faiths or their founders.

ANNEXURE III

GUIDELINES FOR FINANCIAL JOURNALISTS

The Press Council of India has counselled reporters/financial/ journalists/ newspaper establishments to refrain from receiving any gifts/grants/ concessions/facilities, etc., either in cash or kind which are likely to compromise free and unbiased reporting on financial matters.

2. The Council in its Report has observed that the financial journalists today enjoy considerable influence over readers' minds and, therefore, they owe it to them to present a balanced and objective view of the financial dealings, status and prospects of a company. It observed that some companies are given excessive news coverage in the newspapers/magazines because they have issued advertisements to that print media. Sometimes, adverse reports are published of those companies which do not give advertisements to the newspapers or magazines. Again, when a media is not happy with any company/ management for whatever reason, the negative aspects of the company are highlighted, while in the reverse situation, no negative aspects are brought to light. Some companies are also known to given gifts, loans, discounts, preferential shares, etc., to certain financial journalists to receive favourable and positive reports of the companies. At the same time, there is no mechanism for investors' education or for raising public opinion against such unhealthy practices.

3. The Council feeling concerned over the malpractice in the Corporate Sector and after holding detailed deliberations and discussions with the representatives of financial institutions and journalists, has recommended the guidelines enumerated below for observance by the financial journalists :

(1) The financial journalists should not accept gifts, loans, trips, discounts, preferential shares or other considerations which compromise or are likely to compromise his position.

(2) It should be mentioned prominently in the report about any company that the report is based on information given by the

company or the financial sponsors of the company.

(3) When the trips are sponsored for visiting establishments of a company, the author of the report who has availed of the trip must state invariably that the visit was sponsored by the company concerned and that it had also extended the hospitality as the case may be.

(4) No matter related to the company should be published without verifying the facts from the company and the source of such report should also be disclosed.

(5) A reporter who exposes a scam or brings out a report for promotion of a good project, should be encouraged and awarded.

(6) A journalist who has financial interests such as share holdings, stock holdings, etc., in a company, should not report on that company.

(7) The journalist should not use for his own benefit or for the benefit of his relations and friends, information received by him in advance for publication.

(8) No newspaper owner, editor or anybody connected with a newspaper should use his relations with the newspaper to promote his other business interests.

(9) Whenever there is an indictment of a particular advertising agency or advertiser by the Advertising Council of India, the newspaper in which the advertisement was published must publish the news of indictment prominently.

ANNEXURE IV

INTERNATIONAL CODE OF ETHICS
Principles of Professional Values

International and regional organizations of working journalists, representing altogether 400,000 working journalists in all parts of the world, have held since 1978 consultative meetings under the auspices of UNESCO.

The second consultative meeting (Mexico City, 1980) expressed its support to the UNESCO Declaration on Fundamental Principles concerning the contribution of the Mass Media to strengthening Peace and International Understanding, to the promotion of Human Rights and to countering Racialism, Apartheid and incitement to War. Moreover, the meeting adopted the "Mexico Declaration" with a set of principles which represent common grounds of existing national and regional codes of journalistic ethics as well as relevant provisions contained in various international instruments of a legal nature.

The fourth consultative meeting (Prague and Paris, 1983) noted the lasting value of the UNESCO Declaration in which it is stated *inter alia* that "the exercise of freedom of opinion, expression and information, recognized as an integral part of human rights and fundamental freedoms, is a vital factor in the strengthening of peace and international understanding". Furthermore, the meeting recognized the important role which information and communication play in the contemporary world, both in national and international spheres, with a growing social responsibility being placed upon the mass media and journalists.

On this basis the following principles of professional ethics in journalism were prepared as an international common ground and as a source of inspiration for national and regional codes of ethics. This set of principles is intended to be promoted autonomously by each professional organization through ways and means most adequate to its members.

Principle I : People's Right to True Information

Peoples and individuals have the right to acquire an objective picture of reality by means of accurate and comprehensive information as well as to express themselves freely through the various media of culture and communication.

Principle II : The Journalist's Dedication to Objective Reality

The foremost task of the journalist is to serve the right to true and authentic information through an honest dedication to objective reality whereby facts are reported conscientiously in their proper context, pointing out their essential connections and without causing distortions, with due deployment of the creative capacity of the journalist, so that the public is provided with adequate material to facilitate the formation of an accurate and comprehensive picture of the world in which the origin, nature and essence of events, processes and states of affairs are understood as objectively as possible.

Principle III : The Journalist's Social Responsibility

Information in journalism is understood as social good and not as commodity which means that the journalist shares responsibility for the information transmitted and is thus accountable not only to those controlling the media but ultimately to the public at large, including various social interests. The journalist's social responsibility requires that he or she will act under all circumstances in conformity with a personal ethical consciousness.

Principle IV : The Journalist's Professional Integrity

The social role of the journalist demands that the profession maintain high standards of integrity, including the journalist's right to refrain from working against his or her conviction or from disclosing sources of information as well as the right to participate in the decision-making of the medium in which he or she is employed. The integrity of the profession does not permit the journalist to accept any form of bribe or the promotion of any private interest contrary to the general welfare. Likewise it belongs to professional ethics to respect intellectual property and in particular to refrain from plagiarism.

Principle V : Public Access and Participation

The nature of the profession demands that the journalist promotes access by the public to information and participation of the public in the media, including the right of correction or rectification and the right of replay.

Principle VI : Respect for Privacy and Human Dignity

An integral part of the professional standards of the journalist is respect for the right of the individual to privacy and human dignity, in conformity with provisions of international and national law concerning protection of the rights and the reputation of others and prohibiting libel, calumny, slander and defamation.

Principle VII : Respect for Public Interest

The professional standards of the journalist prescribe due respect for the national community, its democratic institutions and public morals.

Principle VIII : Respect for Universal Values and Diversity of Cultures

A true journalist stands for the universal values of humanism, above all peace, democracy, human rights, social progress and national liberation, while respecting the distinctive character, value and dignity of each culture, as well as the right of each people freely to choose and develop its political, social, economic and cultural systems. Thus the journalist participates actively in the social transformation towards democratic betterment of society and contributes through dialogue to a climate of confidence in international relations conductive to peace and justice everywhere, to detente, disarmament and national development. It belongs to the ethics of the profession that the journalist be aware of relevant provisions contained in international conventions, declarations and resolutions.

Principle IX : Elimination of War and Other Great Evils Confronting Humanity

The ethical commitment to the universal values of humanism calls for the journalist to abstain from any justification for, or incitement to, wars of aggression and the arms race, especially in nuclear weapons, and all other forms of violence, hatred or discrimination, especially racialism and apartheid, oppression by tyrannic regimes, colonialism and neo-colonialism, as well as other great evils which afflict humanity, such as poverty, malnutrition and diseases. By doing so, the journalist can help eliminate ignorance and misunderstanding among peoples, make nationals of a country sensitive to the needs and desires of others, ensure the respect for the rights and dignity of all nations, all peoples and all individuals without distinction of race, sex, language, nationality, religion or philosophical conviction.

Principle X : Promotion of a New World Information and Communication Order

The journalist operates in the contemporary world within the framework of a movement towards new international relations in general and a new information order in particular. This new order, understood as an integral part of the New International Economic Order, is aimed at the decolonization and democratization of the field of information and communication, both nationally and internationally, on the basis of peaceful co-existence among peoples and with full respect for their cultural identity. The journalist has a special obligation to promote the process of democratization of international relations in the field of information, particularly safeguarding and fostering peaceful and friendly relations among States and peoples.

Paris : 20th, November 1983.

Source : *Communication Ethics : A South Asian Perspective.*

ANNEXURE V

BROADCAST CODE GOVERNING ALL INDIA RADIO

Broadcasts on All India Radio by individuals shall not violate Broadcasting Code, which prohibits the following :

1. Criticism of friendly country.
2. Attack on religion or communities.
3. Anything obscene or defamatory.
4. Incitement of violence or anything against maintenance of law and order.
5. Anything amounting to contempt of court.
6. Aspersions against the integrity of the President, Governors and Judiciary.
7. Attack on a political party by name.
8. Hostile criticism of any State or the Centre.
9. Anything showing disrespect to the Constitution or advocating change in the Constitution by violence. But advocating changes in the constitutional way should not be debarred.

FOOTNOTE

(i) If a Station Director finds that the above Code has not been respected in any particular or particulars by an intending broadcaster he will draw the latter's attention to the passages objected to. If intending broadcaster refuses to accept the Station Director's suggestions and modify his script accordingly, the Station Director will be justified in refusing his or her broadcast.

(ii) Cases of unresolved differences of opinion between a Minister of a State Government and the Station Director about the interpretation of the Code, with regard to a talk to be broadcast by the former will be referred to the Minister of Information and Broadcasting, Government of India, who will decide finally whether or not any change in the text of the talk is necessary in order to avoid violation of the Code.

ANNEXURE VI

NATIONAL INTEGRATION COUNCIL CODE

In June 1962, the National Integration Council (NIC) drafted a Code of Conduct for the media which goes beyond the traditional responsibilities of the press. Accordingly, the press should :

- take all active steps to develop a feeling of unity, solidarity and cohesion in the hearts of the people and should create a sense of common citizenship and a feeling of loyalty to the nation;
- subordinate group loyalties based on caste, community, religion, region or language to national interest;
- condone no move of any person, party or group to divide the country or to create tension between its peoples;
- condemn unreserved incitement to violence or advocacy of violence as a means of settling conflicts;
- withhold publication of unverified news, which would tend to create discord, and refrain from giving prominent display to such news;
- contradict or rectify all inaccurate reports or comments relating to such news; and
- highlight all activities whether of the State or of the public which promote the progress of the nation and the unity of the country.

ANNEXURE VII

THE TIMES OF INDIA GROUP'S CODE OF ETHICS

October, 1996

1. Journalists of *The Times of India Group* should desist from accepting gifts, favours, concessional benefits such as loans, discounts, preferential shares and the sort from corporate bodies or other entities that they deal within their professional capacity. Though nothing of value should be accepted, a commonsensical approach can be adopted towards accepting, say, a modest box of sweets, inexpensive pens, diaries, calendars and such other tokens of courtesy.
2. All invitations for sponsored trips should come to the Editor for nominating a representative of the newspaper. Under no circumstances should the individual journalist accept such an invitation on his own. The name of the host inviting agency and the fact that the trip was sponsored by it should be mentioned at the conclusion of subsequent articles. Given the sensitive nature of political journalism, no hospitality from an individual politician or party should be accepted. In order to preserve its independence, *The Times Group* would not like its journalists to accept the hospitality of governmental or non-governmental institutions in India. In cases where for convenience in covering a story the transportation provided by the government, a private company or other institution needs to be used, the company will pay an amount equal to the ordinary commercial cost of similar facilities.
3. Every journalist should ensure that professional objectivity is not influenced by personal likes, dislikes, friendship and ideologies. Journalists should refrain from being members of political organisations. Involvement in political activities, community affairs, demonstrations and social causes that could cause a conflict of interest with the discharge of professional duties should be avoided. Any situation of a potential conflict of interest (such as covering

the activities of a club/organisation of which one is a member) should be brought to the attention of the Editor by the journalist concerned.

4. Reports which might be damaging to an individual or organisation should not be carried without every effort being made to contact the affected party and obtain his or its views. In case no comment is available, the effort made to speak to the affected party should be reflected in the report.
5. A journalist should not use the normal requirement of protecting the confidentiality of his sources as a cover to write unsubstantiated or sensational reports. The journalist concerned must be armed with enough information and argument to satisfy the Editor about the authenticity of his report, should the occasion for any doubt or question arise. While a journalist should make every effort to ensure objectivity and accuracy, the newspaper should publish corrections and acknowledge errors.
6. A journalist who holds shares in a particular company must inform his head of department/editor before writing a story related to the company. Insider trading by a journalist on the basis of privileged information is a gross violation of professional ethics.
7. Journalists of *The Times of India Group* should not acquire flats/ houses/land at concessional rates courtesy any government quota. In case, there are any who have already acquired such property out of such a quota, they should declare to the company the acquisition along with the price paid. Accredited journalists occupying government accommodation on rent should conform to the newly announced guidelines of the Press Council of India in this regard : payment of a monthly licence fee to the government plus the house rent allowance given by the employer declaration to the government on March 31 every year of details regarding salary, property acquired, etc.; vacation of accommodation on expiry of allotment, etc. Information on all these aspects should be declared to the Editor.
8. An advisory committee of staff journalists selected by the Editor will be set up to inquire into complaints of misdemeanour or bias against any journalist. The committee may call upon the journalist in question to submit a list of his assets or a record of his investments or any relevant documents, should the need arise. The committee's recommendations will be carefully considered by the Editor before taking action.

ANNEXURE VIII

FINANCIAL EXPRESS'S CODE OF CONDUCT

October, 1996

1. **Gifts :** No FE journalist will accept any gift at press conferences or at any other gathering. This ban excludes routine items like cheap plastic folders and pens. In case a reporter feels that in certain circumstances NOT accepting a gift is embarrassing, the matter should be immediately reported to the Editor/Executive Editor and the gift article obtained will be suitably gifted to charity, or a generally agreed worthy cause. FE journalists should honour this code both in letter and spirit.
2. **Share Investments :** No FE journalists will dabble in share investments of a short-term/speculative nature. By this we mean that it is okay to invest/buy shares, but no one should play the market for short periods like a week or two without taking deliveries. This requirement is very particularly relevant to corporate reporters and those managing the investment section.
3. **Insider Information :** Corporate and market reporters may routinely come to learn about corporate developments of a price sensitive nature. This information, if not used in the paper, should not be disclosed to ANYONE OUTSIDE, especially market sources and brokers, or used for personal profits.
4. **Disclosure :** Journalists involved in market stories, or who are reporting on anything that would affect share prices in general will have to disclose their shareholdings to the Editor/Executive Editor. We expect FE journalists to disclose holdings in any company, wherever the values of their investments exceed Rs. 10,000/- in market value. In the case of those making market recommendations, writers will have to make the following disclosure at the bottom of each article: "Neither the author nor their close relatives have direct or indirect investments in the above company's shares." Or alternatively: 'The author has a small/substantial investment in the

above mentioned share, and his views may, to that extent, be influenced by it'. The idea is to improve the paper's credibility with the reading public. (Here small means investments below Rs. 25,000/- in market value; substantial would be anything above that).

5. **Junkets :** Financial Express may accept junkets/free hospitality from companies both within and outside the country provided it makes editorial sense. All such junkets will have to be cleared by the Editor/ Executive Editor. All invitations will be addressed to the FE Editor, and the Editor/FE reserves the right to send anybody for the trip. If the invitation is specifically directed to any one person, the Editor/ FE reserves the right to decline it.
6. **Balanced Reporting :** FE is a corporate newspaper; what we write affects people's business. Whenever we write about a company, and especially if it involves adverse references to a company, we must make every effort to contact the company/its spokesmen for their point of view. And, where necessary, we must give the companies enough time to respond. It is not right to call up someone at eight in the night and demand an immediate reply to a complex set of allegations. This is not fair reporting.

ALL FE JOURNALISTS WILL BE COVERED BY THIS CODE. VIOLATIONS OF THIS WILL BE TAKEN SERIOUSLY AND DEALT WITH ACCORDINGLY, EITHER THROUGH CENSURE OR IN EXTREME CASES, OUTRIGHT DISMISSALS.

ANNXURE–IX

WORKSHOP RESOLUTION ON MEDIA REGULATIONS FOR THE NEW TIMES
Bangkok, Thailand, April 15-17, 1998

The arrival of the newer services such as the Internet, digital and interactive TV, as a result of convergence has opened a wide debate about how media should be regulated. This workshop on "Media Regulations for the New Times", organised by AMIC, has considered the current state of that discussion in several Asian countries and has formulated the following recommendations.

The crucial role of media in fostering democratic structures and development of the Asian region, leads us to reiterate that the newer services should be considered as an important opportunity for the development of the media and any action which stimulates access to the new technologies should be encouraged. A characteristic of Asia, being a diversity of languages and cultures, the rich possibilities offered by these technologies should be harnessed to enrich these cultures.

If regulation is considered to be necessary, it should conform to the fundamental principles of freedom of speech and the rule of law. When regulation is enacted full accountability of the implementation and enforcement of those regulations must be established.

Freedom of information should be an essential aspect of the relationship between governments, media and the citizens. New technologies, such as the WWW can allow public information more widely and at a lower cost, therefore we recommend that governments desist of perceiving these technologies as a threat but instead treat them as powerful tools of good governance.

While the newer technologies may offer an increased range of services, pluralism remains essential. It must inform the ownership of media and greater diversity of content.

The fast pace of technological developments throw up a complex gamut of regulatory challenges to society. This can be addressed by self regulation which should therefore be considered as the preferred model of regulation.

Although convergence is taking place, we recognize that there is still a need for tailoring regulation to the particular requirements of different media. We, therefore, recommend the following :

Print Media

Acknowledging that the right to publish is an aspect of freedom of speech and as such a fundamental right for every citizen, we recommend that :

- a simple procedure of registration should be sufficient for the press.
- self regulatory mechanisms should be in place such as Press Councils to deal with complaints against unfair practices of the Press.
- where press and media laws inhibit and stifle this fundamental principle, these should be reviewed and liberalised to promote a free press.
- press Councils and similar bodies should have sufficient powers and resources to enable efficient enforcement of their decisions.
- given the public service nature of the press, efforts should ensure the effective representation of diverse sections of the community in the press and similar Councils.
- legislation should be enacted to ensure maximum transparency to avoid abuse of ownership and control.
- wherever there is an attempt to devalue the independence and the role of the editor and the editorial staff by any means, efforts should be made to monitor and discourage such practices by press Councils and other bodies.
- monitoring of the Press coverage by media watch groups is crucial to ensure fairness about the patterns and priorities of such coverage.
- efforts should be made to encourage and promote grassroots and specialised journalism.

Radio and TV

Given the crucial importance to these media in reaching the poor and the illiterate, and their transitional impact we propose that measures be taken to :

- expand audience choices;

- enhance open competition and transparency in the licensing process;
- strengthen professionalism and ethical standards in broadcasting;
- promote greater regional co-operation in the sector;
- build regional consensus on content regulation;
- encourage technologies which facilitate a more efficient use of scarce resources such as the broadcast spectrum.

The Internet

In formulating an Internet policy, governments should set clear priorities, which should be as follows :

- Laws and policies should facilitate and encourage the development of the technological infrastructure and institutions related to the Internet.
- Attempts should be made to promote local hosting of information. Steps should be taken to develop national and regional networks of high bandwidth; to train programmers and users and to encourage the spread of local languages on the Net alongside English.
- A holistic and flexible approach towards regulation must be developed based on a mature understanding of the issues involved in a rapidly changing environment.
- Efforts should be made to clear obstacles to e-commerce given the importance of trade and commercial communications in the global market.

(AMIC Conference–1998)

ANNEXURE X

MODEL ADVERTISEMENT POLICY GUIDE

Under the statute passed by the Parliament in 1978, the Press Council of India is enjoined upon to preserve the freedom of the Press and to maintain and improve the standards of newspapers and news agencies in India. This is further supported by clause (e) of section 13(1) of the Press Council Act, whereby the Council is required to "keep under review any development likely to restrict the supply and dissemination of news of public interest and importance". There have been a number of occasions where the Press Council has been called upon to look into the complaints of improper or arbitrary denial of advertisements by various authorities, severely affecting the economic viability of newspapers, particularly of those in the smaller category.

In disposing of these complaints, the Council has often observed that governmental authorities should not single out a newspaper for discriminatory treatment in the matter of release of advertisements on account of its critical writings. Release of advertisements should be done not on an *ad hoc* basis but on the basis of a notified policy formulated on some rationale criteria. Political consideration should not weight in the issue. Distribution of advertisements should be equitable as far as possible but smaller newspapers which subsist on government advertisement revenue need special consideration of the governmental authorities. While advertisements cannot be claimed by newspaper as a matter of right, they are neither a grant to be released at the whim and discretion of the controlling authority.

Against this background, the Press Council of India has considered the question of formulating basic elements of what may be an advertisement policy for the Central and State Governments to adopt. These model guidelines propose broad principles of uniform applicability governing the release of advertisement by Central and State Government. Union Territory, administration *vis-a-vis* their distribution, rate fixation and payment and canalisation.

Criteria

(1) Newspapers registered with the office of the Registrar of Newspapers for India shall be eligible for inclusion in the approved list for release of advertisements.

(2) Advertisements shall be issued only to such newspapers as have been included in the approved list of Central/State Government for release of advertisements. For preparing the approved list, there should be a committee with due representatives of officials as well as non-officials from among media personalities. For the purpose of selecting the newspapers for release of advertisements of different kinds, the authorities should be guided by the following criteria :

(a) Newspapers will be considered as being eligible for advertisement if it has had regular and uninterrupted publication for four months.

(b) A newspaper seeking advertisement should fulfil the requisite qualification already prescribed by State and Central Government in regard to periodicity and regularity of publication, size of the publication, printing arrangements, editorial and managerial set-up.

(c) The circulation of a newspaper has a bearing on the extent of advertisement released. The sources from which authenticated circulation figures could be obtained are :

(i) The Registrar of Newspapers for India;
(ii) Audit Bureau of Circulation; and
(iii) Chartered Accountant, certifying annual circulation statement.

The figures obtained through anyone of these sources should be acceptable for determining the circulation of a newspaper to be enlisted and no other party should question the certificate issued by either of the three above.

(d) Payment of bills by the government should be made within a period of 45 to 60 days of the publication of the advertisement. The payment could be made at reasonable prevalent commercial rate, less 20% commission in view of the bulk value of release.

(e) It will be desirable that small newspapers having regional content are given some weightage.

(f) Suitable weightage may also be given to language newspaper/periodicals published from remote areas, such as North-East, tribal belts and hilly region and small paper run by linguistic groups.

(g) As far as possible, organs of political parties should not be unduly patronized by the governmental authorities.

General

A list of newspapers eligible for empanelment should be made a public document available on request. The list should be periodically sent to the Press Council of India, the RNI and also to the recognised newspaper associations.

All disputes regarding inclusion/non-inclusion/removal from the approved list for release of advertisements should be referred to an independent body which may consist of representatives of the government and disinterested members of Press from socio-journalistic fields. Alternatively, dispute could be referred to a body created on the pattern of Press and Registration Appellate Board which may consist of the Chairman of the Press Council of India and four other members.

These guidelines are not exhaustive because of the limited nature of the issue involved. They have been prepared with the object to eliminate any possibility of discrimination which may directly or indirectly affect the freedom of the Press.

Press Council of India; 16th Annual Report
(1 April 1994–31 March 1995)

ANNEXURE–XI

INSTITUTIONS IMPARTING TRAINING IN JOURNALISM AND MASS COMMUNICATION

S. No.	Institution	Course offered	Eligibility	Duration	Language
1	2	3	4	5	6
1.	Aligarh Muslim University, Aligarh.	Job Oriented Certificate/Diploma in Journalism.	B. A./B. Com./B. Sc.	One year	English
2.	Andhra Pradesh Agricultural University, Hyderabad.	(i) Process of Communication	-do-	-do-	-do-
		(ii) Mass Media Communication	-do-	-do-	-do-
		(iii) Organisation Communication, Photography and Mass Communication Media as part of Ph. D. and M. Sc. in Extension Education.	-do-	-do-	-do-
3.	Annamalai University, Annamalainagar.	Certificate in Journalism	-	-	-
4.	Assam University, Silchar	PG Diploma in Journalism	Bachelor's Degree	-do-	English
5.	Avinashilingam Institute for Home Science & Higher Education for Women, Coimbatore (Tamil Nadu).	M. A. Journalism (Hindi)	A Degree with Part-I Hindi	Two years	Hindi
6.	Bangalore University, Bangalore.	(i) B. S. (Communication)	Bachelor's Degree	One year	English
		(ii) M. S. (Communication)	IInd Class B. S. Degree or IInd Class Post–graduate Diploma in Journalism/Communication	-do-	-do-
7.	Banaras Hindu University, Varanasi.	(i) Bachelor of Journalism	-do-	-do-	English & Hindi
		(ii) Master of Journalism	Bachelor of Journalism	-do-	-do-

Annexure–XI (Contd.)

1	2	3	4	5	6
8.	Berhampur University, Berhampur, Orissa.	(i) Bachelor of Journalism and Mass Communication	Graduation	One year	English
9.	Bharathidasan University, Tiruchirapally (Tamil Nadu).	PG Diploma in Mass Media	Bachelor's Degree	-do-	English
10.	Bhartiya Vidya Bhawan, Bhawan's Rajaji College of Communication and Management, Madras.	(i) Post-Graduate Diploma in Journalism	Graduation	-do- (Part time)	-do-
		(ii) Post-Graduate Diploma in Public Relations	-do-	-do-	-do-
11.	Bhartiya Vidya Bhawan, Dayanand College of Communication and Management, Chandigarh.	(i) Post-Graduate Diploma in Journalism	-do-	-do-	-do-
		(ii) Post-Graduate Diploma in Public Relations	-do-	-do-	-do-
12.	Bhartiya Vidya Bhawan, Kanpur.	Post-Graduate Diploma in Journalism & Public Relations	-do-	-do-	English & Hindi
13.	Bhavnagar University, Bhavnagar.	Diploma Course in Business Management and Journalism	Bachelor's Degree	-do-	–
14.	Bhawan's College of Communication, Hyderabad.	(i) Post-Grduation Diploma in Journalism	Graduation	-do-	English
		(ii) Post-Graduation Diploma in Public Relations	-do-	-do-	-do-
15.	Dr. Bhimrao Ambedkar Technological University (Distt. Raigarh), Maharashtra.	PG Diploma in Mass Media	Graduation (With Hindi in Inter)	-do-	–
16.	Centre of Advanced Studies in Agricultural Communication G. B. Pant University of Agriculture & Technology, Pantnagar.	(i) Master (Agricultural Communication in Science and Extensions)	B. Sc.	Two years	Hindi & English
		(ii) Ph. D.	M. Sc.	Three years	-do-

Annexure–XI (Contd.)

1	2	3	4	5	6
17.	Chaudhary Charan Singh University, Meerut.	P.G. Diploma in Journalism (Distance Education)	In service Scientists teachers and media professionals	One year	
18.	Chaudhary Charan Singh Haryana Agricultural University, Hisar.	P.G. Diploma in Agricultural English Journalism	–	-do-	English
19.	Delhi College of Art's and Commerce, University of Delhi.	Bachelor's Degree in Journalism	Senior School Certificate (Class XII)	3 Academic years	English
20.	Development & Educational Communication Unit, Indian Space Research Organisation, Ahmedabad.	(i) In Service Diploma in TV Programme, Design Production, Transmission	Not applicable	100 working days	-do-
21.	Film & Television Institute of India, Pune.	(i) Diploma in Film Direction	Graduate	Three years	-do-
		(ii) Diploma in Motion Picture Photography	Science Graduation	-do-	-do-
		(iii) Diploma in Sound Recording and Sound Engineering	-do-	-do-	-do-
		(iv) Diploma in Film Edition	Graduation	Two years	-do-
22.	Film & Television Institute of Tamil Nadu, Madras.	(i) Diploma in Cinematography	Higher Secondary with Science and Photography as a special vocational subject	Three years	English
		(ii) Diploma in Direction and Screen Play Writing	Graduation	-do-	-do-
		(iii) Diploma in Sound Engineering and Sound Recording	Higher Secondary with Science & Electronics as a	-do-	-do-

Annexure–XI (Contd.)

1	2	3	4	5	6
			vocational subject.		
		(iv) Diploma in Film Processing	Higher Secondary	Three years	English
		(v) Diploma in Film Editing	-do-	-do-	-do-
		(vi) Certificate Course in Acting	-do-	One year	-do-
23.	Garhwal University, Srinagar (Garhwal), U. P.	Bachelor of Journalism	Graduation	-do-	-do-
24.	Gauhati University,	Diploma in Journalism	Graduation with relevant subjects	-do-	-do-
25.	Gurukula Kangri Vishwavidyalaya, Hardwar	Diploma in Hindi Journalism	–	-do-	–
26.	Guru Nanak Dev University, Amritsar.	PG Diploma in Mass Media (TV & AIR)	Bachelor's Degree	Two years	–
27.	Hemwati Nandan Bahuguna Garhwal University, Garhwal.	PG Diploma in Journalism	–	One year	–
28.	Himachal Pradesh University, Shimla.	BJ & MC	Bachelor's Degree with 45% marks Admission through Entrance Test	One year	–
			BJMC	One year	English
29.	Horniman College of Journalism, Bombay.	(i) Degree in Journalism, Advertisement & Public Relations	Graduation	-do-	–
		(ii) Diploma in Journalism, Advertisement & Public Relations	-do-	-do-	English
		(iii) Certificate Course in Journalism, Advertisement and Public Relations	Non-Matric	–	-do-
30.	Indian Institute of Mass Communication, New Delhi.	(i) Post Graduate Diploma in Advertising and Public Relations	Graduation	Nine months	-do-

Annexure–XI (Contd.)

1	2	3	4	5	6
		(ii) Post-Graduate Diploma in English Journalism	-do-	-do-	-do-
		(iii) Post Graduate Diploma in Hindi Journalism Post Graduate Diploma in Radio & TV Journalism	Graduation	Nine Months	English
		(iv) Two Diplomas in News Agency Journalism	Restricted to nominees of Non-Aligned countries	Five months	-do-
		(v) Army Course for Media Communication	Army Personnel	Two weeks	-do-
		(vi) Orientation Course for Officers of Indian Information Service (IIS)	Officers of Indian Information Service	11 months	-do-
		(vii) Copy Writing	-do-	One week	–
		(viii) Refresher Course in Broadcast Journalism for Personnel of AIR and Doordarshan	For Personnel of All India Radio and Doordarshan	One month	-do-
31.	Indira Gandhi National Open University, Madidam Goshi, New Delhi.	PG Diploma in Journalism and Mass Communication	Graduate with 2 years experience in Media/Communication organisation	One year	Distance Education
32.	Institute of Correspondence Courses and Continuing Education, University of Mysore, Mysore.	(i) Diploma in Journalism	Pre-University	One year	English
		(ii) Masters Degree in Journalism and Mass Communication	Graduate	Two years	-do-
33.	Jawaharlal Nehru University, New Delhi.	Advanced Diploma in Mass Media	Graduation (with proficiency in Hindi/Urdu)	-do- (Part time)	Urdu

Annexure–XI (Contd.)

1	2	3	4	5	6
34.	Karnataka State Open University, Mysore.	Post PUC Diploma in Kannada and Journalism	10+2	One year	–
35.	Madurai Kamraj University, Madurai.	Diploma in Mass Media and Communication	Bachelor's Degree	One year	–
36.	Maharaja's College, University of Mysore, Mysore.	B. A. with Journalism as an Optional Subject	Pre-University	Three years	English
37.	Mangalore University, Mangalangothri.	M. A. in Mass Communication & Journalism	Bachelor's Degree	Two years	–
38.	Nagaarjuna University Nagaarjuna Nagar (A.P.)	M. A. in Mass Communication	B. A./B. Com./B. Sc.	-do-	–
39.	Nagpur University, Nagpur	Bachelor of Communication	Graduation after Passing B. J. Degree	One year	Marathi
40.	Osmania University, Hyderabad.	(i) Bachelor of Communication & Journalism	Graduation	-do-	English
		(ii) Master Degree of Communication & Journalism	Bachelor of Communication & Journalism	-do-	-do-
41.	Punjab University, Chandigarh.	Bachelor of Journalism	Graduation	-do-	-do-
42.	Press Institute of India, New Delhi.	Computer Journalism	-do-	Two weeks six months (part time)	-do-
43.	Punjab Agricultural University, Ludhiana (Punjab).	MJ	B. A./B. Sc./B. Sc. Agriculture with OGPA of 6.00 out of 10.00 or 60% marks or second class M. A./ M. Sc. with 2nd class graduate degree	2 semesters	English

Annexure–XI (Contd.)

1	2	3	4	5	6
44.	Punjabi University, Patiala.	(i) Bachelor of Journalism & Mass Communication	Graduation	One year	English, Punjabi, Hindi & Urdu
		(ii) Master of Journalism & Mass Communication	Bachelor's Degree of Journalism & Mass Communication	-do-	-do-
45.	Rajendra Prasad Institute of Communication & Management, Guntur.	Post Graduate Diploma in Journalism	Graduation	Nine months (part time)	English
46.	Ranchi University, Ranchi (Bihar).	PG Diploma in Journalism	Degree	Two years	–
47.	Rani Durgawati Vishwavidyalaya, Jabalpur.	Diploma in Journalism	B. Sc./B. Com. (with 50% marks)	One year	–
48.	Sardar Patel College of Communication & Management, New Delhi.	(i) Diploma in Journalism	Graduation	-do-	English
		(ii) Diploma in Public Relations	-do-	-do-	-do-
		(iii) Diploma in Marketing & Advertising	-do-	-do-	-do-
49.	Saurashtra University, Rajkot	Diploma in Journalism	Bachelor Degree	-do-	–
50.	School of Communication & Management Studies, Cochin.	(i) Post Graduate Diploma in Public Relations & Journalism	Graduate	-do- (part time)	English
		(ii) Post Graduate Diploma in Public Relations & Advertisement	-do-	-do-	-do-
		(iii) Post Graduate Diploma in Journalism	-do-	-do-	-do-
		(iv) Post Graduate Diploma in Advertising	-do-	-do-	-do-
51.	Shivaji University, Kolahpur, Maharashtra.	Bachelor of Journalism & Mass Communication	Graduation	-do- (full time)	Marathi

Annexure–XI (Contd.)

1	2	3	4	5	6
52.	Shri Amritlal Delpathbhai Sheth, Department of Journalism, Saurashtra University, Rajkot.	(i) Bachelor of Journalism & Communication	-do-	-do-	Gujarati English
		(ii) Master of Journalism & Mass Communication	Diploma or Degree in Journalism & Mass Communication	-do-	English
		(iii) Ph. D.	M. A.	Two years	-do-
53.	South Gujarat University, Surat.	Diploma in Journalism	Bachelor's Degree	One year	–
54.	Srikrishna Devaryaya University, Anantapur (A. P.)	PG Diploma in journalism	-do-	-do-	–
55.	The Times of India Group, Training Department, Bombay.	Journalism Training	Diploma of Degree in Journalism & Mass Communication	One year	-do-
56.	University of Burdwan, Burdwan (West Bengal).	PG Diploma in Journalism and Mass Communication	Bachelor's Degree	One year	–
57.	University of Calicut, Kerala.	Master of Journalism & Communication	Graduation	Two years	English
58.	University of Kerala, Thiruvananthapuram	Master of Communication & Journalism	-do-	-do-	-do-
59.	University of Madras	(i) M. A. in Journalism	-do-	-do-	-do-
		(ii) M. Phil.	Master of Communication	One year	-do-
		(iii) Ph. D. in Communication	M. A. in Communication & Inter Disciplinary	3 to 5 years	-do-
60.	University of Mysore, Department of Studies in	(i) Diploma in Journalism	Pre-University	One year Correspondance	English
	Journalism and Mass Communication.	(ii) M. A. in Journalism & Mass Comm.	Bachelor's Degree	Tow years	English
		(iii) B. A. with Journalism	Pass in the Pre-	Three years	-do-

Annexure–XI (Contd.)

1	2	3	4	5	6
		as one of the optional subjects	University or equivalent course		
61.	University of Mumbai, Mumbai.	Certificate in Journalism	+ 2 standard	One year	–
62.	University of Poona, Pune	(i) Master of Communication and Journalism	Diploma in Journalism from IIMC	-do-	English
		(ii) Bachelor of Communication & Journalism	Graduation	One year	English
		(iii) Diploma in Journalism	Higher Secondary	Six months (part time)	Marathi
63.	University of Rajasthan, Jaipur.	Post Graduate Diploma in Journalism	Graduation	One year	–
64.	Xavier Institute of Communication, Bombay.	(i) Diploma in Journalism & Development Communication	Higher Secondary	36 weeks (part time)	English
		(ii) Diploma in Public Relations	-do-	-do-	-do-
		(iii) Diploma in Advertising & Marketing	-do-	-do-	-do-
		(iv) Diploma in Film/Video Production	-do-	-do-	-do-

Universities/Institutions offering Journalism/Mass Communication Advertising/Public Relations as one of the subjects for its degree programme; Lalit Narayan Mithila University, Darbhanga, Bihar; Manipur University, Imphal, includes advertising journalism, mass media (Radio & TV as allied subjects for its degree programme; University of Mysore, Mysore South Gujarat University, Surat; Swami Ramanand Tirath Marathwada University, Nanded; Goa University, Goa; Karnatak University, Dharwad; University of Mysore, Mysore.

Sources : Universities Handbook 1997.

GLOSSARY

A.C. Nielsen Company. The world's largest market research firm, best known for network TV ratings.

ABC (Audit Bureau of Circulation). An organisation of independent media owners, advertising agencies and advertisers. Its function is to certify circulation figures for newspapers and magazines, averaged over a six month period.

ABU. Asia-Pacific Broadcasting Union.

Access broadcasting. A scheme by which members of the general public can originate and broadcast television and radio programmes.

Access. In computer terminology access denotes ability to read and make use of electronically stored data.

Account executive (AE). An advertising agency or marketing organization employee responsible for maintaining liaison with particular, ownership and range or requirements of services and their quality.

Account. A general term for the business relationship existing between an advertising agency and its clients.

Accountable. Programming term used in educational television to describe a programme meeting a specified set of instructional objectives.

Actor's equity. The professional stage actor's association in the United States that regulates actors' salaries, working conditions and terms of employment. British Actors' Equity includes film, radio and television actors in its membership.

Adversarial journalism. A style of reporting similar to investigative reporting, especially related to coverage of governmental activity that leads to exposure of wrongdoing.

Advertisement. A written, verbal, pictorial, graphic, etc., announcement of goods or services for sale, employing purchased space or time in print or electronic media.

Advertising. Messages designed to inform and persuade consumers to buy a particular product or service. They are often presented via mass media.

Advertising penetration. The degree to which people in a market have seen a particular advertisement.

Advertising strategy. The planning and directing of an advertising campaign, including research, creative concept and execution, media selection and use and marketing.

Advertorial. (1) A colloquial expression of recent origin, it commonly refers to advertisement features in newspapers on the ground that advertisers have paid for advertising space. It is blurring the distinction between editorial and advertising. This practice is generally considered unethical from strictly journalistic point of view. (2) A blend of advertisement and editorial. A combination of display advertising and editorial comment. Sometimes considered a deceptive form of advertising.

Advocacy advertising. Advertising by a company or industry that takes an editorial position on some subject of public concern, such as the environment, taxes, education, etc.

Agate line. A unit of measurement for newspaper advertising space, 1/14 of a column inch.

Agenda-setting function. The theory that media set an agenda for our thought processes, they tell us what is important and what we should know and need to know.

Aggressive-cues theory. The theory that exposure to violence on television will raise the level of excitement in the viewer.

AIDA (Attention, interest, desire, action). The four-step marketing procedure used in developing some advertising messages : Gain the audience's attention, develop their interest, motivate their desire to purchase and move them to action.

AM. Amplitude modulation of radio waves.

Anchor-person. Co-ordinating presenter of a television or radio programme.

Animation. Giving motion or lifelike appearance to in-animate objects by sequential frame by frame exposure.

Annual billings. Broadcast station's bill to advertisers for commercials carried over a one-year period.

AP (Associated Press). A print and broadcast wire service.

Apogee point at which a satellite is closest to earth.

Art department. The department of an advertising agency or advertiser responsible for the design and execution of layouts, finished arts, and mechanicals, and for the purchase of outside art services.

Artwork. Photographs, drawings, illustrations, etc. prepared for photographic reproduction.

ATS. Application Technology Satellite.

Attitude. A person's pattern of evaluative beliefs (feelings of acceptance or rejection) toward a topic, category of people, or public issue. Attitudes can be measured by attitude scales that ask people to record their patterns of belief.

Audience research. The collection of information in broadcasting to : (1) Define programme objectives. (2) Obtain feedback to evaluate performance. (3) Define commercial potential.

Auteur. A film-maker, usually a director, who creates his or her own personal style. Examples are Alfred Hitchcock, who became famous for his scary movies and Cecil B. De Mille, who developed the big historical epic with a cast of thousands.

Authoritartian theory. The prevailing belief that a ruling elite should guide the intellectually inferior masses.

Auxiliaries. Groups that provide services for media. Examples are wire services, feature syndicates, rating services and research organizations. Essentially, they provide content, feedback, or data needed in decision making.

Backmasking. Technique used to hide a message in a record or tape so that it can be heard only by playing it backward.

Banner. A main headline right across the top of a page.

Bartering. An advertising arrangement in which stations receive programming in return for providing advertising time; widespread in syndicated programming.

BBC. British Broadcasting Corporation.

Beat. A particular subject or area covered by a reporter for gathering news.

Bibliography. The list of documents, articles and books, which are relevant to a certain subject, with details of author, publisher, date of publication etc.

Billboard. The sound-recording industry trade publication that tabulates record popularity.

Bit. (1) The smallest possible unit of information. One bit is enough to tell the difference between two opposites such as yes or no. (2) In the pure binary numeration system either of the digits 0 and 1, synonymous with binary digit.

Bled-off or Bleed. An illustration placed to the edge of a printing area, so that when the paper is trimmed the picture is at the edge without margin.

Bleed (page). To print an illustration so that it goes to the very edge of the page on one or more sides, without a border or margin.

Blow up. A photographic enlargement.

Blurb. A short description of a book, story, article or other piece for promotional purposes.

Bold face. Type having thick lines and presenting a dark and heavy appearance. This type is generally used in headlines or to highlight a particular aspect of news story, feature or an article.

Boutique agency. A relatively small advertising agency that subcontracts many of its services.

Box. A printed rectangle enclosing type set matter or an illustration.

Brainstorm. To meet in a small group to attack a specific problem, usually in a limited time frame. The goal is to come up with as many ideas and solutions to the problem as possible, regardless of the quality of those ideas.

Brand. (1) A graphic symbol, tradesman or combination of both that distinguishes a product or service of one seller from those of others. (2) A line of products or services distinguished by such means as brand name, trademark.

Erand awareness. An assessment oi the number of consumers able to recall or identify a brand. This assessment is useful for evaluating the effectiveness of advertisers and promotional activities.

Brand loyalty. The consistent purchase and use of a specific product by a consumer over a period of time.

Brilliance. Television clarity of a picture i.e. contrasts ratio, audio high fidelity of sound.

Broadcast. Signals sent via radio or television.

Broadcasting. The dissemination of message via transmission over radio or television that provides for reception by the public (as opposed to closed systems).

Broadway. A boulevard in New York city that runs through the Manhattan theatre district; also the generic term for the legitimate theatre, as in the phrase "making it on broadway", implies gaining success as an actor.

Brochure. There is a large variation in bringing out brochures from a few pages to several pages. Quite often, these are attractively designed and produced to promote products or services. These are used by academic and research institutions for disseminating information about their objectives and activities.

Brownlines. Sample copies of the final edition of a magazine.

Business paper. A periodical devoted to a particular industry, trade, occupation, profession, etc.

By-line. A reporter's name at the start of the story. In some situations the author's name appears at the end.

Byte. (1) A binary character operated upon as a unit and usually shorter than a computer world. (2) The representation of a character. (3) A subdivision of a word in a machine, usually comprising eight bits.

Cable TV. A system for sending and receiving television signals by wire from a central facility in a community to homes or other locations. The central facility can pick up signals from satellites or other broadcasting sources, or it can originate its own material. The set owner is charged a monthly fee for the service.

Calligraphy. The art of lettering or writing elegantly by hand, hand lettering or hand writing.

Camera angle. The degree by which a scene is covered by a camera.

Camera-ready copy (CRC). Art work, type composed material, etc. finalized to be photographed for reproduction without further alteration.

Campaign. (1) Generally used in advertising, denotes a series of advertisements or commercials placed in one or more than one media. Before launching a campaign, a general analysis of marketing and media situation is undertaken so as to arrive at proper strategic decisions for planning ads in different advertising media. (2) In advertising, a large number of ads that stress the same theme and appear over a specified length of time.

Catharsis theory. A theory that suggests that viewing aggression will purge the viewer's aggressive feelings.

CBC. Canadian Broadcasting Corporation.

CCTV. Closed-Circuit Television.

CD-ROM. Compact disk read only memory. A high capacity optical disk on which electronic publications can be mounted.

Censor. To delete part of a message in order to prevent receivers from understanding part of its meaning. A person performing the deletions, usually on behalf of a government, is called a censorship.

Central Processing Unit (CPU). (1) A unit of a computer that includes circuits controlling the interpretation and execution of instructions. (2) The principal operating part of computer. It is usually defined as the Arithmetic and Logic Unit (ALU) and the Control Unit (CU) and sometimes (but not always) the primary memory.

Chain. A number of newspapers that are owned by one company.

Channel. The pathway by which a message travels from sender to receiver.

Character. A letter, numeral, symbol or mark of punctuation. This term is used in printing.

Chart of accounts. Ledger used to record stations finances.

Chilling effect. A commonly used term among media analysis and observes to describe the reluctance of journalists to state strong opinions or reach unpopular conclusions for fear of retaliation by the public or by the government.

Churn. In cable TV, the tendency of subscribers to cancel shortly after signing up for cable services.

Circulation. The number of copies sold to people who subscribe to or otherwise purchase a newspaper or magazine.

City editor. An editor of a newspaper who supervises the coverage of news of a local area or city in contrast with national, foreign or state editors. He or she is usually in charge of reporters covering news of a city or metropolitan area.

Class magazine. A periodical intended for a readership with a special range of common interests, which often reflect an above-average income.

Classified advertisements. Small ads generally on column basis. They are grouped under different classifications: public appointments, tender notices, property, situation vacant, educational, company notices, etc.

Classified. Small ads in newspapers without any display and classified by subject, e.g. House sales.

Clearance ratio. The number of network affiliate stations that agree to air a network programme.

CLIP. Existing shot from past video/audio material which can be used as a segment in a programme.

Code. An organised cultural system of signs, languages or symbols and its rules, which govern and allow for the communication of meanings and interpretations.

Cognitive theory. Explanations of the influence of mass communication content on individual members of audiences in terms of psychological variables, such as attitude, belief, selective perception, values, etc.

Cold type. A process in which the elements of a newspaper page are pasted down and photographed; the finished product is then transferred onto a plate for the printing press.

Collage. An illustration made by pasting photographs, line drawing, printed material, etc. used in combinations.

Column inch. A unit of measurement for newspaper advertising space; one inch deep and one column wide.

Comic strip. A panel of consecutive drawings presenting humorious situations and adventures usually found in newspapers.

Commercial. An advertisement on television or radio.

Common carrier. A communication channel that handles interstate and international communications by electronic means, and whose services are open to the public for hire.

Communication policy. Principles and plans in the development of communications technology and other issues related to communication that involve both the public and the private sector.

Communication technologies. Broad term to include all new developments in technological processes and system that aid communication i.e., cellular, radio, satellite, word processor, computer graphics, etc.

Communication. The movement of messages between senders and receivers.

Communicator. Any person who formulates a message composed of one or more symbols that is intended to result in shared meaning and directs the message toward a receiver or receivers.

Compact disc (CD). A sound system using laser technology that reproduces audio quality very precisely.

Complimentary colours. Those colours, which when combined with primary colours, produce white light, e.g. Cyan-Red, Magenta-Green, Yellow-Blue.

Composing. Assembling of types or metallic characters and symbols by hand or by machines into lines of definite measurement.

Composition. (1) The setting of type according to a predetermined layout in a form suitable for printing. (2) Visual components that make up a subjectively pleasing picture.

Compositor. The craftsman who assembles types prior to printing either by hand or by keyboard.

Comprehensive layout. The finished model of a print ad.

Computer personalization. The tailoring of a message to specific individuals by printing letters or other promotional pieces by computer, using names, addresses, special phrases or other information based on data appearing in computer records.

Computerized typesetting. Text rendered in digital form is recorded on a magnetic medium (tape or disk) and run through a computer.

Comsat. Communication Satellite Corporation (USA) formed by the Communication Satellite Act of 1992. The body which supervises international satellite communication traffic.

Concept testing. A type of media-organized feedback in which a one or two-paragraph description for a new series is presented to a sample of viewers for their reactions.

Conglomerate. A corporation or other business group that owns a number of different companies.

Congruency (in meanings). A situation in which all elements of meaning in the message of the communicator are identical with those aroused in the receiver. In other words, perfect accuracy in communication.

Consumer advertising. Advertising directed at the general public.

Consumer society. Modern complex cultures and societies which are defined by a dominant orientation towards the marketing and consumption for goods and services. These play central roles in the lifestyle and cultures of modern times and related processes, which allow for the formation of identities. In consumer cultures, groups and individuals are increasingly defined in terms of their patterns of consumption, choice and expression, as related to leisure, clothing, music, food and many other goods and activities.

Contagion effect. In a media context, the theory that reports of violence can instigate new violence.

Content analysis. A research method used to systematically measure or compare the characteristics of selected samples of media output and content.

Continuity sheet. Shooting details, written on location and used later when editing.

Contrast. The degree of difference between tones in television/film pictures.

Control group. A set of persons used in a research study. They are as similar as possible to another set who serve as an experimental group and receive some form of treatment. Because the control group does not receive the treatment, the two groups can be compared before and after the treatment of the experimental group to see if it had an effect.

Control rooms. Collective areas comprising vision, sound and lighting in a television studio complex.

Controlled circulation. A type of circulation in which publications are sent free or distributed to a select readership, such as airline passengers or motel guests.

Copy. Headlines and message in an ad.

Copyright. (1) Legal and exclusive right to publish a book, article or a work of art to produce music cassettes or make a film. It is generally denoted by the symbol ©. (2) The author, actor or playwright's legal ownership and control over production of his or her writings or play in public, and over reproduction in print of whole or huge portions of the script.

Corporate advertising. (1) Advertising that stresses the resources, skill, and/or character of a company to enhance its image, to establish a favourable market position, to redefine its mission, to pre-sell target markets, to influence the financial community, to establish a position on a specific issue, to build confidence in time of crisis, or to attract and hold quality employees. (2) Also known as institutional advertising which promotes an institution or an organization rather than its products and services.

Countdown. Signal recorded just ahead of the programme start, which provides an aural or visual indication of the number of seconds remaining before the start of the programme.

Counter programming. Airing a programme designed to appeal to a different segment of the audience than those on competing stations.

Continuity. Ensure that such items as dress, actions, backgrounds and time remain consistent when shooting takes place at different times. If incorrect, there are editing difficulties and an unconvincing result.

CPB. Corporation for Public Broadcasting.

CPM. Cost per thousand; the cost of broadcasting a commercial message to 1,000 people.

CPU. Central Processing Unit; the core of a computer, containing the processor and main memory, which reads and interprets the instructions from a computer programme.

Creative boutique. Advertising organization that specializes in the creative side of advertising.

Credibility. The trust that the audience holds for media that perform surveillance functions.

Crop. To edit or delete portions of a photograph to increase interest or change proportions.

Cross-media ownership. A situation in which a person, company or corporation owns both newspapers and broadcasting stations. The extent of such ownership is limited by law.

CRTC. Canadian Radio-Television Commission.

Cue. Signal for a programme or performer to begin.

Culture. Often understood as the 'whole way of life' which distinguishes a society or social group. Culture refers especially to the systems of ideas, beliefs and values which characterise and make up the world of the group and the systems which allow for communication, representation and meaning, from languages to computers, music and digital images.

Cume persons (cumulative audience). The number of different individuals or households watching or listening to a given station or programme at least once during a certain time period.

Cut and paste. The process of cutting up manuscript, proof, illustration, etc. and pasting or affixing the cut up material in a new arrangement.

Cycle. In all-news radio, the amount of time that elapses before the programme order is repeated.

Data base. (1) A collection of data fundamental to a system or enterprise. (2) A set of data that is sufficient for a given purpose or for one or several given data processing systems. (3) A collection of interrelated or independent data items stored together without unnecessary redundancy to serve one or more applications.

Data processing. (1) An unprinted blank version of a paper often in miniature, used for page planning. (2) The systematic performance of operations upon data such as handling, merging, sorting and computing, synonymous with information processing.

Data bank. A collection of information (data), usually held in a computer store.

Dateline. The first words of a story telling the city where the story originated.

Decoding. The activity in the communication process by which physical messages are translated into a form that has eventual meaning for the receiver.

Demography. The study of audience characteristics such as age, sex and socio economic status.

Deregulation. Relaxing the commercial controls and limitations on media imposed by the state.

Descriptive research. Research that describes a current condition.

Developmental journalism. Type of journalism practised by many Third World countries that stresses national goals and economic development.

Diary method. In a rating survey, a method of data collection utilizing a diary.

Direct broadcasting by satellite (DBS). A system in which a home TV set receives a signal directly from an orbiting satellite by installing a small dishantenna.

Direct mailing. Is the use of postal service to disseminate promotional material.

Display advertising. Newspaper or magazine advertisements that announce the availability of goods or services from merchants or other businesses.

Displayed-reward news. News that provides context and background for the consumer; for example, coverage of economic issues. Contrast with *immediate-reward news*.

Dissemination stage. In a news diffusion study, the period of time during which news spreads through a particular society.

Documentary. (1) A film that attempts to portray and explain some real-life situation, usually by filming the actual people in their own setting rather than by using actors and props. (2) A stage production consisting of quick, short scenes depicting current events or problems or modern life, and suggestions for coping with them. Mostly used for educational purposes.

Dry run. Rehearsals prior to camera rehearsals, principally for performers and some of the production teams.

Dummy. (1) A plan or blueprint for upcoming magazine issues that shows the contents in their proper order. (2) An experimental printing, not for public view.

Dysfunction. Consequences that are undesirable from the point of view of the welfare of society.

Earth station. (1) A station that transmits microwave signals to a satellite and also receives those signals. (2) Ground-based terminal of a satellite communication system.

EBU. European Broadcasting Union.

Editorial policies. Guidelines followed by a media organization with regard to certain public issues or political positions.

Editorialise. To include the opinions of a writer in a news story.

Electro magnetic. Wave energy travelling through space at the speed of light; used to transmit radio and television signals.

Electronic compositor. Computer that allows a user to arrange text easily on screen before it is electronically type set.

Electronic news gathering (ENG). Producing and airing field reports using small, lightweight portable TV equipment.

Elite press. Newspapers prepared for and distributed to well-educated and affluent members of society. More emphasis is placed on information and intellectual content than on diversion and entertainment.

Embargo. The stipulated time before which a story should not be published. Generally used in public relations handouts.

Embossing. Forming an image in relief (raised image), as by stamping.

Encoding. The activity in the communication process by which thoughts and ideas from the source are translated into a form that may be perceived by the senses.

ERI. Electronic Response Indicator.

ETV. Educational Television; all non-commercial television programming and commercial programming produced especially for educational purposes, whether or not the programme is used for direct classroom instruction.

Executive editor. The chief editorial officer of a newspaper, who usually supervises other editors and reports to the publisher.

Exit poll. Survey technique in which voters are asked whom they voted for as soon as they leave the polling booth. Used to make computer projections of election winners.

Experimental group. Those subjects in an experiment who receive some form of treatment. They are compared with the control group both before and after the experiment to see if the treatment produced some effect.

Fair use. Under copyright law, people can use copies of the protected work for legitimate purposes.

FCC. Federal Communications Commission.

Feedback. Information received in response to information already imparted.

Field experiment. An experiment that is conducted in a natural setting as opposed to a laboratory.

Field of experience. The accumulation of knowledge, experiences, values, beliefs and other qualities that make up a person's identity.

File. A set of related records treated as a unit; for example, in stock control, a file could consist of a set of invoices e.g. audit review file, back up file details file, inverted file, master file, transaction file.

Fixed position. An advertising term referring to a commercial placed at the same time every day.

Floppy disk/diskette. A thin, flexible magnetic disk and a semi-rigid protective jacket, in which the disk is permanently enclosed. It is used for information storage and retrieval. Data can be directly transferred from one place and terminal to another.

Focus group. A group of ten to fifteen people led by a moderator that discusses predetermined topics.

Font. A complete assortment of a given size and style of type including capitals, small capitals and lower case together with numerals, punctuation marks and commonly used symbols.

Footage. Measurement in feet of film or tape.

Foot-note. An explanatory note placed at the foot of the text on the same page.

Footprint. That area of the earth's surface designated as the reception zone from a satellite.

Forfeiture. The most common sanction imposed on a station by the FCC. It is based on the violation and on the ability of the station to pay.

Format. (1) Consistent programming designed to appeal to a certain segment of the audience. (2) The shape, size, style and general appearance of a book as determined by type, margins, etc.

Franchise. An exclusive right to operate a business in a given territory.

Freebies. Special favours, gifts, or services provided to reporters, magazine writers, or broadcasters in order to influence their reports on the activities of the giver in a favourable direction.

Freeze frame. The repetition of a single television or film frame to produce a stationary image.

Frequency spectrum. The total range of wave frequencies that can be used in broadcasting.

Full-service agency. An ad agency that handles all phases of advertising for its clients.

Gatekeeper. (1) A journalist, including the editor, who filters and regulates the flow of news stories in order to select which stories will be presented to the audience. The term is also applied to other decision-makers within media and cultural industries. (2) A person entrusted with the task of regulating the flow of information.

Geostationary (synchronous) satellite. An orbiting, satellite travelling at a speed proportional to that of the earth's rotation and thus appearing to remain stationary over one point on the earth.

Globalisation/global culture. The results of greatly increased worldwide media and communication systems and the activities of international cultural markets. The local and the national are now linked in many ways to a wider world culture. Globalisation refers to the international economic, political and cultural processes which have accelerated this growth during the nineties.

Global village. A phrase which is used to describe the ways in which modern electronic media have spread around, interconnected and 'shrunk' the world, making possible seemingly immediate forms of communication and cultural relationships.

Golden age of radio. Generally, the period from 1926 to 1948, from the advent of the networks to the decline of network radio.

Graphics. (1) Illustrations/text which enhance a programme. A creative field using computers and other means. (2) Words and figures used on television screens, often specially drawn, as titles, illustration of statistics, etc.

Grazing. Method of TV watching in which a viewer rapidly scans all the available channels using a remote-control device.

Handout. A news item sent around to newspapers by a public relations office.

Hard copy. (1) In computer graphics, a permanent copy of a display image that is portable and can be read directly for example a display image that is recorded on paper. (2) A printed copy or a machine output in a visually readable form; for example, printed reports, listings, documents and summaries.

Hardware. (1) Physical equipment used in data processing as opposed to programmes, procedures, rules, and associated documentation. (2) The physical portion of a computer system including the electrical/electronic components (e.g. devices and circuits), electromechanical components (e.g. disk drive), mechanical (e.g. cabinet) components.

HDTV (High Definition Television). (1) One of a number of competing standards for providing enhanced television images by means of increased scanning lines, higher band width and larger aspect ratio. (2) High-resolution television system that uses over a thousand scanning lines as compared with traditional 525-line system.

Highlights. Maximum brightness of the picture occurring in areas of highest illumination.

Holography. Three-dimensional lensless photography by means of a laser beam.

Home terminal. (1) Receiving set for cable TV transmissions, either one-way or two way (2) Device connecting the drop cable of a cable system to the receiving set.

House drop. The section of the CATV cable that connects the feeder cable to the subscriber's TV set.

House journal. A periodic publication used for informing the various publics of an organisation about its activities.

House magazine. A publication edited and published within a company or organisation, usually, but not always, designed for internal distribution.

HUF. The ultra-high frequency band of the electromagnetic spectrum.

Hyping. Using promotional efforts to increase the size of an audience during a rating period.

Hypodermic needle model. A theory which assets that the media are powerful agents of influence, capable of 'injecting' ideas and behaviours directly into relatively passive audiences of isolated individuals.

Hypothesis. A formal statement that poses a possible independent/dependent relationship between variables under study in a research project.

Indent. To set a line of type so that it begins or ends inside the normal margin..

Independent network. A programme-originating U.S. commercial broadcast network not associated with "the big three" : NBC, CBS and ABC.

Induction process. By which a current in one antenna produces a current in a nearby antenna.

Influence. Changing a person's understandings, feelings, beliefs, opinions, attitude, or even behaviours in any way.

Information society. A society in which more of the labour force is involved in the production, processing or dissemination of information than in the production of goods or crops. The United States passed that point in the early 1980s.

Injunction. A court order that requires an individual to do something or to stop doing something.

Innovations. New ideas, technical intentions, or forms of behaviour that a population adopts.

Institutional advertising. A form of long-range advertising designed to create a particular construction of reality—the image of a company as whole some, responsible or concerned about the important things.

Instrumental surveillance. A media function that occurs when the media transmit information that is useful and helpful in everyday life.

Interactive cable system. An arrangement whereby signals can be sent from the head end to the home and also from home to the head end. Also known as two-way TV.

Interface. The connection among computer hardware, software and people.

International media flow. The patterns of import and export, media production and consumption which result from the operation of world wide media and cultural markets for films, television programmes, music, etc. Some countries and regions produce and export, others import and consume. Such patterns of 'flow' have important consequences for identity and globalisation.

Internet. Globally interconnected telecommunication and computer network systems which allow for diverse forms of interactivity and data interchange. The internet is making rapid headway even in developing countries like India.

Interpersonal communication. A method of communication in which one person (or group) interacts with another person (or group) without the aid of a mechanical device.

Intrapersonal communication. Communication within ourselves.

Inverted pyramid style. A somewhat standardized format for presenting a news story. In this format the reporter explains clearly what happened to whom with what causes and consequences and gives the most important facts first, those next in importance second, and so on to the minor details.

Investigative reporting (or journalism). A style of reporting that emphasizes the careful assembly of facts in order to gain the inside story and expose wrongdoing.

Ionosphere. The upper level of the atmosphere, which reflects radio waves back to earth.

ISBN. An International Standard Book Number (ISBN) is assigned to each book by its publishers. The ISBN identifies the book and facilitates placing the order and computer tracking of inventory.

Jacket. A protective wrapping usually paper for a cloth bound book. It carries the blurb (promotional copy) on its flaps which fold around the front and back covers.

Jargon. The technical or characteristic terminology used by persons of a given industry.

Jazz journalism. A form of *yellow journalism* that persisted into the twentieth century. It was characterized by the *tabloid* format and the extensive use of dramatic photographs.

Jingles. A set of short musical recordings. All designed around a common musical theme and usually related to a station's call letters.

Junk mail. Unsolicited mail just as pamphlets, brochures offering discounts, catalogues marked by organisations to publicise their products or services.

Kitsch. Art forms that are of low quality or are poor imitations of more sophisticated products or styles. Many critics claim that most entertainment produced for the mass media is *kistsch.*

Layout. A diagram or sketch intended to show the planned contents and visual appearance including headlines, text, illustrations, logo, etc. of an advertisement, printed page, poster and so forth.

Leaflets. Usually a one-page printed document containing an announcement or message. They are used mainly as a medium of last resort for disseminating messages under conditions where alternative channels are not available, such as in situations of political repression, war or disaster or wherever more sophisticated media are unavailable or inoperative. They are often presented to their intended audiences by airdrops or are handed from one person to another surreptitiously.

Legacy of fear. A set of beliefs shared by the public that mass communications are powerful and dangerous; that is, that they can and sometimes do produce socially undesirable effects on their audiences.

Letterpress. A printing technique in which the ink is carried by raised surfaces as opposed to intaglio where recessed surfaces carry the ink and planography where the printing surfaces are flush with the non-printing surface.

Libel per quod. Written material that becomes libelous under certain circumstances.

Libel *per se*. Falsely written accusations (such as labeling a person a "thief" or a "swindler") that automatically constitute libel.

Libel. The act of publishing material with the intent of damaging a person's reputation.

Libertarian theory. The assumption that all human beings are rational decision makers and that governments exist to serve the individual.

Linkage. The ability of the mass media to join different elements of society that are not directly connected by interpersonal channels.

Linotype machine. A machine for moulding line of type from hot metal.

Lithography. A printing method in which an image is applied to a stone or metal plate, then washed with an acid solution. Ink is then applied to the surface, adhering to the image portion only.

Live. A studio performance transmitted as it takes place, compared with telecine or video.

Local media. The communications media whose audiences are drawn primarily from the same locality as the media. These media customarily have preferential rate for local advertisers.

Longitudinal study. Research that follows the behaviour of a group of subjects over a long time, such as several years. The study systematically notes changes in the behaviour that can be attributed to known influences.

Lower case. The uncapitalised letters of a font (abbreviated lc).

Low-power television (LPTV). A TV station that broadcasts with lower power than the normal broadcast station and that has a coverage area of twelve to fifteen miles in radius.

M.N.C. Multi-national corporations generally considered to be very large companies with production units in several countries. Several large M.N.Cs have made their presence felt in TV, advertising and film production.

Macroanalysis. A sociological perspective that considers the functions performed by a system (i.e. mass media) for the entire society.

Madison avenue. The highly publicised street in New York city that has become a synonym for the home of the advertising agencies, although few major agencies are still on Madison Avenue.

Magic bullet theory. An explanation of the effects of exposure to mass media content. The explanation assumes that all subjects will receive some critical feature of the message (the magic bullet) that will change them in the same way. Also called *hypodermic needle theory, stimulus-response theory*.

Major-media. The five principal advertising media : Press, Television, Posters, Radio and Cinema.

Makeup. The arranging of type lines and illustrations into page form.

Management By Objectives (MBO). Management technique that sets observable, measurable goals for an organization to achieve.

Market research. Investigations based on applied social science techniques that try to discover what consumers want in a product, why they do or do not buy it and what might lead them to purchase it more frequently. A frequent topic of such research is the effectiveness of advertising.

Market segmentation. The principle that only certain types of categories of people are likely to buy a particular product. For example, it is unlikely that the same segments of the general public will buy yachts, do-it-yourself plumbing parts and rock albums. Their buyers differ in age, income and other variables. Market research can identify these segments, but advertisers must devise messages that will gain their attention and sell the product See *law of right people*.

Marketing approach (to journalism). The practice of making editorial decisions on the basis of market research on readers and their needs and wants.

Mass. Members of a society with a specific set of characteristics : the mass is made up of relatively unorganized people, not members of binding groups or families, who tend to act and react as individuals rather than as members of a group following norms and roles.

Mass communication. The process by which messages are communicated to a large number of people by a mass medium.

Mass media (Mass communication). Organised and specialised modern media institutions such as the press, cinema and broadcasting, whose principal business involves the supply of different forms of information and entertainment. Mass communication is used to describe what these agencies do, what they produce. Attached to both terms and others, for example 'mass audience' is the prefix 'mass'. This carries a series of one-dimensional assumptions about the homogeneity of the audience and the direct influence of the media. In these days of de-massified media the influence of mass media is being seriously questioned.

Mass society. A society in which traditional socialites based loyalty, fealty, and family obligations have eroded due to immigration, industrialization, urbanization and modernization. The society becomes increasingly complex in its structure and its people more differentiated. Under such conditions, informal interpersonal bonds become weak and individuals are more socially isolated. Informal agreements tend to be replaced by more formal contracts backed by the authority of the state.

Master control. Console the heart of a TV control room through which both the audio and the video images are fed, joined together and improved, perhaps by special effects, for the on-air image.

Master control room. Co-ordinating centre for technical facilities of a television/radio complex.

Master print. Master film positive used to produce dupe negatives.

Measure. The length of composed line.

Media. Plural of medium; vehicles used to convey information, entertainment, news and advertising messages to an audience. Includes radio, television, cable television, newspapers, magazines, outdoor boards, etc.

Media access movement. Efforts, largely by minority groups and other special interests, to get access to the media for the purpose of having their views heard.

Media and cultural imperialism. The use of media and communication systems to establish world wide influence and dominance. International media and their markets are significant networks for political and cultural values and forms of identity. Many 'developing nations' face problems maintaining cultural autonomy and independent identity in the face of western and other forms of media export and output. The issues concerning media and cultural imperialism have often been articulated passionately from the Third World perspective.

Media buying service. Organization that specializes in buying media time for advertisers.

Media credibility. The effect of various media on how mass-communication, messages are perceived.

Media production. The organised processes and activities involved in making the distributing media texts and output requiring groups or teams of people working in a variety of commercial, technical and media settings.

Media regulation. The laws, rules and guidelines which operate to define and restrict the parameters of what can be legitimately produced in the media. These may originate from state government, commercial or other bodies and agencies.

Media saturation. The term is generally used to describe the centrality and pervasiveness of the media and of mediated experience in the modern, contemporary society implying increasing involvement of the media in public, national and global life; the growth of time and expenditure spent in private, everyday media involvement, and the popularity of media-related or media-derived activities. As a result, media are held to 'saturate' society, culture and identity.

Media service organizations. A variety of organizations that for a fee provide specialized services for advertising agencies. They buy newspaper space or time on radio or television, and provide talent or other needed services.

Media-originated feedback. Feedback consisting of information about the audience that media industries go out of their way together.

Medium channel of communication. Such as radio or television; singular of media.

Memory. (1) The high-speed, large-capacity storage of a digital computer. (2) A device or medium that can retain information for subsequent retrieval. The term is synonymous with storage or store although it is most frequently used for referring to the internal storage of a computer that can be directly addressed by operating instructions.

Menu. A display of all the options in an interactive computer programme that are available to the user at the computer terminal.

Message. (1) A symbol or configuration of symbols that can arouse similar meanings in both sender and receiver. (2) The actual physical product in the communication process that the source encodes.

Microanalysis. A sociological perspective that considers the functions performed by a system (i.e. mass media) for the individual.

Microprocessor. (1) An integrated circuit that accepts coded instructions for execution; the instructions may be entered, integrated or stored internally. (2) A semi-conductor chip or chip set that implements the central processor of a computer. Microprocessors consist of at a minimum, an arithmetic and a logic unit and a control unit.

Microwave. A very short wave of higher frequency than that of standard broadcast transmission; usually measured in gigahertz (billions of cycles per second).

Millimeter waves. A generic term referring to electromagnetic waves that are between a centimeter and a millimeter long.

Mixed-media performance. A presentation that mixes live performers with electronic elements, such as projected slides, filmstrips, films, videotapes and recorded music. The form is also called multimedia.

Modem. A functional unit that modulates and demodulates signals. One of the functions of a modem is to enable digital data to be transmitted over analog transmission facilities.

Monitor. Television screen in control room or studio so that producers, performers and technicians can see what is being transmitted.

Multinational multimedia conglomerates. Very large commercial organisations whose operations involve competition in world wide markets across a range of television, film, press, music and other information and cultural sectors.

Multiple System Operator (MSO). A cable company that owns more than one cable system.

Multistage flow (of information). A process by which a message is passed on from a person who originally received it from a medium. It passes through a number of additional people, often in complex chains.

Narrowcasting. The opposite of broadcasting, where programmes are aimed at quite specific, special-interest or minority audiences.

National advertiser. Advertiser who sells a product all across the country.

National development. The process of social and cultural change by which traditional societies are modernized.

Network. (1) A national or regional organization distributing radio or television programmes for a substantial part of each broadcast day to stations for simultaneous broadcasting, generally by interconnection facilities. (2) An organization composed of interconnecting broadcasting stations that cuts costs by airing the same programmes.

New media technologies. The large-scale technical developments in communication systems and their cultural consequences. The term is also used to refer to cable, satellite, digital and other computer based media in the current phase.

News diffusion. The spread of information through a society over time.

News perspective. A set of criteria used by news personnel in deciding whether and how to present a news item. They take into account a story's commercial value (that is, its likely effect on their rating), their limited resources, the availability of alternatives, the audience and their competitors' practices.

Newsbreak stage. The time it takes for reporters to transmit the essential facts of a story back to a media organization, which in turn publishes or broadcasts the news.

Newshole. The amount of space available each day in a newspaper for news.

Newspaper. A publication that regularly prints and distributes news of general interest to a broad audience, or of more specialized interest to some category of people. There are dozens of types of newspapers published by various groups for a variety of purposes.

Noise. In communication, anything that interferes with the delivery of a message.

O.B. Outside broadcast, i.e. live transmission from outside a studio.

Objective reporting. An impersonal style of news reporting that emphasizes the facts rather than the reporter's interpretations or opinions.

Observational learning. A form of education in which individuals learn by observing the actions of others.

Offset printing. The method of printing in which the printing is not done direct from printing surface but is done at first by transferring the impression on to a rubber cylinder which in turn gives over the ink on to the paper.

Ombudsperson. An individual in a media organization assigned to handle complaints from audience members.

On air. A 'live' broadcasting source.

On-line editing. High quality process employing sophisticated computer-assisted vision/sound editing/processing equipment.

Opinion leader. (1) One to whom others turn for guidance, advice and information. Substantial communication research has been conducted involving this concept evolved by Paul F. Lazarsfeld. (2) Person interpreting messages originally disseminated by the mass media.

Oridinal measurement. Arranging phenomena with respect to some quantitative attribute, by ranking them from first to last position.

Outdoor advertising. The use of posters, painted displays, billboards, spectaculars and other display advertising along highways, on walls, roofs and so on. See transit advertising.

Output. Pertaining to a device, process, channel involved in an output process, or referring to the data or states involved in an output process.

Page proof. A page-size piece of paper with all the elements–type, photos and illustrations–positioned in their proper places.

Pagination. Page makeup is sometimes referred to as pagination in computer terminology.

Panel study. A research method in which data are collected from the same individuals at different points in time.

Parasocial relationship. A situation whereby audience members develop a sense of kinship or friendship with media personalities.

Participant observation. A method of conducting research in which an observer joins a group (with or without disclosing the true purpose) and makes detailed observations of behaviour while acting as a member.

Partisan paper. A newspaper published or controlled by a political party or interest group and presenting its point of view more or less exclusively.

Pay T.V. A system of distributing television programmes, motion pictures, etc. over the air or by cable, for which subscribers pay on an individual per programme.

Peoplemeter. A mechanical device used to measure TV viewing that electronically records individual TV watching data.

Perception (perceive, perceiving). For human beings, the mental activity of organizing the input of one's senses (sight, hearing, touch, and smell) into interpretations that make sense in terms of one's culture and past experience. In other words, interpreting stimuli in meaningful ways.

Persistence of vision. Quality of the human eye that enables it to retain an image for a split second after the image has actually disappeared.

Personal computer. (1) A low cost, portable computer with software oriented towards, easy, single user applications. (2) A general purpose single user microcomputer designed to be operated by one person at a time. Personal computers range from cheap domestic or hobby machines with limited memory, programme storage on cassette tape, and an ordinary TV as the display device, to extremely sophisticated machines with powerful processors, large capacity disk storage, high resolution colourgraphics, systems and many other options.

Personal influence. Changes in people's beliefs, attitudes, or behaviour brought about by messages received by personal, face-to-face communication.

Photocomposition machine. High-speed, computerized device that translates electronic impulses into images and words.

Physical noise. Breakdown in communication caused by some physical quality or object interfering with the communicative process.

Pictographic writing. An early form of writing in which ideas were represented by simple drawings. Arranged in a sequence, the drawings could tell a story; but because the meanings of the drawings were not standardized, interpretation was not always precise.

Pictorial journalism. Reporting the news or other significant events through photographs.

Pilot testing. A process that involves showing a sample audience an entire episode of a show and recording their reactions.

Pluralism. The theory that power is exercised by interest groups in society, and is reflected in the diversity of ideas and views found in the media.

Point. It is the unit of measurement according to which types are made and is approximately 1/72 part of an inch.

Political advertising. The use of commercials and advertisements to influence elections and government by persuading voters and government officials to behave voluntarily in a recommended manner.

Popular culture. The everyday activities, styles and way of life of ordinary people, including media forms such as pop music and television. It is often dismissed as trashy and throwaway in contrast to the perceived superiority and demands of 'high' culture such as classical music or literature. Popular culture may articulate tensions or challenges to the dominant *status quo*.

Popular press. Newspapers that are prepared for and distributed to people in all levels of society, especially those in the middle and lower levels. They give less emphasis to intellectual content than to entertainment.

Pornography. Printed material, pictures or movies that give explicit portrayals of people in sexual situations. In particular, material of this type that is according to the standards of the community in which it is available, obscene and without redeeming social value such as might be found in a work of art.

Portfolio. A collection of one's personal work.

Portrayal. The representation of some aspect of social life or physical events or situations to which works or other symbols are associated. Portrayals in this sense show the meanings we share for words.

Positioning. In advertising, stressing the unique selling point of a product or service to differentiate it from the competition.

Precision journalism. A form of reporting that makes extensive use of the methods of social science, such as pools, surveys and statistical analysis.

Preface. Part of a book in the preliminary section.

Press Council. An independent agency whose job it is to monitor the day-to-day performance of the media.

Primary colours. In television, red, green and blue are the basic colours from which all other colours can be obtained.

Prime time. (1) The time of the largest audience, when a station charges the highest price for advertising : 7 to 11 p.m. for TV, 7 to 9 a.m. and 4 to 6 p.m. for radio (Radio prime time varies with the market and lifestyle trends). (2) The broadcast periods viewed or listened to by the greatest number of persons and for which a station charges the most for air time.

Print media. The mass media that are not broadcast : newspapers, magazines, periodicals and direct mail.

Producer. Television/Film. (1) Person responsible for the overall production. (2) Financial backer for a production. Radio In-charge of a production.

Professional journal. A journal written primarily for a specific group of individuals, such as lawyers, physicians, or journalists.

Programming. In radio and TV, deciding what programmes to produce and where to place them in the schedule.

Proof. An impression of type taken for comparison with the original copy to determine whether there are typographical mistakes. There are several types of proofs : galley proof is the first proof pulled after setting the matter. Author's proof (page proof) is the proof altered, corrected or passed by the author.

Proof-reader. A person required to mark corrections on the proofs to point out typographical errors.

Proof-reader's marks. The marks made by a proo-freader indicating various corrections. These marks are precisely understood by the compositors and editors and are internationally accepted.

Propaganda. (1) Media images and campaigns which are designed and managed to promote or discredit a particular point of view, ideology or party line. This is achieved through emphasis, manipulation, selection or suppression of information and imagery, with the aim of persuading audiences. (2) Mass communication content–whether news, stories, advertisements, dramas, and so on–that is deliberately designed to change the beliefs, attitudes or behaviour of an audience.

Prosocial behaviour. A general term used by researchers to describe behaviours that are judged to be desirable or worthwhile under the circumstances.

Psychographics. A term referring to such things as the attitudes, values, beliefs, and opinions of an audience.

Public opinion poll. Measures of the public's beliefs or feelings about an issue or topic. These measures are obtained by interviewing various kinds of samples of persons in the population under study, usually with a standardized questionnaire prepared for the purpose.

Public relations (PR). (1) The deliberate, planned and sustained effort to establish and maintain mutual understanding between an organisation and its public. (2) The process of influencing the attitudes and opinions of a group of persons in the interest of promoting a person, product, idea, institution, etc.

Public service broadcasting. The policy enshrined within the BBC under John Reith and carried into all aspects of broadcasting in the UK until the 1990.

Broadcasting act. The policy guaranteed broadcasters a degree of autonomy from both commercial pressures and political interests in their mission to provide services for the national audience that 'informed, educated and entertained'. In the Indian context, Public Service Broadcasting has special significance.

Publicity. A generalised expression often used for public relations, advertising, information, promotion, etc.

Query. A question or clarification addressed to the author or editor on a manuscript or a proof.

Random access. A method of providing or achieving access memory units to retrieve data, is constant and independent of the location of the item addressed earlier.

Random sampling. Selection process in which each unit of the larger portion has an equal chance of being selected.

Rating. The ratio of listeners to a particular station to all people in the market.

Reach. The estimated number of households or individuals in the audience of a television or radio programme, group of programmes or announcement, at least once over some specified period.

Receiver. A person to whom a message has been sent and who perceives and understands that message.

Reinforcement. Support of existing attitudes and opinions by certain messages.

Relay satellite. A satellite capable of bouncing messages back to earth.

Reliability. The degree to which a form of measurement will produce consistent results. For example, a tape measure used repeated to measure a given board will give very consistent (that is, very reliable) results. An IQ test given to a person on different occasions may give less consistent results.

Repeater satellite. A satellite that can both receive signals and retransmit them back to earth.

Representative sample. A sample in which the elements selected for study are distributed into relevant categories in the same proportion as those of the population from which they were selected.

Resonance. In cultivation analysis, the situation in which a respondent's life experiences are reinforced by what is seen on TV, thus reinforcing the effect of TV content.

Review. The announcement in print or broadcast media of a production with some description of the cast, plot and technical aspects. Although the review may offer an opinion, it is not generally considered a piece of serious criticism. However, since a favourable review can make a show a success and a negative one can finish a play, those involved in a production generally take reviews seriously. It is the practice to quote from good reviews in press releases and in paid advertisements for a play. Book reviews are useful source for the readers to keep themselves abreast of the latest publications.

Role-taking. The use of feedback (from a receiver) by a communicator to judge which symbols will best indicate to a receiver the intended meanings of his or her message.

Rough layout. Early version of a print ad.

Run on. Continue the line or para.

Running head. The name of the book or the chapter placed at the top of each page.

Sampling frame. A complete list of the elements in a population from which a sample is to be drawn. An example would be the names of every resident in a community from which a sample of subjects is to be selected.

Sampling the process. Examining a small portion of something in order to estimate its characteristics.

Satellite news gathering (SNG). Using specially equipped vans and trucks to transmit live stories from any location via satellite.

Saturation schedule. The airing of a heavy load of commercials over a short period of time.

Sedition. Committing any act that brings damage to the government; for example, publishing materials that advocate the overthrow of the government. It has on occasion been illegal in the United States to publish anything that scorned, abused or showed contempt for the federal government, its flag or even the uniform of the armed forces (Sedition Act of 1918).

Selective exposure. Exposing oneself to communication believed to coincide with one's preconçeived ideas.

Selective perception. Perceiving only those things that agree with one's preconceived ideas.

Selective retention. Remembering only those things that agree with one's preconceived ideas.

Selectivity. The principle that members of an audience select content from the mass media that is related to their interests, needs, predispositions, and other psychological characteristics.

Semantic noise. Breakdown in communication caused by misunderstanding the meaning of words.

Share. Numerical information provided by rating services concerning the per cent of households who have a television set in use who are tuned into a particular station (viewing a specific programme) during a given time period.

Silk-screen printing. A stencil process in which ink is forced through the pores of a fabric screen bearing a reverse image of the design to be printed.

Simple random sample. A sample in which every element that is selected has exactly the same probability of being included.

Slander. (Spoken defamation). (In many states, if a defamatory statement is broadcast, it is considered to be libel, even though technically the words are not written. Libel is considered more harmful and usually carries more serious penalties).

Small caps. (1) An alphabet of small capital letters, usually the height of the font's normal x-height. (2) Capital letters that are smaller than the regular or full capitals of a font.

SMATV. Satellite Master-Antenna Television; A system that receives signals from satellite.

Snap. A brief news message slightly less important than a Flash.

Soap opera. A dramatic radio or television programme, usually presented daily, with continuing characters and multiple plots. The action deals with contemporary problems and continues from episode to episode. Called soap operas because many of the original sponsors were soap manufactures.

Social categories theory. The view that a person's habits of selecting particular types of media content and responding to them in distinctive ways is heavily influenced by norms and other shared influences that characterize the social categories of which he or she is member (for example, race, education, income, occupation, and so on).

Social learning theory. A general psychological theory that attempts to explain how people acquire behavioural patterns by observing such patterns in social settings. It is a complex theory that involves many assumptions and factors.

Social relationship theory. The view that a person's habits of selecting particular types of media content and responding to them in distinctive ways are heavily influenced by the persons with which he or she has binding social ties (for example, family and friends).

Social responsibility theory. The belief that the press has a responsibility to preserve democracy by properly informing the public and by responding to society's needs.

Socialization. The ways in which an individual comes to adopt the behaviour and values of a group.

Software. (1) Computer jargon for programmes designed to achieve a specific purpose, such as the transmission of information from one computer to another, to use a computer for word processing or to enable it to perform calculations. In computers the machines are referred to as *hardware* and the people who use them as *liveware*. (2) Programmes, procedures, rules and any associated documentation pertaining to the operation of a computer system.

Source. The originator of a thought or idea subsequently transmitted to others in the communication process.

Space. The metal units for spacing out a line of type, namely, hair, thin, mid, thick.

Stand by. Cue that a programme is about to start.

Statistical analysis. The use of specialized mathematical procedures to study the characteristics of a set of data (numerically recorded observations). Various procedures are used to determine averages or other central tendencies, variation (scatter, dispersion), and correlations.

Stet. Let it stand, the term used to denote that the copy or word is to be left as it is. The words affected are underlined with dots and the word 'stet' written in the margin.

Stigma. Any negative quality imposed on someone, such as the assumption that a member of a given racial category may be intellectually inferior or that mentally ill people are dangerous.

Stimulation theory. A theory that suggests viewing violence will actually stimulate an individual to behave more violently.

Story board. (1) Series of rough drawings that show the key shots of a production. (2) A series of drawings depicting the key scenes in an ad.

Straight cash deal. In TV syndication, a station pays a fee to a syndicator and retains the right to sell all the commercial spots in the programme.

Strategic planning. Management technique that sets long-range goals.

Strategy. A communication act planned before hand, which is deliberate and has a clear purpose, is used to deal with a particular group or situation.

Style. Rules of uniformity in matters of punctuation, form of the abbreviations, capitalization, word division, spellings, numerals and other details of expression. House style is the set of rules adopted by a particular publishing house or a newspaper establishment. Style book is a booklet or list of rules stating a newspaper preference about above details. The style book contributes to the uniformity in the style and thus convenience of the readers.

Sub heads. Headings or titles for sections within a chapter or article. Sub heads are usually set in type different from that of the text.

Superscript. In mathematics or tabular material, a small numeral, letter, fraction or symbol that prints partly above the x-height.

Surveillance. The news and information function of the mass media.

Survey. A technique of gathering data that typically uses a questionnaire.

SYNC. Abbreviation for synchronise, synchronisation, etc.

Syndicate (feature syndicate). A group that prepares and provides specialized (feature) material to printed news media for a fee; for example, comics, editorial cartoons, political commentaries, gossip columns, crossword puzzles and serialized books.

Syndicated programming. Programming distributed directly to the stations, not through a network, although it may have first appeared on a network.

Syndicator. Company supplying syndicated programming to local stations.

Tabloid. (1) A newspaper of less than standard page size, normally 14½ inches high by 12 inches wide, with five or six columns and between 1,00 and 1,200 agate lines per page. A small format newspaper characterized by extensive pictorial matter and sensational stores. (2) A newspaper whose pages are usually about five columns wide or about half the size of a standard newspaper page. Tabloids were originally associated with sensationalism; but today the term more commonly applies only to format, not to content.

Tactical planning. Management technique that sets range goals.

Target audience. In advertising, the segment of the population for whom the product or service has an appeal.

Tear sheet. A page cut or torn from a book or periodical.

Technological determinism. An overemphasis on the role of technology and machines as the principal, if not the sole cause of social, cultural and historical change and development.

Telecommunication. Electronic communication involving both wired and unwired, one-way and two-way communication systems.

Telecommuting. Using computers, modems and phone lines to transmit information and data from the home to the office instead of commuting.

Teleprompter. A device, by which a performer is able to read a script optically imaged in front of a camera lens.

Telerecording. The technique of transferring a television programme to film.

Teleshopping. To purchase goods or services from the home; using telephone, interactive videotex, cable television shopping channels.

Teletext. Electronic news delivery system in which the viewer uses a computer to select information from a broad spectrum of electronic pages that can be viewed on a TV screen.

Trade-out. An agreement in which a product or service is traded for advertising on a station.

Transaction. The process whereby information is sent and received and feedback occurs.

Transmit to send information.

Transponder. A receiver/transmitter in a communications satellite.

Transpose. To switch the positions of two words, sentences and paragraphs or to move copy from one position to another, it is used in proofreading and editing.

Trunk cable. The primary cable or main transmission line of a cable-TV system.

Two-step flow of communication. A process by which information, such as an advertising message, is disseminated; the listener, viewer or reader passes on the information or advertising message received from a mass medium to others.

Type. A single metal letter or character. Type family : Various forms of the same type face (roman, bold, italics, condensed, etc.). Type size : size of type calculated in points which refers to the height of printed character. Type face : type style of font or set of characters designed in a certain style and given a special name.

Typographical error. An error made by the compositor also called printers error.

Universe. The whole from which a sample is being chosen. In broadcast ratings, this can be the sample area, metro area, or rating area.

UPI. United Press International; a print and broadcast wire service.

Upper case. The capital letters of a type font.

Uses and gratifications research. The study of psychological variables that provide motivations and rewards for individuals who develop particular patterns of exposure to media content.

Uses-and-gratifications model. A model proposing that audience members have certain needs or drives that are satisfied by using both non-media and media sources.

Validity. An assessment of how well a given form of measurement actually quantifies what it is designed to measure. For example, a common tape measure provides another valid measure of length, but an IQ test may be less valid measure of a person's actual intellectual ability.

Vanity press (or subsidy publishing). The system for publishing an author's work in which he or she pays all the costs of producing the work.

Variety : The entertainment industry trade publication.

VHF. The very high frequency band of the electromagnetic spectrum.

Videodisc. A device such as a long-playing record that produces both a TV picture and sound.

Video-display terminal (VDT). An electronic display keyboard widely used for the composition and printing of news copy. It is capable of storing typed information that can later be called out on the viewing screen for further design and editing.

Videotex. Electronic news delivery system in which the viewer interacts with the computer in selecting the exact content choice desired.

Vision mixer. Control-room technician who at the director's instruction switches from one studio camera to another, introduces film or video-tape, etc. into a programme.

Visualisation. (1) Process by which concepts are translated into visual terms. (2) The process of producing a sketch, layout and so on, from a mental image.

VOA. Voice of America.

Voice over. Narration/dialogue as support to the visual content. The speaker is unseen.

Voyeurism. The practice of gaining pleasure from looking at other people whilst remaining anonymous : most frequently associated with men deriving sexual pleasure from looking at women.

Warning (Beware) Surveillance. A media function that occurs when the media inform the public of short-term, long-term or chronic threats.

Weekly. A newspaper that publishes only one day a week. Many are produced in small communities or rural areas, others appear in suburban sections of large cities. There are many different types.

Wire service. An organization that gathers news, stores, prepares them in a convenient form, and sends them (by wire or other rapid means) to newspapers and broadcasting stations around the country that pay for the service.

Word processor. A text editing unit designed for preparation, storage and dissemination of text initiated on typewriter like devices.

Work station. (1) A configuration of input and equipment at which an operator works. (2) A station at which an individual can send data or to receive data from a computer for the performance of a job.

Writer. A creative and professional individual employed by a company to write literary or technical material or make revisions, modifications or changes. An advertising or continuity writer who works on staff, as a commissioned writer, or as a freelance writer for an advertising agency, public relation firm, network, broadcast station and so forth.

Wrong font (wf). A notation indicting a printer's error in using one or more type characters in a different size or type font.

Xheight. The distance between the base line and the mean line of a type. A type character without ascender or descenders.

Yellow journalism. A late nineteenth-century type of newspaper publishing that placed profit above truthfulness and significance, emphasizing sensationalism, human interest and reader appeal at the expense of public responsibility.

Yuppie. A term coined for young, urban professionals; an upwardly mobile group of people who are the target of extensive advertising.

Zoned edition. Newspaper that has special sections for specific geographic areas.

BIBLIOGRAPHY

Bhatt, S.C. *Indian Press Since 1955*. New Delhi : Publication Division, 1997.

Bittner, John R. *Introduciion to Mass Communication*, New Jersey: Prentice Hall, Englewood Cliff, 1991.

Bittner, John R.. *Broadcasting and Telecommunication*. New Jersey : Prentice Hall, Englewood Cliff, 1991.

Brooks, Brian S. *et al. News Reporting and Editing*. New York : St. Martin's Press, 1988.

Dennis Everette, E. and Melvin De Fleur. *Understanding Mass Communication*. New Delhi : Goyl Saab, 1976.

Dominick, Joseph, R. *The Dynamics of Mass Communication.* New York: McGraw Hill Publishing Company, 1990.

Edward , Bliss, Jr. and James, C. Hoyt. *Writing News for Broadcast*. New York : Columbia University Press, 1994.

Fiske, John. *Introduction to Mass Communication*. New York : Routledge, 1997.

Gupta V. S. and Vir Bala Aggarwal. *Media Policy and Nation Building.* New Delhi : Concept Publishing Company, 1996.

Gupta, Baldev Raj. *Mass Communication and Development*. Varanasi : Vishwavidyalaya Prakashan, 1997.

Jethwaney, Jaishri N. *et. al. Public Relations.* New Delhi: Sterling Publishers, 1994.

Joseph, M. K. *Outline of Reporting*. New Delhi : Anmol Publication Pvt. Ltd., 1997.

Kumar, Kewal J. *Mass Communication in India.* Bombay : Jiaco Publishing House, 1995.

Notes. *Media, Ethics and Laws*. New Delhi : IGNOU, 1995.

Parthasarathy, Rangaswami. *Journalism in India*. New Delhi : Sterling Publisher Pvt. Ltd., 1989.

Rau, Chalapathi, M. *The Press*. New Delhi : N. B. T, 1974.

Report of the Second Press Commission Vol. I, 1982.

Sethi, Patanjali. *Professional Journalism*. Bombay : Orient Longman, 1977.

Sindhwani, Trilok N. *Newspaper Economics and Management*. New Delhi: Ankur Publishing House, 1979.

Singh, D.K. *The Press and the Law*. New Delhi, 1968.

Watson, James and Anne Hill. *A Dictionary on Communication and Media Studies*. New Delhi : Universal Book Stall, 1991.

INDEX